A THEORY OF LEGAL OBLIGATION

The focus of this monograph lies in the construction of a theory of legal obligation, understanding it as a discrete notion with its own defining traits. In this work, Stefano Bertea specifically addresses the question: how should legal obligation be distinctively conceptualized? The conceptualization of legal obligation he defends in this work gradually emerges from a critical assessment of the theories of legal obligation that have been most influential in the contemporary legal-theoretical debate. Building on such critical analysis, Bertea's study purports to offer a novel and unconventional conceptualization of legal obligation, which is characterized as a law-engendered intersubjective reason for carrying out certain courses of conduct.

STEFANO BERTEA is a Deutsche Forschungsgemeinschaft research fellow at the Goethe University Frankfurt and an Associate Professor at the University of Leicester. Previously, he was a Marie Skłodowska-Curie research fellow at the University of Edinburgh, a visiting research fellow at the Max Planck Institute for Comparative Public Law and International Law, an Alexander von Humboldt research fellow at Kiel University, a senior research fellow at the University of Antwerp, a visiting professor at the University of Verona and at the University of Modena and Reggio Emilia, and a visiting researcher at the University of Amsterdam.

A THEORY OF LEGAL OBLIGATION

STEFANO BERTEA
University of Leicester

CAMBRIDGE
UNIVERSITY PRESS

University Printing House, Cambridge CB2 8BS, United Kingdom

One Liberty Plaza, 20th Floor, New York, NY 10006, USA

477 Williamstown Road, Port Melbourne, VIC 3207, Australia

314–321, 3rd Floor, Plot 3, Splendor Forum, Jasola District Centre,
New Delhi – 110025, India

79 Anson Road, #06-04/06, Singapore 079906

Cambridge University Press is part of the University of Cambridge.

It furthers the University's mission by disseminating knowledge in the pursuit of education, learning, and research at the highest international levels of excellence.

www.cambridge.org
Information on this title: www.cambridge.org/9781108475105
DOI: 10.1017/9781108566216

© Stefano Bertea 2019

This publication is in copyright. Subject to statutory exception and to the provisions of relevant collective licensing agreements, no reproduction of any part may take place without the written permission of Cambridge University Press.

First published 2019

Printed and bound in Great Britain by Clays Ltd, Elcograf S.p.A.

A catalogue record for this publication is available from the British Library.

ISBN 978-1-108-47510-5 Hardback

Cambridge University Press has no responsibility for the persistence or accuracy of URLs for external or third-party internet websites referred to in this publication and does not guarantee that any content on such websites is, or will remain, accurate or appropriate.

To Linda,
who has brought the sun along
everywhere we have travelled
for longer than I can remember

CONTENTS

Acknowledgements viii

Introduction   1

1 The Concept of Obligation   13
2 Contemporary Approaches to Legal Obligation: A Preliminary Map   43
3 The Social Practice Account   74
4 The Interpretivist Account   104
5 The Conventionalist Reason Account   135
6 The Exclusionary Reason Account   164
7 A Revisionary Kantian Conception   199
8 Further Dimensions of the Revisionary Kantian Conception   237
9 The Robust Reason Account   263
10 The Method of Presuppositional Interpretation   300

Conclusion   349

Index   354

ACKNOWLEDGEMENTS

> In the elder days of Art,
> Builders wrought with greatest care
> Each minute and unseen part;
> For the Gods see everywhere.
>
> —H. W. Longfellow, 'The Builders'

The amount of time spent researching and writing this book warrants its description as a long-term project. As with any such endeavour, much benefit has come from the support of institutions and people whose role has been essential in developing the original idea into a sustained argument (however much its conclusions will always be open to revision and rethinking).

Funding for the research that has culminated in the book was provided by the Alexander von Humboldt Foundation (through a reintegration grant), the Max Planck Institute for Comparative Public Law and International Law (through an institute grant), the European Commission (through an intra-European Marie Curie Fellowship), the Deutsche Forschungsgemeinschaft (through a DFG research grant), and the Leicester Law School. Under the Alexander von Humboldt reintegration grant I was able to spend three months at the Juristisches Seminar of Kiel University, making it possible for me to engage Robert Alexy and Stanley L. Paulson in important discussions on several of the issues involved in the project. The institute grant funded a two-month research stay at the Max Planck Institute for Comparative Public Law and International Law in Heidelberg. The intra-European Marie Curie Fellowship and the DFG research grant have enabled me to devote myself exclusively to research at the Philosophy Institute of the Goethe University Frankfurt: this period began in February 2015, in a research environment as intellectually stimulating as anyone can hope for, affording several opportunities to share ideas with Marcus Willaschek, a source of invaluable insights, and with the circle of researchers who work at his Lehrstuhl. I am also grateful to the University of Leicester for granting me a semester of study leave in the 2014/15 academic year, and to the Leicester Law School for both providing financial support and showing flexibility in making possible my prolonged absence from the standard teaching and administrative duties that come with an academic position today.

Several academics have influenced my professional, intellectual, and personal development. Here I should like to mention at least those who took my research concerns to heart, gave their time to think through those concerns, and in some cases kindly went through preliminary drafts of parts of this book. Among them are Michał Araszkiewicz, Nick Barber, Francesco Belvisi, Deryk Beyleveld, Bruno Celano, Francois Du Bois, Antony Duff, Jaap Hage, Heidi Hurd, Marisa Iglesias Vila, Andrei Marmor, Jose Juan Moreso, Diego Papayannis, Dietmar von der Pfordten, Thomas Pink, Giorgio Pino, Ralf Poscher, Veronica Rodriguez-Blanco, Corrado Roversi, Claudio Sarra, Aldo Schiavello, Torben Spaak, Nicos Stavropoulos, Daniele Velo dal Brenta, Francesco Viola, Marcus Willaschek, and Andrew Williams. Moreover, I wish to express special thanks to Filippo Valente, who in addition to acting as my copyeditor contributed enormously to clarifying several important threads in my argument.

In recent years at the Leicester Law School, I have had the good fortune of being involved in the doctoral programmes of Maria Paula Barrantes-Reynolds and Daniel Weston: they have been remarkable in embarking into ambitious research projects that in the academic establishment would otherwise wind up yielding to the exigencies of research assessments whose metrics seem to emphasize organizational streamlining and communication skills, while doing little to make for an environment that is actually conducive to quality research. Yet this is precisely the environment occasionally one still finds in some pockets of academia, and the exchanges I have had with Paula and Daniel, thrashing out some challenging theoretical issues, have helped to make my argument much more cogent than it would otherwise have been.

Throughout the course of writing this book a number of people have been wellsprings of encouragement. Among them I should count Mark Bell and Panu Minkkinen, who continued to infuse energy into the project even after the period during which we worked at the same institution. With their attitude and action during their headships at the Leicester Law School, Mark and Panu convinced (even a non-believer like) me that power does not necessarily corrupt, and that, when the leadership is genuine, it requires neither a hierarchy nor a command structure.

Nowadays senior management at different UK universities is informed by a deep-rooted belief that research is a competitive enterprise, not a cooperative one. That view seems to me to carry a misconception. I would not have come fully to this realization had I not met a good many marathoners whose ability to physically sustain a 42 km run and still enjoy the effort has pointed me to a larger truth: that those who commit themselves to the same activity share something, as opposed to competing for something. By the same token, my occasional frequentation with marathoners keeps reminding, that long-distance running is a humble and patient enterprise, and that captured in these adjectives are virtues that need to be valued and nurtured in *any* long-term project (inclusive of academic projects). This, too, is a lesson that seems to me to get lost on most UK senior academic managers, who in referring to themselves as 'leaders' in my view display a genuinely peculiar (one may be tempted to say, idiosyncratic) sense of decorum, intellectual honesty, self-perception, and self-knowledge.

Finally, this project owes much to the supportive presence and constant stream of inspiration that throughout its course have come from people who are little, if at all, embedded in academic institutions. The lives of Linda, Luciano, Miranda, Simone, Fiore, Nina, Vittoria, Ada, Ettore, Stella, Oliana, Sandro, Lilia, and Bruno have enriched mine with more human truths than I will ever be able to put into practice – truths about life itself, about the things that matter, ranging from freedom to respect, from discipline and patience to courage, from love to wisdom, not to mention ethics and integrity as well as friendship, altruism, companionship, and scholarship. For these truths I am deeply indebted to them, even if I will never be able to acknowledge, let alone repay, what I intellectually and affectively owe to them. More than that, I regret that the time spent on this project was time taken away from their company.

Introduction

Within the legal community at large, law and obligation are widely believed to be intimately connected and ultimately inseparable for a number of reasons. To begin with, paradigmatic legal materials, such as statutes, judicial decisions, and doctrinal commentaries, make reference to obligation either directly, by specifying what one is obligated to do, or indirectly, by attributing rights, powers, and privileges – which positions are intrinsically related to the duties of other individuals. Similarly, in legal proceedings practitioners – judges, prosecutors, lawyers, juries – frequently make claims about which obligations under the law certain parties have in specific circumstances. And so do laypeople in their ordinary lives. This means that the deontic language is pervasive in discourses within and about law. Furthermore, the law is deeply shaped by regulative standards, since an important part of the legal domain has to do with norms prescribing courses of conduct and instructing individuals as to how they ought to behave. The very recognition of the prescriptive structure of law provides support to the thesis that key legal statuses can only be expressed through the use of the notion of obligation along with its opposite number, the notion of a right. Finally, law and obligation are taken to go hand in hand as a consequence of the fact that a legal system is commonly understood to be an authoritative institution. The authoritative dimension of law is of some significance in this context in consideration of the fact that an essential component of what is ordinarily meant by having authority, or claiming authority, in practical matters consists in having, or claiming, the legitimate power to affect the normative standing of others. And one of the paradigmatic ways (though not the only way) in which another person's normative standings can be affected consists in creating obligations for them.

This extensive use of obligation-related constructs and terminologies supports the widespread conviction that law purportedly seeks to impose obligations, and on occasion it does in fact affect the duties of those subject to it. This being the case, law and obligation are regarded as conceptually connected by a remarkable number of legal theorists, who maintain that an account of obligation constitutes a central element of the philosophical study of the concept of law and other fundamental legal concepts.[1]

This is not to suggest that the relation between law and obligation is regarded by every jurisprude as a necessary connection or is interpreted in the same way by different legal philosophers. Even the minimalist claim that law seeks to create, enforce, modify, and extinguish obligations has proved to be controversial among legal theorists, who have put forward different accounts of the obligations associated with the existence of a legal system: some regard those obligations as purely and distinctively legal in a merely formal sense; others qualify the obligations engendered by the law as social duties; another group instead takes those obligations to be moral. Which suggests that the necessary link obtaining between law and obligation is at once both a broadly accepted tenet, when framed as a general statement about the law, and a deeply controversial thesis, when its nature is analysed in greater detail. Hence the need for a comprehensive study of the kind of obligation specifically arising out of legal practices.

Considering that legal obligation is a widely theorized notion and that different aspects of the obligation-generating capacity the law arguably possesses have been extensively discussed in the literature, one wants to avoid the misunderstandings this kind of situation is likely to give rise to. To this end here I will be careful to clarify the specific question I intend to address in this book, so as to keep it distinct from other questions that similarly concern the obligatory component of the law. The specific

---

[1] The connection between law and obligation is unambiguously acknowledged in H. L. A. Hart, *Concept of Law* (Oxford, Clarendon, 1994, with a Postscript; or. ed. 1961), p. 82, where it is claimed that 'where there is law, there human conduct is made in some sense non-optional or obligatory'. For more recent statements of this tenor, see, for instance, K. E. Himma, 'Law's Claim of Legitimate Authority', in J. Coleman (ed.), *Hart's Postscript* (Oxford, Oxford University Press, 2001), pp. 271–309; K. E. Himma, 'The Ties That Bind: An Analysis of the Concept of Obligation', *Ratio Juris*, 26 (2013), pp. 16–46; and K. E. Himma, 'Is the Concept of Obligation Moralized?', *Law and Philosophy*, 37 (2018), pp. 203–27; S. Perry, 'Hart's Methodological Positivism', in J. Coleman (ed.), *Hart's Postscript* (Oxford, Oxford University Press, 2001), pp. 311–54; L. Green, 'Law and Obligations', in J. Coleman and S. Shapiro (eds.), *The Oxford Handbook of Jurisprudence and Philosophy of Law* (Oxford, Oxford University Press, 2002), pp. 514–47; R. Alexy, 'The Nature of Legal Philosophy', *Ratio Juris*, 17 (2004), pp. 156–67; R. Alexy, 'The Dual Nature of Law', *Ratio Juris*, 23 (2010), pp. 167–82; and D. von den Pfordten, *Rechtsphilosophie* (Munich, Verlag Beck, 2013).

object of this work is to construct a *theoretical account* of obligation as it applies to the law, and hence to offer a *conceptualization* of legal obligation. I will thus be primarily concerned with the question: how should legal obligation be distinctively characterized? Or, stated otherwise, how is the kind of obligation engendered by the law best conceived? I accordingly propose to contribute to the debate that has sprung up among those who are interested in systematically framing the fundamental features of legal obligation, understood as a notion with its own distinctive defining traits. Those engaged in this debate seek, for one thing, to identify and explore in detail the essential properties that define legal obligation and, for another thing, to establish what specifically distinguishes the specific sort of *legal* obligation from other kinds of obligation.[2]

Once so defined, the subject matter of this research should be kept distinct from a set of other issues concerning the relation between law and obligation that has also been widely studied and discussed in the literature on legal obligation. Of those issues, at least three bear mention here, not only in view of their theoretical significance but also because of the close conceptual connection they bear to the main questions around which the research project here undertaken revolves. First, traditionally legal philosophers studying legal obligation have shown an interest in

---

[2] Contributions to this debate can be found, for instance, in H. L. A. Hart, 'Legal and Moral Obligation', in A. Melden (ed.), *Essays in Moral Philosophy* (Seattle, University of Washington Press, 1958), pp. 82-107; H. L. A. Hart, *Essays on Bentham* (Oxford, Clarendon, 1982), pp. 127-61; Hart, *Concept of Law*, pp. 82-91; K. Baier, 'Obligation: Political and Moral', in R. Pennock and J. Chapman (eds.), *Political and Legal Obligation* (New York, Atherton, 1970), pp. 116-41; A. Gewirth, 'Obligation: Political, Legal, Moral', in R. Pennock and J. Chapman (eds.), *Political and Legal Obligation* (New York, Atherton, 1970), pp. 55-88; C. Johnson, 'Moral and Legal Obligation', *Journal of Philosophy*, 72 (1975), pp. 315-33; D. Beyleveld and R. Brownsword, *Law as a Moral Judgement* (London, Sweet & Maxwell, 1986), pp. 325-81; J. Raz, *Ethics in the Public Domain. Essays in the Morality of Law and Politics* (Oxford, Clarendon, 1994), pp. 194-221; W. Waluchow, 'Authority and the Practical Difference Thesis: A Defence of Inclusive Legal Positivism', *Legal Theory*, 6 (2000), pp. 45-81; J. Finnis, *Natural Law and Natural Rights* (Oxford, Oxford University Press, 2011, 2nd ed., with a Postscript; 1st ed. 1980), pp. 297-350; K. E. Himma, 'Conceptual Jurisprudence and the Intelligibility of Law's Claim to Obligate', in M. O'Rourke, J. Keim-Campbell, and D. Shier (eds.), *Topics in Contemporary Philosophy: Law and Social Justice* (Cambridge (MA), MIT Press, 2005), pp. 311-26; Himma, 'Ties That Bind'; Himma, 'Is the Concept of Obligation Moralized?'; M. Greenberg, 'The Moral Impact Theory of Law', *Yale Law Journal*, 123 (2014), pp. 1288-1342; S. Hershovitz, 'The End of Jurisprudence', *Yale Law Journal*, 124 (2015), pp. 1160-1204; and D. Wodak, 'What Does "Legal Obligation" Mean?', *Pacific Philosophical Quarterly*, 99(4) (2018), pp. 1-27.

determining whether the existence of a system of laws is in itself sufficient to provide those subject to law with a (presumptive) duty of obedience.[3] The mere fact that a norm has been issued in accordance with certain procedures, some argue, is no reason to conclude that there is an obligation to conform to it. Others, by contrast, claim that those living in a country have a prima facie general duty to act in conformity with the laws validly passed by the legal institutions governing that country, at least insofar as the resulting system of law is not extremely unjust.

This concern, traditionally designated as 'political obligation', should be kept distinct from another issue, which is nonetheless partly reminiscent of the former: the issue as to whether either individual legal directives or legal systems in their entirety, by virtue of their own nature, *purport* to create certain obligations for officials and citizens alike. This further theoretical interest can be reformulated in the form of the question: does the law intrinsically make claims on us that entail obligations? This question is part of a more comprehensive investigation of the concept of law, since the issue bears directly on the way one conceives of law. On this basis, the question can be characterized as a conceptual, or metaphysical, question.[4]

---

[3] For some introductory studies of this problem, see R. Wasserstrom, 'The Obligation to Obey the Law', *UCLA Law Review*, 10 (1963), pp. 790-7; M. Smith, 'Is There a Prima Facie Obligation to Obey the Law?', *Yale Law Journal*, 82 (1973), pp. 950-76; J. Simmons, *Moral Principles and Political Obligations* (Princeton, Princeton University Press, 1979); K. Greenawalt, *Conflicts of Law and Morality* (Oxford, Oxford University Press, 1987); J. Horton, *Political Obligation* (Basingstoke, MacMillan, 1992); N. O'Sullivan, *The Problem of Political Obligation* (New York, Gardland, 1987); R. Higgins, *The Moral Limits of Law* (Oxford, Oxford University Press, 2004); and S. Perry, 'Law and Obligation', *American Journal of Jurisprudence*, 50 (2005), pp. 263-95.

[4] The question is treated in J. Raz, *The Authority of Law* (Oxford, Oxford University Press, 2009, 2nd ed.; 1st ed. 1979), pp. 28-33; P. Soper, 'Legal Theory and the Claim of Authority', *Philosophy and Public Affairs*, 18 (1989), pp. 209-37; P. Soper, 'Law's Normative Claims', in R. George (ed.), *The Autonomy of Law* (Oxford, Clarendon, 1996), pp. 215-47; R. Alexy, 'Law and Correctness,' in M. Freeman (ed.), *Legal Theory at the End of the Millennium* (Oxford, Oxford University Press, 1998), pp. 205-21; R. Alexy, *The Argument from Injustice* (Oxford, Clarendon, 2002; or. ed. 1992), pp. 35-9, Himma, 'Law's Claim of Legitimate Authority'; Himma, 'Conceptual Jurisprudence'; S. Bertea, 'On Law's Claim to Authority', *Northern Ireland Legal Quarterly*, 55 (2004), pp. 396-413; S. Bertea, *The Normative Claim of Law* (Oxford, Hart, 2009); C. Heidemann, 'Law's Claim to Correctness', in S. Coyle and G. Pavlakos (eds.), *Jurisprudence or Legal Science?* (Oxford, Hart, 2005), pp. 127-46; N. MacCormick, *Institutions of Law* (Oxford, Oxford University Press, 2007), and J. Gardner, 'How Law Claims, What Law Claims', in M. Klatt (ed.), *Institutionalized Reason* (Oxford, Oxford University Press, 2012), pp. 29-44, among others.

Thirdly, a lively debate has sprung up between those who investigate the conditions under which the law can be considered a legitimate source of obligation and so is justified in imposing its rule over a group of people, in some circumstances even by recourse to coercive force, or the threat of sanctions. This concern leads one to deal directly with the issue as to whether the law has some practical authority over its addressees, and under which conditions the authority of law should be regarded as legitimate and so binding on those subjects.[5]

It is scarcely necessary to add at this point that the different debates on the obligatory dimension of the law just mentioned are closely linked to one another as well as to the distinctive issue this book is specifically devoted to: the issue of how legal obligation ought to be conceptualized. Indeed in dealing with any of the basic questions framing those debates – the conceptualization of legal obligation, the duty to obey the law, law's claim to obligate, and the practical authority of law – we will often have to give at least some consideration to the other questions as well. But this interconnection does not mean that the debates have no distinguishing features and cannot stand on their own. And this is why I have specified the distinctive debate I take up in this study in my effort to argue for a given conception of legal obligation.

In working towards an encompassing conceptualization of legal obligation, I will defend a number of claims which constitute the

---

[5] See Raz, *Authority of Law*, pp. 3–27; J. Raz, *The Morality of Freedom* (Oxford, Oxford University Press, 1986), pp. 23–105; Hart, *Essays on Bentham*, pp. 243–268; J. Finnis, 'The Authority of Law in the Predicament of Contemporary Social Theory', *Notre Dame Journal of Law, Ethics and Public Policy*, 1 (1984), pp. 115–38; L. Green, 'Authority and Convention', *Philosophical Quarterly*, 35 (1985), pp. 329–46; L. Green, *The Authority of the State* (Oxford, Clarendon, 1988); D. Regan, 'Law's Halo', *Social Philosophy and Policy*, 4 (1987), pp. 15–30; D. Regan, 'Authority and Value', *Southern California Law Review*, 62 (1989), pp. 995–1095; M. Moore, 'Authority, Law and Razian Reasons', *Southern California Law Review*, 62 (1989), pp. 830–96; Soper, 'Legal Theory and the Claim of Authority'; L. Alexander, 'Law and Exclusionary Reasons', *Philosophical Topics*, 18 (1990), pp. 153–70; R. Friedman, 'On the Concept of Authority in Political Philosophy' (1973), now in J. Raz (ed.), *Authority* (Oxford, Basil Blackwell, 1990), pp. 56–91; R. Ladenson, 'In Defense of a Hobbesian Conception of Law', *Philosophy and Public Affairs*, 9 (1980), pp. 134–59; H. Hurd, 'Challenging Authority', *Yale Law Journal*, 100 (1991), 1611–77; J. Cunliffe and A. Reeve, 'Dialogic Authority', *Oxford Journal of Legal Studies*, 19 (1999), pp. 453–65; S. Shapiro, 'Authority', in J. Coleman and S. Shapiro (eds.), *The Oxford Handbook of Jurisprudence and Philosophy of Law*, (Oxford, Oxford University Press, 2000), pp. 382–439; A. Marmor, 'An Institutional Conception of Authority', *Philosophy and Public Affairs*, 39 (2011), pp. 238–61; A. Marmor, 'The Dilemma of Authority', *Jurisprudence*, 2 (2011), pp. 121–41, just to mention a few.

fundamental steps of the argument I deploy in what follows, and which provide the main contents of this book. In Chapter 1, I set the stage for my substantive inquiry into the obligatory dimension of the law by asserting that a conceptualization of obligation *in general* is the preliminary step for constructing a comprehensive theory of the kind of obligation *engendered by the law*.[6] In a nutshell, thus, the overall strategy I will follow in working towards the objective just set out – putting forward an account of legal obligation – consists in, first, (a) introducing a concept of obligation in wide currency today, and then (b) critically considering a number of different theoretical accounts of legal obligation that have so far been defended in jurisprudence. Accordingly, in Chapter 1 I seek to establish the fundamental characteristics of obligation understood as a conceptual construct with its own distinctive defining traits. In that context, I will defend the view that obligation is best conceived as a practically normative requirement that makes a noticeable and yet resistible claim on us, who in turn are bound to, and accountable for, conforming to it, since acting otherwise would be prima facie wrong. This concept of obligation will also be presented as the essential means enabling us to critically assess the contemporary theories of legal obligation as well as to move beyond the current debate in legal theory and put forward an original conception of legal obligation.

The discussion of existing theories of legal obligation begins in Chapter 2, where I introduce a basic distinction between approaches to legal obligation, or paradigms for an understanding of it: the distinction between the 'empirical model' (with its main variants consisting in the 'predictive account' and 'imperative account') and the 'normative model'. There I will also defend the view that, without too much oversimplification, the basic conceptions of legal obligation advocated in jurisprudence today can be reduced to those two paradigms. However, I will go on to claim only the normative model offers a presumptively sound interpretation of the kind of obligation engendered by law. The normative model comes in different versions, irreducible one to another,

---

[6] In turn, the basic insight orienting this line of research on legal obligation is that obligation singles out a general idea used in different realms and takes on different meanings in distinct contexts. This difference is attested, for instance, by the fact that we ordinarily speak not just of obligation per se, but also of moral obligations, social obligations, legal obligations, religious obligations, and natural obligations, just to name a few. The question thus arises as to whether these obligation-invoking phrases refer to altogether disparate notions or whether there is a general overarching idea – the idea of obligation *simpliciter* – to which the specific kinds of obligation can be traced.

the most significant of which are the 'formal account', the 'social practice account', the 'interpretivist account', and the 'reason account'. Not all those accounts can be regarded as having the resources needed to accommodate the general concept of obligation and so as being an apt tool for explaining legal obligation, though. This, it will be argued, is not the case with the formal account, which will accordingly not be of concern in the rest of the study. In this way, the discussion undertaken in this chapter sets the stage for the remaining part of the book, where I will critically evaluate what I take to be the most sophisticated theories of legal obligation.

Chapter 3, which revisits and updates an argument that originally appeared in *Canadian Journal of Law and Jurisprudence*,[7] specifically discusses the social practice account of legal obligation, an account that characterizes legal obligation as a social bond linking together those who are subject to the law. This account is paradigmatically defended by those espousing the so-called conception of law as a shared activity, which accordingly will constitute the main target of the discussion carried out in this chapter. In addressing this theoretical approach, I will contend that the social practice account faces insurmountable difficulties in conceptualizing the obligatory dimension of law and that even the most nuanced versions of the social practice account explain legal obligation in ways that range from incomplete to internally incoherent.

With that done, I will pass in Chapter 4 to present an alternative model for the study of legal obligation: this is the interpretivist account, on which legal obligation is construed as having both a social component and an evaluative one. On the interpretivist account, legal obligations are construed as duties fundamentally determined by the political morality underpinning a given institutional practice. I will argue that in fleshing out this theory interpretivists fail to appreciate the intrinsic connection between legal obligation and the fundamental standards of practical rationality. As a result, they allow for the possibility that legal obligations may be regarded as genuine even if they diverge from practically rational requirements. In this way, they wind up having to subscribe to the twofold view that (a) one may be under a legal obligation to act against the demands of practical rationality, and (b)

---

[7] See S. Bertea, 'Law, Shared Activities, and Obligation', *Canadian Journal of Law and Jurisprudence*, 27 (2014), pp. 357–81.

legal regimes can make claims on how one ought to act even if the justification for such claims is not fully rational. Neither of those two commitments seems palatable.

The different criticisms I level at the social practice account and interpretivist account can ultimately be reduced to the statement that legal obligation cannot adequately be conceptualized without making practically rational considerations, or reasons for action, a central part of the explanation of the obligations engendered by law. This conclusion should not be taken merely as a negative statement, namely, a claim about what an insightful theory of legal obligation is *not*. For in addition to meaning, in the negative, that the views of legal obligation introduced in Chapters 3 and 4 are fundamentally flawed, it also suggests, in the positive, that a thorough scrutiny of the main standing alternative to the social practice account and the interpretivist account – namely, the reason account – can legitimately be expected to secure a better explanation of legal obligation.

On the reason account, the basic notion we need to appeal to for adequately characterizing legal obligation is that of a practical reason, as opposed to that of a social practice or that of an institutional and evaluative practice. In the literature we can find not just one but several versions of the reason account of legal obligation. I will accordingly devote Chapters 5 and 6 to the critical discussion of two influential variants of this paradigm – the 'conventionalist reason account' and the 'exclusionary reason account' – before (a) building on that critical discussion to introduce my own alternative reason conception of legal obligation (in Chapters 7 and 8) and (b) assessing its relation to a third popular version of reason account – the 'robust reason account' – which I regard as conceptually close to my own theory (in Chapter 9).

More specifically, by building on the positions defended in my critiques of the social practice account, the interpretivist account, the conventionalist reason account, and the exclusionary reason account, I will put forward a different conception of legal obligation. This conception, which is alternative to any other existing theory, I will call the 'revisionary Kantian conception' of legal obligation. Such conception embodies both the features constitutive of the general concept of obligation *simpliciter* (the concept introduced in Chapter 1) and the views on legal obligation theorized in contemporary legal philosophy (the views criticized in the discussion from Chapters 3 to 6), on which it seeks to improve. So, by combining the claims defended in the positive in defining a concept of obligation with the claims made in the negative in rebutting the main contemporary theories of legal obligation, one gets the materials out of which I construct an alternative theoretical account of legal obligation.

The resulting theory of legal obligation I present as the revisionary Kantian conception can be summarized thus: legal obligation is a reason for carrying out certain courses of conduct, a reason engendered by the law and stating that such conduct is required as a matter of intersubjective considerations. This concise formulation can be more analytically spelled out in the following terms. Firstly, legal obligation, as I conceive it, describes a *normative* kind of necessitation – an ought – *requiring*, as opposed to simply recommending, that those who are subject to law act in the prescribed way. Secondly, fulfilling one's legal obligations should *presumptively* be understood as the *right* thing to do, whereas departing from what a legal obligation prescribes is legitimately regarded as pro tanto wrong. Relatedly, legal obligation holds *categorically*, such that an obligee's subjective states and personal commitments do not affect its bindingness. As a result, for one thing, legal obligations bind us in a *genuine* sense, as opposed to a merely perspectivized one, and, for another, they operate as intrinsically *rational* requirements, rather than as social, institutional, or technical 'oughts'. In addition, the distinctive kind of ought attached to legal obligation has a *defeasible*, or variable, force, as distinct from an exclusionary, or invariant, force. Finally, legal obligations are best understood as reasons addressing the *generality* of legal subjects, namely, the legal community as a whole, rather than just a subclass of it, such as legal officials, meaning those who occupy certain institutional roles or who otherwise commit to, accept, or take an internal point of view to the legal enterprise.

Having so introduced and discussed my substantive conception of legal obligation, I will conclude my argument by introducing and consolidating the specific methodological principles and assumptions that underpin the revisionary Kantian conception. Those principles and assumptions, I will contend in Chapter 10, shape a specific methodology – I will call it the method of 'presuppositional interpretation' – that is akin, but irreducible, to methods traditionally used in legal and political philosophy, such as conceptual analysis, reflective equilibrium, transcendental argument, and Kant's analytic method. As a distinctive method of inquiry, presuppositional interpretation describes a process through which we identify (a) the defining traits of legal obligation and (b) the essential presuppositions that make it possible for us to even conceive of legal obligation, in such a way as to (c) provide a systematic and coherent scheme for interpreting the fundamental features of legal obligation and its basic conditions of intelligibility.

A comprehensive study of legal obligation of the kind just outlined can be argued to be of both *theoretical* and *practical* significance. Understanding legal obligation is essential to a *theoretical* account of law because obligation is a central notion in the legal domain. Accordingly, the discussion of legal obligation affects a number of overlapping debates that occupy a central position in legal philosophy. An engagement with legal obligation should thus be of interest to theorists with different backgrounds and philosophical orientations. This conclusion applies a fortiori to the argument I will be unpacking in this work, where I flesh out the concept of obligation by proceeding from a perspective that is deeply shaped by broadly philosophical concerns. From this perspective of inquiry, mastering and comprehensively accounting for obligation as such is instrumental to arriving at a better grasp of the legal domain, which is taken to be an inherently complex and multidimensional realm.[8] And by studying legal obligation as part of the general class of which it is part – that is, as issuing from a concept of obligation *simpliciter* – we can make our discussion of legal obligation theoretically significant in both a focused and a broad sense, making it useful in the specific study of law as well as in our reasoning on a broad range of ethical issues at large.

The reason for this being the case can be better appreciated by considering that obligation is commonly regarded as a central normative term, and its analysis is widely seen as an essential component of any project aimed at advancing our knowledge in a vast range of normative and action-related investigations, as in morality, society, religion, politics, and to some extent economics. The notion of obligation is in particular regarded as the fundamental issue in moral theory, at least by those who adhere to the so-called law conception of moral theory, a tradition that has been greatly influential since the post-classic age in Greek

---

[8] Central to my approach, in other words, is the view that only a broad and interdisciplinary framework can put us in a position to compare and contrast different and yet connected features, properties, and phenomena relating to the obligations generated by the law, which might otherwise be mistakenly perceived as thoroughly heterogeneous. Relatedly, at least insofar as we acknowledge that legal theorists are entrusted not only with *describing* current uses of legal concepts – such as the uses that legal practitioners make of *obligation* – but also with *critically approaching and assessing* those concepts, we should think it of paramount importance to have a general philosophically informed framework of thought that may be used to assess and evaluate particular, context-embedded uses of notions of wider currency.

philosophy.⁹ In this tradition, moral principles are regarded as ultimately reducible to principles of duty and obligation. Consequently, the study of obligation is widely regarded as essential to an understanding of morality and of its basic principles. Insofar as obligation is regarded as the central normative concept in moral theory, a study of legal obligation grounded in the recognition of the conceptual connection between legal obligation and obligation *simpliciter* is to be deemed of wide theoretical significance, in that it is instrumental to a thorough treatment of theoretical problems in ethics.¹⁰ Therefore, from the point of view of this influential tradition, the approach to legal obligation taken in this work will be regarded as functional to enhancing our awareness that legal philosophy and moral theory are connected in a number of important respects, and that the study of legal issues is of paramount significance in a number of ethical sub-disciplines, too.

In addition to being of theoretical importance, a study of legal obligation carried out from the broadly philosophical perspective I take in this work should be considered of *practical* significance. Support for this view can be extracted from the argument set out by Ernest Weinrib in his work *The Disintegration of Duty*. Weinrib observes that we are moving away from a general conception of obligation, and he undertakes to work out what this means for the way in which cases in tort are decided. In this context, he criticizes the case-by-case, policy-based approach the courts use as the standard method of adjudication in common law systems, arguing instead for a more systematic approach where the legally correct outcome of a case is arrived at on the basis of some statement of general application about duty. Weinrib's main argument against a piecemeal approach to tort cases is ultimately based on the view that the law is by nature systematic. So even in common law systems, the law, 'by its own internal logic and dynamism, cannot treat the particular instances of duty

---

⁹ As pointed out by Elizabeth Anscombe, the law conception of moral theory marks a break with the classic tradition, and especially with its Aristotelian version. See G. E. M. Anscombe, *Ethics, Religion and Politics: The Collected Philosophical Papers of G. E. M. Anscombe, Vol. 3* (Oxford, Blackwell, 1981), pp. 29–31. This conception can be traced back to Stoic moral theory, but only within Christianity did it find a full statement. It can be argued to still be the dominant view among moral thinkers today, though it certainly is not the generally accepted view.

¹⁰ For further statements of the importance of obligation in normative thought, see W. Quillian, 'The Problem of Moral Obligation', *Ethics*, 60 (1949), p. 40; J. Hems, 'What is Wrong with Obligation', *Philosophy and Phenomenological Research*, 22 (1961), p. 50; and D. Richards, *Reasons for Action* (Oxford, Oxford University Press, 1971), pp. 95–6, among many others.

as a chaotic miscellany of disparate and independent norms'.[11] The coherence of a legal system – a coherence that is not always a reality in actual legal systems but nonetheless should at least be regarded as an ideal – requires specific legal obligations to be thematically unified through one or more common underlying principles. In this view, courts engaged in adjudication need to rely on a general conception of legal obligation in deciding cases – a general conception that in tort law will take the form of an account of the duty of care. In making the case that we should refer to this conception of legal obligation and reject a policy-led approach, fragmenting the notion of legal obligation into separate factors and features, Weinrib thus appeals to the need to preserve and contribute to the systematic nature of law, arguing as well that we ought to implement an ideal of (corrective) justice in legal adjudication.

Although Weinrib's argument is specifically intended to critically assess the case law in Canadian tort law, it can be generalized to show that the systematic nature of law calls for a general conception of legal obligation. Which general conception is demanded as well by the legitimate aspiration to both generality and justice as two characteristic features of legal systems. A general conception of obligation should make it possible to identify those traits which are common to all uses of obligation not only in law but also in the broader practical realm. Different kinds of obligations are, in other terms, systematically related by their own internal logic and dynamics. So, if we conceive of legal obligation as a separate and independent class, we will jeopardize its internal unity and transform it into a loose assemblage of disparate items conceptually incapable of any cohesion. And, as Weinrib has convincingly argued, such fragmentation and disintegration of the notion of legal obligation is not only theoretically unsound but also practically dangerous, for it puts at risk the very possibility of pursuing a coherent and just ordering of society through law. Hence the practical relevance of a comprehensive study of legal obligation of the kind I undertake in this book.

---

[11] E. Weinrib, 'The Disintegration of Duty', *Advocates' Quarterly*, 31 (2006), p. 213.

1

The Concept of Obligation

1.1 Introduction

In this chapter, I set out to pinpoint the *concept* of obligation, by which I mean the arrangement of features and properties that those who systematically reflect on the obligatory dimension of human experience essentially associate with the existence of an obligation. This task will bring me to engage with the existing literature, where I will search for the *meaning* of obligation, namely, for the widespread *sense* of how an obligation should be understood, or is best conceived.[1]

Before dealing with the concept of obligation, however, I need to clarify why that concept, as opposed to (directly) the concept of *legal obligation*, is fundamentally relevant to my construction of a *theory of legal obligation*. This will be done in Section 1.2, as part of a broader introduction to the basic assumptions that shape the research project undertaken in this monograph. In that context, I will focus on three claims in particular, each of which plays a significant role in my argument. First, I will emphasize the fact that my study is concerned with pro tanto obligation. Accordingly, whenever I discuss issues relating to either obligation per se or obligation in the legal sense, I will only be interested in advancing our understanding of what one is *presumptively*, as opposed to conclusively, obligated to do. Second, I will explain why in my theoretical framework determining the concept of obligation per se is regarded as the premise of, or introductory move in, the argument that I intend to offer in support of a comprehensive theoretical account of legal obligation. That account, in other words, will be argued to be established on firm grounds (only) insofar as it does proceed from the

---

[1] This is not to say that the concept of obligation is readily available, or that it is 'out there' waiting for us to pick it up. Despite the fact that the concept (mostly implicitly) underpins many views of obligation, it still needs to be constructed. This is what I will do in this chapter.

conceptualization of obligation *simpliciter*. Finally, I will draw attention to the fact that a theoretical account of legal obligation grounded in the assumption just mentioned can reasonably be expected to be shaped by deep philosophical concerns. That is to say, in arguing for a theory of legal obligation from a conceptualization of obligation per se, I am naturally led to engage with debates concerning general philosophical ideas, both substantive and methodological, and so I end up dealing with issues that extend beyond the specifically legal domain and studies. In this work, then, philosophical debates – in particular discussions central to practical philosophy – can be claimed to be as relevant and central as the domain-specific debates that interest the legal theorists who are engaged in establishing how legal obligation should be conceived.

It is only after I have thus introduced the overall context within which my argument proceeds that I will specifically identify the fundamental features, or defining properties, of the notion of obligation, as most scholars depict that notion (Section 1.3). The objective of Section 1.3 will, therefore, consist in isolating the concept of obligation, namely, in determining the essential characteristics of obligation understood as a concept with its own distinctive defining traits. The project I will embark on in that section, however, should not be interpreted as an attempt to either offer a conceptual analysis or provide a formal definition of obligation, by thus uncovering the set of necessary and sufficient conditions that govern the use of the concept-term 'obligation'. In fact, I am sceptical about the potential that conceptual analyses and formal definitions may have in contributing to our understanding of obligation. One important reason for this scepticism has to do with the fact that obligation is a pervasive component of our ordinary practical experience and comes in a wide typological variety.[2] Such pervasiveness and typological variety render any effort to conceptually analyse and formally define what an obligation is theoretically dubious, if not altogether hopeless.

To briefly elaborate on this statement, obligations surround us and stay with us in the most diverse settings. For instance, etiquette and courtesy insist that it is our duty to carry out certain acts even when we are not inclined to do so; social exchanges with both acquaintances and strangers more often than not come with demands directing us to take others' needs, wishes, and interests into account, despite the fact that this

---

[2] Further grounds of this scepticism are introduced in some detail in my systematic discussion of the methodology underpinning this project, which can be found in Chapter 10.

may mean that we have to sacrifice our well-being; legal norms, whose presence is so ubiquitous that we ordinarily fail to notice them, establish patterns of behaviour we have to account for in our deliberating about what we are required to do within a given jurisdiction; and once we, finally alone, feel entitled to shut down and get some well-deserved rest in the comfort and privacy of our homes, obligations obstinately refuse to desert us and, by making appeals to who we are or should be, filter into the intimacy of our space and continue to make claims on us. Indeed, there is barely any sphere of life that is obligation-free: whenever we embark on action – such as meeting up, driving around, shopping, playing, working, engaging in politics, debating, pondering, and so on – we unremittingly bump into obligations. The ubiquity of obligations is also reflected in the fact that a number of practices we engage in are defined, constrained, shaped, and indeed made possible by the very obligations they set forth for the individuals taking part in those practices. Since obligations consistently pop up in different contexts and take the most diverse forms, the possibility that one single conceptual analysis or formal definition summarizing the basic characters of obligation in terms of some necessary and sufficient conditions may become available and turn out to be theoretically insightful strikes me as highly implausible.

This belief fundamentally informs and decisively orients my search for the concept of obligation. Indeed, it explains why the concept of obligation I will arrive at is not meant to be a statement of the necessary and sufficient conditions that establish the nature of obligation. In other words, in providing a concept of obligation I do not intend to embark on any formal exercise aimed at defining what obligation is. Nor do I align myself with the tradition, ultimately tracing back to Jeremy Bentham and finding a paradigmatic formulation in the study of Wesley N. Hohfeld,[3] which is meant to grant us a conceptual analysis of obligation and the mutual relations obtaining between the fundamental legal positions related to obligation – such as right, privilege, and non-right, to stick to Hohfeld's findings. In contrast to Hohfeld's analysis of the concept of obligation, which is directed at individuating and consolidating the logical (or quasi-logical) relationships between obligation and other fundamental legal notions primarily by making use of the so-called

---

[3] Here I specifically refer to J. Bentham, *Of Laws in General* (London, Athlone, 1970; or. ed. 1782), especially appendix B; and W. N. Hohfeld, *Fundamentals Legal Conceptions* (New Haven, Yale University Press, 1964; or. ed. 1919).

square of oppositions, my engagement with the concept of legal obligation is intended to disclose a shared sense in which those who have systematically engaged with the obligatory dimension of human practices understand, or conceptualize, obligation.

In doing so, I aspire at singling out a general concept that, far from merely fixing, or even sanctifying, some ordinary meaning of the term 'obligation' or determining what obligation is in some logical fashion, enables us to appreciate remarkable similarities between senses of what is obligatory – the social sense, the moral sense, the legal sense, the political sense, etc. – that otherwise would be erroneously perceived as conceptually heterogeneous and so largely unrelated, or disconnected. The direction, scope, and target of the two research projects – the project undertaken by conceptual analysts as well as by those searching for a formal definition of obligation, on the one hand, and the project I purport to carry out here, on the other – are, therefore, hardly comparable, despite the fact that both are presented as contributions to establishing how legal obligation is best (or even necessarily) conceived.

On the basis of the preceding remarks, it can be claimed that my treatment of obligation should be interpreted as an inquiry into the traits and elements that competent users associate with standard, or typical, instances of what is obligatory. Those traits and elements are not claimed to apply to every instance, including the most marginal and peripheral examples, of obligation that one can imagine. They are rather presented as the general and necessary (but not sufficient) conditions of conceivability of an idea – obligation *simpliciter* – that provides the ground layer of any other, specific, instantiation of what is obligatory in different contexts, such as law, politics, morality, society, etc. And this is the way in which should be read my statement, which I will introduce and argue throughout Section 1.3, that obligation, qua a distinctive concept, is best conceived as a practical and normative requirement legitimately demanding obedience.

1.2 Basic Assumptions

In this section, I will introduce the basic assumptions underpinning not only the discussion concerning the concept of obligation offered in this chapter but also, more generally, the discourse about legal obligation I will carry out in the rest of the book. I intend to focus in particular on three of those fundamental assumptions. The first of them concerns the character – presumptive, as opposed to conclusive – of obligation as

I scrutinize it. The second assumption I discuss here concerns the relationships between obligation in general and obligation within the law. The last assumption I will deal with in what follows pertains to the overall approach shaping my treatment of obligation as it arises out of the law – an approach that can be defined as broadly philosophical, vis-à-vis specifically bound to jurisprudence as a distinct field of theoretical inquiry.

The first of the fundamental assumptions orienting my study is that here I will only be concerned with discussing and characterizing the notion of presumptive (prima facie, or pro tanto) obligation, as opposed to conclusive (all-things-considered, or actual) obligation.[4] The difference between presumptive obligation and conclusive obligation can be stated thus: a presumptive obligation is one we are expected to perform unless other standards come up that, by virtue of their greater force or cogency, compel us to behave otherwise. A conclusive obligation, by contrast, admits of no such exception – it simply establishes that this is how the agent ought to act, no matter what.

The difference between the two types of obligation can be restated in terms of the epistemic conditions under which the associated ought-judgements – namely, presumptive ought-judgements and conclusive ought-judgements – are made.[5] An all-things-considered judgement about obligation gives us an indication of what we ought to do after taking into account all the relevant information concerning the whole *spectrum* of claims that are made on us in a particular circumstance. A conclusive obligation then establishes what we have an obligation to do on balance, that is, in the light of all the obligations applying to us in the relevant situation and potentially pulling us in different directions – it determines what we ought to do once all the applicable prima facie obligations are taken into account (along with the attendant demands) through an assessment of their relative force. By contrast, a pro tanto judgement about obligation is a judgement made under conditions of uncertainty and so on the basis of a limited set of available information and applicable standards. A judgement of this kind does not express what

---

[4] Throughout this work, I will use the phrases 'presumptive obligation', 'prima facie obligation', and 'pro tanto obligation' as synonyms. Similarly, 'conclusive obligation', 'all-things-considered obligation', and 'actual obligation' are taken to express the same idea.

[5] This way of describing the difference can be found in J. Hage, 'Legal Transactions and the Legal Ought', in J. Stelmach and B. Brozek (eds.), *Studies in the Philosophy of Law* (Krakow, Copernicus, 2011), pp. 183–6.

we ultimately ought to do when acting in compliance with all our obligations. It only directs us to act based on the requirement that judgement reflects. Hence, when we are under different prima facie obligations we may, in fact, find ourselves in a predicament in which some of these obligations direct us to act in one way, while others demand that we act in another way.

Because my exclusive concern in this work is with presumptive obligation, that is henceforth how I will be using the term 'obligation' (both in general and in relation to law). Unless stated otherwise, accordingly, obligation and legal obligation will be taken to mean anything we are required to do under certain circumstances so long as no countervailing considerations intervene that compel us to act differently. As it can be appreciated from this characterization, a presumptive obligation does not necessarily determine any final practical outcome, precisely because it does not take all ought-related judgements into account, such as they may apply to the matter at hand. For this reason, a pro tanto obligation may well come into conflict with other requirements calling for a different behaviour. Still, even when a presumptive obligation conflicts with, and is possibly defeated by, stronger demands pertinent to the issue in the given circumstances – meaning that its force does not turn out to be conclusive and so it does not determine what an agent ought to do in the end – it nonetheless stands as an obligation in its own right. That is, the possibility of its losing out to other relevant considerations does not make it void, or insignificant: it will still be complete in itself. This is why not only do we need an account of presumptive obligation but also such an account logically precedes the one of conclusive obligation. For it is only once we understand presumptive obligation – simpler and more basic than conclusive obligation as it is – that we can make sense of conclusive obligation – which can be explained as the result of a complex of prima facie obligations in a relation of either contrast or mutual support.

The second assumption shaping my study concerns the strategy that, in my view, one is best advised to rely upon when constructing a theoretical account of legal obligation. This strategy consists of working out the defining, or essential qua necessary (although typically less than sufficient), traits of legal obligation from the general idea of obligation. That is to say, I start out, not from legal obligation, but rather from the broader and more fundamental idea, or genus, legal obligation is a species of, namely, obligation *as such*. In this work, then, legal obligation will enter the stage only *after* the concept of obligation has been introduced and clarified. This choice – taking obligation, rather than legal obligation directly, to be the entry point in the discussion – is based on, and justified by, the assumption that legal obligation is a specific kind of a more general and far-reaching construct of thought, to which it directly owes, and from which it ultimately borrows, its fundamental features and necessary conditions of intelligibility.

To elaborate on this point, in my conceptual framework different species of obligations are not understood to refer to a disparate collection of ideas, only partly connected and only partially resembling each another. Obligation is, by contrast, regarded as one reasonably unified notion, which is ordinarily used in different settings and can take on different meanings in different contexts. In consideration of this typological variety, obligation is best understood not as a monolith but instead as a notion referring to a 'family' of ideas, each bearing some resemblance to the others as well as showing certain discontinuities with them. The typological varieties of, and possible relations of family resemblance between, obligations of different sorts, however, should not be radicalized to the point of denying the existence of a general overarching concept – obligation per se, or obligation *simpliciter* – to which the different specific kinds of what is obligatory can be traced and from which they ultimately derive their fundamental features and conditions of conceivability. While that overarching concept is broad and open-ended – it is arguably capable of accommodating certain departures from its paradigmatic instantiation – it is a unified notion absent which we would lack the fundamental benchmark against which to appreciate and critically assess the core quality of what is presented as, and claimed to be, a specific type of obligation.

As a result, from the standpoint of the assumption behind my inquiry, each type of obligation is not an irredeemably free-floating construct unrelated to the other species of the same kind. By contrast, each different species of obligation, with its distinctive traits, will be understood to share a few fundamental features with the other species of what is obligatory. These common features are the traits constitutive of obligation *simpliciter*, which should be expected to be found at least in the standard instances, or paradigmatic cases, of each specific type of obligation.[6] Accordingly, it is potentially misleading to ignore those features and focus exclusively, or directly, on the type-specific traits of a

---

[6] For statements in the same tenor, see K. E. Himma, 'The Ties That Bind: An Analysis of the Concept of Obligation', *Ratio Juris*, 26 (2013), pp. 18–19.

given form of obligation (such as legal obligation, moral obligation, or social obligation). For, unless we preliminarily consider the traits describing what an obligation *in general* is, we will not be able to provide an adequate characterization of any specific type of obligation. The flexible, and yet unified, concept of obligation *simpliciter* thus constitutes the essential dimension of all forms of obligation (which in turn are understood as particular instantiations of that broader genre), such that this general concept fixes the basic traits and conditions of conceivability of each peculiar instantiation of what is obligatory.

From this view that specific types of obligation are dependent on a general idea of which they are types – the idea of obligation *simpliciter* – it follows that legal obligation should be understood as having no special advantage over other forms of obligation just by virtue of its being legal. Far from providing the paradigm of obligation, legal obligation is just one among several possible types of obligation.[7] Significantly, this is a position my approach has in common with Kant's treatment of legal obligation, which is also shaped by the same thesis. Kant defends a comparable view in particular in his 'Doctrine of Right' – 'right' being one of the two main parts into which he divides 'morals' (which in Kant's work has a broad meaning, encompassing not only morality but also the legal realm and, more generally, the practical sphere).[8] For Kant claims that obligation, understood by him as 'the necessity of a free action under a categorical imperative of reason', is one of the basic concepts that different domains of practical philosophy share, such that we must gain a correct understanding of obligation (in general) before we can begin to

---

[7] For a contrary statement, see H. L. A. Hart, 'Legal and Moral Obligation', in A. Melden (ed.), *Essays in Moral Philosophy* (Seattle, University of Washington Press, 1958), pp. 83–4. However, Hart changed his mind later on. See, in particular, the treatment offered in H. L. A. Hart, *Concept of Law* (Oxford, Clarendon, 1994, with a Postscript; or. ed. 1961, pp. 82–91). In that context, Hart explicitly takes up the 'general idea of obligation', understood as 'a necessary preliminary to understanding [obligation] in its legal form' (Hart, *Concept of Law*, p. 85).

[8] Statements of this position can be found not only in *The Metaphysics of Morals* but also in the lectures Kant gave while working on that book. See, for instance, Gottlieb Feyerabend's lecture notes on Kant's course on 'Natural Rights', available in F. Rauscher *Kant: Lectures and Draft on Political Philosophy* (Cambridge, Cambridge University Press, 2015) and corresponding to volume 27 of the Berlin Academy Edition, at 1325–32, where the thesis that legal obligation is best understood as a specific instantiation of obligation *simpliciter* constitutes the first step in Kant's criticism of the sanction theory of legal obligation.

address the fundamental legal concepts and the specific obligations associated with the existence of a legal system.[9]

These observations show that the thesis underpinning one of the key assumptions of my argument is entrenched in Kant's philosophy, where that very thesis is also used to criticize the sanction theory of legal obligation. That is, for Kant as well as for me a comprehensive account of obligation *simpliciter* should be regarded as an essential preliminary step towards any correct understanding of legal obligation and of legal issues at large. Namely, establishing how obligation in general is to be conceived should be regarded as vital to any critical approach to the current uses and practices involving legal obligation.[10] Likewise, it is arguably not possible to recognize whether certain appeals to obligation and obligation-related notions in law are appropriate unless we can draw on a concept of obligation per se, a concept that sets the overarching standard against which actual obligation-related uses and practices can be assessed.

This set of assertions – (1) the claim that obligation as a concept does not refer to a mere disparate arrangement of ideas, only partly connected one to another and only partly mutually resembling, and so obligation singles out one reasonably unified and overarching construct looming behind the more specific uses and the different meanings obligation may take in different contexts, and (2) the thesis that a correct understanding of obligation is a necessary preliminary step in any comprehensive study of legal obligation – provides the justification for the strategy that I intend to follow in this work. This strategy consists in extracting the specific notion of *legal obligation* from the general idea of *obligation*, and

---

[9] I. Kant, *The Metaphysics of Morals* (Cambridge, Cambridge University Press, 1996), AK 6:222; see also AK 6:221–8.

[10] This statement is revealing of the fact that my approach to legal obligation presupposes at least the possibility of (what Daniel Wodak characterizes as) the 'Generic View', namely, the claim that 'there is a univocal meaning of *obligation*, and adjectives like *legal* and *moral* modify obligation in the exact same way; by modifying the "standards used in determining what acts are obligatory"' (D. Wodak, 'What Does "Legal Obligation" Mean?', *Pacific Philosophical Quarterly*, 99(4) (2018), pp. 1–2; original emphasis). Wodak distinguishes the Generic View from two alternative conceptions: the 'Ambiguity View' (that is, the statement that 'there is no univocal meaning (or "unitary concept") of *obligation* as it is used in moral and legal contexts', 'What Does "Legal Obligation" Mean?', p. 1; original emphasis) and the 'Moralized View' (or the thesis that '*obligation* has a distinctively moral meaning in legal contexts', 'What Does "Legal Obligation" Mean?', p. 2; original emphasis). For a detailed discussion of all three positions and a defence of the Generic View I refer the reader to Wodak, 'What Does "Legal Obligation" Mean?'.

so in constructing a theoretical account of legal obligation out of the material that fundamentally defines what obligation is. As a result, by the end of the path I begin covering in this chapter I should be expected to conceptualize legal obligation as a combination of a set of general elements constitutive of obligation per se with an arrangement of traits associated with obligation of the distinctively legal type, understood as the kind of obligation specifically arising out of law.

A final assumption shaping my exploration of obligation, which is closely related to the one just introduced, concerns the kind of approach I embrace. My approach can be characterized as broad and interdisciplinary, as opposed to domain-specific and primarily intra-sectorial. As already mentioned, I take obligation to be a normative idea of wide currency – a notion we appeal to in social contexts, moral settings, and legal frameworks, among others – and one that establishes the necessary conditions of conceivability of (the paradigmatic instances of) each type of what is obligatory – social obligation, moral obligation, legal obligation, and so on. For this reason, in order to account for any specific kind of obligation we need to take up a broad, or philosophical, approach enabling us to put in place a general framework for the study of the obligatory dimension of human experience. In the absence of such a broadly philosophical approach one may well be able to grasp the specific traits of a given kind of obligation, but, at the same time, one would run the risk of missing the general features that kind of obligation typically shares with the other instantiations of what is obligatory. As a result, my strategy for accounting for legal obligation is fundamentally driven and deeply shaped by general philosophical concerns. That is to say, my study of the obligatory component of legal practices proceeds from a general philosophical basis, as opposed to a specifically jurisprudential, or sectorial, basis, and it assigns a central role to essential wide-encompassing philosophical questions, conceptions, debates, and methods.

This strategy does not mean that either I disregard insights and perspectives specifically originating in jurisprudence or I uncritically import into the legal domain ideas and views worked out within the broader philosophical debate. For, on the one hand, the picture of both obligation *simpliciter* and legal obligation that I draw in what follows also heavily relies on contributions offered by legal theorists; on the other hand, I do not try to superimpose a purely philosophical model onto the jurisprudential debate concerning legal obligation. Instead, my use of philosophical constructs – especially those originating in practical philosophy broadly understood – is intended to be instrumental to establish a relation of mutual interaction between philosophy and legal theory. Consequently, the conception of legal obligation I am aiming for should be understood as the outcome of a combined effort where jurisprudence and philosophical studies both stand in the foreground.

On this basis, it can be concluded that from the perspective of my analysis there is a close and mutual dependence between practical philosophy and theory of law, whose concerns more than occasionally overlap with those of practical philosophy. For one thing, practical philosophy can be used to revisit and frame traditional debates concerning the kind of obligation engendered by the law that occupy a central position within legal theory, and possibly to find answers to legal questions that have so far eluded jurisprudence. For another thing, the debate in legal theory is taken to have implications for the broader philosophical discussion of practical matters. That way the approach I devise ultimately sets the stage for a fruitful cross-pollination between philosophical disciplines and legal studies. It is with the aim of exploring the potential inherent in the exchanges between theory of law and practical philosophy that this project about legal obligation is framed. And this is why the nature of my theoretical engagement with obligation as it applies to the legal world can be qualified as genuinely interdisciplinary. Namely, my treatment of legal obligation is the outcome of a theoretical reflection engaging with different areas of study. For a set of debates on which my discussion of obligation in general and legal obligation in particular specifically draws is not surprisingly that developed within mainstream jurisprudence. Indeed, the subject of my investigation is widely regarded as fundamental to the theory of law, understood as a distinct legal discipline devoted to the philosophical study of the concept of law and to the other concepts taken to be fundamental and common to legal systems having a comparable degree of maturity and organization. My construction, however, also benefits from a close engagement with discussions that go beyond the boundaries of legal philosophy. Since I understand obligation as a fundamental component of the normative dimension of human experience, my study of legal obligation heavily relies on, and should be expected to have implications for, a number of debates concerning the normative component of our experience. It is through this relation that my conception acquires a distinctively multidisciplinary character. For if, on this view, we are to put forward a general account of legal obligation, we will have to take up a number of issues framed within different fields of practical philosophy. As much as these fields may be distinct, offering ideas and theories worked out in different contexts, I will bring them together in my attempt to arrive at a rigorous account of obligation as it is originated by legal practices. In sum, my study is grounded on the assumption that we cannot have a full understanding of legal obligation unless we engage in an authentically interdisciplinary endeavour combining insights originally developed by researchers with different interests and a broad range of expertise.

1.3 The Essential Components of Obligation

The chief aim of the remaining part of this chapter is to determine the set of traits commonly ascribed to obligation. This is expected to give us the general meaning of obligation and so the concept of obligation as distinct from a conception, or theoretical account, of obligation. As anticipated in Section 1.2, in my framework of thought the *concept* of obligation is meant to mark the *boundaries* within which the theoretical debate concerning obligation is to take place. It thus refers to the *ground* common to otherwise conflicting, or at least alternative, theoretical views. By contrast, a *conception* of obligation identifies a far more *controversial view* of what is obligatory, a view closely aligned with the particular philosophical preferences underlying one's approach to obligation as well as with the specific contents, criteria, and conditions of existence that different theorists attach to obligation.[11] The idea that I will delineate in

---

[11] This distinction between concept and conception has been made popular by J. Rawls, *A Theory of Justice* (Cambridge (MA), Harvard University Press, 1999, rev. ed.; or. ed. 1971), p. 5. The distinction should not be conflated with the distinction between intension (or sense) and extension (or reference) of a term. In a nutshell, in literature by 'intension' it is meant the set of logical, or definitional, properties that are implied by an idea. Intension, in other words, specifies what the relevant idea *signifies*, or stands for. By contrast, the extension of a term refers to the arrangement of all existing instances of that term – the host of items the term describes. The extension, then, individuates the actual referent of the relevant term – namely, the whole of occurrences to which that term applies. Despite the fact that one may find some superficial similarities between concept and intension as well as between conception and extension (e.g. it may be claimed that both concept and intension are largely context-independent, whereas both conception and extension are context-sensitive ideas), the two distinctions – concept vs. conception, on the one hand, and intension vs. extension, on the other – do not map one unto the other. The discontinuity setting the two distinctions apart can be appreciated, for instance, by considering the fact that intension is regarded as analytic in quality, whilst the quality of extension is synthetic, or so the traditional view goes. By contrast, no such difference in quality characterizes the pair concept–conception, both of which are to be understood as synthetic and a posteriori constructs of thought. I am grateful to Daniel Weston for bringing this point to my attention. I remain of course solely responsible for the errors and misconceptions contained in this footnote.

the following subsections will then be theoretically lightweight: rather than presenting a potentially controversial and partisan picture, I will extract from the literature the current views of what an obligation is so as to reduce them to a common core encapsulating a broad understanding of obligation, or a general framework within which to think about obligation.

To briefly expand upon these introductory remarks, in my framework of thought, the concept of obligation singles out the elements needed to think about obligation as a distinctive idea. Those elements are in turn understood to be the ones inherent in the understanding of obligation that is widespread among those who systematically reflect on what is obligatory. As I define it, therefore, the concept of obligation is established by the *learned* discourse about obligation, that is, by the *educated* people's shared knowledge of what is obligatory, or, to put it otherwise, the specialist *rational* cognition of obligation.

By thus taking a consolidated and ecumenical notion as the starting point of my argument, I intend to protect my approach from the charge that it may be parochial and one-sided. Indeed, the premises of one's inquiry need to be statements of the kind that can be acknowledged as constitutive of the subject matter by all those involved in the debate (or at least by the vast majority of them); otherwise the whole exercise can be accused of being arbitrary and idiosyncratic. Relatedly, if the outcome of my theoretical exploration is to be regarded as reliable and non-partisan, the basis of that exploration needs be such that anyone taking part in the debate and thinking straight should be compelled to accept it. That way the argument avoids the risk of incorporating its potentially controversial and theory-laden conclusions about the subject matter from the very outset. Likewise, the resulting theoretical account cannot be accused of having been smuggled into the starting point and then illicitly presented as the conclusions of the study itself. As a consequence, the whole project will not amount to a concealment of my theoretical preferences, which, far from being already baked into the premises the exploration departs from, can be claimed to be the output of a rigorous process of inquiry. By taking a consolidated and generally shared characterization of obligation as the point of departure of my investigation, I therefore intend to make sure that the whole argument cannot be seen as constructing a contentious picture in its very premises and so as being vitiated *ab ovo*.

It should also be noted in this context that taking the concept of obligation as the initial object of my discussion means choosing a theory-dependent notion as the entry point in the current debate on legal obligation. For the concept of obligation, as I construct it, is the product of the *theoretical* efforts of those who have systematically engaged with the obligatory dimension of human practices and have devoted themselves to advancing our understanding of what is obligatory. By its very construction, such a product is a theory-laden construct and so a philosophically charged piece of knowledge.[12] As a specialist rational understanding of what is obligatory, therefore, the concept of obligation occupies a peculiar position. On the one hand, it is meant to summarize a *less than partisan* framework for the study of obligation; on the other hand, it results from a *theoretical* engagement with the obligatory dimension of our practices. On this basis, the starting point of my exploration can be characterized as a *thin*, or *generic*, theoretical construct. That is to say, such a starting point is not a theory- or philosophy-independent idea, and yet it is sufficiently ecumenical and shared among those debating issues of legal obligation to be understood as non-idiosyncratic and non-arbitrary.

In turn, the choice of relying on a lightly theoretical construction as the premise of the argument that I expect to lead at a comprehensive theoretical account of legal obligation can hardly be regarded as capricious. First, the rationale behind this choice is warranted by the recognition that there are no such things as theoretically neutral judgements in the normative sphere, and so theory is inescapable. For it is sensible to maintain that in the normative domain one can hardly count on some set of 'hard' data: an arrangement of theory-independent elements supported by, and anchored in, something that is verifiable independently of any theory.[13] And, in the absence of a set of premises which are beyond dispute, like hard facts, or which can be independently proved and so are backed by evidence that no one can reasonably challenge, it seems appropriate to rely on the next most trustworthy thing available. Which arguably is the set of convictions that are most widespread within the community of those participating in the relevant

---

[12] This feature depends on the fact that the concept of obligation, as I understand it here, is defined by the traits that theorists, as opposed to laypeople, widely agree to be associated with obligation. Therefore, no matter how widespread the shared views instantiated by the concept of obligation may be, they still reflect a theoretically informed understanding of obligation.

[13] This belief is hardly uncontested and yet several writers will find it at least presumptively tenable. For a statement of this tenor, see, for instance, R. Stern, 'Transcendental Arguments', in E. N. Zalta (ed.), *The Stanford Encyclopedia of Philosophy* (Summer 2015 ed.), http://plato.stanford.edu/archives/sum2015/entries/transcendental-arguments.

debate. After all, what else, if not the considered judgements shared by those who have devoted time and intellectual energy to understanding obligation, can be regarded as the least subjective and reliable entry point for an argument aimed at constructing a comprehensive account of legal obligation? As much as the considered judgements shared by experts in the study of obligation may be fallible and culturally indexed, they provide us with a repository of wisdom, namely, an established and consolidated knowledge, about the obligations associated with our social practices that it would be unreasonable to ignore.[14]

In sum, the premises I will be departing from when constructing a theory of legal obligation consist in the statements constitutive of the concept of obligation. This concept is meant to capture a rationally defensible understanding of obligation, an understanding endorsed by those who take part in the theoretical discussions of issues relating to obligation. Insofar as we recognize that in the normative realm one can only aspire to establish the indispensable character of some features, or traits, within a given domain, and to do so in a way that is limited to a certain community, the concept of obligation, as I define it, can be claimed to be the most catholic, promising, and authoritative point of departure for a theoretical treatment of legal obligation, since there is hardly anything more widely agreed on (perhaps only implicitly) by those whose frame of thought is delimited by the literature concerning the obligatory dimension of our practices. Hence the rationale for my choice to use the concept of obligation as the entry point of the argument that in this study is used to build a theoretical account of legal obligation.[15]

For the reasons just set out, I regard the general understanding of obligation that will be introduced in what follows as sufficiently plausible and non-arbitrary. Hence, I will deem such understanding as requiring no sustained argument in support. By this, I mean that I will consider the concept of obligation to reflect a widely enough shared view of obligation,

---

[14] Insofar as the concept of obligation I take as the starting point of my exploration incorporates the views of obligation shared by those who have systematically reflected on that notion, it cannot be equated with any set of universally compelling, necessary, or objectively valid truths about obligation. It should rather be understood as a historical and contextual understanding of obligation. The exploration I carry out in this work should therefore be understood to start out from a contingent and historical conceptual construct that has gained consensus within the relevant community.

[15] A more systematic discussion of this methodological choice essentially shaping my project can be found in Chapter 10.

asking the reader to follow along, at least for the sake of argument. I am not suggesting, however, that the concept of obligation as it is presented in the rest of this chapter should be taken for granted as a self-evident proposition. For there is no thesis that can hold its ground as uncontroversial in philosophy, much less in the study of obligation, which is a topic with a long tradition enriched by many diverse voices. What I am rather saying is that discussions are necessarily shaped by the initial premises around which they are organized, and this discussion will be framed by the general understanding of obligation soon to be introduced. All I expect, then, is that the general traits of obligation I will single out here will be accepted as reasonable enough to serve as a 'port of entry' into the argument. If they should later turn out to be unreasonable, one can always go back and revise the argument accordingly.[16]

A final caveat is in order before I begin my characterization of obligation as a distinctive concept. My reasoned critical review of the literature is an exercise in judgement and so it is an inevitably selective and non-mechanical process. In order to flesh out the general meaning of obligation I will not make use of logical deductions: what I claim to be the defining traits of obligation are not derived by means of syllogistic operations applied to the bulk of the material in which the current views are set out. In order to identify the concept of obligation I will rather reflect on an understanding of obligation that is widely shared among practical philosophers, thus aiming for a carefully constructed and overall coherent synthesis of the existing positions defended by those who have systematically reflected on that concept. Through this non-deductive exercise in judgement, which both is based on and combines a range of views put forward in the literature, I will work towards a meaningful picture that marks the conceptual boundaries of what is obligatory, thus making it possible for theorists with different

---

[16] The point has famously been stated by Charles Sanders Peirce in his criticism of Cartesian doubt: 'We cannot begin with complete doubt. We must begin with all the prejudices which we actually have when we enter upon the study of philosophy. These prejudices are not to be dispelled by a maxim, for they are things which it does not occur to us can be questioned. Hence this initial skepticism will be a mere self-deception, and not real doubt; and no one who follows the Cartesian method will ever be satisfied until he has formally recovered all those beliefs which in form he has given up. . . . A person may, it is true, in the course of his studies, find reason to doubt what he began by believing; but in that case he doubts because he has a positive reason for it, and not on account of the Cartesian maxim. Let us not pretend to doubt in philosophy what we do not doubt in our hearts.' (C. S. Peirce, 'Some Consequences of Four Incapacities', *Journal of Speculative Philosophy*, 2 (1868), pp. 140–1).

philosophical backgrounds and legal-theoretical preferences to engage in the debate concerning obligation.

In this vein, here I do not intend to offer a (mere) list of the traits that different theorists have regarded as central, or even as essential, to the definition of obligation. As a matter of fact, one can hardly find even a handful of features uncontroversially viewed by everyone as defining obligation. Since almost no element that has been claimed to be constitutive of obligation has gone unchallenged, the attempt to find a set of core traits everyone considers necessary to a sound definition of obligation is hopeless. For this reason, instead of recording all that has been said about obligation in the existing literature, I will take the point of view of someone who should be considered a competent user of the concept-term 'obligation'; and from this viewpoint I will consider what general components something must have in order to be qualified as an obligation. This way, I intend to characterize obligation at a very general and non-partisan – albeit certainly not pre-theoretical – level of analysis, thus attempting to single out the elements lacking which nothing would be regarded as an obligation by a competent speaker.

In sum, in the rest of this chapter, I will be discussing the traits and properties that define obligation as a distinctive concept. The resulting characterization – to be interpreted as providing us with the general meaning of obligation – will be thin and widely acceptable. In this sense, the concept should be able to accommodate a vast range of specific accounts of obligation reflecting the distinct philosophical perspectives endorsed by those who have defended those accounts. At the same time, the general meaning of obligation is neither pointless nor irrelevant. While it does not give a comprehensive answer to the basic questions about obligation, as these questions are debated among those who study obligation, to the same extent to which a specific theoretical account can do, it does make sense of these questions. Accordingly, the concept of obligation will be framed in terms sufficiently clear and precise to render intelligible such questions as: what is the nature of obligation?, how are obligation and 'ought' related?, what is the distinctive force of an obligation?, is the existence of an obligation independent of the specific perspective, goals, interests, and desires of those who are subject to that obligation, or is it rather necessarily tied to those persons' cognitive and volitional attitudes?, how is obligation related to other paradigmatic normative instances like imperatives, requests, and recommendations?, what is the kind of justification, if any, that should be associated with the existence of obligation?, is obligation essentially linked with sanction and coercion, or at least with the possibility of sanctioning and coercing deviant conduct?, how are obligation, wrongness, and accountability connected?, and, finally, what kinds of entities – persons, institutions, states of affairs – intrinsically have or lack the capacity of obligating? The features and properties that match these sweeping and encompassing criteria, by thus defining the general meaning of obligation, as such features and properties emerge from a critical review of the literature, are introduced analytically and discussed separately in the following subsections.

1.3.1 Obligation and Practical Normativity

Obligation is widely acknowledged to incorporate a distinctively normative and practical dimension. Revealing in this context are, for instance, Kenneth Einar Himma's statements that obligations are associated with 'claims about what someone (or some class of persons) *ought to do* in some state of affairs' and that 'obligations arise only where there are *prescriptions* that guide and enable the appraisal of *human acts*.'[17] Thus, obligation can be so described: (a) on the normative side, obligation involves reference to *standards* providing guidance and enabling appraisal, by thus securing a basis for judging one's performance as correct or incorrect, and, (b) on the practical side, obligation serves as a means by which our *conduct* is guided and assessed, and so is *action-centred* – obligation is concerned with one's doing, or acting. That is to say, obligation sets itself up as a *practical norm* – it indicates that which *an agent ought to do* – and can accordingly be broken down analytically into an '*ought*' component (the normative part) and a '*do*' component (the practical part).[18] Both these components are essential to conceiving of something as obligatory.[19]

---

[17] Himma, 'Ties That Bind', p. 20 and p. 21, respectively (emphasis added).

[18] Let me specifically clarify that here 'ought' stands for a conceptual category, as opposed to a mere verbal-semantic expression. 'Ought', in other terms, refers to a category of thought distinct from and irreducible to the category of 'is'. And insofar as 'ought' is understood as a conceptual category it can be expressed by a number of different terms and phrases, such as 'has to' and 'should' (just to name a few), which indicates the same idea without using the word 'ought'. I should like to thank Dietmar von der Pfordten for bringing this point to my attention.

[19] These two traits are recognized as essential to obligation in H. A. Prichard, *Moral Obligation* (Oxford, Clarendon, 1949), pp. 87–163; K. Baier, 'Moral Obligation', *American Philosophical Quarterly*, 3 (1966), p. 210; and, more recently, D. Owens, 'Rationalism about Obligation', *European Journal of Philosophy*, 16 (2008), p. 406, too. That

To briefly elaborate on these points, on the one hand, obligation is normative, vis-à-vis descriptive, since it provides us with a standard for guiding, appraising and justifying.[20] In the same vein, obligation is best conceived as a guideline that is *normatively* effective but need not be *causally* so. That is, obligation is concerned with the normative statuses of agents, and so it refers 'to the products of an exercise of *normative power*.'[21] Likewise, the relation between those who are under an obligation and those who are in the position to make claims on those persons by virtue of that obligation is not primarily empirical: it is a relation based on considerations about what certain individuals *have to do*, as opposed to what those individuals *in fact do* or are *likely to do*. On the other hand, obligation is distinctively *practical* in that it exists, to borrow some words Thomas Pink uses in his characterization of moral obligation, as 'a standard on agency – action or omission.'[22] As a result, Pink continues, we can only be under an obligation 'to do or omit doing things' and can hardly be claimed to have an obligation in relation to things that 'happen independently of our own action.'[23] Since obligations are ultimately designed to operate within the realm of action – inherent in what is obligatory is an action-guiding and action-justificatory component – we cannot

---

practicality too (not just normativity) should be recognized as essential to obligation finds a clear statement also in Jaap Hage's work, where the 'ought' is distinguished into two kinds – which he calls the 'ought-to-do' and the 'ought-to-be' (see Hage, 'Legal Transactions and the Legal Ought', pp. 178–83). Obligation, Hage argues, is an instance of the former kind, in that it determines what *ought* to be *done*, and so provides constraints on behaviour. On this basis, what is obligatory should not be confused with what 'ought-to-be' – that is, with some instantiation of non-practical normativity – 'which expresses how the facts should lay without necessarily implying that somebody in particular ought to make the facts comply with this ideal' and so has 'little to do with action' (Hage, 'Legal Transactions and the Legal Ought', p. 179). In this framework, the category of what ought to exist, on the one hand, and the category we use to state what ought to be done, on the other, are distinct. Accordingly, resolving obligation in an instantiation of what ought to exist would amount to the conflating of two different categories of thought, namely, to incur into a category mistake.

[20] The connection between normativity and ought is widely accepted today. For a couple of recent exemplary statements of this connection, see J. Dancy, 'Editor's Introduction', in J. Dancy (ed.), *Normativity* (London, Blackwell, 2000), p. vii; and J. Broome, 'Reasoning', typescript (with the author), pp. 8–10).
[21] Owens, 'Rationalism about Obligation', p. 408; original emphasis.
[22] T. Pink, 'Moral Obligation', in A. O'Hear (ed.), *Modern Moral Philosophy* (Cambridge, Cambridge University Press, 2004), p. 160.
[23] Pink, 'Moral Obligation', p. 160.

legitimately conceive of obligation as a notion falling outside the practical sphere or as a notion having no practical reach or effect.

This breakdown helps us to distinguish obligation, on the one hand, from that which is practical but *descriptive* (indicating not what agents *ought to* do but what they, *in fact*, do or are most *likely* to do) and, on the other hand, from that which is normative but *theoretical*, or even *epistemic*, by virtue of its depicting an account of the world as it ought to *be* (not necessarily implying any agency or action on our part but mere contemplation). The latter realm can, in turn, be distinguished from the world such as it *is*, which places us in a domain diametrically opposite to that of obligation, a sphere at once theoretical and descriptive – the sphere of the '*is*'. Hence, at a conceptual level obligation can be initially described in terms of a breakdown that works by way of two conceptual oppositions: normative, as opposed to descriptive, and practical, as opposed to theoretical. These two conceptual oppositions yield four kinds of dimensions, or categories, namely, (i) the theoretical and descriptive dimension (which has to do with the world such as it is); (ii) the theoretical and normative dimension (which concerns the world as it ought, or has, to be); (iii) the practical and descriptive dimension (which relates to what agents do); and (iv) the practical and normative dimension (which refers to what agents ought, or have, to do). Only in the fourth class can obligation be found.

1.3.2 Obligation as a Requirement

In the normative and practical realm, which is a domain inhabited by different kinds of standards for guiding and appraising action, obligation is taken to specifically single out a *requirement*, or *necessity*.[24] That is, associated to obligation is a *specific* normative quality: the quality of a *demand*. What is obligatory is prescriptive and mandatory – obligation makes conduct exactable and compulsory. Which is to say that an obligation places us under a directive and, related, obligatoriness stands for requiredness, or necessitation, as opposed to reasonableness, or commendableness. In other terms, what is obligatory cannot be reduced

---

[24] On the idea of obligation as a requirement, see R. Brandt, 'The Concepts of Obligation and Duty', *Mind*, 73 (1964), p. 374; Pink, 'Moral Obligation', pp. 159-61; Owens, 'Rationalism about Obligation', p. 403; and S. Darwall, 'Moral Obligation: Form and Substance', *Proceedings of the Aristotelian Society*, Supplementary Volume 110 (2009), pp. 31-6.

to something practically normative qua desirable, advisable, or generically good. Nor does an obligation simply constitute a point in favour of what it instructs one to do. Similarly, disregarding an obligation is considered not just to be foolish, insensible, or worthless as, by contrast, acting against the good advice, counsel, suggestion, or recommendation of someone may be. The condition that those who have an obligation finds themselves in can, on this basis, be differentiated from the circumstance experienced by those who are merely commended to do something. For the former subjects, unlike the latter, are *required* to do what the relevant obligatory standard directs them to do.

To rephrase this point, inscribed in obligation is a specific kind of 'ought': binding, or mandatory, 'ought', since being under an obligation is tantamount to be compelled, bound, expected, or urged (in a normative sense, vis-à-vis a physical sense and psychological sense) to act in the prescribed way. That the notion of demand is constitutive of, or essential to, obligation can be appreciated by considering the circumstance that presenting an obligation as an inherently, or even primarily, advisory standard, rather than as a prescriptive principle, would strike most students of obligation as not only odd but also ultimately untenable. Namely, direction, not recommendation, best describes what an obligation commits us to: an obligation encapsulates a requirement that, if recognized as valid, has the quality of a pronouncement normatively *urging* one to engage in some course of conduct. So, for one thing, obligation is conceptually connected to a necessity, making any alternative course of conduct ineligible and unviable; for another thing, when an obligation exists, just one course of action is, normatively speaking, available to the agent. On this basis, it can be claimed that our having an obligation and our being bound to do something are not only etymologically related terms – 'obligation' derives from the Latin word *ligare*, 'to bind' – but they are also conceptually interlinked: obligation identifies a bond, or *vinculum*, something that fetters an agent by making certain courses of action compulsory in the relevant circumstances. Obligation, in sum, is a kind of normative necessitation issuing from a binding standard whose nature is mandatory.

Insofar as obligation is defined by requiredness, it applies a distinctive pressure on its addressees. The distinctiveness of the pressure attached to obligation is twofold.[25] On the one hand, it is widely recognized that we

---

[25] The peculiarity of the pressure associated with obligation is discussed in A. Gewirth, 'Obligation: Political, Legal, Moral', in R. Pennock and J. Chapman (eds.), *Political and*

cannot be said to have an obligation if we are under no constraint, or similarly if we can *effortlessly* free ourselves of it. In the presence of an obligation, it is noted by Margaret Gilbert for instance, 'people may feel trapped', since an obligation cannot be shrugged off or modified by 'a simple change of mind.'[26] In that sense, obligation comes with some built-in resistance limiting the options available to an agent – an obligation is 'something that takes the matter out of your hands', as David Owens phrases it.[27] This is also why an imperceptible or insignificant constraint would hardly count as an obligation. For an impalpable and hardly tangible constriction would exert no discernible pressure on those who are under such constraint and so ultimately it would amount to no compulsion at all – not even a normative one – by thus not being qualifiable as an obligation, to begin with. On the other hand, the (noticeable) pressure we are under when we have an obligation need not be inexorable. This dimension of obligation is due to the fact that the necessity of obligation – its demanding that one does something – is neither naturalistic nor metaphysical nor logical, but rather distinctively normative. Precisely because what is obligatory does not consist of any natural and conceptual kind of necessity, obligations can as a matter of practical possibility be ignored, disposed of, or violated. Hence, ordinarily we do have the capacity to act against the claims made by our obligations. In performing such act, we disobey, or even challenge, a genuine and substantial constraint imposed on us. And a decision to so act will not typically come without consequences. But the act through which one infringes upon an obligation is neither naturalistically nor metaphysically nor logically impossible.

In combination the two dimensions of the pressure associated with obligation just introduced – tangibility and escapability – mean that the realm inhabited by obligations marks off the sphere of a resistant and yet violable necessity. This feature of obligation – its presenting itself as a normatively significant but empirically ignorable imposition on us – can be further conceptualized in a number of more specific ways. But the specific way in which we choose to do so is going to depend largely on the

---

Legal Obligation (New York, Atherton, 1970), pp. 55–6; M. Forrester, 'Some Remarks on Obligation, Permission, and Supererogation', *Ethics*, 85 (1975), p. 219; and G. Cupit, 'How Requests (and Promises) Create Obligations', *Philosophical Quarterly*, 44 (1994), pp. 439–41.

[26] M. Gilbert, *On Social Facts* (Princeton, Princeton University Press, 1992), p. 34.

[27] Owens, 'Rationalism about Obligation', p. 404.

particular theory of obligation we espouse and the philosophical preferences we have. An introduction to the concept of obligation, therefore, cannot set out in any further detail the sense in which obligation takes the form of a distinctive normative pressure (a form of pressure distinct of, and irreducible to the kind of pressure that, say, suggestions and recommendations put on us). Indeed, any further characterization would lead one to move from a description of the *concept* of obligation to an argument for a *conception* of obligation. Whereas I do in Chapter 7 provide such an argument (at least in relation to the type of obligation engendered by the law), for the time being it suffices to point out that the idea of obligation as a discernible and yet resistible normative necessitation may find, and in fact it currently finds, a range of interpretations in the literature.[28]

1.3.3 Obligation, Wrongness and Accountability

An implication of the conceptual connection that is widely thought to exist between what is *obligatory* and what is *required* (as distinct from what is sensible) is that obligation and wrongness too are widely regarded as essentially associated. As mentioned above, obligation sets out (i) a normative standard the compliance with which (ii) can be legitimately demanded of, or is exactable from, those placed under it. The normative quality of obligation (i) means that the claim what is obligatory makes on us is intended to be valid, or justified (as opposed to being merely effective, operative, or efficacious) in the domain to which the obligatory standard applies. Hence the pressure obligation exerts on us is, at least

---

[28] Examples are the conception of obligations as (a) a compelling demand supported by protected reasons for action insulated from at least some countervailing reasons, (b) a requirement having either entrenched force or a particular additional inbuilt strength, and (c) an overriding constriction. The idea of an obligation as a protected reason following an exclusionary logic is owed to Joseph Raz (see J. Raz, *Practical Reason and Norms* (London, Hutchinson, 1990; 1st ed. 1975), pp. 73-84). Stephen Perry appeals instead to the idea of reasons of different weights to explain the difference between an obligation and a statement supporting but not requiring a course of action (see S. Perry, 'Judicial Obligation, Precedent and the Common Law', *Oxford Journal of Legal Studies*, 7 (1987), pp. 215-57; and S. Perry, 'Second Order Reasons, Uncertainty and Legal Theory', *Southern California Law Review*, 62 (1989), pp. 913-94). The idea of overridingness is central to David Gauthier's account of obligation (see D. Gauthier, *Practical Reasoning* (Oxford, Clarendon, 1963), p. 201) as well as to Darwall's, which specifically describes *moral* obligation in this way (see S. Darwall, 'Moral Obligation and Accountability', in *Oxford Studies in Metaethics*, 2 (2007), pp. 111-12).

prima facie and within the relevant context, legitimate and defensible. In addition, it was claimed, within the normative realm obligation takes the shape of a requirement (ii): obligation configures a course of action as demanded, vis-à-vis generically worth, reasonable, or advisable. Now, this twofold dimension of obligation is the basis on which obligation can be said to be essentially connected with wrongness. For the combination of those two components of obligation – normativity and requiredness – renders what is obligatory something demandable, that is, something that can be *legitimately required*, not merely *de facto exacted*, from the obligated party. This statement means in turn that those who fail to comply with an obligation should be regarded as doing something wrong, when measured against the applicable normative standard. Namely, it is (at least presumptively) wrong not to do what is demandable, or exactable, in accordance with the normative patterns those placed under an obligation (ought to) underwrite, or commit to. Which remark indicates that obligation and wrongness are conceptually connected via the idea of one's being *normatively bound* to do what an obligation directs one to do.[29] Likewise, it is hardly arbitrary, capricious, or unreasonable to treat those who do not fulfil their obligations as wrongdoers – after all, they are subjects who act against a presumptively justified demand placed on them.[30]

From what precedes it can be concluded that there is a close, or analytical, link between obligation and wrongness. For a conceptual correspondence exists between (a) one's being obligated to perform a given conduct and (b) being presumptively wrong for that one to act otherwise. And, since it is prima facie wrong for someone to act contrary to an obligation, doing what one has an obligation to do is pro tanto right, whilst failing to comply with an obligation – and so refraining from performing what a normative standard demands – is tantamount to acting wrongly unless that action contrary to the obligation at stake is accompanied by an adequate justification. Therefore, someone is typically acknowledged to be (presumptively) guilty of wrongdoing whenever

---

[29] Crucially, the same (close and strict) relation does not obtain between what is advisable, or reasonable, and what is wrong, since it is not necessarily the case that failing to do what is advisable, or reasonable, is also wrong (although it is intrinsically foolish, or insensible).

[30] For a statement of the link between obligation and wrongness, see Pink, 'Moral Obligation', pp. 173–5; and Owens, 'Rationalism about Obligation', pp. 403–4, for instance. Similarly, Christopher Essert includes that link among the 'set of intuitions or platitudes about obligation' any theoretical account of obligation need be consistent with (C. Essert, 'Legal Obligation and Reasons', *Legal Theory*, 19 (2013), p. 68).

she does less than she can be legitimately expected, qua justifiably required, to do. That is to say, wrongness and obligation essentially imply each other, to the effect that if an agent has a presumptive obligation to act in a certain way then it is prima facie wrong for that agent to act differently.[31]

Crucially, once it is combined with the widespread assumption that those who have an obligation are purposive and intentional agents, the analytic connection linking obligation and wrongness discloses a further component of obligation: its correlation with accountability. Obligation and accountability are intrinsically related, since those having an obligation can also be held accountable for any infringement of that obligation they may carry out. This conceptual relationship stems from the fact that violating an obligation is (at least pro tanto) wrong and those performing an act of (presumptive) wrongdoing are (at least prima facie) accountable for failing to comply with the claims obligations make on them. To put this point otherwise, since someone acting in breach of an obligation is one who does something wrong and one who does wrong can be called to account for one's wrongdoing, a conceptual connection obtains between obligation and accountability.

This connection is paradigmatically made to emerge by Stephen Darwall, who qualifies it as an 'intrinsic' link.[32] True, in his study not only is Darwall concerned just with a specific type of obligation – moral obligation – as distinct of obligation per se, but also he takes up a peculiar perspective. For Darwall builds on Peter Strawson's theory of reactive attitudes to theorize a general account of moral obligation from what he expressly characterizes as the 'second-person standpoint.'[33] A number of claims Darwall defends in his construction, therefore, reflect a specific theoretical framework and so they should be regarded as primarily meant to give us a (potentially controversial and divisive) conception of a specific type of obligation, vis-à-vis an ecumenical concept of obligation per se. Nonetheless, it seems to me, Darwall's point that moral obligation and accountability are intrinsically connected can be generalized. Even those who do not approach obligation from the second-person standpoint and

---

[31] As Himma ('Ties That Bind', p 22) puts it, 'an unexcused and unjustified non-performance of a *j*-obligation is *j*-ly wrong'.

[32] S. Darwall, *The Second-Person Standpoint* (Cambridge (MA), Harvard University Press, 2006), p. 91. The link is discussed in detail in Darwall, *Second-Person Standpoint*, pp. 91–118.

[33] The reference is, in particular, to P. Strawson, *Freedom and Resentment, and Other Essays* (London, Methuen, 1968), pp. 1–28.

are concerned with obligation *simpliciter*, as opposed to moral obligation, should be expected to acknowledge the role accountability plays in defining obligation. For, as long as obligation is conceptualized as a requirement – a claim that many philosophers are willing to uphold – those who have an obligation can be called to act as the obligation directs and so they are both answerable for what they are obligated to do and, similarly, accountable for any breach of their obligations.[34]

The statement that obligation is essentially related to accountability is, hence, best understood as a general assertion about obligation, namely, a claim that is neither conditioned on the acceptance of a given theoretical perspective nor dependent on the specific type of obligation at stake. The statement is rather owed to, and justified by, the general fact that obligation is analytically linked to (at least presumptive) wrongdoing and an agent is prima facie accountable, or answerable, for her doing what is wrong. Because one acting in breach of her obligations is not simply performing an unreasonable conduct – she is rather failing to do what she is legitimately demanded to do – she can, on this basis, be called to answer for her conduct and held accountable for failing to meet her obligations. Namely, anyone who has an obligation, moral or otherwise, should be taken to be accountable for what she does about that obligation. Or, to put it differently, for one thing, what we are obligated to do cannot be conceptually distinguished from what we are accountable for doing and, for another, we are accountable for compliance with the obligations we have, since acting in accordance with our obligations is presumptively the right thing to do (qua a token of abstinence from wrongdoing).

In conclusion, obligation is essentially tied to accountability by virtue of its being analytically linked to wrongness. Relatedly, the trio – obligation, wrongness and accountability for compliance – form a closely knit and tightly interwoven conceptual cluster.

1.3.4 *Is Obligation a Relational, Qua Personal, Notion?*

The preceding remarks might be taken to lead to the conclusion that obligation has a relational, qua personal, structure. For, I indicated,

---

[34] The independence of the link between obligation and accountability from the standpoint one takes – and more generally from the specific account of obligation one is committed to – is noticed by Darwall himself (see Darwall, 'Moral Obligation: Form and Substance', pp. 31–4).

obligation designates a normative status where some individuals are accountable for performing certain actions. On this ground, it could be argued that in order for an obligation to exist, it must be the case that some people are in the position to be able to exact certain things from others (those bound by the obligation in question). More to the point, it may be thought that, when an obligation is in place, someone must be entitled to expect from the person having an obligation either (a) some kind of behaviour by virtue of that obligation or (b) some kind of restitution for that person's failure to comply with that obligation.

Although one can hardly deny that a basic relational structure is inscribed into obligation, we should not write too much into it, especially when obligation is understood (as it is here) in a generic sense. For, insofar as the notion of obligation is conceived in a generic sense, we should allow for the possibility that what one is obligated to do (and is accountable for doing) is not owed to a specific person – and so it does not, strictly speaking, have a definite relational, or personal, structure – but is rather generically expected of indeterminate others. This means that obligation in its generic sense is not necessarily concerned with personal relations between individuals and to that extent is a relational notion only in a loose sense of the term.

One can express the same idea by relying on the distinction between directed and imputed obligation.[35] Obligation in the *directed* sense is a narrow notion of obligation that refers to the position of someone bound to do something for someone else, who in turn has a legitimate claim to that thing. A directed obligation is an obligation owed to a particular person and so is correlative to a claim or right that person has. From this it follows that a directed obligation is intrinsically relational by virtue of the specific bond it sets up between individuals. This notion of obligation can be contrasted with a broader notion: the idea of *imputed* obligation, understood as a requirement that is not necessarily owed to another person bound by a special relationship to those placed under the obligation but is rather owed to others generally. Thus, the counterparty in cases involving an imputed obligation needs to be neither specified nor specifiable. An obligation can be due simply because compliance with it is in the general interest, rather than being understood to satisfy the rightful claim of a specific individual accordingly entitled to exact compliance from those placed under the

---

[35] This distinction is introduced in Gilbert, *On Social Facts*, pp. 35–42.

obligation. In imputed obligations, therefore, the relational aspect of obligation is only indirect and devoid of practical import. This, in turn, justifies the claim that a broad and tolerant concept of obligation should refrain from incorporating any reference to the relational structure of the bond constitutive of obligation.

1.4 Conclusion

In this chapter, I introduced the concept of obligation, which, when characterized as the set of features specialists widely regard as defining the obligatory dimension of human practices, was argued to be the least controversial starting point for the construction of a theoretical account of legal obligation. This was claimed to be the case for two reasons. First, the concept of obligation was constructed as a constitutively tolerant and ecumenical notion. True, obligation qua concept is a theoretically loaded idea and, as such, it can hardly be known and defined without reference to the learned discourse about obligation that has been carried out within the philosophical literature. Nonetheless, the concept of obligation is an idea that is not compromised by, and so is independent of, a specific theoretical perspective. Which means that theorists with the most diverse philosophical backgrounds and preferences can concur in endorsing the concept of obligation, whilst at the same time remaining free, and indeed being expected, to disagree when they argue for a more specific account, or conception, of obligation. Secondly, the concept of obligation is concerned (not with some specific type of obligation but rather) with the general notion of obligation, or obligation per se. Now, even the theorists who fail to agree over the specific quality of legal obligation – is it an autonomous kind of what is obligatory, or rather does it instantiate a type of social tie, or is it reducible to a moral duty, or else? – at a deep conceptual level should reasonably be expected to understand legal obligation as a variant of what is obligatory per se and so to acknowledge it as an obligation to begin with. And, insofar as they concede as much, they are committed to incorporate in their specific theory of legal obligation the traits constitutive of obligation as a concept – traits that, accordingly, should be regarded as necessary, although not sufficient, conditions of the conceivability of legal obligation qua a kind of what is obligatory. Hence the significance of introducing the concept of obligation and regarding it as a safe initial premise in the argument directed at the construction of a conception of legal obligation.

In this context, I engaged in a critical review of the literature concerning obligation and claimed that the features and properties essentially attached to obligation are practicality, normativity, requiredness, wrongness-relatedness, and linkage to accountability. On this basis, I concluded that obligation is best conceived as a practically normative (Section 3.1) requirement that makes a perceptible and yet empirically resistible claim on us (Section 3.2), who in turn do something presumptively wrong, for which we can be held accountable, insofar as we fail to abide by it (Section 3.3). This I regard to be the fundamental, or essential, and so minimal characterization of obligation. This characterization is also broad, tolerant and generic enough to be used as the very starting point of the argument I deploy in the rest of this book in support of my theory of legal obligation. Since legal obligation is a kind, or instantiation, of what is obligatory and the concept of obligation defines what is obligatory at its most basic level, no theoretical account of legal obligation can refrain from incorporating (and providing an interpretation as well as a specification of) the traits I pinpointed in this chapter as defining, and constitutive, of obligation. For disregarding those traits would mean to characterize the requirements set out by the law as not being obligatory. To put this the other way round, in order for any conception of legal obligation to be theoretically tenable, that conception must account for the fact that the kind of obligation engendered by the law partakes of the concept of obligation, as I have introduced it in this chapter. For this reason, in the rest of my argument, I will feel entitled to use the concept of obligation set out in this chapter as the elemental standard against which the main accounts of legal obligation theorized so far can be critically assessed.

Importantly, the treatment of the concept of obligation undertaken in this chapter has also provided me with the opportunity to clarify two other basic assumptions underlying my engagement with legal obligation. I focused in particular on (1) the fact that I will embrace a broad, or philosophical, approach, by thus engaging not only with the legal-theoretical literature but also with contributions coming from other branches of practical philosophy, and (2) the fact that I am interested in offering a conception of presumptive, as opposed to conclusive, legal obligation. In doing so, I implicitly admitted the programmatic, or constitutive, limitations of my argument concerning legal obligation. Such argument is ambitious, since it deals with an idea – legal obligation – that has attracted the interest of several theorists at different times and it aims at providing a general conceptualization of that idea from a broad and philosophically oriented perspective; and yet the argument is limited, for it is not meant to address all the disputes concerning legal obligation and is rather concerned with conceptualizing that notion when the notion is understood as the merely pro tanto demands legal systems place on those living under their jurisdictions.

2

Contemporary Approaches to Legal Obligation
A Preliminary Map

2.1 Introduction

In Chapter 1, I looked at obligation as a concept capturing the essential traits of the human experience of all things obligatory – a barebones statement of that experience. Since any instantiation of what is obligatory will contain those defining traits, the same traits can be understood to capture the conditions that need to obtain in order for obligation to be intelligible to us. But precisely because these defining traits are understood to be necessarily present in any particular instance of what is obligatory, they cannot exhaustively explain every single type of obligation. They are not, in other words, sufficient conditions for the conceivability of all such types, which in addition to having the constitutive traits of *obligation simpliciter* will also have further defining features. As anticipated, this way of framing obligation entails the thesis that in developing an account of *legal obligation* aspiring to be sound and comprehensive, we will need our conception of legal obligation to include both the defining traits of the concept of obligation and some additional traits distinctive to obligation as it is engendered by the law.

This thesis will guide my inquiry and shape the main argument that will be unpacked in the rest of the monograph, serving as the basic benchmark against which to assess the tenability of the most influential views of legal obligation currently defended in the literature. That is to say, in Chapters 3 to 6 those views will be reinterpreted as possible alternative inflections of the general concept of obligation introduced in Chapter 1, thereby reframing this concept for the legal domain and filling it with contents specific to it, while using the same general (albeit necessarily incomplete) concept as a preliminary litmus test making it possible to see whether the inflected conceptions of legal obligation in the literature can qualify as instantiations of the general concept of obligation.

The strategy I will be following in this work can be more specifically restated thus. The main hypothesis underpinning my treatment of legal obligation is the proposition that in order for a conception of legal obligation to be theoretically tenable, it must show that, as a bare minimum, legal obligation (a) is *normative* in a *practical* way (Section 1.3.1); (b) *requires* us to do (or not do) something in this or that circumstance by making a claim on us (Section 1.3.2); (c) entails that any disregard of, or non-compliance with, such claim would amount to a wrong on our part such we can be held accountable if we do fail to comply with that (Section 1.3.3); and (d) has its source in law. On this view, an account of legal obligation should be able to explain how certain requirements can arise out of law to begin with, but in a way that is practical and normative. Which is to say that while the law can prescribe certain courses of action as mandatory, we can still choose to act otherwise (thereby failing to comply with its demands) but not without normative consequences (meaning that in that case we can be said to have committed a wrong and can accordingly be held accountable for our actions). Conversely, a conception that fails to account for these traits of what is legally obligatory will be regarded as theoretically inadequate, considering that the point of introducing the same traits is to offer a picture of what the *essential* components of obligation are, before we even turn to obligation such as it arises in this or that context or domain.

An important caveat is in order here: in the rest of this work I will not assume that the general concept of legal obligation introduced in Chapter 1 has actually served as a starting point for the accounts of legal obligation so far found in the literature. Nor do I assume that these accounts were ever explicitly intended to address the concerns which the general, barebones concept addresses. We need to recognize and accept that in legal theory today we find a range of different conceptions of legal obligation concerning different issues. But, and this is the basic hypothesis informing my critical engagement with the jurisprudential accounts of legal obligation passed in review from Chapters 3 to 6, no conception of obligation can be regarded as theoretically sound unless it can be shown to be an instance of obligation per se.

To expand on the caveat, in using the concept of obligation as a benchmark or litmus test (however much a preliminary and non-exhaustive one) by which to judge whether different conceptions of legal obligation are adequate, I take up a perspective that is neither historical nor strictly internal to the debates I engage with. What it means to characterize my benchmarking as *non-historical* is that my interest here is mainly conceptual. In other words, I am not interested in discussing the intellectual process and motivations that have led a given legal theorist or tradition of legal thought to characterize legal obligation in a certain way. I am rather concerned with the question of whether the theory at hand ultimately succeeds in presenting legal obligation as a type of obligation and so whether it carries the minimum content of obligation (in accordance with the concept set out in Chapter 1). What it means to characterize my benchmarking as *not strictly internal* to the theories of obligation I will critically assess in what follows, then, is that we need to recognize that these theories may well regard as unimportant what in this exploration is instead taken to be fundamental, namely, that a conception of legal obligation needs to reflect and explain a set of traits understood as essential to the *concept* of obligation. Accordingly, the advocates of those theories may well regard the criteria I use to assess and criticize their conceptions of legal obligation as in large part foreign to the criteria that matter to the research programmes out of which their theories and conceptions originate. The kind of critique undertaken here may therefore be claimed to some extent to be conducted from a standpoint external to those research programmes. But that is to be expected with any radical critique, namely, with any criticism levelled by someone that does not share the same premises with the conception they set out to criticize.

With these clarifications in place in this chapter I proceed to paint the backdrop against which to set the research project undertaken in this book, namely, to provide an overview of the accounts of legal obligation that in Chapters 3 to 6 will more specifically be discussed and evaluated in light of the benchmark, or litmus test, just mentioned. The discussion in this chapter will therefore be predominantly interpretive, concisely reconstructing the most ambitious theories of legal obligation currently championed and locating them on a preliminary rough map designed to bring out the fundamental conceptual relationships that hold among these theories. As tends to be the case with interpretive hypotheses, the reconstructions offered in this chapter will not only be tentative but also open to challenge. Indeed, in introducing the existing theoretical accounts of legal obligation we could envision other taxonomies, and so other ways of providing a bird's-eye view of the current debate on how legal obligation is best conceptualized. So, the map offered in this chapter partly reflects my own theoretical interests and research objectives, and not everyone may share these interests and objectives. But for all that, I submit that the reconstruction offered here does not in any significant way distort the landscape of existing accounts of legal obligation, to the effect that the resulting map is hardly arbitrary.

As suggested, in addition to being theoretically charged, the reconstruction offered in this chapter will provide no more than an outline view of the theories of legal obligation framing the current debate. This is to be expected in a work of this kind, where the purpose of giving the 'lie of the land' is not to granularly account for every conception of legal obligation defended in jurisprudence but to locate my own conception within contemporary legal theory so as to convey a clear sense of how it relates to the other views of legal obligation that have been advanced so far and become established. In fact, any more comprehensive and detailed reconstruction would require a separate work of considerable length. For, as mentioned in the Introduction, the problem of explaining the kind of obligation generated by the law has engaged legal philosophy from the outset and so has been attacked by theorists working in different philosophical traditions in a debate spanning across the centuries. It is therefore a complex picture that would have to be painted in providing an exhaustive account of that body of work. And, no study of reasonable length could realistically aspire to do that. The project taken up in this chapter is thus limited in both scope and ambition: I will merely identify the main conceptions of legal obligation advanced in recent jurisprudence, in such a way as to set the stage for the discussion in Chapters 3 to 6, where these conceptions will be subjected to punctual critical analysis by looking at whether they can work as instantiations of the concept of obligation introduced in Chapter 1. It is for this reason that the accounts of legal obligation presented in this chapter will not be discussed in any thorough manner but will be reduced to a map of their basic models or paradigms.

2.2 Models of Legal Obligation: A Basic Dichotomy

Legal obligation has been conceived in many different ways by legal theorists with diverse philosophical backgrounds. And, even though this rich variety of conceptions will not be reflected in this overview, the discussion that follows will serve a critical purpose in reducing this many-hued landscape to a map of the basic models on which basis legal obligation is conceptualized today. There is a broad fundamental distinction that can be usefully introduced in this connection between two models – an empirical model and a normative one – to which I submit all conceptions of legal obligation can, without oversimplification, be reduced.

An approach to legal obligation can be qualified as *empirical*, as opposed to normative, insofar as it seeks to explain legal obligation entirely in terms of the way people in fact behave or are likely to behave when they are said to be under an obligation. Obligation, on this model, is a concept that pertains to the conceptual category of 'is' as opposed to the conceptual category of 'ought'. Here the 'is' and the 'ought' are understood as two frameworks of thought rather than as two distinct ontological kinds. Ontologically speaking, the reality that surrounds us and that we experience is one. But, in order to understand this reality and make sense of it, we use two different vocabularies: that of the 'is' and that of the 'ought' – the former is a descriptive vocabulary fit to explain the world in empirical terms; the latter is a normative vocabulary framing the world in evaluative or prescriptive terms.

Bearing that distinction in mind we have the elements needed to define an empirical approach to legal obligation. Indeed, given that (i) the language of 'is' is a language of facts and probabilities, (ii) obligation involves our behaviour or can be observed and measured by looking at the way we behave, and (iii) legal obligation restricts the range of our behaviour to the way we behave under the law, an approach to legal obligation can be described as empirical if it views legal obligation in terms of our actual or likely behaviour under a system of laws. On this empirical model, we have a legal obligation insofar as (a) the law requires us to behave in some way and (b) we behave accordingly, or are likely to behave accordingly, or at least there is some probability of our doing so, since (c) undesirable consequences will follow or are likely to follow any failure on our part to do so, i.e., any non-compliant behaviour.

An approach to legal obligation can, by contrast, be considered *normative* if it frames obligation as an 'ought': legal obligation, on this view, is defined not by the course of action we *in fact* take or are more or less *likely* to take in light of the consequences of failing to do what the law requires, but by these requirements themselves, singling out the course of action we *ought to* take (or ought not to take), regardless of whether we actually act accordingly or are likely to do so.

Let us, then, have a closer look at these two opposite models of legal obligation, taking them up in turn in the next two sections.

2.3 The Empirical Model

In an empirical definition of legal obligation, no mention is made of what ought to be done: the claim that a legal obligation exists only means that either certain courses of conduct are set forth as a code of behaviour and that we are likely to incur sanctions for failing to comply with that code, that is, if we fail to behave in the manner described. As a consequence, that something is a legal obligation does not in itself mean that we should act accordingly: any connection between what we have a legal obligation to do and what we ought to do is either contingent or a construction built on top of what a legal obligation has us do. In legal theory, we find at least two different basic variants of the empirical model of legal obligation: the predictive account and the imperatival account.

An account of legal obligation can be qualified as *predictive* insofar as it describes legal obligation in terms of the likelihood of our being sanctioned for disobeying the behaviours described in a legal system. That is, we have a legal obligation to do something if we are likely to otherwise be legally sanctioned. In order to determine whether a legal obligation exists, then, we have to determine whether we are likely to incur a penalty for failing to behave in the manner set forth in law. Conversely, no legal obligation can be said to exist without such likelihood, even if the required behaviour is formally on the books.

Crucially, the connection between obligation and punishment in law is, on this account, purely probabilistic: legal obligation says what people can expect to suffer in consequence of their acting inconsistently with what is stated in the law. In short, legal obligation is conceived as a factual notion: it is framed in terms of regularity of compliance and consistency in the use of punishment for non-compliance, making this a firmly empirical idea expressing the capacity of a system to coerce people and its effectiveness in doing so. This makes legal obligation a *dependent*, or derivative, notion – a by-product of law's ability to coerce. On this model, in sum, legal obligation ultimately comes down to the sanction one is likely to suffer for breaking the law and failing to act in conformance with legal standards.

The account of legal obligation in accordance to which to be under a legal obligation is nothing but to be likely to incur into a sanction provided by the system and imposed under the law was originally theorized within the pragmatic and instrumentalist strand of legal realism. Which account was based on the premise that, in the words of Oliver Wendell Holmes, law can be reduced to 'the prophecies of what the courts will do in fact'.[1] Relatedly, 'a legal duty' was conceived by

---

[1] O. W. Holmes, 'The Path of the Law', *Harvard Law Review*, 10 (1896), p. 461. On this broad approach to legal issues, 'when we study law we are not studying a mystery but a

Holmes as 'nothing but a prediction that if a man does or omits certain things he will be made to suffer in this or that way by judgement of the court'.[2] Legal realists à la Holmes thus explain legal obligation by referring to the legal system's coercive ability and its amenability to probabilistic prediction. In this way, claims about legal obligation can be reduced to factual propositions about the likelihood that the legal system will react to and punish unlawful behaviour. On this view, to claim that a behaviour is obligatory under the law is to assert that law (a) describes that behaviour, (b) specifies a punishment for failing to act that way, and (c) will likely enforce that punishment or at least can be expected to do so with a certain degree of probability.

In contemporary jurisprudence a similar conception can be found in the so-called law and economics movement.[3] Like legal realism, the law and economics movement not only sets out to purge all metaphysical elements from the legal domain but also endorses a form of reductionism about normativity in human practices. Accordingly, it claims that the power of a legal theory can be measured by its capacity to make accurate predictions about the way law influences behaviour.[4] This makes the account of legal obligation espoused by the advocates of the law and economics movement a variant of the predictive account,[5] where the

---

well-known profession. We are studying what we shall want in order to appear before judges, or to advise people in such a way as to keep them out of court ... People want to know under what circumstances and how far they will run the risk of coming against what is so much stronger than themselves, and hence it becomes a business to find out when this danger is to be feared. The object of our study, then, is prediction, the prediction of the incidence of the public force through the instrumentality of the courts' (Holmes, 'Path of the Law', p. 457). The primary concern of this strand of legal realists, then, is to predict what decision-making bodies are going to do. Accordingly, this variant of legal realism emphasizes the social efficacy of rules, while downplaying their authoritative issuance, in giving an account of what law is. This means that for a proper understanding of the law, we have to look not only at enacted or formal law (referred to as 'paper rules' or 'law in books') but also, and even more importantly, at what officials actually do as they set about applying that law: only if we understand the behaviour of judges - along with the underlying worldview, value system, and mindset - can we predict what those officials will decide when a case is brought before them by thus gaining a grasp of the law (the 'real rules' or 'law in action').

[2] Holmes, 'Path of the Law', p. 458.
[3] For an introduction highlighting all the different nuances found within the predictive account of legal obligation advanced in the law and economics movement, see L. Kornhauser, 'The Normativity of Law', *American Law and Economics Review*, 1 (1999), pp. 3-25.
[4] This point is explicitly made in Kornhauser, 'Normativity of Law', pp. 3-4, for instance.
[5] On this description, see R. Cooter, 'Prices and Sanctions', *Columbia Law Review*, 84 (1984), pp. 1523-59.

penalty for non-compliance is reframed as an additional cost for the lawbreaker and so as an economic disincentive to disobeying the rules of law. From this perspective, then, legal obligation is modelled as a reward, or an advantage we stand to gain from, as a result of complying with the law; conversely, non-compliance is modelled not as a prohibition, but as a cost the lawbreaker is likely to incur as a result of that course of action. So, if legal rules are essentially incentives to act as prescribed in a legal system, such obedience can be understood not as a civic virtue but as an act that, other things being equal, will reduce the financial costs associated with our social conduct. Legal obligation is therefore framed in terms of self-interest: even if we comply with the law out of a concern with its inherent value, that is not how, on this model, legal obligation works and ought to be understood – it is rather understood as the cost or benefit of an agent's decision about whether or not to comply with the law. Which statement is ultimately revealing of the fact that, in the picture offered by the advocates of the economic approach to law, legal obligation is conceptually associated with self-interest-based motivational power.

The second variant of the empirical model – the imperatival account – provides a different definition of legal obligation, which too is purely fact-based. An account can be qualified as imperatival if it ties obligations to what the law *requires* us to do (either by command or by any other means of specifying the behaviour we imperatively *must* have). Thus, to have a legal obligation, on this view, is to be required to behave in certain ways by those in power. The idea of a legal requirement is in turn tied to the idea of a sanction, whether real or potential, since those who set out these requirements are usually in a position to enforce them. This means that, for a legal obligation to exist, there must be some kind of pressure, whether physical or psychological, that someone (the enforcer) makes on someone else (the person or persons bound by that obligation). Imperatival theories of legal obligation accordingly see a close, conceptual connection between legal obligation and the coercive means by which to ensure compliance with what any given obligation requires. On this view, then, a legal obligation is a requirement the legal system imposes and enforces on legal subjects, regardless of whether these subjects are willing to comply.[6]

---

[6] As hinted at in passing a moment ago, coercion is understood here in the broad sense of a background threat, meaning that it *implies* the use of force for the purpose of compliance, without necessarily having to actually *use* force. For an analytic discussion of coercion in law, see G. Lamont, 'Coercion and the Nature of Law', *Legal Theory*, 7 (2001), pp. 35–57.

The imperatival account finds a paradigmatic statement in the works of Jeremy Bentham and John Austin. The core idea behind their versions of the imperatival account is that the law would cease to be recognized as such without a political sovereign issuing commands backed by the threat of sanction for failing to comply with those commands. A political sovereign is a subject – a person or body – that within a given territory enjoys a higher status in virtue of which it alone can wield decision-making power and force. The sovereign's superiority is, in turn, defined in terms of habits of obedience: someone is politically superior insofar as they habitually receive obedience from the rest of the population – in that their commands are consistently complied with by those to whom they are addressed – while the converse is not true, in that the sovereign is not in the habit of obeying anyone else. In this framework, we have a legal obligation to do something insofar as we are subject to the political sovereign's commands and these commands are backed by a system of sanctions. Relatedly, a behaviour is obligatory if we are ordered to perform it and can be forced to do so if we do not spontaneously comply. In the imperatival account, legal obligation is thus framed as a purely *empirical* notion: something becomes obligatory simply in virtue of its being required under a system that can enforce that behaviour or in virtue of its being commanded by someone who has the power to force unwilling addressees to comply. As the reader can appreciate, all of the elements in this definition of legal obligation – sovereignty, commands or imperatives, and sanctions – are purely empirical: one is a political superior, or sovereign, so long as they have the power to impose requirements or commands on others subject to that power, and so long as that power is effective, meaning that it can actually be exercised by punishing those who fail to act as required or to obey the commands issued. Because all the ingredients that go into this definition of legal obligation are empirical, so is the nature of legal obligation (in this imperatival narrative).[7]

The imperatival account of legal obligation does not as such find much support today. At least some elements of this historically prominent account of legal obligation, however, can be seen to shape the approach to legal obligation taken up by contemporary legal theorists who lay emphasis on the imperatival component of the law as a whole. Consider,

---

[7] This notion of legal obligation is paradigmatically advanced in Lecture One of Austin's *The Province of Jurisprudence Determined* (see specifically J. Austin, *The Province of Jurisprudence Determined* (London, Dartmouth, 1998), pp. 11–15).

for instance, Matthew Kramer's engagement with the so-called Hart–Raz debate on the nature of the obligations engendered by the law.[8] Joseph Raz's account of legal obligation as existing essentially in virtue of the *reasons* that may be proffered for compliance is criticized by Kramer on the basis of the imperatival view that legal norms are not necessarily prescriptive and so do not necessarily amount to practical reasons.[9] Raz's claim that a conceptual connection exists between the rules of law and the reasons by which they are supported is so criticized by Kramer, who argues that Raz disregards the fact that legal norms need not function prescriptively:[10] they can also function in a starkly *imperative* manner. Hence, whereas prescriptions are understood by Raz as creating *reasons* for acting accordingly (and in this sense they belong in the realm of the 'ought'),[11] for Kramer imperatives inhabit a realm that is categorially different: the realm of 'must', where reasons are not essential. Imperatives, Kramer claims, 'do not necessarily lay down or presuppose reasons-for-action for their addressees', since they are the 'products of the overwhelming superiority – the actual superiority or the presumed superiority – of the addressors over the addressees'.[12] Therefore imperatives result from the exercise of an overwhelming coercive power. Insofar as the law consists of imperatives – moving us away 'from the sway of "ought" to the sway of "must"' – any connection between law and practical reasons has to be understood as merely accidental, and not as intrinsic, or analytic.[13]

Now, this argument can be made compatible with an empirical model explaining legal obligation in the imperatival fashion. Being detached from the 'ought', imperatives give rise to obligations in a purely non-normative sense; and because the law consists of stark imperatives, it belongs not in the sphere of what *ought to* be but in that of what *must* be. Any duties a system of this kind will generate will thus be grounded in the requirements set forth in law and in the commands issued by legal powers. Relatedly, a connection can be established not only between legal obligations and legal imperatives but also between the act of breaching a legal obligation and the penalty one incurs for failing to fulfil it or for

---

[8] See M. Kramer, *In Defense of Legal Positivism* (Oxford, Oxford University Press, 1999), pp. 78–112.
[9] See Kramer, *In Defense of Legal Positivism*, pp. 83–9.
[10] Kramer, *In Defense of Legal Positivism*, p. 87.
[11] Kramer, *In Defense of Legal Positivism*, p. 84.
[12] Kramer, *In Defense of Legal Positivism*, p. 85.
[13] Kramer, *In Defense of Legal Positivism*, p. 85.

disobeying a command. Crucially, these are views central to the imperatival account theorized by Bentham and Austin. The picture of legal obligation that emerges from Kramer's critique of Raz's account of legal obligation therefore stands in a relation of conceptual continuity with the standard imperatival account of legal obligation.

At the same time, it should be noted that Kramer's conception of legal obligation cannot be reduced to that of Bentham and Austin. For, to begin with, Kramer explicitly states that no legal system, even a despotic one, can be made to rest *exclusively* on stark imperatives.[14] While the interaction between legal officials and the community of legal subjects at large can, but need not, be governed by imperatives alone, the interaction among officials themselves takes an altogether different form. In their internal discourse officials speak a language of reasons, norms, prescriptions, and 'oughts', as opposed to one of commands, imperatives, and 'musts'. In so doing, Kramer does not only reject the all-encompassing imperatival conception of legal obligation theorized by Bentham and Austin,[15] he also underscores that the nature of legal obligation can be investigated and grasped in isolation from the penalties set forth in law. In combination, these aspects of his account move it away from the imperatival account, since, in contrast to strictly Austinian theorists, who 'must submit that no legal obligations are imposed by norms that are seldom implemented', Kramer's theory 'enables us to see that those norms do indeed impose such obligations (albeit largely uneffectuated obligations)'.[16] And this means that, for Kramer, 'even a regime of stark imperatives will always leave open the potential for situations where having legal obligations to perform φ does not involve any likelihood of being obliged to perform φ'.[17] In conclusion, even if Kramer's theory of legal obligation incorporates some key imperatival theses, it cannot in the outcome be considered strictly imperatival.

2.4 The Normative Model

Unlike the empirical model, in either the predictive version or the imperatival version, the normative model rests on the view that

---

[14] Kramer, *In Defense of Legal Positivism*, pp. 92–101.
[15] This is explicitly claimed in Kramer, *In Defense of Legal Positivism*, p. 99, even though Kramer seems more concerned here with what I am calling the predictive account of legal obligation than with the imperatival account as here characterized.
[16] Kramer, *In Defense of Legal Positivism*, p. 99.
[17] Kramer, *In Defense of Legal Positivism*, p. 99.

obligation is conceptually linked with what we *ought* to do, where 'ought' at least implicitly carries a value judgement of right and wrong, meaning that implicit in a claim that something is obligatory and so ought to be done is the idea that it is the right thing to do. This view – an obligation to do something implies a prescription saying that this is what we properly ought to do – finds broad common-sense support, for it seems intuitive that an obligation means that the behaviour it prescribes ought to be carried out. And so it is that legal theorists with diverse backgrounds and philosophical agendas conceive legal obligation as a practical and normative necessity.

Directly flowing from the normative model so construed are two related implications about the way legal obligation is to be defined and characterized. Firstly, the model rejects any purely empirical account of legal obligation, on the reasoning that an empirical theory is constitutively unable to secure an inherent connection between 'ought' and obligation. Secondly, insofar as an analytical connection does get recognized between 'ought' and obligation, there is no way that legal obligation can be satisfactorily characterized without bringing a normative standpoint into the picture. Since what is normative points to what *should* be done, as opposed to what *in fact* is done or is *likely* to be done, it is only by taking a normative perspective that legal obligation can adequately be explained.

The thesis that the connection between legal obligation and the practical 'ought' is not contingent but analytical can be recognized as the common trait unifying the different forms the normative model has taken in the legal-theoretical debate. Beyond that, however, there is not much in common among the different variants of the normative model. The survey of the normative model offered below, where the variety of normative models will be broken down into four basic types – the formal account, the social practice account, the interpretivist account, and the reason account – will make this apparent.

2.4.1 *The Formal Account*

In the formal account, legal obligation is constructed as essentially dependent on the formal validity of law. Something becomes legally obligatory by virtue of its being required in a legally valid provision, regardless of how its addressees behave or are likely to behave relative to that provision, and regardless as well of whether those empowered to enforce it actually do so. This makes a legal obligation an entirely formal condition, one existing simply in virtue of a rule of law. An obligation so construed also entails the enforcement of a sanction for non-compliance, but crucially, in distinction to the empirical model, such consequences are *normative*, meaning that what matters in defining an obligation is not whether the relative sanctions are likely to materialize but whether they are set forth as a rule of law. It is by making the *stated* rule essential to obligation – rather than the rule such as it is applied: law in books rather than law in action – that an account of legal obligation becomes formal. And since no rule of law can exist on its own, apart from the other rules making up the system of which the rule is a part, the formal account should also be properly characterized as intra-systemic.

From this intra-systemic perspective, legal obligation is defined as (a) something its addressees ought to do because (b) it is stated in a rule that (c) forms part of an interlocking set of rules in virtue of which (d) a system of laws is in place governing the way in which to enforce the sanctions prescribed for failing to fulfil the obligation in question. An account so described, then, is at once *normative* and *formal*: it is normative in that it views legal obligation as stating the way its addressees *ought to* behave (versus do behave) and what consequences *ought to* be applied (versus do get applied) for any non-compliant behaviour; it is formal in that it views legal obligation as existing only in virtue of its being stated as a rule of law (rather than in virtue of whether it is actually complied with and enforced).

This conception is paradigmatically theorized in the Kelsenian tradition of legal thought.[18] The concept of legal obligation defended by Hans Kelsen and his contemporary epigones is aptly summarized in the claim that one has a legal obligation to perform a given action 'in so far as the contradictory of that behaviour appears in the legal norm as the condition of a compulsive act, described as the penalty (consequence of tort)'.[19] This formal characterization of legal obligation can be further specified and enriched when read in conjunction with Kelsen's

---

[18] The main reference here is Hans Kelsen's extensive and influential body of work. See, for instance, H. Kelsen, 'The Pure Theory of Law', *Law Quarterly Review*, 50 (1934), pp. 474–98; H. Kelsen, *General Theory of Law and State* (Cambridge (MA), Harvard University Press, 1945); and H. Kelsen, *Pure Theory of Law* (Berkeley, University of California Press, 1967). A contemporary legal theorist who draws heavily on Kelsen's approach is Christoph Kletzer. See, in particular, C. Kletzer, 'Absolute Positivism', *Netherlands Journal of Legal Philosophy*, 42 (2013), pp. 87–99; C. Kletzer, 'Primitive Law', *Jurisprudence*, 4 (2013), pp. 263–72.

[19] Kelsen, 'Pure Theory of Law', p. 495.

conception of a legal norm. A legal norm is formally understood by Kelsen as a power-conferring provision, that is, a proposition in virtue of which certain individuals – legal officials – are authorized to impose sanctions when the behaviour described in the norm is not performed.[20] From an intra-systemic perspective, if (i) a legal norm contains a power-conferring provision of this sort and (ii) legal obligations are established by legal norms, then a legal obligation is simply the counterpart of a legal conferral of power, or *empowerment*: it is the mirror image of an official's power, or competence, to impose and enforce legal sanctions.

Importantly, in Kelsen's legal theory it is this legal empowerment, and not obligation, that functions as the basic distinguishing element of law as well as the pivotal notion on which basis a science of law can be constructed. The reason why Kelsen takes empowerment to be the fundamental legal concept, making obligation secondary or derivative, is deeply rooted in his legal project, which is based on, and justified by, the possibility of keeping law separate from morality. The idea of empowerment enables him to do just that. For empowerment works with the complementary concepts of imputation and competence, which in combination make it possible to characterize a system, or order, as dynamic. Dynamic systems so conceived are in turn distinct from static systems, which instead make obligation the central organizing idea around which the rest of the system revolves. Now, a paradigmatic case of a static system is morality. Therefore, by defining law in terms of empowerment, as against obligation, Kelsen intends to support the view that law – a standard case of dynamic order – cannot be reduced to morality, the nature of which is instead static.[21]

In Kelsen's theory legal obligation accordingly figures as neither a primitive nor an independent concept but is rather derivative, being based on a more fundamental one: the notion of (legal) empowerment. A legal obligation, in other words, can be said to exist when certain individuals are empowered by the legal system to impose sanctions on other individuals for failing to comply with certain norms of that system. In Kelsen's paradigmatic statement of the formal account, therefore, legal

---

[20] As Stanley Paulson aptly comments, this means that 'many of Kelsen's references to the legal "ought" and to legal obligation ... turn out to be thinly disguised references to the imposition of sanctions by the legal official' (S. L. Paulson, 'A "Justified Normativity" Thesis in Hans Kelsen's Pure Theory of Law?', in M. Klatt (ed.), *Institutionalized Reason* (Oxford, Oxford University Press, 2012), p. 77).

[21] For a sophisticated and insightful reconstruction of this aspect of Kelsen's theory, see Paulson, '"Justified Normativity" Thesis', pp. 78–92.

obligation tends to be ultimately conceived as a placeholder referring to the conditions under which a legal official is empowered, or competent, to impose a penalty on those who infringe legal norms.[22] That is to say, obligation is not conceived by Kelsen as a self-contained modality; it is rather a by-product resulting from a combination of empowerments, or norm-creating powers. As may be appreciated, this characterization of obligation is purely formal. Indeed, no special content or substantive element, needs to be brought into the picture in order for an act to be qualified as obligatory. An act is so qualified simply in virtue of its being the object of a rule of law setting out the conditions under which legal officials are empowered to issue formally legitimate sanctions.

The formal nature of legal obligation so characterized can be further appreciated in light of Kelsen's nomological conception of normativity.[23] As previously mentioned, the formal account constructs legal obligation as a *normative* concept. Now, normativity is understood by Kelsen as a purely formal idea, an idea formulated without bringing any content into play. On this purely formal, or nomological, view, normativity exists simply as that which is lawlike. This definition of normativity supports the claim that legal obligation – a paradigmatic normative notion – should likewise be regarded as a formal concept.

On the formal conception, in addition, normativity figures as a category of thought distinct from, and irreducible to, causality. In this distinction lies the core of Kelsen's anti-naturalism, anti-empiricism, and anti-psychologism, which, in the positive makes his theory normative. As a normative system, then, law is itself taken to have its own constitutive principles and shaping notions, differing from those that frame the causal domain, and irreducible to them. Central among these principles and notions distinguishing the normative from the causal is the idea of imputation, with which the notions of competence and empowerment work in tandem. For imputation plays in the normative domain the same role that causal connection between facts plays in the empirical. On this basis, Kelsen keeps normativity neatly distinct from causality, thus preventing any empirical, naturalist, or psychological element from filtering into the normative realm, a realm of norms and forms as distinct from that of facts and contents. Which is to say, in conclusion, that, as the

---

[22] This statement can be found in Kelsen, *General Theory of Law and State*, p. 59, for instance, and can be said to express Kelsen's considered view of the matter.

[23] For a detailed treatment of this conception of normativity, see Paulson, '"Justified Normativity" Thesis', pp. 102–11.

counterpart of empowerment and competence, legal obligation is conceived as deriving from one of the basic concepts keeping the normative apart from the factual, and so law as a normative practice apart from the world of facts. On these grounds legal obligation is claimed to be categorically separate and autonomous from both (a) commands and the probability of incurring sanctions for non-compliance (two factual notions), and (b) *moral* obligation, in defining which the ideas of imputation, competence, and empowerment play no role. In light of these features, the formal account of legal obligation cannot be likened to either the empirico-positivist conception of legal obligation or the moralist conception of legal obligation espoused by hardcore natural lawyers.

2.4.2 The Social Practice Account

A second way of framing the normative model other than through the formal account is through the social practice account, on which legal obligation is understood as a social bond by which different people or entities are connected under the law. On this view, the law binds legal subjects in the same way that social rules bind individuals and groups in society, that is, in a substantive rather than a formal way: one has a legal obligation since the law is a distinctive social normative institution and institutions of this kind impose obligations on those who are subject to their rules.

The contemporary stream of social practice account of legal obligation traces its theoretical roots to H. L. A. Hart's jurisprudence. Hart's account of legal obligation is based on the idea of a social rule, for it is premised on the view that a legal obligation arises through the existence of a legal rule understood as a social practice coupled with a widespread attitude to that practice (by which is meant any widely practised pattern of behaviour).[24] This means that a legal rule cannot exist unless it is underpinned by a corresponding practice and this practice is widely accepted in the relevant community. Stated otherwise, a legal rule exists when the behaviour it prescribes is both regularly performed and regarded as legitimate, to the effect that deviations from it are criticized and criticism of any

---

[24] While Hart's theory of legal obligation did change over time, its core claims remained relatively constant and are concisely summarized in H. L. A. Hart, *Concept of Law* (with a Postscript, Oxford, Clarendon, 1994; or. ed. 1961), pp. 82–91. For a detailed reconstruction of the evolution of Hart's account of legal obligation, see A. Oladosu, 'H. L. A. Hart on Legal Obligation', *Ratio Juris*, 4 (1991), pp. 154–69.

deviation is seen as justified. A legal rule, in other words, is a standard by which to guide and judge courses of conduct – a standard at once broadly practised and accepted within a social group, and which is framed in a distinctively normative language.

It is out of legal rules that legal obligations originate – legal rules that, as just suggested, are characteristically and peculiarly social in nature. Indeed, at least some legal rules are meant to provide their addressees with instructions on how they ought to behave. And when certain further conditions are met, the prescriptions contained in those rules give rise to obligations. More specifically, a legal obligation, for Hart, arises when the behaviour a legal rule requires to be observed within a community is regarded as valuable and is accordingly accompanied by an insistent demand for conformity.[25] That compliance with the behaviour prescribed by a legal rule is regarded as valuable means that those who hold that view – the committed members of the social group to which the rule applies – are reasoning from what Hart calls an internal point of view, which in turn means that the rule and the behaviour it prescribes are *critically* endorsed by those who have that point of view. This critical endorsement ultimately confers normativity on what would otherwise be a normatively inert notion (the habit of obeying the rule) as well as on the broader practice of generalized compliance with standards of behaviour.

In sum, on Hart's account, it is in virtue of an internal point of view that plain social conformity – the mere fact of acting in accordance with a standard of behaviour – turns into a structured and considered pattern of justified behaviour, which can be described as an example of rule-following and thus as a paradigmatically normative practice. This means that legal obligations become such in virtue of a practice that the committed members of the relevant social group regard as setting justified standards for guiding and assessing conduct. In Hart's theory, therefore, the nature of legal obligation – the kind of obligation that comes with law – is specifically social: a rule of law is at its core deeply rooted in the social structure of the group governed by the relative legal system. At the same time, a rule as constructed by Hart is inherently normative, and so consequently is rule-following – a normative phenomenon in distinction to a merely factual one, as is the mere habit of obedience among the members of a social group.

---

[25] For a statement of this thesis, see H. L. A. Hart, 'Legal and Moral Obligation', in A. Melden (ed.), *Essays in Moral Philosophy* (Seattle, University of Washington Press, 1958), pp. 87–92, for instance. See also Hart, *Concept of Law*, pp. 85–8.

Hart's theory lies at the origin of the currently dominant social practice account of legal obligation: the one associated with the so-called conception of law as a shared activity. On this conception, the ability of law to obligate is rooted in the existence of practices jointly undertaken within a given community.[26] As an activity endorsed by participants, a joint practice hinges on a mutual reliance that gives rise to expectations among participants. It is on this basis that the activity can give rise to obligations by which the same participants are bound. And law, once conceived as such an activity, can do precisely the same.[27]

The key insight here is that once legal obligation is understood to rest on a shared activity, its nature becomes distinctively and specifically *social*. This means that, on this account, legal obligation cannot be reduced without misrepresentation to *moral* obligation. In contrast to moral obligation, which paradigmatically originates in a critical attitude, legal obligation is claimed to derive from an arrangement of social facts. Indeed, in the recognition of the social origin and nature of legal obligation lies the distinctive and unifying trait of any social practice account: what unifies the different instantiations of this account is the view that legal obligation originates in patterns of group behaviour and so is social in nature. This means that legal obligation need not coincide with moral obligation, and indeed it need not even be analytically related to it: when legal standards are understood as shaped by social practices – as activities shared within a group – their content may or may not overlap with those of moral standards. Thus, on the one hand, the social practice account of legal obligation does not deny the possibility that what morality requires (its content) should coincide with what is required by the social practices understood to lie at the core of law and to define what counts as law. On the

---

[26] This social practice model is defended in J. Coleman, *The Practice of Principle* (Oxford, Oxford University Press, 2001), pp. 67–148; S. Shapiro, 'Law, Plans, and Practical Reason', *Legal Theory*, 8 (2002), pp. 387–441; S. Shapiro, *Legality* (Cambridge (MA), Harvard University Press, 2011); and S. Shapiro 'Massively Shared Agency', in M. Vargas and G. Yaffe (eds.), *Rational and Social Agency: Essays on the Philosophy of Michael Bratman* (New York, Oxford University Press, 2014), pp. 257–93.

[27] See Coleman, *Practice of Principle*, pp. 92–4. Different declinations of similar views are defended in E. Lagerspetz, *The Opposite Mirrors* (Dordrecht, Kluwer, 1995); N. MacCormick, *Institutions of Law* (Oxford, Oxford University Press, 2007), pp. 11–20; C. Kutz, 'Acting Together', *Philosophy and Phenomenological Research*, 61 (2000), pp. 1–31; C. Kutz, 'The Judicial Community', *Philosophical Issues*, 11 (2001), pp. 442–69; and Shapiro, 'Law, Plans, and Practical Reason'; Shapiro, *Legality*; Shapiro 'Massively Shared Agency'.

other hand, the account does not posit a *necessary* overlap in content between moral requirements and legal requirements: any such overlap is only possible and merely contingent. For, on this conception, legal obligation and moral obligation are two different kinds – the former being social, the latter critical – and so cannot be reduced to each other. For the same reason, although nothing prevents social practices from incorporating moral standards and content – in fact this is to be expected – any overlap between the two kinds of content, or between what social practices require and what morality requires, is not necessary but only possible. The social practice account can thus be said to draw a neat conceptual separation between legal obligation and moral obligation.

This unifying trait of the numerous variants of social practice account makes it possible to classify them as voluntarist, as they all advance a kind of 'will theory of obligation'. On the will theory, obligation is a practical directive brought into existence by someone expressing their will, or intention, which primarily determines the content of legal obligation and its validity.[28] By the same token, 'the method for finding out whether someone has an obligation to do a particular thing is ... simply to find out whether his case comes under an appropriate directive'.[29] The reason why the social practice account of legal obligation can be marked down as an example of will theory is that social rules and practices incorporate practical directives whose validity and content are established by what the relevant social group willingly commits to. On this account, then, different communities are entitled to shape their own rules, answering their needs, interests, and aspirations without any restriction of content. Social rules accordingly exist not in virtue of the (moral or rational) contents they embody but simply in virtue of their having been willed – that is, agreed upon and accepted – by the relevant community. And this is the sense in which, on the social practice account, legal obligation can be described as will-dependent and said to be a direct issue of the lawmaker's will.

---

[28] In John Finnis's words, the will theory explains legal obligation 'by reference to the moving force of [the lawmaker's] will', to the effect that a legal obligation 'can be imposed or withheld by [the lawmaker] at his choice' (J. Finnis, *Natural Law and Natural Rights* (Oxford, Oxford University Press, 2nd ed., with a Postscript, 2011; 1st ed. 1980), p. 330). For a clear reconstruction of the will theory, see K. Baier, 'Moral Obligation', *American Philosophical Quarterly*, 3 (1966), pp. 213–18.

[29] Baier, 'Moral Obligation', p. 214.

2.4.3 The Interpretivist Account

The interpretivist account of legal obligation is closely bound up with the conception of law developed by Ronald Dworkin and his followers. This conception, interpretivism, proceeds from the premise that legal propositions – or assertions about what law is – can be true or false, and that the truth of one makes it obligatory, while its falsity deprives it of obligatory, or directive, force. Hence the concern of interpretivism to explain what makes it the case that certain legal propositions are true, and so obligatory, and others false, and so lacking in obligatory force. This is why, interpretivists reframe most of the classic questions of jurisprudence in terms of what legal rights and obligations are. On the same basis, interpretivism is to be understood as 'a thesis about the fundamental or constitutive explanation of legal rights and obligations (powers, privileges, and related notions)'.[30] Central to interpretivism, thus, is the thesis that the different theoretical approaches to legal issues can be defined and distinguished from one another by their conception of legal obligation.

The interpretivist theory of the nature of legal obligation heavily depends on the statement that law is an interpretive concept, namely, a combination of the social facts constitutive of a given institutional arrangement and the underlying principles of political morality on which basis those same facts and arrangement are justified. Indeed, in recognizing that law is an interpretive concept, one need also appreciate that the institutional dimension cannot on its own afford an accurate picture of the law, for there is no practice that stands on its own without an accompanying set of justificatory principles, or view of why the institutional arrangement is set up in specifically the way it is. Therefore, no matter how analytically and exhaustively we may describe the institutional arrangement, we will not be able to get to the core of law by description alone: we do need to interpret it. And to interpret the set of social practices constitutive of the law is, on this view, to reconstruct these practices through a hypothesis at once explanatory, evaluative, and justificatory. This means that in the very act of explaining the whole set of social facts and institutional practices in which the law is embedded, we need to not only identify the facts and practices that are essential to its working but also discern the values, standards, and principles in light of

---

[30] N. Stavropoulos, 'Legal Interpretivism', in E. N. Zalta (ed.), *The Stanford Encyclopedia of Philosophy* (Summer 2014 ed.), http://plato.stanford.edu/archives/sum2014/entries/law-interpretivist/, section 1.

which those facts and practices make sense to those who engage in them and on which basis they can be held up as legitimate.

On an interpretivist account, then, law is understood as the resultant of two fundamental components, one of which is institutional and social, while the other is evaluative.[31] The relation between the two components is one of mutual feedback: on the one hand, social rules and institutional practices cannot be understood in isolation from the values that lend those rules and practices a point, or rationale; on the other, the values that go into the explanation of law are specifically the evaluative considerations intended to make the best sense of the social rules and institutional practices associated with the existence of a system of laws. In this picture, interpretation plays a crucial role, since it establishes which social events are relevant to the making of law and, at the same time, determines which principles of political morality should be appealed to when identifying legal propositions. On this basis, interpretivism recognizes law to be neither a mere social practice nor simply a set of evaluative standards governing the conduct of a community. They instead understand law as an arrangement of *interpretive* facts, which in turn are irreducible to either social practices or values taken in isolation from each other.

From this conception of the nature of law emerges a distinctive picture of legal obligation. As a product of law – in itself an interpretive concept – legal obligation too is conceived as an interpretive concept. On the interpretivist account, in other words, legal obligation is a genuinely practical requirement generated by the social practices that shape a given institutional framework, as these practices and framework are interpreted in light of, and are justified by, the scheme of principles underlying those social practices and that institutional framework themselves. On this conception, institutional and evaluative components combine to give rise to legal obligations, which accordingly are the resultants of social facts and political practices, on the one hand, and values and normative considerations, on the other. And this means, among other things, that legal obligation is conceived by interpretivism as an inherently justified demand and so as a genuine claim made on legal subjects.

---

[31] To put it in Dworkin's terms, law 'includes not only the specific rules enacted in accordance with the community's accepted practices but also the principles that provide the best moral justification for those enacted rules. Law then also includes the rules that follow from those justifying principles, even though those further rules were never enacted' (R. Dworkin, *Justice for Hedgehogs* (Cambridge (MA), Harvard University Press, 2011, p. 402).

For interpretivism, in sum, legal obligation is not something that can be understood by reducing it to either mere social and institutional facts or moral and political principles alone. In fact, it is the reference made to political morality – the space where social practices and moral principles merge – that specifically distinguishes the interpretivist conception of legal obligation from those defended in both the social practice account and the reason account. For, on the one hand, as much as the standards of law may be rooted in social practices, they are by their constitution *critical*, vis-à-vis social. Hence the irreducibility of the interpretivist account to the social practice account. On the other hand, the standards of law do not necessarily amount to rational principles, since those standards in part depend on the institutional framework the legal system is embedded in. And this framework is not necessarily designed to meet the demands of practical rationality, but rather to address the political concerns of the community governed by the law.[32]

2.4.4 The Reason Account

As the name suggests, the reason account argues that a legal obligation can be said to exist and have binding force only if it meets certain rational standards. On this account, legal obligation is conceived as being in the first place a *rational* demand: what we have a legal obligation to do is what practical rationality requires us to do. From this thesis it follows that it is only by recognizing the inherent rationality of what a legal obligation exacts from us that this notion can be properly grasped and explained. This means establishing an analytical, or conceptual, connection between legal obligation and practical reasons. Or, stated otherwise, it is the notion of a practical reason, as opposed to the notion of a social practice or the idea of an arrangement of interpretive facts that becomes essential to defining legal obligation.

This broad thesis – the view that the fulfilment of certain standards of rationality is regarded as essential to the existence of legal obligation, which is accordingly conceived as primarily a rational requirement – characterizes all versions of reason account that have been theorized in the literature and distinguishes this account from the other conceptions of

---

[32] On the interpretivist account, therefore, there is a conceptual distance between legal obligation and what practical rationality demands. It is this view of legal obligation as conceptually distinct from the demands of rationality that sets the interpretivist account apart from the reason account of legal obligation.

legal obligation so far introduced. The reason account, however, is a diversified camp. The fundamental feature that keeps one reason account apart from the others is the way in which each reason account specifically conceives of the kind of reason that shapes its distinctive view of legal obligation. Since the literature offers a vast variety of conceptions of a reason, equally plural will be the variants of the reason account of legal obligation. In what follows I will focus on the three strands of the reason account that have proved to be the most influential in contemporary jurisprudence. They are what I will be referring to as the 'conventionalist reason account', the 'exclusionary reason account', and the 'robust reason account'.

These three strands of the reason account can be introduced in snapshot form as follows. The conventional reason account defines legal obligation in terms of the conventions law is claimed to consist of. In turn, conventions are understood as practical reasons of a special kind, that is, as considerations, given in support of certain statements, rooted in practices enjoying widespread support in the community at hand. The other two variants of the reason account that will be discussed in this work – the exclusionary reason and robust reason accounts – are both non-conventionalist. This means that they both espouse the view that legal obligation does not originate in an arrangement of conventions but is rather shaped by considerations whose nature is critical and moral. That is to say, on the exclusionary reason and the robust reason account alike legal obligation and moral obligation are conceptually inseparable, for they share the same nature, which is moral. The differences between the two accounts are mainly owed to the way they interpret the claim about the conceptual continuity between legal obligation and moral obligation. On one account, the relationship between legal obligation and moral obligation is exclusionary, whereas on the other account it is inclusionary.

The exclusionary interpretation proceeds from the view that the force of legal obligation is invariant (or non-defeasible), and that the obligations arising out of law accordingly function as exclusionary reasons for action. The notion of exclusionary reason has been influentially theorized by Raz. In his exploration of practical reasons, Raz defines exclusionary reasons as negative second-order reasons, namely, reasons for not acting in a certain way or, to put it otherwise, directives to disregard certain considerations supporting a course of action. An exclusionary reason, then, is a statement instructing one not to take certain substantive grounds into account in determining what one ought to do. Accordingly, in the face of an exclusionary reason an agent can well end up not acting on the balance of the applicable reasons, as instead is the case when the practical landscape is governed only by first-order reasons. A reason account will thus be labelled exclusionary if, on the one hand, it claims that both moral obligations and legal obligations are ultimately rational requirements – they are directives supported by practical reasons – but, on the other hand, it recognizes that there may be divergences between what morality requires us to do and what the law demands from us.

The implication of this claim is twofold. Firstly, the exclusionary reason account recognizes a conceptual connection between the obligations generated by legal practices and the obligations set forth by rational morality. This connection rests on the view that the mandatory norms of law are not independent from, and in fact originate in, moral considerations. Which is why every statement of a legal obligation is claimed to be grounded in a moral proposition justifying what law requires. Yet, once a legal obligation emerges out of moral considerations, as these have been crystallized in the relevant mandatory norm of law – and this is the second implication of the view of legal obligation associated with the exclusionary reason account – the contents, or substance, of the resulting obligation is independent of morality. Accordingly, legal obligations may occasionally differ in content and scope from moral obligations. Whilst inseparable from the obligations generated by rational morality, legal obligations as conceived on the exclusionary reason account will not necessarily coincide with the former. That is, whereas the nature of legal obligation is rational and moral, the content of legal obligation – what is demanded by law – may not only differ from, but also conflict with, the content of the obligations that rational morality imposes on us. Law and legal obligation are thus set in a realm that is distinct and separate from that of rational morality and the obligation it generates.

This means that the exclusionary reason account frames law as a peculiar and distinct subset of practical rationality whose underpinning logic is autonomous from, and irreducible to, the logic of rational morality. So, even though legal obligation and the obligations generated by rational morality pertain to the same genus – both notions being grounded in the same kind of practical reasons – they do not necessarily coincide, and may occasionally not only diverge but also stand in direct conflict. This means, among other things, that on this view it is far from necessarily the case that one has a *legal* obligation to do what on the balance of moral considerations one *rationally* ought to do. In this way, a distinction is maintained between the contents of legal obligation and those of moral obligation.

This last claim keeps the exclusionary reason account apart from the robust reason account, which denies just that distinction, thus coming close to fully identifying legal obligation with moral obligation. This version of the reason account can be qualified as robust since it establishes a strong connection not only between moral reasons (as opposed to conventional standards) and legal obligation – by grounding both in practical rationality, in this being indistinguishable from the exclusionary account – but also between the contents of legal obligation and those of moral obligation, in which respect the robust account distinguishes itself from the exclusionary one. From this standpoint, then, there is an almost complete identification of moral and legal obligations, an identification that the exclusionary model instead emphatically rejects. That is, on the robust reason account obligation has the same meaning in law as it does in morality. Relatedly, legal obligation is understood as a requirement set forth in law, which in turn is understood as a constitutively moral (or at least non-immoral) enterprise.[33] This combination of claims means that no legal obligation can contradict a requirement of rational morality. The robust reason account, then, is deeply shaped by the thesis that legal requirements are *moral* requirements.

To put it in slightly different terms, on the robust reason account legal validity and moral validity are theorized as being inseparable, since only morally valid propositions can be legally valid, and no proposition can be regarded as legally valid unless it satisfies a standard of rational morality. From this it follows that legal obligations are generated by legal standards, which as such (as valid legal standards) constitutively are norms backed up by rational morality, too. Hence the conceptual impossibility for legal obligations – the obligations arising out of law – to come into conflict with moral obligations – the obligations arising out of rational morality. This is to say that on the robust reason account legal obligations are moral claims made on us, because anything that is legal is equated with anything that is moral (where *legal* is understood to include legal validity and legal obligation, which in this theoretical framework are inseparable). The conceptual scheme framing the robust reason account

---

[33] For a paradigmatic statement of the robust reason view, see D. Beyleveld and R. Brownsword, 'The Practical Difference between Natural-Law Theory and Legal Positivism', *Oxford Journal of Legal Studies*, 5 (1985), pp. 1–32; D. Beyleveld and R. Brownsword, *Law as a Moral Judgement* (London, Sweet & Maxwell, 1986), pp. 324–41 and 352–6; H. Hurd, 'Challenging Authority', *Yale Law Journal*, 100 (1991), 1611–77; and H. Hurd, *Moral Combat* (Cambridge, Cambridge University Press, 1999).

can thus be summarized in the statement that law and the fundamental legal concepts are subcategories of morality and the fundamental moral concepts, respectively. More specifically, what is legally valid is such because of its being in the first instance morally valid. And the validity of proposition in turn rests their bindingness: only valid propositions can give rise obligations. From which it follows that only legally valid norms can give rise to legal obligations.[34] Because legally valid norms are morally valid norms, legal obligations – the obligations established by legally valid norms, which by definition are also morally valid norms – amount to moral obligations. As the resultant of a legally valid provision, legal obligation is an obligation arising under a morally valid standard. Which is why legal obligations cannot clash with moral obligations. The robust reason account, therefore, frames obligation as a unified field, or discourse, which is homogeneous and not internally differentiated.[35]

As significant as the differences may be which set apart the two main non-conventionalist strands of the reason account of legal obligation, equally significant are the claims which, by contrast, they share,

---

[34] See Beyleveld and Brownsword, *Law as a Moral Judgement*, pp. 326–8.

[35] It follows that the robust reason account also commits one to the unity of obligation: obligation singles out an internally compact and undifferentiated whole, to the effect that legal obligation is ultimately indistinguishable from moral obligation. As Beyleveld and Brownsword put it, 'being legally bound is being morally bound; having a legal reason for action is having a moral reason; appeals to legal obligation are appeals to moral obligations' (Beyleveld and Brownsword, *Law as a Moral Judgement*, p. 329). Beyleveld and Brownsword introduce some exceptions to this principle, which in its pure form they consider far too rigid. They acknowledge, for example, that one may have a collateral obligation to comply with legally invalid rules, and so immoral rules, so as to avert greater moral evil. The exceptions they allow for, however, are not meant to deny the basic idea underpinning the robust reason view. Accordingly, for Beyleveld and Brownsword, 'legal obligations arise only under legally valid rules; legally valid rules are morally legitimate rules; there may be an obligation to comply with a legally invalid rule but the legal obligation in such a case will be generated by a background [rule shaped by the Principle of Generic Consistency, which in Beyleveld and Brownsword's construction is the most fundamental moral principle] rather than by the legally invalid rule itself. The *only* case of legal obligation is obligation arising under a morally legitimate rule' (Beyleveld and Brownsword, *Law as a Moral Judgement*, p. 328; original emphasis). From this reconstruction we can also appreciate that the robust reason account of legal obligation is derivative, in that it locates the source of legal obligation *outside* the law positivistically defined. A legal obligation is understood to arise only insofar as the demands made by law conform to standards that are external to, and independent of, the law narrowly constructed. Legal rules are on this view obligatory because they coincide with other, extralegal standards – that is, moral standards – which are intrinsically obligatory. The ability of the law to give rise to obligations is thus not internal to the law itself but is instead borrowed from outside the law.

distinguishing them from the conventionalist strand of the reason account. Two of these shared claims are in particular worthy of mention. Firstly, key to all non-conventionalist versions of the reason account is the claim that the nature of the practical reasons at the root of legal obligation is moral.[36] This claim can be supported by an argument that Raz has articulated. Raz observes that obligation has the same meaning in legal and moral discourse alike, in that the rules of law and the standards of morality both direct their addressees to act in certain ways. And the only way one can get others to act as directed is by providing them with reasons for action that they can acknowledge to be a legitimate guide for their behaviour. For the appeal to *one's own* self-interest cannot grant justification to the requirement that *another* individual acts as that individual is directed.[37] This means that the reasons for action supplied by the law cannot be self-interested, responding solely to the interests of the lawgiver, and hence prudential. The reasons for action supplied by the law need instead to be *other-regarding*, such that they can be considered legitimate by those to whom they are addressed. Now, if we accept that proposition – namely, that if the rules of law, including obligation-imposing rules, can fulfil their distinctive guidance function only so long as they appeal to interests broader than those of the rule-makers themselves – then we must also accept that the nature of the obligations engendered by these rules cannot but be moral as opposed to being prudential.

The argument can be succinctly restated as follows: (a) the reasons backing the requirements set forth in the rules of law need to apply to the generality of all those to whom such rules are addressed; (b) if a reason is to apply to all those subject to a corresponding rule – each of whom may have different interests – it cannot be self-interested, that is, it cannot be tailored to advance the self-interest of any one group or person in particular; (c) only *moral* reasons satisfy that criterion – addressing the interests of *all* those concerned, rather than only the interest of those by whom they are put forward (that is, only moral reasons are other-regarding) – since these reasons alone are constitutively such that anyone may be willing, or can reasonably be expected, to acknowledge their value or point; hence, (d) no rule of law can generate obligations unless it

---

[36] To put it in Raz's concise formulation, 'legal obligations are real (moral) obligations arising out of the law' (J. Raz, 'Hart on Moral Rights and Legal Duties', *Oxford Journal Legal Studies*, 4 (1984), p. 131).

[37] This clam is defended in Raz, 'Hart on Moral Rights and Legal Duties', where Hart's social practice account of legal obligation is criticized on this ground.

appeals to moral reasons so defined – that is, reasons detached from the self-interest of those who put them forward, as well as from the interest of particular groups or people (or any subset of those affected by the rule which the reason at issue is supposed to support). The thrust of this four-part argument is that law can generate obligations only insofar as it brings *moral* considerations to bear, and hence that legal obligations are ultimately moral obligations, for they need the backing of moral reasons if they are to be binding. As a result, to have a legal obligation is to have a practical reason to act accordingly – a reason whose nature is moral but which is established by law.

The second trait shared by both main strands of the non-conventionalist reason account is that neither of them subscribes to the will theory of obligation. The tradition to which the non-conventionalist reason accounts belong is not the voluntarist tradition of legal thought – which instead deeply shapes the social practice account and informs the picture of legal obligation offered by the interpretivist account as well as the conventionalist reason account – but rather the rationalist tradition of legal thought. Rationalism, in this context, is a position that, in the negative, does not condition the existence of legal obligation exclusively on what the lawmaker wills and, in the positive, connects legal obligation to the rational merits of the conduct required as a content of obligation.

To expand on this statement, the reason account, in all its non-conventionalist variants, does not reject outright the idea that legal obligation needs to have a basis in an expression of will by those in power – in fact it views this as a necessary condition for something to count as a legal obligation. But it does not understand this condition to be the *only* condition, or a sufficient condition, for the existence of a legal obligation. On the non-conventionalist reason accounts, thus, a legal obligation can stand, or be said to exist, only if it can ultimately be shown to be *rational*. Because no act of will, whether carried out in isolation or set in a conventional social practice, can succeed in making obligatory a course of conduct that is not rational, the lawmaker's will has no *intrinsic* role to play in giving rise to a legal obligation. It is rather the rationality of the required act that provides the genuinely defining element of legal obligation. Therefore, while on the non-conventionalist reason accounts it takes a number of conditions to make a legal obligation, and all of these conditions are necessary, they do not all stand on the same footing. Some of these conditions – among which is an official statement of what law requires – are necessary but not sufficient to even initiate the process of establishing a legal obligation. For this process has its origin (not in an authoritative expression of will or intent, but rather) in the recognition that the legal requirement at hand stands up to rational scrutiny. It is only because the lawmaker's intention to create obligations is expressed in the context of a normative framework perceived as rationally justified that on the non-conventionalist reason accounts the same intention can be regarded as an essential part of the process of bringing a legal obligation into being. In other terms, it is the practical instantiation of rationality, and not an official statement of intentions or an expression of will, that plays a key role in creating and shaping legal obligation.

On all non-conventionalist reason accounts, in sum, the obligatory force of a legal requirement should essentially be explained by referring to its rational justification and not to its underlying act of will. It follows that, from this perspective, the ability to create, modify, or extinguish a legal obligation does not entirely or ultimately depend on the lawgiver. True, having legal authority is a precondition for one to be able to create legal obligations. But this precondition will prove not only insufficient but also irrelevant unless it is coupled with a recognition of the intrinsic rationality of the required behaviour – an intrinsic rationality that is not determined by, and is ultimately independent of, the will of those in power. To conclude, the ultimate source of legal obligation does not lie in a decision – which cannot on its own establish an obligation – but rather in its rationality, that is, in its ability to be recognized as having a rationally appreciable point, or as being sound and valuable from the standpoint of practical rationality.

2.5 Interim Conclusion

In this chapter I looked at some fundamental theoretical models that have been championed in contemporary jurisprudence in addressing the problem of legal obligation. At the ground level were identified two basic and irreducible models – an empirical one and a normative one – and their main instantiations (which in the empirical camp are the predictive account and the imperatival account, and in the normative camp are the formal account, the social practice account, the interpretivist account, and the reason account). It was also suggested that the concept of obligation introduced in Chapter 1 can be used as a test for assessing the adequacy of any model and account of legal obligation (however much incomplete and preliminary this test may be). This idea of a benchmark concept sets the agenda for the following chapters, where the accounts of legal obligation defended in contemporary jurisprudence will be evaluated against that benchmark by considering whether they can adequately explain the concept of legal obligation.

Crucially, three of the accounts of legal obligation I looked at in this chapter – the imperatival account, the predictive account, and the formal account – fail that adequacy test straightaway and so will not require any detailed discussion in the following chapters. To briefly elaborate on this statement, of the defining elements of the concept of obligation consider (a) the normative nature of what is obligatory and (b) its practical nature. The inclusion of these elements means that obligation singles out a specific kind of necessitation, one that is (a) normative, rather than empirical (physical or psychological), and (b) action-guiding, rather than purely formal, or nomological. These traits are shared by, and necessarily define, any kind of obligation, including legal obligation.

Once we take into account the specific nature of the necessitation associated with obligation – normative necessitation – we can conclude that no non-normative conceptualization of legal obligation is theoretically tenable. For according to the concept of obligation, legal obligation is a *normatively* necessitating force. And normative necessitation cannot without distortion be reduced to any empirical compulsive force, be it actual or just probable. This means that neither the predictive account nor the imperatival account can adequately explain legal obligation. More specifically, in light of the concept of obligation introduced in Chapter 1, the predictive account and the imperatival account can be shown to issue from a categorial mistake: they both interpret a *normative* requirement as a form of *factual*, or *empirical*, necessity. By so doing, they mix up two different categories of thought: the normative, or 'ought', and the factual, or 'is'. This categorial mistake shapes and so disqualifies any empirical model of legal obligation that, in virtue of its very construction, lacks the conceptual resources needed to provide a satisfactory account of legal obligation, which, as a species of obligation, is to be qualified as a distinctively normative force.

Likewise, by recognizing the practical nature of obligation, we can appreciate that among the accounts of legal obligation belonging to the normative family – outside of which we cannot reasonably aspire to explain legal obligation in a theoretically credible way – the formal account occupies an uneasy position. And in this way we can see the crucial failing of the formal account without embarking on any detailed discussion. For, as was argued in Section 2.4.1, the formal account sets up an analytical connection between legal obligation and the formal validity

INTERIM CONCLUSION

of law: to claim that a legal obligation exists means, from this perspective, to assert that a valid legal norm has been issued which formally empowers certain subjects to administer a given sanction whenever the legal norm is violated. Therefore, the ground on which the formal account of legal obligation can be criticized, when it is assessed against the concept of obligation, is that of its practical irrelevance. The formal account does not explain how law, once recognized as obligatory, can succeed in guiding conduct. After all, the fact that from the formal point of view a norm is in place, thus officially conferring on someone the power to punish non-compliant behaviour, does not in itself provide any indication as to whether we ought to do what law requires: no formal conferral of power suffices to this end unless it is integrated with substantive considerations by which to legitimize the requirement to behave as prescribed. This means that the formal account leaves the practical aspect of legal obligation largely unexplained, thereby proving constitutively incapable of explaining legal obligation as a *practical* demand. From which it follows that the formal account is unable to explain how the law can claim to obligate those subject to it – for on this view the law cannot show them why they should behave as required.

In summary, if we accept the concept of obligation constructed in Chapter 1 – a concept essential to which are both the normativity and the practical guidance of legal obligation – we should be able to see, in the first place, that only the normative accounts have a shot at explaining that concept, and, in the second place, that the only viable accounts within that normative camp are the social practice account, the interpretivist account, and the three basic versions of the reason account, namely, the conventionalist reason account, the exclusionary reason account, and the robust reason account. Since none of these accounts blatantly fail the preliminary adequacy test set up in Chapter 1 in order for any conception of legal obligation to be considered at least presumptively sound from a theoretical point of view, they all bear further critical scrutiny to assess their ability to explain legal obligation. Which is what I will be doing in the following chapters, looking to see whether the normative accounts just mentioned can explain the normative and practical concept of legal obligation not only prima facie but also in an insightful way that holds up to a deeper critical scrutiny.

3

The Social Practice Account

3.1 Introduction

This chapter is devoted to the discussion of the social practice account of legal obligation, which, as anticipated in Chapter 2, conceives of the obligations generated by the law as socially grounded requirements to act in the way prescribed by a system of legal norms. On this view, the kind of obligations the law engenders is claimed to be social in quality since the law itself fundamentally is a social institution.

The theoretical approach that has most systematically and consistently defended this position, by so arriving at a paradigmatic statement of the social practice account of legal obligation, is a general theory of law I will henceforth refer to under the label 'conception of law as a shared activity'. This view, which has increasingly gained ground in jurisprudence in recent years, finds a comprehensive and sophisticated theorization in the works of the legal philosophers who conceptualize of law as an enterprise jointly engaged in by a given community of individuals, or, stated otherwise, as a peculiar and distinct form of 'acting together'.[1] The conception of law as a shared activity, then, connects the existence and obligatoriness of law with its specific constitution, in turn elucidated in

---

[1] Some of the most influential works that theorize the conception of law as a shared activity are J. Coleman, 'Constraints on the Criteria of Legality', *Legal Theory*, 6 (2000), pp. 171–83; J. Coleman, 'Incorporationism, Conventionality, and the Practical Difference Thesis', in J. Coleman (ed.), *Hart's Postscript* (Oxford, Oxford University Press, 2001), pp. 99–147; J. Coleman, *The Practice of Principle* (Oxford, Oxford University Press, 2001); S. Shapiro, 'Law, Plans, and Practical Reason', *Legal Theory*, 8 (2002), pp. 387–441; S. Shapiro, *Legality* (Cambridge (MA), Harvard University Press, 2011); S. Shapiro, 'Massively Shared Agency', in M. Vargas and G. Yaffe (eds.), *Rational and Social Agency: Essays on the Philosophy of Michael Bratman* (New York, Oxford University Press, 2014), pp. 257–93; C. Kutz, 'Acting Together', *Philosophy and Phenomenological Research*, 61 (2000), pp. 1–31; C. Kutz, 'The Judicial Community', *Philosophical Issues*, 11 (2001), pp. 442–69; and R. Sanchez Brigido, 'Collective Intentional Activities and the Law', *Oxford Journal of Legal Studies*, 29 (2009), pp. 309–24.

terms of the structure of a practice undertaken together within a given social group.

In consideration of the fact that today the social practice account of legal obligation finds its most polished and thorough theorization in the works of those who espouse the conception of law as a shared activity, in this chapter I intend to submit the social practice account of legal obligation to systematic critical scrutiny by specifically dealing with the theory of legal obligation endorsed by the champions of the conception of law as a shared activity. So the particular question that I will discuss in this chapter is: can the conception of law as a shared activity provide a thorough explanation of the quality and scope of legal obligation, and can it in this way – as a rigorous and internally coherent form of the social practice account – adequately explain the ability of law to impose pro tanto obligations?

The conception of law as a shared activity can be interpreted as an attempt to systematically account for the Janus-faced nature of law – its being at one and the same time a social institution and a normative practice – while holding fast to the claim that the existence of law is exclusively a matter of social practices (a claim that in the literature is called the 'social fact thesis').[2] In this chapter, the discussion of such approach to law and its obligations is structured as follows. I will first introduce the conception of law as a shared activity in some detail and reconstruct it as a general theory of law and its normativity (Section 3.2). Then, I will turn specifically to the account of legal obligation theorized by the advocates of the conception of law as a shared activity (Section 3.3), which I take to be offered by its very proponents as a paradigmatic instantiation of the social practice account of legal obligation. In this context, I will notice that the view of legal obligation associated with the conception of law as a shared activity is rendered by giving legal obligation two fundamental senses: a full-blooded sense and a perspectivized one. The rest of the chapter will be devoted to showing why the account is flawed in. More specifically, in Section 3.4 I will argue that the account of legal obligation in a full-blooded sense theorized by the advocates of the

---

[2] On this basis, it can be appreciated that the conception of law as a shared activity is a paradigmatic form of legal positivism. For the social fact thesis is one of the fundamental claims differentiating legal positivism from non-positivist theories of law, to the effect that any theory underwriting the social fact thesis is best understood as a form of legal positivism.

conception of law as a shared activity is at once limited and partial, since it can explain legal obligation only in relation to those who are committed to the legal enterprise. This means that we are left to wonder why everyone else – namely, the bulk of the (non-necessarily-committed-to-the-law) population living under the jurisdiction of a legal system – can also be claimed to have obligations arising out of the law. Furthermore, the proponents of the conception of law as a shared activity do not present us with a compelling argument that the obligations the law gives rise to are *social* obligations, namely, requirements entirely grounded in social practices. Yet, it is precisely this sort of argument that an advocate of the social practice account of legal obligation needs to make. Finally (in Section 3.5), I turn to the perspectivized sense of legal obligation, arguing that this construction of obligation overlooks the normative import the legal enterprise is widely acknowledged to have, and thus fails to explain the ability of legal institutions to play their typical guidance function through the obligations they set forth.

3.2 The Conception of Law as a Shared Activity

Every day we each carry out many acts: some of these we perform individually, but some we execute in concert with others, whose activities either provide the conditions for our own, or form the background to our own, or constitute specific components of our own. In all cases where our action is not individual (that is, in all cases of shared undertaking), the activities of others are indispensable to our own, in that what we do is either impossible or meaningless in isolation from what other people do. Therein lies the basic idea of the conception of law as a shared activity. Analytically speaking, this is a twofold idea: it consists in (a) describing law as a practice jointly undertaken by a group of individuals, each of whom contributes in a distinct way to the collective undertaking; and (b) observing that this practice and the legal system it props up cannot, without distortion, be interpreted as the outcome of the activities of a collection of individuals each acting separately, because legal practice results from the concerted action of a collectivity. Legal actors should, then, be regarded as partners in a joint project, namely, individuals who have certain ends and a participatory intent in common.

Those who espouse the idea that we should conceive of law as a special kind of shared activity give legal specificity to it in different ways. But before getting into the differences, I will first lay out the features that these variants have in common. This can serve as a useful introduction, not least because the conception of law as a shared activity has not yet received any systematic and consolidated treatment. The conception of law as a shared activity is a form of legal positivism developed as an attempt to deal with some core issues that H. L. A. Hart first identified and that have since become central to Anglo-American legal philosophy. It will therefore be useful to bring this conception into contrast with the other main strand of post-Hartian legal positivism defended in analytical jurisprudence, namely, legal conventionalism. For some time the argument has been that legal conventionalism is what analytical legal positivism essentially comes down to and that the two approaches can in this sense be identified.[3] The conception of law as a shared activity rejects this understanding of legal positivism by denying that conventionalism is a necessary element of a legal-positivist account of law. On this alternative interpretation of legal positivism, joint action (not convention) serves as the fundamental legal criterion, the one that (directly or indirectly) determines what counts as law, or the element lacking which something cannot be said to count as law. That is, something is law to the extent that, necessarily, it can be described as a collective practice consisting in a group acting together and sharing a goal. Since those who act together may, but need not, do so on the belief that this is required by, and is in accordance with, a social convention, the resulting practice is not necessarily conventional in character. In other terms, what specifically distinguishes a shared activity, which on this conception figures as the

---

[3] As even one of the torchbearers of the conception of law as a shared activity once believed, contemporary legal positivism 'is committed to explaining law as ultimately resting on social convention' (Coleman, 'Incorporationism, Conventionality, and the Practical Difference Thesis', p. 103) and hence it is committed to the view that the conditions for the existence of law are established by convention. See also Coleman, *Practice of Principle*, p. 68. This claim goes under the name of the conventionality thesis, a thesis defended by contemporary analytical legal positivism and stating that the criteria of legality are conventional. The connection between legal conventionalism and legal positivism finds a thorough theorization in A. Marmor, *Positive Law and Objective Values* (Oxford, Oxford University Press, 2001), pp. 1–48; A. Marmor, 'How Law Is Like Chess', *Legal Theory*, 12 (2006), pp. 347–71; A. Marmor, *Social Conventions* (Princeton, Princeton University Press, 2009); A. Marmor, *Philosophy of Law* (Princeton, Princeton University Press, 2011), pp. 35–83; and J. Vilajosana, *El derecho en acción* (Madrid, Marcial Pons, 2010), pp. 139–78. For a critique of this connection, see L. Green, 'Authority and Convention', *Philosophical Quarterly*, 35 (1985), pp. 329–46; L. Green, 'Positivism and Conventionalism', *Canadian Journal of Law and Jurisprudence*, 12 (1999), pp. 35–52.

basic criterion of legality, is that this activity may be social but need not be conventional.[4]

This conception of the legal enterprise owes much to a body of work on the theory of action where the effort has been to understand the dynamics characterizing interpersonal interaction and collective action. A connection can thus be established between the conception of law as a shared activity and contemporary studies in the philosophy of social action. Looming large among these studies in particular is Michael Bratman's theory of social action, since to a large extent the conception of law as a shared activity (such as it has so far been theorized) can be interpreted as an attempt to extend Bratman's specific account of shared intentional activity, or some revision of that account, to the study of the law. This means that the law is specifically defined in terms of an activity engaged in by individuals who (a) are mutually responsive to the intentions and actions of others, (b) are committed to the joint activity, (c) share the plans (and sub-plans) instrumental to performing the relevant joint action, and (d) are aware that others intend to act jointly in the relevant way, and thus expect these other participants to contribute to the common activity. On this conception, those who take part in a collective practice are not required to have the same *reasons* for participating in it. They need share only certain goals. Likewise, the possibility of having shared activities depends on our capacity to have certain objectives in common, even though the reasons we each have for pursuing those objectives may not coincide or even overlap.

In bringing this account of shared activities to bear on law, however, its advocates do not simply reproduce and merely contextualize the insights originally theorized in the philosophy of social action: they expand on, and partly modify, them. What makes it necessary to tweak these insights and revise the account is essentially the different subject matter to which they apply. Whereas the model case for the investigation of joint action involves personal interaction among small groups in the absence of authority, neither of these two elements aptly describe legal practice. For legal practice (a) does not depend on the ability of

---

[4] On this point, see Kutz, 'Judicial Community', pp. 453–5; and M. Bratman, 'Shapiro on Legal Positivism and Jointly Intentional Activity', *Legal Theory*, 8 (2002), pp. 515–16. This gives that conception an edge over other versions of legal positivism, especially in view of the problems by which legal conventionalism is plagued. For a statement of these problems, see C. Dahlman, 'When Conventionalism Goes Too Far', *Ratio Juris*, 24 (2011), pp. 335–46, among others.

individuals to interact face to face as members of small groups, and (b) involves activities carried out under the regulation of an authority. To draw on the philosophy of social action, thus, the proponents of the conception of law as a shared activity require a new model case.

In this revisionary process, the conception of law as a shared activity has been shaped in a variety of ways, with different interpretations of what social philosophers take to be the core elements of joint action. What all these variants of the conception of law as a shared activity have in common is the idea of law as a distinct mode of 'acting together' – an idea that frames the legal domain as a social practice jointly engaged in by certain individuals. But, they take different paths in the way they construct the collective undertaking understood to uniquely characterize the law. In fact, in contemporary analytical jurisprudence, among those who defend the conception of law as a shared activity we find two broad groups: those who offer a 'thick' account of this collective undertaking and those who instead offer a 'thin' account of it.

In the first camp one can locate Jules Coleman, who construes the conception of law as a shared activity in a theoretically robust and demanding way.[5] For Coleman turns to what Bratman calls a shared cooperative activity in explaining the rule of recognition. Accordingly, for Coleman at the foundations of any systems of law we find a *cooperative* practice undertaken by the members of a social group.[6] Noticeably, Coleman considers that the members in question are (just) the legal officials. That is because Coleman, following Hart, looks to the rule of recognition as the essential legal practice in explaining the nature of law. And the rule of recognition is the official practice through which the criteria of validity are established, determining what counts as law in any given jurisdiction. Since this practice, in Coleman's view, is best understood as a Bratmanian shared cooperative activity among legal officials, it follows that at the core of any system of laws there is a practice shared

---

[5] See especially Coleman, 'Incorporationism, Conventionality, and the Practical Difference Thesis', p. 114–21; Coleman, *Practice of Principle*, pp. 74–102.
[6] This is where Coleman's theory reveals its robustness, because unlike the champions of the conception of law as a shared activity who embrace a thin version of that conception by defining the law only in terms of a shared *intentional* activity, Coleman views this activity as intrinsically *cooperative*. This means that those who participate in and shape the legal practice are understood to have a commitment to mutually support one another's effort to do their share in the legal system. This is *in addition to* their having a shared participatory intent. So we have an added layer of commitment here: the participants' shared intent is also a commitment to cooperate in making the joint activity a viable enterprise.

among (just) legal officials – the rule of recognition – that takes the distinctive form of a cooperative activity jointly carried out by those administering the legal system. Stated otherwise, a legal system is best understood as the outcome of a citizen-addressed project shared and pursued cooperatively by a specific group of individuals: legal officials.

A version of the conception of law as a shared activity comparatively thinner than Coleman's is theorized by Scott Shapiro.[7] In his main body of work Shapiro defends an original account of law significantly revising the positivist stance from within. What sets Shapiro's theory of law apart from other positivist theories is that Shapiro regards legal activity as a distinctive form of shared activity. As an instantiation of the activity of social planning, the law is understood to embody what might be called 'massively shared agency with authority'.[8]

This idea of massively shared agency with authority draws on Bratman's model of shared agency but makes some significant changes to it, by thus amounting to a considerably thinner mode of collective undertaking. In Shapiro's view, insightful though Bratman's model may be in several respects, it cannot be applied to legal institutions straightaway, for it does not as such recognize the role that impersonal authorities play in the governance of social affairs. Only when it is made to recognize that role can it be used to shed light on the nature and mechanisms of legal systems. In this way, shared agency can be said to hold even when some agents in the group stand in a relationship of superiority to the others, some participants do not take up a cooperative attitude, and not everyone in the group is committed to the joint enterprise. In addition, on Shapiro's revised model, coercion is not an obstacle for a group of individuals jointly performing an activity, at least not to the extent that coercion is used as a backup strategy to promote general conformism.[9] Those distinctive features render Shapiro's model of shared activity more inclusive than Bratman's and Coleman's, since that model expands the notion of acting together so as to bring within its scope situations where individuals in a group (a) can still be regarded as engaging in joint action despite the fact that they do not necessarily relate to one another on an

---

[7] Even thinner approaches have been theorized in Kutz, 'Acting Together'; Kutz, 'Judicial Community'; and Sanchez Brigido, 'Collective Intentional Activities and the Law'. Nonetheless, for all their differences and partial divergences, Kutz's and Sanchez Brigido's models can be claimed to be substantially in line with (the spirit of) Shapiro's overall project.

[8] Shapiro, *Legality*, p. 195

[9] See Shapiro, *Legality*, pp. 161–73.

equal footing, (b) may be alienated from the overall enterprise they contribute to, and (c) work towards a vaguely specified purpose without even knowing who the other participants in the project are.

Shapiro proceeds from the notion of massively shared agency with authority and sets out his 'planning theory of law' by thus construing law as a kind of collective planning activity.[10] This activity – the law itself – is described by him as 'an incremental process whose function is to guide, organize, and monitor behaviour through the settling of normative questions and which disposes its addressees to comply under normal conditions'.[11] In this conceptual framework the law is a large-scale, hierarchically structured activity carried out by those entrusted with planning for the wider community – namely, the legal officials. The planning theory, accordingly, reconstructs legal systems as institutions of social planning, legal rules as plans or planlike norms, and, consequently, legal officials as planners. On this account, thus, by creating, implementing, and enforcing social plans, legal officials guide the behaviour of individuals and groups, thus helping them 'lower their deliberation, negotiation, and bargaining costs, increase predictability of behaviour, compensate for ignorance and bad character, and provide methods of accountability'.[12]

3.3 The Social Practice Account of Legal Obligation

On the conception of law as a shared activity, legal obligation is explained as part of a broader account of the normative dimension of law. The account is framed in terms of the existence of a social practice lying at the foundations, and being constitutive, of law. So the challenge facing those defending the conception of law as a shared activity is to explain legal obligation as a social requirement. Namely, they will have to present legal

---

[10] For a summary statement of this legal theory, see Shapiro, *Legality*, pp. 193–233.
[11] Shapiro, *Legality*, p. 203.
[12] Shapiro, *Legality*, p. 200. What makes the planning theory a *positivist* theory of law is that the plans are mere social facts, rather than morally driven arrangements. They may have a moral component, to be sure; but that is not what makes them operative. Their active existence is owed not to any moral worth they may claim or embody, but to their de facto acceptance, meaning that, having been designed, they are made publicly accessible and gain acceptance within a social group. If the effective currency and content of social plans is not *essentially* dependent on moral considerations, and if law consists in the activity of social planning, then, the existence and authority of law can be said to be exclusively a matter of social facts, which is precisely the legal-positivist argument.

obligation as grounded (not in evaluative considerations, but rather) in constellations of social facts and patterns of social behaviour, to the effect that the nature of legal obligation can be acknowledged to be social, vis-à-vis moral.

In the literature there are two fundamental ways in which this challenge has been addressed by those who espouse the conception of law as a shared activity. First, there is the view of legal obligation in a full-blooded sense, or obligation as a *practical* requirement associated with the existence of legal institutions, activities, and provisions. Secondly, there is the perspectivized view of legal obligation as a demand arising in a situation where one is asked to do something from a given *point of view*, namely, from the standpoint of the legal enterprise itself. These two senses of legal obligation may look quite similar, but the difference between them is substantive not cosmetic. This section will be devoted to showing in what way this is so.

What legal obligation in the full-blooded sense has in common with legal obligation in the perspectivized sense is its originating not from any evaluative standard but from that specific form of joint social practice, which (on the conception of law as a shared activity) is where we must locate the legal phenomena. But this is as far as the comparison will go, because in the full-blooded sense, legal obligation gives rise to a genuinely practical demand, in a way that legal obligation in a perspectivized sense does not. For legal obligation in a full-blooded sense stands for a requirement that competes with general practical reasons and so figures in a determination of what one ought to do generally, vis-à-vis what one ought to do in accordance with the law – law, which is, in turn, understood as a discrete domain set apart and disconnected from the rest of the practical domain. So, in the full-blooded sense, legal obligation is a rationally related requirement: the norms offered by the law affect our practical life – what we (ought to) do – and choices in general – how we (ought to) behave.

How this comes about has been explained in a comprehensive way by Coleman. Hence, it is to his account that I will now turn for a better understanding of the full-blooded sense of legal obligation.[13] Coleman relies on Bratman's theory of shared cooperative activity to explain not

---

[13] See Coleman, *Practice of Principle*, pp. 86–102 and 143–7. The account no longer reflects Coleman's view but, since there is no competing account that is as thorough in explaining what full-blooded legal obligation is on the conception of law as a shared activity, I will take Coleman's view as paradigmatic in that respect.

just the *existence* of the law – the law exists insofar as a certain group of individuals engages in such an activity – but also the *mechanism* through which the legal system so conceived can give rise to genuine obligations. Coleman's basic premise is that the shared activity in which the law is explained is a network of interacting agents whose individual activity depends on there being some form and degree of cooperation. And those who engage in this network of relations come to depend on one another for a range of vital activities that would not otherwise be possible if they were not so networked and cooperative. *Ergo*, each participant in this network has a legitimate expectation that everyone will do one's part or fulfil some role in the cooperative scheme which is the shared activity itself. This expectation gives rise to an obligation to act accordingly – or, rather, it gives rise to a set of mutual obligations the participants each owe to one another. And these can be considered genuine practical demands made on the relevant participants.

An essential ingredient in this construction (serving to complete the explanation) is that of *endorsement*. In Coleman's theory, the shared cooperative activity to which the rule of recognition owes its structure is not just a pattern of behaviour that people in the group at hand happen to conform to, but rather a practice they are *committed to* because they recognize that it involves a mutual interdependence and renunciation of freeriding. Crucially, an endorsed practice is one that generates *reasons* for its participants to act in accordance with the prescriptions arising out of the practice itself. And insofar as these reasons entail corresponding obligations at least occasionally, to the extent that law can be defined in terms of a shared cooperative practice, we can explain its capacity to generate (full-blooded) obligations for the social group engaged in that practice.

The key to this account apparently lies in its specification of the nature of a reason for action engendered by a shared practice, because a reason so conceived is taken as the basis for an obligation to act in accordance to the law. Reasons for action, as we have seen, are understood on this account to arise out of a cooperative social practice, and it is to this source that they owe their validity and practical relevance. However, what makes them valid and relevant is not their content (that is, the particular *ethos* or substantive values a given cooperative practice happens to embody) but the social nature of that practice, namely, its formal structure as a network of interdependent individuals mutually committed to the enterprise itself.

This explains three features of the reasons for action and obligations associated to the law understood as a shared practice. First, these reasons are content-independent (in the sense that they do not owe their status to the content of the conduct they call for). Second, they are peremptory, in that they bar any independent deliberation and argument, preventing their addressees from critically questioning the value of engaging in the required behaviour. This, too, is a feature deriving from the nature of the practice as an enterprise whose survival is predicated not on the content of its *mores* but on the nature of its form as a network of cooperative and hence mutually interdependent activities. Third, in the context of that cooperative social practice which is the law, reasons for action are *genuine*, meaning that even though they are distinctly legal, and so cannot be reduced to moral reasons, they work just like moral reasons in that they too are practical demands and enter into competition with moral requirements. In other words, if, on the one hand, the reasons for action and the obligations generated by the law are in virtue of that fact specifically legal, on the other hand, they are grounded in a broad enough way that they also enjoy an extended practical relevance – a sense in which they can be said to compete with *non-legal* practical demands, including moral ones.[14]

This last feature captures the sense in which this account of legal obligation can be described as full-blooded. Legal obligation is understood as making a *genuine* claim on us as agents, and legal obligation can do so because of the way in which it is extracted out of law as a social scheme of cooperation one commits to. This means that, while legal obligation (as the adjective suggests) is distinctly *legal* – for it *originates* in law – it is not on account of law qua some formal code of rules but on account of law qua shared social practice. This makes it possible for legal obligation to move into the realm of the practical at large while retaining a specifically legal core that makes it irreducible to rational and moral obligations.[15]

---

[14] As Coleman puts it, these reasons, along with the associated obligations, 'are not tied to the institution of law in the way, for example, many of rights and duties created by the rules of a game are ... Legal duties arise in law, but they are duties that figure in our determination of what we ought to do generally and not just in our deliberations about what we ought to do in playing the game "law"' (Coleman, *Practice of Principle*, p. 143).

[15] Despite the frequent references to reasons for action it makes, the account associated with the conception of law as a shared activity is best qualified as a social practice account, as opposed to a reason account, because the considerations triggering the obligation-generating capacity of law are purely social, vis-à-vis rational, in quality. Namely, the law is claimed to engender obligation by virtue of the social practices of which it is constituted, vis-à-vis some rational component. And this means that the ultimate ground of legal obligation is the fact that certain individuals, as a group, endorse the legal framework – and this is a social fact. The account, in other terms, essentially relies on the social acceptance of the law to explain how the law can succeed to generate obligations.

Both of these features – the genuine quality of legal obligation and its being grounded in social practices – can be used to contrast the account of full-blooded legal obligation theorized by the advocates of the conception of law as a shared activity with their account of *perspectivized* legal obligation. To this end I will refer to Shapiro's recent work and his theory of law as a form of social planning. In fact, this theory gives us not one but *two* accounts of legal obligation: one which applies to agents in their capacity as legal officials – the people engaged in the activity of social planning – and the other which applies to agents in their role as ordinary citizens. This distinction is significant because while legal obligation as it applies to agents in the former group can be described as genuine, it cannot be so described in relation to agents in the latter group – and it is here that obligation in a perspectivized sense comes into play.

Let us start from the activity of social planning in relation to legal officials. According to Shapiro's account, there are two reasons why legal officials can be said to have full-blooded obligations under the law. The first is rooted in their commitment to the master plan that lies at the foundations of law – this is the social fact of acceptance. The second is rooted in the principle of instrumental rationality and coherence under which an agent ought to act consistently with past resolutions, for otherwise that agent can be criticized either as irrational – resolving to do something only to subsequently proceed along a course that contradicts that choice – or at least as inconsistent – disregarding the very plan one has had a part in designing in an official capacity or has otherwise accepted. As Shapiro puts it, if a 'subject has accepted the shared plan', then they are 'bound to heed the plan' as a matter of instrumental rationality.[16] Which is why 'legal officials are rationally required to conform to their shared plan'.[17] These two considerations combine to give rise to a presumptive *genuine* obligation of legal officials to do what law requires. This obligation can be construed as both legal and genuine because it arises out of law (and is thus distinctly legal) and yet it also finds a practical basis in the principles behind acceptance and commitment.

But now we ask, what about those who have no part in framing the shared plans constitutive of law or who do not endorse these plans? As Shapiro argues, 'those who do not accept the law are not similarly bound'.[18] We cannot apply to them the same argument we apply to legal

---

[16] Shapiro, *Legality*, p. 142.
[17] Shapiro, *Legality*, p. 182.
[18] Shapiro, *Legality*, p. 182.

officials. But a legal obligation need not be rationally grounded in that way: it can also be understood in a *perspectivized* sense. In this perspectivized sense – the second important sense in which the conception of law as a shared activity understands legal obligation – what it is to have a legal obligation is *not* to be bound by any broad principle of practical rationality, but only to be bound *from a legal point of view*, that is, from the standpoint of one who merely *acknowledges* the legal system rather than fully committing to it.

A legal obligation in this perspectivized sense – the sense arising from the standpoint of one embedded in the context of the legal system and who takes the distinctive perspective of the master plan forming the foundations of law – is not an obligation in a genuine sense, because it stands only so long as we wall off any (practical) considerations not specific to the shared practice or master plan itself. An obligation so constructed comes down to the rather prosaic-sounding statement, 'You are *in* this practice, so you are expected to behave in the manner that everyone else does who is similarly situated.'

This is why legal obligation in the perspectivized sense is less demanding than legal obligation in the full-blooded sense and it applies *regardless* of whether one is a legal official. The two understandings of legal obligation, thus, share the social fact of people being situated in a given shared practice. Where they depart is in the kind of commitment they presuppose. Legal obligation in a full-blooded sense presupposes that individuals have an active role in shaping the relevant practice and to endorse its form of life. This makes it a genuine obligation consequent on what it means to accept a shared practice to which others are also committed. By contrast, legal obligation in a perspectivized sense presupposes not so much a *commitment* as an *understanding* of what is expected of one who happens to be embedded in the context of a given practice framed by a specific set of rules. This makes it a context-specific obligation having no authentically general practical foundation, that is, no foundation outside that specific practice.

3.4 The Social Practice Account of Genuine Legal Obligation: A Twofold Critique

In this section, I will engage critically with the account of genuine legal obligation theorized by the advocates of the conception of law as a shared activity so as to assess whether it is (a) sufficiently encompassing, and (b) coherent with the basic tenets fundamentally shaping the social practice account of legal obligation – the tenets setting such account apart from other kinds of accounts of legal obligation. The main claim I intend to make in what follows is that there are two serious weaknesses in the theory of legal obligation put forward by the defendants of the conception of law as a shared activity: in the first place, the theory is severely limited, or insufficiently far-reaching; in the second place, it can be shown to be ultimately irreconcilable with the fundamental tenets defining the social practice account and so it can be considered internally incoherent. Let us consider these two issues in turn.

3.4.1 A Limited Theory

The limitation of the theory of (full-blooded) legal obligation available through the conception of law as a shared activity can be traced back to the very nature of that theory, which is ultimately voluntarist. On this view, no legal obligation is said to arise unless we bring into play the principles of instrumental rationality: means-end coherence, cross-temporal consistency among one's plans, consistency between one's plans and one's beliefs, and coherence between one's plans and the acts performed in execution of those plans. However, these principles cannot *alone* explain legal obligation. We still need an agent's commitment to the relevant joint activity for a legal obligation to arise, since it is only through this combination – an agent's participative willingness coupled with an espousal of rational instrumentality – that, on this account, legal obligation can be explained.[19] This means that legal obligation in the full-blooded sense is constructed as essentially dependent on an agent's commitment to the joint activity constitutive of law. For this reason, legal obligation can be held to apply only to those who are committed to that system and so only to those who accept the rules of the system whose underlying joint activity they participate in – hence the voluntarist nature of the social practice account.

Now, what is especially limiting about this approach to legal obligation is the restriction on those who are under a duty to act as legal norms demand. For most of the individuals the law is concerned with do not fulfil what, on the conception of law as a shared activity, is argued to be the primary condition for an obligation to arise in connection with (law

---

[19] See M. Bratman, 'Taking Plans Seriously', in E. Millgram (ed.), *Varieties of Practical Reasoning* (Cambridge (MA), MIT Press, 2001), pp. 204–19.

as) a shared activity, namely, an individual *commitment* to this activity. Indeed, for most legal subjects – ordinary citizens, residents, and more generally anyone who is not a legal official – the existence of a legal system is just a fact of life – something over which they have little (if any) control and of which they have (almost) no knowledge. Therefore, legal subjects cannot be *expected* to have any commitment to the law. Nor can these individuals either be *presumed* to have such a commitment or be *implicitly attributed* such a commitment. This conclusion follows from a view of agency as autonomous rationality on which we cannot expect others to comply with a scheme they have played no part in designing – a view that those adhering to the conception of law as a shared activity do not challenge. Even if the system is designed with those individuals' best interests in mind, therefore, this is still not a basis on which to hold them committed to any provisions issued in accordance with the rules the system is governed by, since that would be tantamount to a violation of their individual autonomy.[20]

Thus, since the population placed under the jurisdiction of a legal system is not directly involved in shaping the shared activity lying at the foundations of law, it cannot be said to come under any full-blooded obligation to comply with the rules framed through such an activity. That is to say, the account theorized by the advocates of the conception of law as a shared activity constructs legal obligation as a requirement that applies only to legal officials: in this theoretical construction, only individuals acting in an official capacity have genuine obligations to act in conformity with the relevant system of legal norms. For exclusively those individuals who control the levers of the legal powers or who have an active role in maintaining the legal system can be considered participants in, and so committed to, the shared activity constituting the law.

As a matter of fact, it is not even clear who exactly the champions of the conception of law as a shared activity single out as the participants in the legal enterprise and so those who are under a legal obligation in the genuine sense.[21] On a narrow interpretation, the class of the legal

---

[20] A fully developed argument in support of this claim can be found in B. Celano, 'What Can Plans Do for Legal Theory?', in D. Canale and G. Tuzet (eds.), *The Planning Theory of Law* (Dordrecht, Kluwer, 2013), pp. 129–52.

[21] The lack of clarity on this point has been noticed by M. N. Smith, 'The Law as a Social Practice', *Legal Theory*, 12 (2006), pp. 265–92. The same problem is also discussed in G. Pino, 'What's the Plan?', in D. Canale and G. Tuzet (eds.), *The Planning Theory of Law* (Dordrecht, Kluwer, 2013), pp. 187–205.

obligees is so closed as to encompass only the constitutional framers and maintainers, whereas on a broad interpretation that class also includes legal officials at large. That is, legal obligees may well comprise not just those who originally designed the legal system – and, thereafter, those responsible for interpreting the basic constitutional provisions and modifying the constitution when needed – but also those responsible for enacting new norms in accordance with the constitutional architecture (typically, the legislators) and those entrusted with applying the rules (law-enforcement and administrative officials). However, even on the broad interpretation the class of those who are regarded to be under legal obligations in the full-blooded sense still designates a limited group of individuals and is far from inclusive of the bulk of the population, namely, it does not extend to all those residing in the territory regulated by the system of laws.

Hence, legal obligation in the full-blooded sense, as it is constructed by the champions of the conception of law as a shared activity, does not bind every legal subject: its binding force only concerns legal officials, who constitute a small subset of all legal subjects. Which is to say that legal obligation does not apply to the vast majority of those who stand to be deeply affected by the existence of a legal system. That way, the theory of legal obligation under review fails to clarify how the people as a broad group (including the officials themselves when *not* acting in an official capacity) are under some genuine obligation to act in accordance with the prescriptions issued by a system of laws. That is precisely because, on the conception of law as a shared activity, legal subjects are best understood not as participants in, and committed to, the legal enterprise but (in the best possible scenario) as *beneficiaries* of that enterprise.

Patently, unless one is content with concluding that the obligatory capacity of law only affects, and concerns, a small minority of legal subjects and, consequently, a legal system can set forth no obligation for the large multitude of those who live under its jurisdiction, the social practice account of legal obligation, as it is paradigmatically instantiated in the works of the advocates of the conception of law as a shared activity, will have to be considered a theoretically flawed option. For an account that can at most tell us how the law can impose duties on certain subjects, but is structurally unable to explain how the law obligates all individuals living under a given jurisdiction should be regarded as a partial and significantly incomplete theory of legal obligation. Indeed, it is difficult to embrace that theory and still defend the widespread view of law as an institution that influences the practical deliberation of *all* legal subjects (also) by creating obligations for them.[22]

The reason why the broad ability the law is recognized to have in shaping our practical deliberation cannot easily be squared with the theory of legal obligation put forward by the proponents of the conception of law as a shared activity is that setting forth of obligations is widely acknowledged to be an essential way for law to provide practical guidance – it may not be the only way, but it is certainly an essential way. An account of the action-guiding function of law, therefore, cannot hold much interest if it fails to explain the sense in which the obligations it engenders are genuine for the totality, or at least the vast majority, of those living under the law. And yet the conception of law as a shared activity fails precisely in that respect, since it only allows for legal obligations to bind legal officials, who are a minority of legal subjects. This means that the very statements through which the law sets out obligations are deprived of direct practical relevance in relation to the community at large. Namely, on the social practice account, for a significant part of the population the practically normative function of law – that of guiding, assessing, and justifying action – will have to be fulfilled in a way that does not involve a recourse to obligation. And this picture runs contrary to the widespread intuition that the law goes hand in hand with obligations (in the full-blooded, or genuine, sense of the term). For it is commonly accepted that the law is a system capable of *generally* shaping the behaviour of those under its jurisdiction and that one fundamental and paradigmatic way it does this is by engendering obligations. Which is precisely the feature contradicted by the social practice account of legal obligation offered by the conception of law as a shared activity.

The statement of the inability to explain how the law generates full-blooded obligations for legal subjects at large is deeply counterintuitive. Although there is no denying that the law relies on a variety of methods in governing behaviour – this can be achieved by conferring powers, designating certain actions as permissible, and so on – it is commonly agreed that imposing obligations is a fundamental and basic way in

---

[22] This widespread view of law as a practical institution is arguably endorsed by (at least some of) the proponents of the conception of law as a shared activity. For a statement of the thesis of the action-guiding dimension of law, see, for instance, Coleman, 'Incorporationism, Conventionality, and the Practical Difference Thesis'; Coleman, *Practice of Principle*, pp. 67–73 and 134–48; and Shapiro, *Legality*, pp. 113–15.

which the law affects our conduct. For the use of obligations can be regarded, not just as one of several ways for law to shape our modes of conduct, but as a standard, or paradigmatic, way to do so. What is more, imposing obligation is widely understood to be central to the practically normative function of the law – indeed, it is hard to see how the law could possibly work as a practical institution without generating at least some obligations for all legal subjects. Yet this straightforward intuition finds no recognition in the theoretical framework provided by the conception of law as a shared activity.[23]

By the same token, the advocates of the conception of law as a shared activity end up denying the proposition that most of us can, or should, regard moral obligations and legal obligations as demands that may occasionally come into conflict. Any such conflict is explained away as merely apparent, since in contrast to moral obligation – recognized to be binding on the generality of (legal) subjects, qua agents and so creatures whom the principles of practical rationality apply – legal obligation is claimed not to be binding on the bulk of the population. So, apart from legal officials, no legal subject can be said to be under two practical pressures possibly pulling in opposite directions, that of morality and that of law. On this conception, then, for the vast majority of us moral obligations and legal obligations are mistakenly understood to be potentially conflicting standards of conduct whereas in fact they never enter into conflict. The two kinds of standards cannot conflict, because on the social practice account of legal obligation moral duties do apply to us all while legal obligations do not concern most of us – the two types of requirements, in other terms, cannot really intersect, let alone clash, at least for most legal subjects. That is, on the social practice account only legal officials can experience some authentic conflict between the obligations arising out of law and the demands of morality. By contrast, as far as legal subjects who are not legal officials are concerned, on this account there is no convergence in scope of legal demands and moral prescriptions, which is why the obligations established by law and the duties generated by morality cannot overlap, to the effect that any appearance of conflict between the two is just an illusion (and one that will go away once we realize that we are not looking at conflicting demands within the

---

[23] This counterintuitive aspect of the theory is in itself a problem if we consider that the theory is cast within the paradigm of analytical jurisprudence and that in this paradigm a prominent role is recognized for ordinary intuitions and common assumptions. For a detailed account of this role, see Shapiro, *Legality*, pp. 13–22, among others.

same sphere but we are instead switching between spheres that are heterogeneous rather than just different). And this means that, on the social practice account a dilemma widely considered central to our practical existence and commonly perceived as real is made out to be illusory.

On these bases I consider the social practice account of legal obligation that can be extracted from the works of those endorsing the conception of law as a shared activity to be theoretically questionable.

3.4.2 Still a Social Practice Account?

Aside from being limited in scope, the explanation of full-blooded legal obligation offered by the conception of law as a shared activity sits uncomfortably with other claims that are essential to a theory proposing to construct legal obligation as a requirement whose binding force is ultimately social. This is because, as I will elaborate in this section, the shared activities from which legal obligations are derived cannot be *reduced* to social facts, or be characterized solely in terms of such facts. By contrast, these activities embody evaluative considerations that are not entirely socially based, in that values – whose status is partly independent of social considerations – are directly and fundamentally involved in extracting genuine obligations from the practices which the conception of law as a shared activity makes constitutive of the law. This feature of the practices which, on that conception, are understood to lie at the foundation of law – their having a kind of obligatory force at least partly dependent on their embodying evaluative principles that are not entirely based on social practices – is ultimately irreconcilable with the social fact thesis. And the social fact thesis is both essential to the conception of law as a shared activity, as a general theory of law, and distinctive to the social practice account of legal obligation. These are the points around which this section is structured, where I intend to show that (a) the kinds of obligations associated with joint activities are not exclusively social, and that (b) once legal obligations are so construed (as not entirely social), we will have to let go of two theses central to the social practice account, namely, (i) the thesis that legal obligation is a type of social obligation, and (ii) the related thesis that legal obligations are qualitatively different from moral obligations as obligations rooted in evaluative standards whose basis is not entirely social.

To elaborate on these preliminary remarks, I should note that the obligations generated by shared activities may well have a social basis – that is, these obligations *primarily* owe their existence and contents to the presence of some social practice. Indeed, it would be arbitrary to deny the social basis of an obligation that comes into being through a collective practice one participates in. An obligation to contribute to an enterprise one shares with others undeniably is to some extent established by that very reason. That is, an obligation of this kind can legitimately be claimed to owe *part* of its validity and content to the fact that the enterprise in question engages a group of participants interested in pursuing that very enterprise. But this does not mean that such obligations can thereby be *exhaustively* explained by pointing out their social basis. Nor does it mean that the binding force of such obligations has *no* dependence on the value of the shared activities by which they are engendered, to the effect that whatever value those activities have or lack plays no more than a marginal role in explaining the nature of the obligations so engendered. Accordingly, it is arbitrary to conclude that because one's participation in a collective practice and the existence of a shared activity are both social facts, then the nature of the ensuing obligations must likewise be social. Indeed, it does not follow from the factual premises just introduced – from the fact that a joint enterprise exists, coupled with the fact that an agent supports the enterprise and participates in it – that one has an obligation to do one's fair share in that enterprise. For, even when an activity has the endorsement of a participating agent, it is still not in itself a sufficient basis on which to ground an obligation of the agent to satisfy the demands issuing from that shared activity. To this end we also need to bring into the picture evaluative principles whose basis is not entirely social. Let me expand on this point.

To begin with, if the basis of obligations arising in connection with joint activities is not entirely socially based (and their nature is accordingly not entirely social), that is due to the *meaning* associated with those activities as parts of a collective practice, and, more to the point, to the mutual expectations that people come to form as participants in such a practice. When we take part in a joint activity, we come to rely on everyone's contribution to the enterprise itself. And this mutual reliance means that we can expect people to do their part or to act in accordance with what the practice requires. The relationships so structured thus bring into being a network of mutual reliance and expectations that not only distinguish joint activities from other sorts of activities (such as the practices one embarks on in isolation from and without collaboration with others), but also constitute a necessary condition and the essential source of the obligations a collective enterprise may give rise to.

This means that there is no obligation to contribute to an existing social practice just because that practice exists and you have decided to conform to it. Rather, this obligation comes about because, by joining the practice, you have led others to count on your contribution – this by giving everyone else assurance (however implicit it may be) that you will do the things required by the practice you have joined. And going back and reneging on an assurance you have previously given, even if it is only an implicit assurance, is objectionable as a matter of principle. In other words, we are dealing with more than just a social fact: at stake here is, rather, an evaluative standard, because the course of conduct at issue remains wrong even in social environments where it may be widely accepted. That is to say, while the obligations the practice brings into being are inherent in the practice itself – they would not exist without the practice itself – they are not just based on the social fact of the practice's existence. They rather come into being through (a) the general evaluative principle prescribing us to honour the expectations we have led others to have in regard to our own behaviour and commitment to the practice – and as a general principle, this standard is not entirely socially based – in combination with (b) the fact that by participating in a given joint activity we have justified others in having those expectations about us (which expectations can therefore justifiably be relied on).[24]

In addition, there is also a distinct way in which evaluative considerations whose basis is not entirely social can be claimed to figure into the explanation of the obligations associated with the existence of joint activities. Even on a voluntarist approach to obligation, such as the approach underpinning the social practice account of legal obligation paradigmatically encapsulated in the conception of law as a shared activity, it is acknowledged that the fact of acceptance – the fact that those who participate in a joint activity do so because they commit to that activity – cannot *alone* explain what it takes for such an activity to give rise to obligations. On a social practice account, endorsement is a necessary but not a sufficient condition for an activity to bind its participants to an ensuing range of obligations. A shared activity may be fully and broadly endorsed, and still it will not generate any genuine

---

[24] A similar point is made in N. MacCormick, 'Voluntary Obligations and Normative Powers I', *Proceedings of the Aristotelian Society*, Supplementary Volume 46 (1972), pp. 59–78; M. Bratman, *Faces of Intention* (Cambridge, Cambridge University Press, 1992), pp. 135–40; and F. Alonso, 'Shared Intention, Reliance, and Interpersonal Obligations', *Ethics*, 119 (2009), pp. 444–75.

requirement if there is something questionable about it from the standpoint of a code grounded in rationality, vis-à-vis a social code. Otherwise stated, even from the perspective of the will theory, the endorsement of a shared activity is indispensable for such an activity to be able to give rise to obligations, and yet that endorsement is not a sufficient condition to turn an activity into an obligation-generating practice. That is so because the endorsement of an unprincipled, or unworthy, practice is conceptually incapable of grounding genuine obligations.[25] Hence, it takes a combination of conditions for a collective practice to be a source of full-blooded obligations: there needs to be (i) some configuration of social facts, namely, a joint activity that you are committed to, coupled with (ii) compliance with some evaluative standard grounded in rationality in relation to which the activity may be determined to be worthwhile. In summary, the full-blooded obligations associated with a shared activity are conditional not only on social facts – on the existence and endorsement of the activity itself – but also on evaluative considerations whose basis is not entirely social – that is, on whether the activity is seen to comport with a principle of action grounded in rationality.

These remarks have two conceptual implications that are related to each other. First, even if the law is conceived as a shared activity, this does not mean that the obligations grounded in that activity are independent of evaluative considerations whose basis is not entirely social. Quite the contrary: legal obligations, to the extent that they are said to find their basis in a collective practice, are not reducible to social elements. For not every joint activity enlisting the commitment of its participants as a matter of social fact thereby generates full-blooded obligations for those persons. Only those activities that are both factually endorsed and rationally valuable constitute sources of genuine obligation. And the same goes for the law when construed as such a practice: no genuine requirements can issue from the law unless the law, aside from enjoying the commitment of those who participate in it, can also on the whole be

---

[25] Support for this claim can be found in Bratman's work (see, for instance, Bratman, *Faces of Intention*, pp. 132–5), which, as the reader will recall, is the main reference point for the most influential variants of conception of law as a shared activity. In fact, it is noteworthy that the claim is commonplace in contemporary practical philosophy. Remarks of similar tenor can be found, for example, in J. Rawls, *Collected Papers* (Cambridge (MA), Harvard University Press, 1999), pp. 121–3; and J. Simmons, *Moral Principles and Political Obligations* (Princeton, Princeton University Press, 1979), pp. 109–14.

regarded as worthwhile, or at least permissible, in light of the principles of practical rationality.

Second, if we are to judge whether a legal obligation exists, we have to make evaluative considerations whose basis is not entirely social, thereby engaging in evaluative reasoning that goes beyond a consideration of social facts. For if what ultimately determines whether or not an activity can give rise to legal obligations is an evaluative feature of that activity, and the basis of evaluation is not entirely social, then it takes an evaluative argument to determine whether or not those obligations exist. Or, at least, there is no way to exclude such an argument, which therefore proves necessary to that end. This second implication reinforces the conclusion that the conception of law as a shared activity cannot confine the nature of legal obligation to the social sphere. True, we can, on this conception, appreciate the social reasons why those who are committed to the shared activities instantiating the law should have a genuine obligation to do what the law requires. But we cannot characterize this obligation as a purely social obligation.

This conclusion is of paramount theoretical importance, for it cannot easily be reconciled with the basic tenets underlying the social practice account of legal obligation. What is key to, and distinctive of, that account is the claim that legal obligations can be reduced to social requirements. For, on this account, legal obligation is conceived as a socially grounded requirement whose basis and binding force are independent of evaluative considerations whose quality is not entirely social, even when its contents can accidentally replicate or partially overlap with the contents of certain valuative frameworks. However, as previously argued, this conceptual reduction of legal obligation to social obligation melts away in the treatment that legal obligation undergoes in the conception of law as a shared activity.

Crucially, this difficulty is made even more significant by the fact that those who propound the conception of law as a shared activity present it as a coherent instantiation of a legal theory broadly in line with Hart's distinctive interpretation of legal positivism.[26] Indeed, Hartian legal positivism is organized around the social fact thesis, which in turn is closely bound up with the claim that the nature of legal obligation is social – a claim that, as shown, cannot find a sufficient basis in the

---

[26] See, for instance, Coleman, 'Incorporationism, Conventionality, and the Practical Difference Thesis', where he explicitly describes his project as an attempt to coherently develop Hart's jurisprudence.

conception of law as a shared activity. The specific difficulty in question may not emerge with immediate evidence, especially because the social fact thesis is generally interpreted as a view concerned with the *existence* of the law rather than with its *obligatoriness*. So it will be useful to consider this point further here.

The social fact thesis is a claim about the criteria of legality: it tells us what counts as law in a given system. For this reason, the social fact thesis, per se, can be understood as agnostic about the questions relating to legal obligation, which questions concern the *normativity* of law as distinct from its *existence*. However, the separation between claims about the existence of law and claims about its normative dimension can be shown to be less clear-cut than it may appear at first sight and is commonly understood. This is particularly the case if we conceive of law as a practical institution, that is, as an institutional framework whose basic function consists in providing action-guidance and justification by supplying agents with genuine reasons for action. On this conception, it is unviable to maintain a rigid separation between the existence and the obligatoriness of law. The reason for this is not hard to see. If law is understood as a practical institution, then its validity cannot be determined solely on the basis of whether its legal provisions exhibit certain relevant properties whose import is just socially factual. Instead, the validity of law must also be predicated on the ability – normative in kind – of its statements, whether in isolation or in mutual combination, to guide and justify action. And one way in which law guides action, while justifying the action it calls for, is by imposing obligations. From this it follows that we cannot go about determining which legal statements exist as valid elements of a practical institution without also considering which of those statements are normative as obligation-engendering demands. Only when we know which statements of law are *both* valid *and* obligatory can we conclude that a given legal system exists as an institution capable of shaping its addressees' deliberation on how to act.

So, even though *in abstracto* the concept of legal validity can be *distinguished* from that of legal obligation – the former relating to the existence of law and the latter to its normativity – any attempt to push the distinction beyond what is needed for analytical clarity, by actually *separating* the two dimensions of law, will ultimately lead to an artificial understanding that is likely to obfuscate the role of law as a practical institution. Since this is precisely how the advocates of the conception of law as a shared activity view the law (they view it as a practical institution),[27] it is artificial for them (and indeed for anyone proceeding from that understanding of law) to separate the question of which legal statements are obligatory from the question of which statements are valid, and so exist, as practical directives.

In sum, I just argued that, on the understanding of law as a practical institution – as a system providing practical guidance – the question of the existence of law is seen to be interdependent with that of its obligatoriness. This is because we cannot determine whether the law exists as a practical institution without first considering whether the law shapes action. And the way law does this is in part by setting forth obligations. So, insofar as the obligations imposed by the law cannot be understood as conceptually insulated from evaluative standards whose basis is not entirely social, even the existence of law cannot be established without also engaging in evaluative considerations whose basis is not entirely social. This view, however, is inconsistent with the social fact thesis – a thesis not less essential to the conception of law as a shared activity than the thesis that law is ultimately a practical institution. Insofar as these two fundamental tenets are incompatible, any attempt to hold them together is bound to fail. Yet this is precisely what the conception of law as a shared activity seeks to do when it presents itself as a theory of legal obligation that, for the reasons previously explained, does not succeed in anchoring legal obligation exclusively to social facts and practices. That is, in framing legal obligation as a kind of obligation whose status cannot be shown to be exclusively social, and so cannot be shown to be independent of evaluative principles whose basis is not entirely social, the proponents of the conception of law as shared activity jeopardize the internal coherence of their theory of law and undermine the social practice account of legal obligation they set out to theorize.

3.5 A Critique of the Social Practice Account of Perspectivized Legal Obligation

In what precedes I argued that the genuine obligations the law gives rise to on the conception of law as a shared activity only bind legal officials and are grounded in evaluative standards that are partly independent of the social facts constitutive of law. The first element gives us a limited theory of legal obligation, whereas the second element is hardly

---

[27] See, for instance, Coleman, *Practice of Principle*, pp. 134–48; and Shapiro, 'Law, Plans, and Practical Reason', pp. 437–9.

compatible with a social practice account of legal obligation. But I also mentioned the fact that legal obligation is understood by the proponents of the conception of law as a shared activity in a perspectivized sense. A perspectivized legal obligation is characterized as a domain-specific requirement whose implications do not go beyond the specialized 'game' in which law consists. In the perspectivized sense legal obligation is said by the proponents of the conception of law as a shared activity to apply to every legal subject as well as to be completely social in quality. That way, the two main difficulties I ascribed to the social practice account of legal obligation could be claimed to be overcome. Although the introduction of perspectivized legal obligations is ingenious, it has its own problems, or so I will argue here. The most serious of these problems lies in the *normative irrelevance* of perspectivized legal obligations. Perspectivized legal obligations, I intend to emphasize in what follows, are normatively inert, since perspectivized statements are by construction *descriptive* statements, as opposed to being normative statements.

The descriptive quality is a characteristic that flows directly from the way perspectivized legal obligation is framed, namely, as a legal obligation that one has from a certain point of view. Any statement that is so framed need be understood not as a *norm* in itself but rather a *description of a norm*. By claiming that from a given perspective a subject ought to undertake a certain course of conduct, we are *describing* the normative standards – or 'oughts' – that apply to (the action of) such subject, vis-à-vis *directing* that subject to act so and so. This formulation indicates that ultimately perspectivised legal obligations are statements about what is obligatory that have a *normative object* (namely, certain standards directing one's action) and (yet) a *descriptive* quality. In other terms, a statement expressing a perspectivised obligation describes the condition, or accounts for the state of affairs, of one who is taking the point of view of the legal system. Such statement can then be said to have the status of a *report*: it informs us of the fact that, barring interfering circumstances, individuals taking a given perspective view themselves as being under the requirement to perform a certain course of conduct. And, qua reports about what is obligatory in accordance to the law, perspectivised legal obligations are descriptive through and through:[28] they pertain to a

---

[28] This descriptive quality of perspectivized obligation is acknowledged in Shapiro, *Legality*, pp. 184–8. See also S. Hershovitz, 'The End of Jurisprudence', *Yale Law Journal*, 124 (2015), pp. 1167–73. In the context of a broader discussion Scott Hershovitz emphasizes the fact that an obligation from the law's point of view is 'a descriptive claim, not a

sphere of human experience – descriptive, as opposed to normative – that is conceptually distinct from the domain inhabited by genuine obligations.

We can so see what it is that makes legal obligations in a perspectivized sense normatively inert: perspectivized legal obligations have no straightforward connection with the 'practical ought' and therefore have no necessary bearing on the question of why one ought to act in the ways the law requires. This is because obligation, when it is understood through the lens of a report stating how individuals view their own position, is going to come across as a statement that does not have any direct, or immediate, implication on the decision of which courses of conduct those individuals ought to take.[29] That is to say, on this conception legal obligations remain *external* to the deliberative process aimed at determining what one ought to do. Likewise, a legal system putting forth perspectivized legal obligations cannot shape our conduct through the obligations it generates. Therefore, even if we acknowledge that the law succeeds in setting up perspectivized legal obligations with a general scope and purely social basis, this will not help us determine whether and how the law makes demands, justifies this or that action, or assesses behaviour.

This conclusion is of considerable theoretical importance especially when it is read in conjunction with my statement of the concept of obligation, as this concept has been introduced in Chapter 1. There I noticed, among other things, that practicality – the property of being action-related – and normativity – the property of being concerned with the 'ought'-dimension of human experience – are constitutive of obligation. Statements of obligations, I claimed, have to do with how someone *ought* to *act*: they refer to one's acting as well as providing guidance and enabling appraisal. These two components – practicality and

---

normative one' and, relatedly, 'claims about legal obligations are, on this picture, quasi normative; they appear to be normative, but they are not really' (Hershovitz, 'End of Jurisprudence', p. 1169). See also Kutz, 'Judicial Community', pp. 463–5.

[29] This dimension is explored in detail by Veronica Rodriguez-Blanco, who qualifies the 'legal point of view' as 'a distance viewpoint that does not commit itself to action'; accordingly such a point of view 'is not a deliberative or practical point of view, but merely a theoretical viewpoint' (V. Rodriguez-Blanco, 'The Moral Puzzle of Legal Authority', in S. Bertea and G. Pavlakos (eds.), *New Essays on the Normativity of Law* (Oxford, Hart, 2011), p. 89). Likewise, the statement of a perspectivized obligation, namely, the statement that one has an obligation from the legal point of view, occupies a territory that lies outside the boundaries of an agent's (or even a legal agent's) deliberative process.

normativity – keep obligation apart from both descriptive practical statements – statements establishing what agents *in fact* do or are most *likely* to do – and normative theoretical statements – statements showing how matters ought to *be*. Neither descriptive practical statements nor normative theoretical statements, I argued, amount to obligations.

Now, insofar as legal obligation is claimed to have a perspectivized sense and perspectivized statements are non-normative statements that do not enter one's deliberation about what one ought to do, it can be legitimately concluded that strictly speaking perspectivized legal obligations are not obligations at all. That is, a perspectivized obligation is an obligation in a Pickwickian sense only, for it cannot be acknowledged to incorporate any direct normative dimension. And without this normative dimension a statement cannot play the action-guiding and justificatory role that legal obligation, qua an instance of what is obligatory *simpliciter* as per the concept of obligation introduced in Chapter 1, should be recognized to have. So, despite any appearance to the contrary and some surface convergence with obligation proper, perspectivized obligation cannot be conceptualized as an obligation. What the champions of the conception of law as a shared activity label 'perspectivized obligation' can hardly be considered an instance of obligation, given that as a conceptual matter obligations are normative requirements, whereas perspectivized obligations are descriptive statements that can be shown to have no (direct) bearing on how an agent ought to act.

A perspectivized legal obligation, in other words, pertains to a different sphere of human experience when compared with genuine legal obligations. The latter is normative, whilst the former is normatively void and irrelevant. That is, on one side is the normative sphere – that of full-blooded legal obligation – to which obligation proper belongs; on the other is the descriptive sphere, to which perspectivized legal obligation is confined. Because of this altogether different quality – its not partaking of the normative domain – the notion of perspectivized legal obligation is, despite the terminology used by those theorizing the conception of law as a shared activity, irreducible to the concept of obligation and, consequently, to the standard meaning of legal obligation.

In sum, any appearance of continuity between the two senses of legal obligation – perspectivized legal obligation and full-blooded, or genuine, legal obligation – is merely illusory: perspectivized legal obligations cannot be regarded as legal obligations in any proper sense of the phrase, since in a perspectivized legal obligation the link between obligatoriness and normativity – a link that is conceptually essential to the definition of something as an obligation – is severed. And this means that a theory of legal obligation qua perspectivized obligation is no account of legal obligation at all.

3.6 Conclusion

My main concern in this chapter was to point out some significant shortcomings of the social practice account of legal obligation, such as this account has influentially been theorized within the conception of law as a shared activity. As the name suggests, the core of this conception lies in the idea of construing a legal system as something that is built and maintained through a joint undertaking, to wit, as that which a group does when acting in pursuit of some common goal. Through this lens the concept of a legal obligation is presented as a requirement arising out of one's participation in the shared activity lying at the foundation of law, and thus as something that becomes mandatory by virtue of such participation.

In my critical treatment of the conception of law as a shared activity I noted that such conception offers a bipartite account of legal obligation, insofar as there emerges from it a dual understanding of such obligation: we have *genuine* legal obligation – carrying normative force (by virtue of its purporting to guide and justify conduct) and accordingly liable to come into competition with other sources of practical guidance – and we have legal obligation *in a perspectivized sense*, whose purpose is not to engage with us in reasoning about what we ought to do but simply to state, or describe, what we are expected to do if we should embrace the perspective of the legal system whose jurisdiction we are subject to.

This dualistic construction of legal obligation was found to be liable to three lines of criticism: the account of legal obligation offered by the conception of law as a shared activity (i) is limited in its scope; (ii) does not make allowance for the evaluative components of the obligations arising out of the law as a shared activity, which components cannot be reduced to social facts; and, when it presents legal obligation as a perspectivized statement of what is obligatory under the law, (iii) fails to illustrate the sense in which the law is recognized to be a normative institution.

In summary, the argument I presented indicates that even the subtlest and most sophisticated theories of legal obligation that endeavour to provide an account of legal obligation based on the idea of social practice end up explaining legal obligation in ways that range from incomplete to inconsistent with the basic tenets of a social practice approach to law and its obligatory dimension. For, as much as it may make perfect sense to think about legal obligation by looking at the concept in its proper setting – that of the social practices out of which legal obligations arise – conceptualizing legal obligation primarily in terms of the shared activities the law is made of has proved to be misleading.

The conclusions one can draw from the preceding discussion are not, however, entirely negative. At least three important positive lessons can be extracted from what precedes, and in what follows each of these lessons will be used in the process of constructing a sound account of legal obligation. First, the argument offered in this chapter suggests that legal obligation ought to be understood as a *general* standard: the obligations engendered by the law are meant to address the whole community of those living under the relevant legal system, vis-à-vis a minority of those subject to the law. The second positive lesson one can draw from the foregoing discussion can be stated thus: whereas the *contents* of legal obligations are deeply and decisively shaped by the social practices lying at the foundation of law, the *sources* of legal obligation – the grounds making a legal obligation binding – consist of values, as distinct from social facts. Which is to say that, even if the *substance* of legal obligation is largely, or even exclusively, established by some social fact, the *force* of legal obligation is owed to evaluative features that cannot entirely be reduced to their social existence. Legal obligations, in other words, bind by virtue of their being anchored in values of a certain kind, that is, values having some kind of bearing on the law as a collective enterprise, but not reducible to such an enterprise or scheme understood as a mere social fact. And third, what precedes reveals that legal obligation can be properly understood only as a practically normative statement, as opposed to a perspectivized one. Legal obligations, in other words, are genuine directives – full-blooded, as I have called them – and as such they make normative claims on the subjects they address: far from merely stating what one is expected to do insofar as one takes up a given perspective, or occupies a certain role or position, legal obligations provide direction to agents in a practical and non-domain-specific sense.

4

The Interpretivist Account

4.1 Introduction

In the previous chapter I argued that even the most sophisticated versions of the social practice account of legal obligation lack the conceptual resources needed to supply a theoretically sound and sufficiently comprehensive explanation of the kind of obligation engendered by the law. For, while the social practice account of legal obligation sheds light on some central features of legal obligation, it is plagued by a major problem: it regards legal obligation as primarily a matter of social facts and institutional practices by thus downplaying its evaluative dimension, which consequently is turned into a merely derivative and secondary component of obligation as it is produced by the law.

In this chapter, I intend to discuss an account developed as a programmatic attempt to avoid this problem: interpretivism. On the interpretivist view, legal obligation is claimed to result from a combination of a social, or an institutional element, and an evaluative, or political, one. The latter is understood to be closely dependent on the social and institutional dimension and inextricably bound up with it. This coupling of components endows the interpretivist account of legal obligation with a distinctness in virtue of which the place it occupies in the jurisprudential debate is not shared with any of the other accounts discussed in this work. Hence the interest in the interpretivist research programme – a programme that requires independent discussion and separate engagement, owing not only to its *originality* but also to its theoretical *significance*.

The *originality* of the interpretivist theory of legal obligation specifically lies in the way in which such theory understands and combines the fundamental traits of legal obligation. On this view, legal obligations are inseparable from the social dimension and institutional history of the political arrangements put in place in a specific community. This position is qualified by two related claims. The first one is that the nature of legal obligation is not exhausted by its social and institutional dimension; the second one is, consequently, that essential to explaining legal obligation is an appeal to evaluative and political considerations. On the interpretivist account, then, a legal obligation arises out of a compound of social facts, institutional practices and (predominantly context-dependent) evaluative standards. These facts and standards, however, are neither self-evident nor immediately accessible to us: they need to be interpreted. Hence the view of legal obligation as an interpretive concept, one that we can only arrive at by means of applying hermeneutical processes to a given institutional practice.[1]

The *theoretical significance* of the interpretivist approach to legal obligation lies in the way in which it conceives the task of explaining legal rights and duties. This explanation is understood to constitute the core of any comprehensive theory of law.[2] It is accordingly a fundamental assumption of interpretivism that different legal theories can be distinguished from one another by their answers to such questions as: What makes it the case that legal obligation exists?, or What sorts of facts does legal obligation fundamentally depend on for its existence?, or, again, What facts make true the assertion that a legal obligation obtains? And, if legal obligation can be said to exist only so long as certain facts are ascertained, the question – What is the nature of the relation between legal obligation and its underlying facts? – becomes central to any project in jurisprudence. Since a number of questions about legal obligation play an essential role in defining the interpretivist approach to law and distinguishing this approach from alternative legal theories, we can expect to find a sophisticated and innovative view of legal obligation in the interpretivist theory. Hence the need to, and theoretical

---

[1] The notion of interpretive concept is discussed in R. Dworkin, *Justice for Hedgehogs* (Cambridge (MA), Harvard University Press, 2011, pp. 158-70) for instance, where it is also compared with, and distinguished from, the notions of 'criterial concept' and 'natural kind concept'.

[2] This has been the case since Dworkin's early works, through which interpretivism was first introduced into legal theory. Thus Dworkin argues that since 'lawyers lean heavily on the connected concepts of legal right and legal obligation', and yet 'our understanding of these concepts is remarkably fragile', it becomes essential for us to be able to explain in legal theory 'what legal rights and obligations are' (R. Dworkin, *Taking Rights Seriously* (London, Duckworth, 1978), p. 14). On this basis, Dworkin reformulates the classic questions of jurisprudence in terms of the concepts of legal right and legal obligation. See also N. Stavropoulos, 'Legal Interpretivism', in E. N. Zalta (ed.), *The Stanford Encyclopedia of Philosophy* (Summer 2014 ed.), http://plato.stanford.edu/archives/sum2014/entries/law-interpretivist/, section 1.

justification of, critically engaging with this theory in the path towards a comprehensive account of legal obligation.

For all these reasons, this chapter will be devoted to a systematic discussion of the interpretivist claims about legal obligation. I will begin, in the next section, to introduce the basics of the interpretivist account of legal obligation, which in turn is firmly rooted in, and justified by, the interpretivist legal theory at large. Having introduced the basic elements of the interpretivist account of law and legal obligation, I will pass to critically assess whether interpretivism has the conceptual resources necessary to make full sense of legal obligation as a distinctive notion. In this context, I will focus on what I take to be the fundamental problem besetting the interpretivist theory of legal obligation. This problem can be summarized as follows. The account defended by interpretivism presents legal obligations as duties fundamentally determined by the *political morality* underpinning a given institutional practice. On this view, legal obligation is claimed to be a species of moral obligation (where morality is conceived as a scheme of political principles that fits a specific institutional framework, while offering the best justification for the same framework). Patently, this claim establishes no conceptual connection between what is legally obligatory and what is morally obligatory in the sense of being required by *critical morality* as a scheme of normative standards warranted by *practical rationality*. The problem with this statement is that while, on the interpretivist account, legal obligation is a kind of *moral* requirement, the fundamental principles of *rational* morality are not necessarily regarded as components of legal obligation. And insofar as that is the case, the interpretivist account allows for the possibility that legal obligations diverge from obligations grounded in practical rationality, while at the same time qualifying them as genuine obligations. Which is puzzling, because in this way we end up legitimizing both the view that one may be under a legal obligation to act against the demands of practical rationality and the conclusion that legal regimes may make claims on how we ought to act even if they require us to act irrationally, namely, even if they require us to perform courses of conduct that do not have the backing of a justification grounded in practical rationality.

4.2 The Interpretivist Account of Legal Obligation

In this section I start out by introducing the basics of interpretivism as a conception of law, and then I clarify the theoretical implications of this conception for an understanding of legal obligation. The reconstructive task I embark on here is made difficult by the fact that interpretivism is a nuanced view that over the years has taken more than just one variant. This aspect of interpretivism is apparent in the body of work produced by the founder of this tradition of legal thought, Ronald Dworkin. To be sure, the fundamental ideas Dworkin sets out to defend in his early works are restated in his most recent writings.[3] But these theses have nonetheless stressed different aspects of interpretivism and drawn on different concepts.[4] So, even if Dworkin's interpretivism has been reasonably stable over time, a number of the views Dworkin originally defended have been fine-tuned, contextualized and revised in sometimes significant ways in his recent restatements of them. Add to this the fact that Dworkin's ideas have deeply influenced the contemporary debate in jurisprudence. Predictably, those who have engaged with Dworkin's scholarship have not confined themselves to merely applying his insights to a specific problem. Indeed, even those who follow in Dworkin's lead have elaborated on Dworkin's own theoretical approach in original and creative ways. Most notably, Nicos Stavropoulos has clarified the conceptual underpinnings of the interpretivist project and drawn the most consequential implications of interpretivist legal theory even beyond the territory Dworkin originally envisaged.[5] This means that in any attempt to bring interpretivism to bear on current legal issues, we will also have to take Stavropoulos's work into account. The combined effort of Dworkin and Stavropoulos (as well as a few others) has yielded a legal theory that is not only extremely rich and philosophically

---

[3] Among Dworkin's most influential and theoretically original contributions to interpretivism one should at least mention Dworkin, *Taking Rights Seriously*; R. Dworkin, *A Matter of Principle* (Cambridge (MA), Harvard University Press, 1985); R. Dworkin, *Law's Empire* (Cambridge (MA), Harvard University Press, 1986); R. Dworkin, *Justice in Robes* (Cambridge (MA), Harvard University Press, 2006); and Dworkin, *Justice for Hedgehogs*.

[4] For a statement of one fundamental change his theory has undergone over time, see Dworkin, *Justice for Hedgehogs*, pp. 400–2.

[5] See in particular N. Stavropoulos, *Objectivity in Law* (Oxford, Oxford University Press, 1996); N. Stavropoulos, 'Obligations and the Legal Point of View', in A. Marmor (ed.), *The Routledge Companion to Philosophy of Law* (New York, Routledge, 2012), pp. 76–92; N. Stavropoulos, 'Words and Obligations', in A. Dolcetti, L. Duarte d'Almeida, and J. Edwards (eds.), *Reading HLA Hart's The Concept of Law* (Oxford, Hart, 2013), pp. 224–81; and Stavropoulos, 'Legal Interpretivism'.

sophisticated but also constantly evolving, and which still lacks any definitive overarching statement.[6]

For all its nuances, the core idea behind interpretivism is nonetheless quite straightforward. Interpretivism offers itself as a theory about the truth of legal propositions and the grounds on which such truth may be claimed. And its basic contention is that a legal proposition, or statement of law, is true insofar as (a) it sets forth legal rights and obligations for those it is addressed to and (b) it justifies such rights and obligations to the same addressees. By elaborating on this contention, interpretivism is meant to provide a 'philosophical explanation of how institutional practice ... modifies legal rights and obligations'.[7] The fundamental insight, in providing such an explanation, is that 'the law is determined by certain principles that explain why the practice should have that role'.[8] Two components of this concise formulation need to be emphasized.

First, interpretivism is explicitly organized around the objective of providing a sound explanation of the facts constitutive of law, thereby clarifying what makes it the case that the law requires what it does. The basic aim of the interpretivist project, in other words, is to explain what determines our legal obligations (and rights). This brings legal obligations (and legal rights) front and centre in the interpretivist inquiry into the law. Law and obligation are then presented as interlinked notions: in the interpretivist conceptual framework, on the one hand, any claim about law bears on the way in which legal obligation is conceived and, on the other hand, the study of legal obligation has implications for our understanding of the law as a whole.[9]

Second, it is a core claim of interpretivism that certain moral principles figure prominently among the determinants of law and legal obligation. This claim is not meant to deny that law is largely dependent on certain institutional practices, which mainly consist of social facts, namely,

---

[6] The main contemporary contributions made in theorizing interpretivism include M. Greenberg, 'How Facts Make Law', *Legal Theory*, 10 (2004), pp. 157-98; M. Greenberg, 'Hartian Positivism and Normative Facts: How Facts Make Law II', in S. Hershovitz (ed.), *Exploring Law's Empire* (Oxford, Oxford University Press, 2006); G. Letsas, *A Theory of Interpretation of the European Convention on Human Rights* (Oxford, Oxford University Press, 2007); S. Guest, *Ronald Dworkin* (San Francisco, Stanford University Press, 3rd ed., 2012); and D. Kyritsis, *Shared Authority* (Oxford, Hart, 2014), to name but a few.

[7] Stavropoulos, 'Legal Interpretivism', section 1.

[8] Stavropoulos, 'Legal Interpretivism', section 1.

[9] These claims are defended in Dworkin, *Taking Rights Seriously*, p. 14; and Stavropoulos, 'Legal Interpretivism', section 1.

arrangements, decisions, deliberations, and the like. In the interpretivist view, however, we are not to understand these as *brute* social facts and institutional practices, for in that case we would not be able to explain what makes law and what determines our legal obligations. In other words, unless normative standards are brought into the picture and appealed to in showing the relevance of institutional practices and social facts, the latter cannot determine what obligations (and rights) exist in a given jurisdiction.

If the truth of legal propositions, and so the binding force of the obligations put in place through any complex of institutional acts, cannot be made to depend (just) on brute social facts and institutional practices, it must have (also) another basis. On the interpretivist account this basis consists of the principles of political morality that can best explain, make sense of, and provide justificatory support for such facts and practices (however complex this explanatory and justificatory relation may be). Interpretivism is thus fundamentally committed to the thesis that principles of political morality are constitutive of law. Since these principles are evaluative standards, interpretivism ultimately views law as a combination of social facts (viz. institutional arrangements) and value judgements. This means that neither social facts and institutional practices alone nor values, if taken in isolation from their broader political context, have the resources needed to make legal propositions true and so to act on their own as determinants of law. The two need to work in tandem if law is to have any force and work as intended.[10]

Crucially, it is through interpretation that social practices gain meaning. They do so in the process of bringing evaluative principles to bear on them. This interpretive process consists in the activity of making sense of the political practice – or any institutional practice that forms part of the public discourse – in light of principles and values drawn from that very forum, or sphere of understanding. More analytically, the interpretive process makes it possible to determine (a) what the *point* of the practice at issue is, or what values it is meant to model or embody, and (b), in light of that determination, what contents the practice should take, that

---

[10] To put it in Dworkin's own words, the law 'includes not only the specific rules enacted in accordance with the community's accepted practices but also the principles that provide the best moral justification for those enacted rules. The law then also includes the rules that follow from those justifying principles, even though those further rules were never enacted' (Dworkin, *Justice for Hedgehogs*, p. 402).

is, what policy it should be shaped by, and so what it actually should consist in.

As can be appreciated from this snapshot, interpretive activities aimed at teasing out the point of the institutional and social practices from which the law can be derived are not just descriptive, that is, they are not intended as a value-neutral form of inquiry concerned with social facts existing prior to and independently of the interpretation itself. On the contrary, these activities are aimed at *reconstructing* the practices they interpret. So interpretation accounts for institutional and social practices such as they present themselves to the observer. At the same time, interpretivism singles out certain such practices as relevant to law, or as practices that need to be taken into account in shaping the contents of law. Interpretive activities, then, both explain and justify the institutional practices they turn to: an institutional practice becomes valuable and relevant to law only as a practice shaped by the very activity through which it is interpreted. Finally, interpretation clarifies the role that social facts play in establishing legal obligations: it singles out the facts in virtue of which one can be deemed to have an obligation under the law, and in so doing it turns otherwise brute facts into grounds of law.[11]

The essential role of interpretation in determining the truth of legal propositions means that social practices and the principles of political morality do not serve the same function in the constitution of law. The principles of political morality come logically first in the order of explanation, for they select those elements of a social practice and institutional arrangement that are legally relevant by thus elucidating 'how it is that institutional and other nonmoral considerations have roles as determinants of the right or obligation' in question.[12] On this view, they are the principles of political morality that govern when one has to determine how the institutional framework and political practice affect legal contents and obligations, since 'one cannot see the practice except through

---

[11] For a statement to this effect, see Stavropoulos, 'Legal Interpretivism', section 4; and Greenberg, 'How Facts Make Law', pp. 173–84.

[12] Stavropoulos, 'Legal Interpretivism', section 1. For interpretivism, then, 'the explanation of how legal practice matters to legal rights and obligations is an ordinary explanation of the normative effects of action by appeal to the substantive normative considerations that give it that role' (Stavropoulos, 'Obligations and the Legal Point of View', p. 77). This is to say that it is the principles of political morality, and not bare facts, that 'justify some particular aspect of the institutions' action having a role as a determinant of rights and obligation. By doing so, they aim to establish, for each candidate determinant of law, its precise impact on the law' (Stavropoulos, 'Legal Interpretivism', section 4).

the lens of morality; the facts are not there independently to constrain. ... facts are only there through their moral status; they are moral propositions in the interpretive story (or they have no moral status within that story)'.[13] The (explanatory) pride of place that evaluative considerations – the principles of political morality – have in the interpretivist account of law and legal obligation is thus owed to the fact that the evaluative component, as singled out by way of interpretive processes, justifies why an institutional practice has a bearing on legal requirements and thus why certain social facts (and not others) are legally relevant.[14]

In light of these last remarks it can be appreciated that interpretation is baked directly into the law and into the obligations the law engenders. This means that institutional arrangements, social practices, and the facts of political life can shape the content of law and give rise to obligations, not as such – in virtue of some inherent property – but only as *interpreted* arrangements, practices, and facts. This is also true of the facts that play any role in determining how the law is made:[15] not only is this a determination that presupposes a political morality, but political morality forms a background in light of which the social facts themselves are selected through interpretive processes. Which social facts therefore do not come in to being as neutral entities to which evaluative criteria are then applied for the purpose of culling what is to count as legally relevant; rather they come with an evaluation already packaged into them. So, in arguing that the social facts of law are inescapably interpreted, interpretivism also says that law is an indissoluble amalgam of facts and values, neither of which can be separated from the other.

Because the facts that make up law are a combination of institutional practice and evaluative principles, those facts are understood by interpretivism as facts of a metaphysically distinctive kind. Accordingly, they are termed 'interpretive facts'. What makes interpretive facts unique is

---

[13] S. Guest, 'How to Criticize Ronald Dworkin's Theory of Law', *Analysis*, 69 (2009), p. 356. On this basis, these principles are regarded by interpretivists as elements establishing 'how institutional practice determines the law, i.e., which precise aspect of the practice is relevant to the practice's contribution to the law' (Stavropoulos, 'Legal Interpretivism', section 4).

[14] The account from which this picture is derived can on this basis be regarded as a 'substantive' account, insofar as the business of identifying legal obligations has no non-normative part, and insofar as normative facts figure in any explanation of the binding force of social practices.

[15] As Stephen Guest remarks in this regard, determining what counts as law is an activity that is not 'constrained by facts even though it makes use of facts' (Guest, 'How to Criticize Ronald Dworkin's Theory of Law', p. 352).

that they can neither be reduced to institutional practices nor portrayed as purely evaluative entities. The reason why, on the one hand, interpretive facts cannot be equated with bare social practices is that, as noted, there is no such thing as an inert fact waiting to be evaluated. The reason why, on the other hand, interpretive facts cannot be reduced to evaluations is simply that evaluation is not self-validating, in that it still has to reckon with what we would ordinarily recognize as fact, however pre-interpreted all facts (on this conception) may be. What is distinctive about interpretive facts, then, is that in coupling a factual dimension and an evaluative dimension – or social practices with an evaluation of them grounded in principle – they cannot exist outside the frame of these two dimensions thus inseparably welded: the truth of the relevant social fact depends on the validity of its evaluation as much as the latter depends on the former.

Shift over to the realm of law, and this means that law can neither be (a) collapsed into an institutional arrangement – namely, into a complex of practices and decisions framing social facts along a timeline that runs from the past to the future – nor (b) understood to consist only of the scheme of principles that best fit and justify that practice. For both of these elements – (a) and (b) – concur in determining what law is, such that neither can exist without the other.

On this basis interpretivism argues that in order to determine what law requires, we have to look at the political history that forms its background, a background inclusive of legislative and judicial decisions.[16] We thus need a theory that tries to make the best sense of the historical background of the law and shapes the law accordingly. To this end, that background needs to be assessed in light of the principles of political morality. And these are in turn condensed in what Dworkin calls ideal of integrity.[17] Integrity is a political virtue requiring 'that the public standards of the community be both made and seen, so far as this is possible, to express a single, coherent scheme of justice and fairness'.[18] In virtue of this appeal to fairness, integrity demands that all members of a political community be treated with equal concern and respect. It importantly

---

[16] See R. Dworkin, '"Natural" Law Revisited', *University of Florida Law Review*, 34 (1982), pp. 165–6.

[17] For a treatment of integrity, as it applies to law, see Dworkin, *Law's Empire*, pp. 225–75. See also Dworkin, '"Natural" Law Revisited', pp. 168–73. An insightful account of integrity that is most Dworkinian in spirit is also offered in G. Postema, 'Integrity: Justice in Workclothes', *Iowa Law Review*, 82 (1997), pp. 821–55.

[18] Dworkin, *Law's Empire*, p. 219.

follows from this requirement that the arrangements made in the past by those in authority ought to shape court decisions and institutional arrangements going forward. A political institution bears the mark of integrity insofar as the acts and decisions forming the underlying practice adhere to the fundamental principles that justify the institution over the course of its development. The practice of integrity endows the institutional record with a principled coherence over time, so that the institution will not fall prey to the vagaries of political contingency. In this way, in a political order based on integrity, those who are subject to the law can be confident that their mutual engagement in the practical sphere unfolds within a relatively stable and coherent framework. The basic idea here is that by so reconstructing the background political history and practice as a coherent scheme unified under the principle of integrity, the institutional arrangement as a whole gains moral justification. For integrity makes the institutional arrangement and its evolution both intelligible and morally attractive by putting it in its best light and thus turning a mere record of events into a framework in which facts and values come together so as to achieve the closest possible fit with the idea of a political order in which all members are treated fairly and are respected as individuals.

The moral justification that comes by way of integrity is peculiar in its method, for here the justification of institutional arrangements is pursued by conferring unity on these arrangements. The principles that secure this unity are arrived at by publicly and coherently interpreting the acts and decisions that over time have been carried out by those in power. This makes the justifying principles inherently historical and socially situated: far from superimposing an abstract ideal on a community's political experience, integrity grounds the justifying principles in the institutional arrangement it seeks to justify, looking not only at its current make-up but also at the history behind it.

It is this analysis of how law works and how its content is shaped that, on an interpretivist account, shows how legal obligation comes about: legal obligation is the outcome of (a) identifying the facts and practices that ought to tell us who we are as a society and how we have historically evolved as a political community, and (b) interpreting these facts and practices in light of the principle of integrity, so as to arrive at a coherent understanding of ourselves as such a community. In a word, legal obligation emerges out of the activity of reconstructing an institutional framework as a coherent whole and showing that the principles through which that coherence is achieved are ones that fit our self-understanding and ought to therefore guide and govern our interaction as members of a society where matters of public interest are at issue.[19] What counts as obligatory in a given jurisdiction, then, is determined by the activity through which the formative acts of its institutional history are publicly interpreted under a principle of integrity, in such a way that their content is legitimized and thus recognized as binding on the members of the political community over the future course of their interactions. Integrity thus acts at the same time as a principle of coherence and as one of justification, for in unifying our social facts, institutional practices, and political decisions into a coherent view of how we ought to understand our life as members of a single polity, it makes those facts and practices normative and thus capable of giving rise to obligations as part of the institutional framework they make up.[20]

As these remarks suggest, legal obligations are principled requirements that we have because of our political history and institutional framework. Likewise, they are duties that 'can be forced on official demand in and through [adjudicative] institutions' and to which correspond certain rights 'people are entitled to enforce on demand, without further legislative intervention, in adjudicative institutions'.[21] Related to this, legal obligations cannot, on the interpretivist conception, be understood to simply issue from an institutional practice per se but are rather inextricably bound up with the values and justifications underpinning that practice. In other words, before a requirement set out within an institutional practice can become binding as law – before it can carry force as a legal obligation – it needs to be recognized as something that hews to the principles of political morality espoused by the community subject to the jurisdiction at hand. For this reason, legal obligation cannot be conceptualized as simply an institutional demand, in turn understood as a brute social fact: it cannot be reduced to the fact that some requirement is issued and institutionally enforced. It is instead to be conceptualized as an inherently *justified* requirement, that is, a requirement for which *normative support* is offered as part of the institutional practice through

---

[19] See Dworkin, *Law's Empire*, pp. 240–50.

[20] Compare Stavropoulos, 'Obligations and the Legal Point of View', p. 89, where the same point is summarized by saying that, on the interpretivist view, 'the role of institutional action as a determinant of legal obligation is explained by some distinctive political virtue that is realized or some purpose that is served by institutional action's having that role. Thus, the legal relevance of institutional practice is derivative from the moral relevance of some of its aspects to the problem of coercive enforcement.'

[21] Dworkin, *Justice for Hedgehogs*, p. 406.

which it is put into place.²² Justification ought therefore to be understood as essential to legal obligation – for otherwise we are left with brute social facts or uninterpreted institutional practices, which cannot alone act as grounds of legal obligation.²³

In sum, legal obligation is a compound of social practices coupled with the reasons and values by which such practices are justified. These are the reasons and values that serve as a justifying basis of an institutional arrangement and its requirements only by making it possible to interpret the propositions of law so that they cohere with and even clarify the self-understanding of the political community subject to those propositions, such that the same propositions are shown to qualify as true for that community. This brings up a final point, which is that legal obligations are conceived by interpretivism as *genuine* obligations.²⁴ This means that legal obligation is a kind of moral obligation – indeed it is a special variant of moral obligation in that it specifically arises out of certain institutional arrangements and political practices.²⁵ Accordingly, legal obligations occupy the same space as the obligations rooted in (other branches of) morality. The reason why legal obligation can carry such genuine practical force is that the institutional structure out of which it emerges – the law – is in turn political, and hence moral:²⁶ if the law is an enterprise rooted in political morality, and hence is genuinely practical, so are the obligations emerging out of the law. As such, they stand on an equal footing with the requirements establishing how we ought to behave as a matter of practical necessitation, and occasionally may therefore clash, compete, and even trump, outweigh, or prevail over, such other requirements.

---

[22] Thus any sound explanation of legal obligation must include the considerations that assign to the practice some reason-giving role, since the determinants of legal obligation include 'normative facts, which are independent of the practice and give some of its aspects normative relevance' (Stavropoulos, 'Words and Obligations', p. 128).

[23] This point is expressly made in Dworkin, '"Natural" Law Revisited'; and Dworkin, *Justice in Robes*, pp. 13–18, among other places.

[24] The law, Dworkin claims, is 'a source of genuine obligations' (Dworkin, *Law's Empire*, p. 191). Similarly, in Stavropoulos, 'Legal Interpretivism', section 4, it is emphasized that legal obligation is not a duty in a mere perspectivized sense.

[25] On this aspect – legal obligation as belonging to a special branch of political morality – see Dworkin, *Justice for Hedgehogs*, p. 407.

[26] This point is made by Mark Greenberg, who argues that 'legal obligations are a certain subset of moral obligations' (M. Greenberg, 'The Moral Impact Theory of Law', *Yale Law Journal*, 123 (2014), p. 1290) and, more to the point, the subset of moral obligations 'created by the actions of legal institutions' (Greenberg, 'Moral Impact Theory of Law', p. 1306).

4.3 How the Interpretivist Account Gets Legal Obligation Wrong

Interpretivism marks an advance on the social practice account in providing a unified and prima facie conceptually sound account of legal obligation that duly recognizes the role evaluative considerations play in explaining how the law can make demands on us. Unlike the social practice account, the interpretivist account does not *underplay* that role. As a result, it does not only elucidate how law *as a matter of collective activity* gets us to behave in keeping with its rules, but it also emphasizes that there is an essential *justificatory* component involved in this activity. For in requiring us to behave in one way or another, the law also *justifies* why we should do so, thus providing normative support for its demands. Indeed, interpretivism recognizes justifications as essential to law, noting that even when they point to facts in virtue of which we are legally bound to do something, these facts are always *interpreted*. Now, since on the interpretivist account there is no such thing as an uninterpreted fact or practice, and since to interpret is always to make a value judgement – and one that is intended to justify the practice or the fact adduced as grounds for behaving as prescribed – it follows from interpretivism that the fact of our having an obligation under the law is not just a brute fact of circumstance but is also at the same time a *normative* fact. In pointing out this fundamental feature of law, interpretivism also recognizes that law develops as a *normative* social practice, institutional framework, and political culture, a practice, framework, and culture whose history is itself a rich repository of foundational values and justificatory considerations absent which the practice, framework, and culture could not exist to begin with. And in so doing interpretivism captures what is distinctive about legal obligation, namely, its inextricably combining two elements: on the one hand is the fact of our being required to do what law says, on the other is the interpretive activity that necessarily comes with that fact, an activity that brings a whole range of evaluative and normative considerations into play in imposing such a requirement.

Although the overall architecture of the interpretivist account of legal obligation seems sound, especially in recognizing an essential connection between facts and values in law, the kinds of values brought into play in justifying the obligations we become subject to under the law stem from a background justificatory assumption that is open to criticism, or so I will argue in this section, where I make explicit the interpretivist view of justification and proceed to criticize it. This is the view that moral standards are wholly internal to the practice out of which they arise, such that a coherent interpretation of this practice needs only to bring out its inherent values to justify the obligations associated with the practice. I will claim that a stronger, independent justification is instead needed for a proper grounding of legal obligation. Indeed, if the obligations engendered by the law are genuine obligations, as the proponents of the interpretivist account theorize – that is, if legal obligations are requirements with general practical relevance, and the claims they make are claims on our practical deliberation at large – they need a kind of justification conceived in that broad practical framework, rather than one contingent on the practice in which they are embedded, for otherwise any practice, once duly interpreted, can act as a self-authenticating source of justification. Likewise, what the law requires of us can no longer be evaluated in light of standards shaped by the principles constitutive of practical rationality, the kind that – I submit – stands behind any genuine obligation, one that appeals to our powers of reasoning in pointing out why we should act accordingly.

In order to spell out and expand on this critique, we need to look more closely at the basic interpretivist proposition that legal obligation results neither from an institutional practice as such, nor from any set of moral values, but from a combination of the two, that is, from a practice as interpreted in light of the principles of political morality that are understood to legitimize that practice. As this framing of the conception suggests, the relevant principles are not external to the practice but organic to it. The relation between the two is thus one of interdependence: just as the social facts constitutive of an institutional practice cannot have any meaning before they are viewed through the lens of a political morality, this political morality is not a freestanding standard of evaluation pre-existing, and superimposed on, the practice. It rather emerges out of the practice itself and is offered as the best understanding of that practice – the best ideal fit for that practice. But to arrive at such an understanding we have to look at the institutional record and political history of decisions that have shaped the practice over the course of its formation and development. For the principal point of interpreting the practice is to mould its constitutive facts and decisions into a coherent whole attractive to those to whom they apply. What seems to come into view here is the full picture of the hermeneutical circle involved in giving legal obligation an interpretivist account. Namely, first, from the institutional and social practice through which the content of legal obligation is established we extract the values and principles in light of which to make sense of the practice itself; then, we use these principles to shine the best light on the practice, enabling it to reflect back to us what it is ideally meant to achieve. We can see, thus, that the social and institutional practice out which legal obligation arises decisively contributes to determine the principles in light of which that same obligation is to be interpreted and understood.

Despite its initial attractiveness, this framework strikes me as forming a rather closed loop. This is because of the controlling influence exerted by the background against which the principles of political morality are worked out. On the one hand, it would be unreasonable to pretend that these principles existed in a vacuum, for they are *practical* principles designed to guide the action of people *in a political community*: they accordingly have to be *embedded* in that community, for otherwise it would be impossible to achieve the fit needed for them to work properly. But, on the other hand, this fit between political principles and the community for which they are designed seems to leave little room for independent judgement, the kind needed to subject them to critical scrutiny. I will call this state of affairs the 'predicament of fit'. Such predicament can be formulated thus: we want a political morality that will make rational sense to *us*, rather than to some impartial spectator sitting in high judgement on our practice – that is, we want our principles to be true to our practice; but at the same time we should not be complacent in achieving such a fit, for that would make it impossible to steer our practice towards a course that is not only coherent with past and current practice but also open to rational scrutiny. It is in this territory of self-reinforcing, path-dependent thinking that the interpretivist approach lands us. Or at least this is what we risk in adhering to its premise of fitness for purpose. The risk is inherent in the fact that on the interpretivist account interpreting a practice – with its history, background, and foundational values – is functional to make the best sense of it to those who engage in it. And if we pursue this course closely enough, we will wind up with principles that are socially and historically conditioned to a degree that squeezes out the possibility of seeing the same practice through other lenses.[27]

The same applies to legal obligation: its content needs to be set in the context of a practice, its history woven into a coherent narrative that

---

[27] This much is acknowledged in Dworkin, *Law's Empire*, p. 203, stating that 'there is no guarantee ... that the interpretive attitude will always justify reading some apparently unjust feature of an associative institution out of it'. See also Dworkin, *Law's Empire*, pp. 403–7.

pushes it forward into the future; but not to such an extent that the narrative gains a momentum of its own, pulling all interpretation along in its slipstream. This is precisely what the interpretivist account suggests in claiming that 'the fact that a given principle figures in the best justification of legal practice as a whole provides a reason for extending that principle into the future'.[28] On that same basis, we would also have to proceed in shaping the obligations we want to be bound by under the law. But if this 'best justification' resolves itself into the 'closest fit' between a principle and the underlying legal practice with its accompanying obligations, we will have little room in which to manoeuvre in detecting anything in the practice that may not seem right, qua less than rational. In other words, the principles we wind up committing to will be so internal to the practice that we lock our interpretation of it into an airtight system that cannot be assessed in light of any standard of practical rationality.

In summary, in grounding legal obligation in principles of political morality, and requiring that these principles be true to the institutional arrangement they are intended to guide, interpretivism sets up between legal obligation and its enveloping political framework an internal relation in virtue of which legal obligation not only reflects the contingencies of that framework but also seems justified as long as its form and content cohere with the same framework and core values as interpreted through the lens of the political morality in which legal obligation itself is grounded. But this seems too comfortable a fit between legal obligation and the institutional practice out of which it emerges, for it seems to rule out the possibility of subjecting legal obligation to a test of practical rationality, or critical morality, thereby allowing for the possibility of a gap between what one is *legally* obligated to do and what one is *rationally* required to do. Indeed, if legal obligation needs to be consistent with its embedding institutional practice, it may not be amenable to any critical scrutiny outside the range of what is allowed by the interpretation designed to achieve that fit and consistency.

Crucially, this circuitousness can be claimed to constitute not just a likely outcome of interpretation but an inherent part of it. This is because behind the requirement of coherence – which on the interpretivist approach seems to foreclose a deep, rational, independent scrutiny of the political principles on which legal obligation is based – is the previously mentioned ideal of integrity. In the interpretivist framework,

---

[28] Dworkin, '"Natural" Law Revisited', p. 182.

integrity is the central ideal and guiding criterion of interpretation, requiring that an institutional practice be shown to be stable and fair to all those who engage in it. Since this means showing the practice to be consistent with the values and ideals participants in the practice already espouse and with its own legacy, interpretation of law and legal obligation as justified on this basis ends up being self-referring.

This dimension of the interpretivist account of legal obligation can be further explored and restated by pointing out that in such account interpretation is not meant to be a *deconstructive* process but a *constructive* one:[29] interpretation (re)constructs and (re)frames an institutional and political practice by bringing it into line with its own founding ideals, in a sort of reflective equilibrium. Now, to be fair, to so interpret a practice – that is, to make it coherent with the principles espoused by its participants – is not just to shine the best light on it in such a way as to hide its less palatable aspects. For the effort, in making sense of the practice, is to make it fair and equitable in the eyes of the same participants. So there is room for improvement in interpreting a practice. But the range of improvement is bound by what the practice already understands to be fair and ideal. Accordingly, in the interpretivist framework the coherence requirement seems to weigh heavily on what can be done in the way of rational criticism, since it brings in the dead hand of the past, so to speak. To rephrase this point, constructive interpretation, in the sense just outlined, looks more like a rationalization of the practice at hand than a critical assessment of it in light of independently validated principles. Its corrective power under the ideal of integrity is limited, being confined within the bounds of what the requirement of securing internal coherence allows.[30] Nor does it help that the notion of integrity

---

[29] This emerges clearly in Dworkin's account of how interpretation establishes what counts as law in a given jurisdiction (see Dworkin, *Law's Empire*, pp. 45–86). For a thorough critical discussion showing how the hermeneutical activities involved in shaping the contents of the law are not deconstructive but reconstructive and rationalizing, see E. Christodoulidis, '"End of History" Jurisprudence: Dworkin in South Africa', in F. Du Bois (ed.), *The Practice of Integrity: Reflections on Ronald Dworkin and South African Law* (Cape Town, Juta, 2004), pp. 64–85; and S. Levinson, 'Hercules, Abraham Lincoln, the United States Constitution, and the Problem of Slavery', in A. Ripstein (ed.), *Ronald Dworkin* (Cambridge, Cambridge University Press, 2007), pp. 136–67.

[30] In fact, as Emilios Christodoulidis has argued, settled iniquities are resilient to interpretation so construed, which, if anything, may even end up making iniquities deeply entrenched in the system's institutional history. See Christodoulidis, '"End of History" Jurisprudence'; and also E. Christodoulidis, 'The Suspect Intimacy between Law and Political Community', *Archiv für Rechts- und Sozial-Philosophie*, 80 (1994), pp. 1–18.

at stake here is of the *inclusive* sort, as opposed to the more demanding 'pure integrity', as Dworkin calls it,[31] that would make it possible to look at a set of institutional practices and arrangements from an external viewpoint. Indeed, it is precisely this external viewpoint that would be needed for a sound critical assessment of a practice.[32]

So, as much as Dworkinian integrity can be used in order to temper rulings and political decisions that by most measures have proved to be unreasonable and unjust – leading to practices such as slavery and torture or to conditions of deep and entrenched economic inequality – it cannot show them to be inherently wrong or unreasonable. This is because it is committed to ensuring continuity with the existing content and historical record of the institutional framework within which such rulings and decisions are made. And the same shortcoming will also be reflected in the legal rights and obligations established through the same rulings and obligations.[33] Integrity, in other words, may interpretively make coherent a set of institutional, political, and economic arrangements that seem unintelligible. It may even serve as a useful guide in revising such arrangements for the better. But integrity does not necessarily bend them into conformity with rational standards.

Nowhere is this gap between political and critical rationality more conspicuous than in the laws and rulings of what in jurisprudence are referred to as wicked legal systems, understood as institutional arrangements that, on the one hand, are set up as legal systems proper – they formally qualify as such by way of their structure – but, on the other hand, become a vehicle for issuing rationally indefensible directives.[34] Often cited as examples are the antebellum South in the United States

---

[31] On this aspect, see Dworkin, *Law's Empire*, pp. 404–7.

[32] By external viewpoint I do not mean a view from nowhere imposed on the practice at hand, but rather a standard of rational correctness – what I am calling practical rationality – which the participants in the practice are assumed to espouse, for they are understood to have an interest in following rational patterns when making their own decisions in shaping the practice they are subject to, without necessarily having to submit to the legacy of the past.

[33] The historical conditioning of legal obligation emerges most clearly in Dworkin's treatment of the question. See Dworkin, '"Natural" Law Revisited', pp. 181–7, among other places.

[34] The example of a wicked legal system is being used here only to dramatize a point already made, namely, that interpretivism fails to close the gap between political morality and critical morality. But there is no conceptual difference, in this respect, between a wicked legal system and one that would not qualify as wicked. So the argument does not turn on there being any wicked systems to point out as examples. The question of rights and duties under a wicked legal system is addressed from an interpretivist perspective in

and the Third Reich, where slavery and genocide, respectively, were practices consistent with law. Here the courts would have to validate practices that do not stand up to critical scrutiny – practices that may have been consistent with the *political* morality underpinning those legal systems, but not with any rational standard. And yet the best a judge could do in these cases, on an interpretivist approach, is strike a balance between the status quo, with its legacy of subjection and unspeakable practices, and what practical rationality can bear.

As I have argued, interpretivism ties legal obligation to moral standards rooted in the specific institutional structure, practice, and history out of which it arises, in such a way that it need not pass a test of practical rationality. A conception so construed carries implications of considerable theoretical moment. For what we are to distil from it is that the justification of legal obligation does not depend on conventional standards, nor does it rest squarely on the principles of practical rationality, but is rather centred on the community, and in particular on a reconstruction of it that makes the best sense of its institutional arrangement in light of its foundational values and other widely shared values. In short, legal obligation is understood as neither a conventional nor a rational construct but as a political one. Now, on the one hand, this means that legal obligation does not come into being simply in virtue of a provision having been authoritatively issued: it cannot be reduced to the fact of our having to do or refrain from doing something as a result of a political authority having issued a demand, to that effect in keeping with its rules of procedure, for it also needs the support of justificatory principles.[35] But, on the other hand, these principles are not the standard

---

R. Dworkin, 'Review of R. Cover, Justice Accused: Antislavery and the Judicial Process', *The Times Literary Supplement*, 5 December 1975; Dworkin, *Taking Rights Seriously*, pp. 338–45; Dworkin, '"Natural" Law Revisited', pp. 183–7; Dworkin, *Law's Empire*, pp. 101–8; and Dworkin, *Justice for Hedgehogs*, pp. 410–12. For a critical discussion of Dworkin's position, see E. Mureinik, 'Dworkin and Apartheid', in H. Corder (ed.), *Essays on Law and Social Practice in South Africa* (Cape Town, Juta, 1988), pp. 181–217; D. Dyzenhaus, 'Why Positivism Is Authoritarian', *American Journal of Jurisprudence*, 37 (1992), pp. 83–112; D. Dyzenhaus, *Hard Cases in Wicked Legal Systems* (Oxford, Oxford University Press, 2010), pp. 22–33; D. Dyzenhaus, *Dworkin and Unjust Law*, in W. Waluchow and S. Sciaraffa (eds.), *The Legacy of Ronald Dworkin* (Oxford, Oxford University Press, 2016), pp. 131–64; Christodoulidis, '"End of History" Jurisprudence'; and P. Soper, 'In Defense of Classical Natural Law in Legal Theory: Why Unjust Law Is No Law at All', *Canadian Journal of Law and Jurisprudence*, 20 (2007), pp. 201–23, among others.

[35] This point is taken up in Stavropoulos, 'Obligations and the Legal Point of View', pp. 86–9.

constitutive of practical rationality. So, while legal obligation, on an interpretivist account, cannot be based solely on our endorsement of it as a matter of conventional morality – for it needs to be supported by values, and these values need to stand independently of the collective agreement that may materialize within a social group – they need not be so independent as to have their own foundation in practical rationality.

The first of the two theses just outlined seems to me to be unexceptionable. In fact, as mentioned earlier, it strikes me as an important advance on the social practice approach to legal obligation. The second thesis, by contrast, falls subject to the criticism I have so far been considering. Which is to say that in grounding legal obligation in *political* morality – the kind embraced by the political community whose institutions make legally binding claims on its members – interpretivism is essentially saying that legal obligation need not be responsive to any *critical* morality, in turn understood as a rational code of conduct. This clearly shapes the kind of practical justification we require for legal obligation: one grounded not so much in the rational *acceptability* of obligation as in its institutional, or political, *acceptance*.

To be fair, as we just saw, interpretivism is best understood as trying to chart a middle course between these two standards – acceptability and acceptance – for it grounds legal obligation not in any sheer commitment to an institutional practice but in a reconstruction of it meant to make it coherent with its own founding values – a reconstruction in light of which the practice and the obligations arising out of it ought to prove intelligible and shareable to its participants. But this via media, I submit, is not compatible with the assumption that these participants are agents capable of independent thinking informed to the principles constitutive of practical rationality. So, as much as interpretivism may have a principled understanding of legal obligation, requiring it to be justified on moral grounds, these are the very moral grounds that those who are subject to legal obligation accept from the outset. Which means that their institutional and political morality will trump any rational morality that may prescribe a different set of practical choices. It is this grounding of legal obligation in an institutional *political* morality, rather than in an independent *rational* morality, that in my view undermines the justificatory force of legal obligation such as it is conceived on the interpretivist account.

That is to say, on the one hand, the interpretivist account sets up a defining, or analytical, relation between legal obligation and the principles of political morality by which it is underpinned – in that legal obligation is justified insofar as it rests on a political morality embedded in an existing institutional practice. On the other hand, the same account asserts that the practice justifies ultimately itself. And this is questionable because (genuine) justification entails the possibility of *independently* validating that which it is meant to justify – here the obligations rooted in an institutional practice. Which in turn entails the possibility of *rejecting* such a practice, if the practice fails to pass the independent test of justification – whereas justification-as-interpretation does not allow for this possibility, or at least not to the extent we can achieve by proceeding from a critical standpoint.

Indeed, the interpretivist account is essentially premised on the view that in order for the law to make claims on us, its obligations need to be ultimately rooted in the community that forms within a polity, a polity whose history, mores, founding values, and political principles endow those obligations with a fuller meaning and deeper force and justification than that which may come from formal enactment.[36] A polity cannot act as a ground of obligations simply in virtue of its issuing provisions in keeping with a set procedure; it needs the backing of its own values and principles. And the connection between this back-end content and our front-end duty of obedience is established by the ideal of integrity. Integrity fastens the institutional framework to its underlying values and principles, and in so doing it endows with genuine force the duty of obedience owed by those who are subject to its jurisdiction. What binds these subjects, therefore, is not any imagined role they may have as parties to a contract they have entered into on terms that all agree to as fair, but rather their concrete status as members of a community of principle, a community held together by a set of moral values and political principles they are committed to and in virtue of which they gain a sense of mutual equal concern.[37]

---

[36] On this role of the political order in grounding genuine legal obligations see, for instance, Dworkin, '"Natural" Law Revisited', pp. 183–7. For a statement of the view that this duty of compliance we have as participants in a polity ultimately rests on its principles of political morality, see Dworkin, *Law's Empire*, pp. 190–216.

[37] As Dworkin states this contrast, 'the best defense of political legitimacy – the right of a political community to treat its members as having obligations in virtue of collective community decisions – is to be found not in the hard terrain of contracts or duties of justice or obligations of fair play that might hold among strangers, where philosophers have hoped to find it, but in the more fertile ground of fraternity, community, and their attendant obligations' (Dworkin, *Law's Empire*, p. 206). A community of principle is a polity inhabited by individuals 'governed by common principles, not just by rules hammered out in political compromise' (Dworkin, *Law's Empire*, p. 211).

In summary, the reason why a polity can act as a source of obligation lies not in its bare political structure (in the mere fact of its enacting provisions in accordance with an agreed practice), nor in any contractual principle of justice, but in the moral and political ideals espoused by its members, whose 'general commitment to integrity [as grounded in those ideals] expresses a concern by each for all that is sufficiently special, personal, pervasive, and equalitarian to ground communal obligations'.[38] Yet – and herein lies what I take to be the critical failure of the interpretivist account of legal obligation – the moral values and political principles an associative community needs to commit to as a matter of integrity in order for the legal obligations they are bound by to count as obligations to begin with need not be congruent with any standard of practical rationality. Integrity may explain the ability of a community to commit to a set of values and principles, but it does not secure for such values and principles any grounding in practical rationality. Integrity, in other words, may well be consistent with an espousal of values and principles that would not pass a test of critical morality. And this cannot be countenanced as a possible outcome of a theory of legal obligation, when legal obligation is presented as a genuine requirement.

To conclude my critique of interpretivism, while this account correctly understands legal obligation as a claim that needs to be justified, the form of justification employed to this end cannot guarantee that the provisions we are asked to subscribe to are rationally sound. They may be directives we ought to support as a matter of integrity, and they may even be subject to improvement if interpreted consistently with their underlying values; but there is no way to ensure that they will pass an independent assessment carried out by practical rationality, since (on the interpretivist approach) we are stuck with reasoning within the bounds of those underlying values, or of whatever foundational values happen to be espoused by the political community in question. And this feedback loop ultimately deprives the interpretivist account of legal obligation of the ability to fully rectify the potential injustices of the legal systems out of which it arises, thereby making the account theoretically questionable.

---

[38] Dworkin, *Law's Empire*, p. 216.

4.4 Addressing a Potential Objection

In response to the criticism of the interpretivist account of legal obligation levelled in the previous section, it could be pointed out that the theoretical framework within which the criticism is raised is insufficiently sensitive to the fact that the law belongs to a *particular* sphere of practical rationality. It is true that interpretivism conceives of law as a collective enterprise at once practical and rational, thereby acknowledging that law and practical rationality are intrinsically connected. But law is not regarded by interpretivists as a mere instantiation of, or a direct derivation from, practical rationality. On the contrary, the interpretivist view is that the practical and rational dimensions of law are specific and unique: while it is understood (on the interpretivist legal theory) that a central role in shaping the law is played by moral considerations – especially considerations appealing to standards of public, or institutional, morality – the law as an enterprise is largely understood to be autonomous from practical rationality in general.[39] On the interpretivist account, in other words, the justification for legal obligation does not have a generic rational basis but is rather conceived as distinctly based on political argument.

The specificity of the justification for what is legally obligatory is owed in particular to the distinctively political and institutional nature of the law as a whole: in the legal domain, justifications do not make any direct appeal to the general standards of practical rationality, and that is because the law unfolds in the more delimited and peculiar space of political discourse. In the context of interpretivism, this statement is ultimately supported by the view that law is a social and interpretive practice shaped by the basic values underpinning a specific community and rooted in a given institutional arrangement or power structure. In providing a justification for the use of coercive force across a certain territory, the law appeals to normative considerations which the community of people inhabiting that territory should be expected to accept and support. This explains the way the interpretivist account understands the justificatory standards that apply to the law, meaning the standards against which the law as a practice and the requirements the law issues need to be assessed: these are understood as standards not of *rational* morality but of *political* morality and institutional justice.

---

[39] This thesis has been consistently defended by Dworkin over the years. For a recent restatement of this position, see Dworkin, *Justice for Hedgehogs*, pp. 405–9.

A related part of this counter-objection to my argument is that Dworkin's interpretivism can be claimed to be distinctively *political*. Dworkin is not proposing a legal theory of universal reach: in conceiving law as an interpretive practice, he does not view law as implementing a set of universal values, or a code of conduct grounded in principles of rationality that apply to legal subjects by virtue of their being human. Accordingly, interpretivism is not properly understood as a humanist doctrine purporting to show that the obligations generated by the law are owed to our fellow human beings. Nor is a legal system conceived, on the interpretivist view, as an instrument put in place to realize pre-existing ideals of justice and principles of cooperation that can be identified independently of legal institutions themselves. For Dworkin, the interpretive practices making up the law are embedded in a specific polity's institutional history and political framework. Moreover, these practices are essential to defining the relevant standards of justice and collective well-being of those subject to the law. These standards are thus specific to, and dependent on, each legal system's distinctive make-up, history, and context.

A potential counter-objection to my critique, in sum, is that such critique is off target, since the law endogenously establishes its own justificatory standards, as opposed to deriving these standards from the outside (for instance, from practical rationality conceived as a body of principles we can apply to ourselves as human beings regardless of the specific culture we happen to identify with or to have been raised in). That is why, on the interpretivist account, the *sources* of legal obligation cannot be located in the humanity or rational agency we all share but must instead be traced to our shared background and history as members of a specific political community governed by particular institutions; and, likewise, the *justification* of legal obligation needs to appeal not to moral standards and principles of practical rationality whose scope covers the whole of humanity but to the values that underpin and structure the polity we have formed under the jurisdiction of the law.[40]

My reply to this potential counterargument departs from the statement that the criticism which in the last section was levelled at the interpretivist account of legal obligation is not intended to deny that under certain conditions the best or most compelling justification for

---

[40] An argument along these lines can be found in M. Iglesias Vila, 'De la justicia como equidad al derecho come equidad', in J. M. Bermejo and M. A. Rodilla (eds.), *Jurisdicción, interpretación y sistema jurídico* (Salamanca, Aquilafuente, 2007), pp. 11–38.

the specific requirements issued by a legal system may be found in the complex of political values and institutional ideals shared within the community of individuals subject to the jurisdiction of the law and underpinning its shared life. Whereas personally I am not convinced that intrinsically contingent human interactions and geographical proximity can decisively establish the force of legal obligation and so conclusively determine the nature of what is legally obligatory, in Section 4.3 I did not challenge this dimension of the interpretivist account of legal obligation. Indeed, the argument deployed in that section did not call into question the special significance of political arrangements in giving rise to the obligations one is subject to the jurisdiction of the law. Nor was the argument aimed at denying that these subjects can come under different systems of obligations, such as moral obligations as distinct from social or legal obligations.[41] Instead, the argument was specifically meant to call into question the theoretical soundness of any account on which legal obligations can contradict the requirements grounded in practical rationality, thus allowing for the possibility that the local practices and specific commitments by which the law is underpinned can give rise to genuine obligations to act against the principles of practical rationality. Or, to put it differently, my claim was that practical rationality sets the broad boundaries of what can be legally obligatory, such that anything done in contradiction with the requirements of practical rationality will have to be regarded as *ipso facto* unjustified and so constitutively non-obligatory. This means that, for one thing, the *ultimate* and *conclusive* justification for what is legally obligatory must appeal to the fundamental principles of practical rationality; and, for another, our legal subjectivity does not replace our rational agency but rather combines with, and integrates, it. That is to say, we do not bracket our practical rationality or put it on hold by virtue of our being subject to the law, since the law presupposes such practical rationality: true, the law addresses us as members of a community, but it does so whilst also assuming that we can exercise the powers of reason that make us rational agents.[42]

---

[41] Again I personally doubt that radical differentiation is tenable; but this personal conviction is not granted by any argument I offered in this chapter.

[42] This is, after all, the very core of the so-called conception of law as practical reason – a conception interpretivists too champion (as it emerges, for instance, from Dworkin, *Justice in Robes*, pp. 1–35). By conception of law as practical reason I mean the broad and encompassing view conceiving of the law as a normative system aimed at providing its addressees with practical guidance. On this view, legal norms are argued to figure in an

To further elaborate on this dense formulation of my reply, I find it perfectly reasonable to claim, as the interpretivist account does, that the requirements issuing from a legal system cannot be justified in the abstract – that is, without considering (also) the values that underlie such system and its polity. Likewise, I agree that those political values play an essential role in justifying the requirements of the law, thereby helping to make them binding. However, it is not reasonable to suppose that the justificatory power of this political morality, however deeply rooted it may be, is all-controlling, since no political morality can contradict the principles of practical rationality without losing its justificatory import. Accordingly, practical rationality acts as an important broad constraint on what can be justified on a political basis. In other words, the justification by which a coercive demand imposed by the law becomes obligatory can be based on considerations of political morality only to the extent that they comport with the principles of practical rationality. For those who are subject to the law are to be regarded rational agents, to begin with. That is, they should be acknowledged to have the capacity to deliberate on a course of conduct and offer reasons why such course of conduct should be undertaken, avoided, proscribed, prescribed, and so on. It would therefore be inconsistent for legal subjects to act contrary to the principles of practical rationality. Related to this, no legal provision requiring one to act contrary to these principles can rank as a genuine obligation, since it would deny our rational agency, thereby lacking practical justification.

In other terms, I find nothing objectionable in the interpretivist claim that the law is a *special* case of practical rationality and so there is something distinctive about legality and the obligations attached to the

---

essential way into one's reasons for action. Law should then be conceived as an institution which bears on practical deliberations by changing an addressee's reasons for action (see S. Burton, 'Law as Practical Reason', *Southern California Law Review*, 62 (1989), pp. 747–93; G. Postema, 'The Normativity of Law', in R. Gavison (ed.), *Issues in Contemporary Legal Philosophy* (Oxford, Clarendon, 1987), pp. 81–104; and J. Raz, *Engaging Reason* (Oxford, Oxford University Press, 1999). Relatedly, on this view legal subjects are regarded as persons having the 'capacity to perceive and understand how things are, and what response is appropriate to them' as well as the 'ability to respond appropriately' to situations and inputs (Raz, *Engaging Reason*, p. 67). Accordingly, the subjects of law are taken to be able to determine their lives 'in accordance with their appreciation of themselves and their environment, and of the reasons with which, given how they are, the world presents them' (Raz, *Engaging Reason*, p. 67). On this basis, it is also argued that law is inseparable from practical rationality in the specific sense of being a particular instantiation, or species, of it.

law, when compared to pure practical rationality and the obligations pure practical rationality engenders. However, I also believe that one cannot coherently push the speciality, or autonomy, of the legal sphere up to the point of severing any link such sphere has with practical rationality, by thus arriving at possibly justifying the requirement to disregard, and infringe upon, the fundamental principles of practical rationality. And yet this is what the champions of interpretivism end up doing when they establish a conceptual connection between legal obligation and political morality, whereas at the same time defining political morality as a domain that is not conceptually constrained by the fundamental principles of practical rationality. It is the endorsement of this position – freeing legal obligation from its intrinsic justificatory connection with practical rationality – that produces a distorted conception of the nature of legal obligation and, relatedly, prevents interpretivism from arriving at a theoretically sound account of the nature of the kind of obligation engendered by the law.

In summary, while the interpretivist account of legal obligation correctly sees the need for legally mandated courses of action to have some kind of *justification* before they can count as legal obligations proper, it restricts the range of justification by appealing exclusively to the political or institutional basis of those requirements, without recognizing that any such justification needs to also be consistent with the fundamental principles of practical rationality. This is problematic because, while the political or institutional justification of the kind envisioned by the interpretivist account may work well for a given polity, it need not be consistent with the more basic rational agency or capacity for reason-giving by which we are enabled to work out the political differences that may set us apart within our own polity. Indeed, as long as legal obligation is acknowledged to be a *justified* demand and, at the same time, legal subjects are taken to be *rational agents*, the conclusion follows that practical rationality plays a fundamental role in establishing how legal obligation ought to be conceived. This is the case, since from the perspective of a rational agent considerations concerning the political structure and institutional arrangements framing a given legal order can provide some justification to the legal demands (by thus turning those demands into obligations) only insofar as those considerations are aligned, and do not conflict, with the fundamental standards of practical rationality. Otherwise a legal subject would be claimed to be under the legal obligation – namely, the *justified* requirement issued by the law – to undertake courses of conduct that are prohibited by the basic standards of practical rationality and so challenge the very rational status of such subject. Which conclusion is incompatible with the recognition that legal subjects should constitutively be treated as agents endowed with rational capacities, since for any rational agent the breach of the fundamental principles of practical rationality is inherently self-defeating and so inherently unjustifiable. Accordingly, by exclusively appealing to political values and institutional considerations when characterizing legal obligations, whilst at the same time leaving the basic standards of practical rationality out of the picture, interpretivists, on the one hand, fail to acknowledge the existence of a core of fundamental rational principles that ought to orient the conduct of those living under the jurisdiction of the law and, on the other hand, arbitrarily radicalize the autonomy, or differentiation, of the legal domain within the sphere of practical rationality.

The root of this difficulty, it seems to me, lies in the boldness of the interpretivist claim. That is to say, the interpretivist account does not confine itself to recognizing the possibility that a legal system's political history and institutional framework can work within the interstices of practical rationality so as to complement the latter in justifying the claims a legal system makes on us: this seems perfectly reasonable, for neither is practical rationality so complete as to be able to guide our conduct in every practical situation without the aid of more specific forms of practical reasoning nor can practical rationality be the sole basis on which to justify such courses of conduct in every situation. On the contrary, interpretivism seems to be making the stronger and more sweeping claim that legal obligations are justified *primarily* or even *essentially* by the political history and institutional framework of a legal system, in turn conceived as independent of any constraint originating in the basic principles of practical rationality. The interpretivist claim, thus, is not just that the law issues requirements *on top of* those of practical rationality – drawing on political and institutional values with which to integrate the principles of practical rationality, and justifying such requirements on the basis of this enriched set of principles – but rather that the law can *independently* justify its own requirements, and, as a result, it can introduce requirements in conflict with those of practical rationality by justifying them on its own terms, without forfeiting its claim to guide action. The interpretivist account therefore allows for the possibility of acting contrary to reason if that is what political morality requires. But the only way we can accept this conclusion is if we are prepared to accept that the law is not purportedly concerned with, and does not characteristically address, rational agents. Which is an unusual view at best.[43]

4.5 Closing Remarks

In a sophisticated and original account, interpretivism presents legal obligation as a genuinely binding demand generated by the law understood as an interpretive practice. The interpretive nature of law carries over to what law produces, including legal obligation, which consequently should be understood to be likewise interpretive, and hence to

---

[43] A final comment is in order that has to do with the question of monism versus dualism in political philosophy as it relates to my own account of legal obligation. On a monist conception, the practical principles by which we judge our own lives and those of others in the personal sphere of individual action are the same ones by which we ought to judge our political and institutional arrangements in the public sphere. As Liam Murphy puts it, 'any plausible overall political/moral view must, at the fundamental level, evaluate the justice of institutions with normative principles that apply also to people's choices' (L. Murphy, 'Institutions and the Demands of Justice', *Philosophy & Public Affairs*, 27 (1999), pp. 253). On a dualist conception, by contrast, these two domains (the personal and the public/political/institutional) are governed by *different* sets of principles. In this camp we find J. Rawls, *A Theory of Justice* (Cambridge (MA), Harvard University Press, 1999, rev. ed.; or. ed. 1971) and T. Pogge, *Realizing Rawls* (Ithaca, Cornell University Press, 1989), for example, as well as T. Nagel, 'The Problem of Global Justice', *Philosophy & Public Affairs*, 33 (2005), pp. 113–47, noting that 'there is no inconsistency in governing interpersonal relations by principles very different from those that govern legal institutions' (Nagel, 'Problem of Global Justice', p. 125). Now, because the argument presented in this chapter against the interpretivist account of legal obligation assumes that there must be a coherent set of general principles governing the practical sphere – the principles of practical rationality, which rationality in turn defines our human agency – one may be tempted to think that the whole argument entails a monist view of the practical sphere. But this impression would be wrong: the argument *cuts across* the distinction between monism and dualism because, like monism, it understands the need to integrate the fundamental principles of practical rationality (the monist foundation) with other principles and values that are specific to the political sphere (see Murphy, 'Institutions and the Demands of Justice', p. 254), and like dualism it accepts these political principles (or the need for them) without denying that they must rest on a set of basic principles (of practical morality) that apply across the board (see Nagel, 'Problem of Global Justice', pp. 126–30). Monism and dualism alike, then, understand there to be a set of fundamental principles governing the whole of the practical sphere, such that no legal or political conception can plausibly introduce obligations that run contrary to this foundation, for that would amount to accepting the possibility of justifying that which is irrational or has no basis in human agency. In this idea – that legal obligation must have some foundation in practical rationality, and that this foundation cannot be contradicted – lies the kernel of my counter-objection to the interpretivist account of legal obligation, and the idea stands regardless of whether we seek to solve the problem from a monist perspective or a dualist one.

result from an interpretation of our institutional practices, or from these practices as enriched with evaluative considerations. This account of legal obligation was claimed to be neatly distinguishable from, and indeed incompatible with, the social practice account of legal obligation. For, whereas like the social practice account interpretivism acknowledges the essential role that institutional practices play in defining legal obligation, in contrast to the social practice account the interpretivist account takes the view that the practices out of which legal obligation arises cannot be reduced to social practices. In fact, central to the interpretivist project is the thesis that the practices shaping the law combine a social component with an evaluative one. It is this evaluative component that rules out the possibility of qualifying the resulting obligation-determining practice as purely social.

Crucially, it was pointed out, the evaluations in light of which a social practice is taken by interpretivists as capable of giving rise to obligations are internal to the practice itself and so to the institutional framework through which those obligations are put into place. The relevant evaluations are accordingly designed to support and justify this institutional framework and the political acts carried out within it. This justification rests on an interpretive ideal of integrity that combines notions of fit, sense, and fairness, for the point is to show that the obligations arising out of a social practice fit with the political principles by which the practice is underpinned, and thus make sense in light of these principles, which in turn are understood as principles of fairness, qua equal concern and respect, or otherwise as principles on which basis to publicly reason in working out what fairness, qua equal concern and respect, means where legal obligations are at issue. These principles of political morality, however, like the obligations they are meant to support, are not seen by the advocates of interpretivism as independent of the practice they underpin. Rather, they form an integral part of the practice and thus cannot themselves be assessed in light of any other evaluative standard through which to look at the practice critically. This is where a reason-based account of legal obligation comes in, offering a rational benchmark by which to evaluate a practice and its underlying principles of political morality by looking to see, not just how or whether they fit together and are to be accepted within the community governed by the law, but also whether they can pass a test of practical rationality. The point, in other words, is not just to interpret and evaluate a practice in light of own principles of political morality, but to make sure that they satisfy a standard of rationality, thus showing that the obligations arising out of the practice and put into place through its institutional framework, in addition to making sense to those who participate in the practice, also carry a genuine binding force.

In summary, as much as the interpretivist account of legal obligation deserves credit for recognizing that we cannot be bound by a legal directive simply in virtue of its arising out of a social practice (this was the gist of the social practice account) – for a social practice is an inherently principled enterprise and the principles it feeds on need to be worked into any account of why we ought to accept a legal provision as obligatory – the kind of justification envisioned by interpretivism is internal to the practice itself and so is construed as something of an 'institutional' justification of the practice, closer to showing how it comes to be accepted than why it *should* be endorsed. The interpretivist account therefore does not move far enough in justifying the practice and the obligations arising out of it: instead of connecting legal obligation to rational morality, the account connects it to an institutional code of values, thus failing to explain how it can be genuinely binding. So, while the interpretivist account of legal obligation moves in the right direction, representing an advance on the social practice account, it stops short of providing a full, or genuine, justification of legal obligation, one that is based on practical rationality as a freestanding criterion of judgement. But what does such alternative account relying on practical rationality exactly look like and how can it uncover the nature of legal obligation by also vindicating the genuine bindingness of law's demands? To these questions I will devote the discussion in the rest of the book.

5

The Conventionalist Reason Account

5.1 Introduction

The criticisms I levelled at the social practice account and interpretivist account can ultimately be reduced to the claim that legal obligation is not adequately conceptualized without making rational considerations, or justificatory *reasons* for action, a central part of the conceptualization. This conclusion should not be taken merely as a negative statement, namely, a claim about what an insightful theory of legal obligation is *not*. Indeed, in addition to meaning (in the negative) that the accounts of legal obligation discussed so far in this book are fundamentally flawed, it also suggests (in the positive) that a thorough scrutiny of the main alternative to those accounts, namely, the *reason account*, can legitimately be expected to secure a better explanation of legal obligation. For, as noticed in Chapter 2, on (all the different variants of) the reason account, the fundamental notion for defining legal obligation and framing a discourse about it is that of a rational consideration, or a reason, as opposed to that of a social practice or that of an interpretive fact. That is to say, the very claim setting the reason account of legal obligation conceptually apart from the social practice account and the interpretivist account is the thesis that legal obligation is a notion defined by justificatory, or normative, practical reasons of a specific kind. From the theoretical perspective of those endorsing the reason account, thus, the fulfilment of certain standards of practical rationality is considered essential to the existence of legal obligation. By virtue of their conceptualizing legal obligation as justificatory practical reason with a special structure, the reason account is, at least presumptively, well positioned to provide an explanation of the capacity the law has to issue requirements with genuine normative force. As a result, (any version of) the reason account can legitimately be expected to avoid the shortcomings that (as previously argued) taint social practice account and interpretivist account, by thus offering valuable insights into the kind of obligation generated by the law.

In this chapter, I intend to scrutinize a specific variant of the reason account that has proved to be cutting-edge and original: the theory of legal obligation put forward by Andrei Marmor. The version of the reason account of legal obligation theorized by Marmor is built on a rigorous and comprehensive form of legal conventionalism. In a nutshell, Marmor intends to explain the nature of legal obligation in terms of the *normative reasons* engendered by the *conventions* the law is made of. Since in his explanation of legal obligation Marmor appeals to the reasons generated by conventions – namely, social and institutional standards – his theory of legal obligation should be understood as the reason account conceptually closest to the social practice account and interpretivist account, both of which provide an explanation of legal obligation that explicitly acknowledges the fundamental role social frameworks and institutional arrangements play in establishing the nature of what is obligatory. And this is why my critical exploration of the reason account begins with Marmor's conception of legal obligation.

This chapter will be organized as follows. I start out by introducing the basics of Marmor's legal conventionalism and his view of legal obligation, which I will qualify as a minimalist statement of the reason account. Then, in Sections 5.3 and 5.4 I will critically engage with a distinction that I take to be central to Marmor's study of legal obligation: the distinction between obligations within a practice, or internal obligations, and obligations that are external to it. Marmor claims that legal obligations are obligations of the former type: they are merely internal obligations, and so obligations the bindingness of which is ultimately conditioned on the existence of extra-institutional, or external, reasons, that one may have to participate in the obligation-engendering practice. I will argue that a conception constructing legal obligation as an internal demand cannot account for the characteristically genuine bindingness of the duties arising out of the law. The objection that I level at Marmor's theory of legal obligation in this context is modest: I do not claim that internal obligations *necessarily* fail to rank as genuine requirements. I will instead argue that legal obligations as conceptualized by Marmor *may well* amount to less than genuinely binding statements. This conclusion means that Marmor's conceptual framework is incapable to provide a firm ground to his thesis that legal obligations, as he depicts them, are both internal and (of necessity) genuinely binding. With that done, in Section 5.5 I will take a more radically critical stance by arguing that, at least on one plausible interpretation, Marmor's account of legal obligation depicts legal obligation as a perspectivized duty, namely, a demand that is justified exclusively 'from a certain point of view'. This picture is objectionable, since, as I argued in Chapter 3, perspectivized obligations inherently lack genuine binding force. Related to this, I will claim that ultimately Marmor's theory is unable to take our understanding of legal obligation any further than the social practice account, as this account is defended by the champions of the conception of law as a shared activity.

5.2 Legal Conventionalism and the Obligations Imposed by the Law

The primary aim of this section consists in introducing Marmor's theory of legal obligation. This theory is rooted in Marmor's statement of a form of legal conventionalism that depicts law as a practice consisting of a set of interlocked social conventions, which differ in kind, occupy different layers, and perform distinct functions. The interlocked social conventions law is made of explain the *social existence* of law, which for Marmor is a *normative institution*. As a normative institution, law not only seeks to provide legal subjects with sound *normative reasons for action* but also purports to give rise to *obligations* to act as prescribed.[1] Thus, for Marmor any general theory about the nature of law needs to take seriously the task of systematically elucidating how obligations are generated by the law and so how a legal obligation should be conceptualized. The project of explaining how the law can give rise to obligations and what the fundamental characteristics of legal obligation are is accordingly central to Marmor's legal-theoretical project. In consideration of the strict dependence that Marmor establishes between legal obligation and the conventional practices underpinning the law – Marmor's theory of legal obligation is part and parcel of an explanation of the nature of law as a conventional normative practice – in this section I will first present Marmor's general account of conventions and then pass to elucidate the view of legal obligation Marmor defends.

Marmor sets out three defining features of a convention.[2] First, a convention is not just a regularity of behaviour; rather it is a *norm*,

---

[1] This dimension of law is discussed in A. Marmor, *Positive Law and Objective Values* (Oxford, Oxford University Press, 2001), pp. 25–6.
[2] These are understood by Marmor as necessary conditions 'for the applicability of the concept-word [*convention*] to all its *standard* examples, but not to every example one can think of' (A. Marmor, 'On Convention', *Synthese*, 107 (1996), p. 351; original emphasis). Marmor is therefore only interested in identifying the *fundamental* features of a convention – those that characterize its paradigmatic case – rather than in attempting a *formal*

meaning that it provides normative *reasons* for acting as it directs. The practical reasons that make conventional practices normative are compliance-dependent, and that is the second defining element of conventions. We have a reason to act as a convention instructs only so long as the convention is generally followed within the community we belong to.[3] That is because a convention has an essentially *social* character: it exists as a norm only insofar as there is a group of individuals who consistently follow it.[4] And, third, as social rules or standards that provide reasons to act accordingly by virtue of a broad compliance with the rule or standard itself, conventions are also *arbitrary* social rules. A social rule is in this sense arbitrary if its core function can be preserved by an alternative rule the group could conceivably follow.[5]

Marmor distinguishes his own account of a convention as an arbitrary social rule from two other influential theoretical models: Margaret Gilbert's and David Lewis's. The most important difference between Marmor's conception and Gilbert's lies in the normative force the former acknowledges conventions to have. Gilbert's conception is characterized by Marmor as purely sociological.[6] A convention, as it is understood by Gilbert, cannot be distinguished from a collective pattern, or regularity, of behaviour. The problem with Gilbert's view, then, is that if we define a convention merely in terms of behavioural regularities, as opposed to rules, we will not be able to distinguish our reasons for acting in accordance with a convention from our beliefs about such reasons.[7]

---

definition of a convention as the set of necessary and sufficient conditions applicable to *every* convention. In fact, Marmor is skeptical about formal definitions of conventions (see Marmor, 'On Convention', pp. 350-1).

[3] On this defining element of conventions, see Marmor, 'On Convention', pp. 352-5; and A. Marmor, *Social Conventions* (Princeton, Princeton University Press, 2009), pp. 5-8 and 13-15.

[4] This point is made in Marmor, 'On Convention', pp. 356-9; and Marmor, *Social Conventions*, pp. 2-4.

[5] On the arbitrariness of conventions, see Marmor, 'On Convention', pp. 351-3; A. Marmor, 'Deep Conventions', *Philosophy and Phenomenological Research*, 74 (2007), pp. 590-1; and Marmor, *Social Conventions*, pp. 8-12.

[6] A more detailed account of the differences between Marmor's account of conventions and Gilbert's can be found in Marmor, *Social Conventions*, pp. 25-30.

[7] Marmor specifically addresses this issue by distinguishing between what a reason for action *is* – namely, a fact – and what one *believes* or takes it to be, which is not a fact but an attitude towards fact (see Marmor, 'On Convention', pp. 362-3). It bears pointing out that Gilbert does address the normativity of conventions, but she does so taking a different route than Marmor (see M. Gilbert, 'Social Conventions Revisited', *Topoi*, 27 (2008), pp. 5-16).

The main problem with Lewis's theory of conventions is that it is a one-dimensional view. All conventions, on this theory, can be conceptualized as ways of solving the problem of coordination among people by securing some uniformity of behaviour.[8] Marmor objects that conventions can emerge for other reasons, too. They can be introduced not only to solve pre-existing coordination problems but also to establish hitherto inexistent practices, for instance. Conventions may thus have a constitutive role, as distinct from a coordinative one. Conventions of this kind – whose existence and normativity are irreducible to coordination conventions – are described by Marmor as constitutive.[9] A constitutive convention brings into being an autonomous practice that typically responds to a social group's need or interest. It is therefore informed by values that have wide currency among those who are subject to the convention (even if these values are not so controlling as to 'determine' the convention, which therefore retains some autonomy).

There is, finally, a third type of convention (distinct from both coordination and constitutive conventions) that Marmor considers to be important and that Lewis fails to account for. Coordination and constitutive conventions, for all their differences, are alike in being *surface* conventions. However, typically surface conventions are not standalone normative practices capable of either providing their own solutions to pre-existing coordination problems (coordination conventions) or responding directly to the basic needs and interests from which those problems originate (constitutive conventions). That is because, in Marmor's theory, in a number of instances 'surface' conventions exist on a more abstract conventional layer: the layer that Marmor calls 'deep' conventions.[10]

Deep conventions grow organically and gradually as normative responses to fundamental psychological needs, social concerns, and practical interests profoundly involved in defining who we are and what kind of world we live in or wish to live in. They accordingly have a direct connection to those needs and interests in so that they occupy an

---

[8] Lewis's account is systematically presented in D. Lewis, *Convention: A Philosophical Study* (Cambridge (MA), Harvard University Press, 1969). For a discussion of the ways in which Marmor understands his account of conventions as different from Lewis's, see Marmor, *Social Conventions*, pp. 19–25.

[9] See Marmor, *Social Conventions*, pp. 31–57.

[10] Deep conventions are discussed in Marmor, 'Deep Conventions', pp. 586–610; and Marmor, *Social Conventions*, pp. 58–78. As examples of deep conventions, Marmor mentions competitive games, genres of art, and legal traditions.

intermediate space between those needs and interests, on the one hand, and surface conventions, on the other. Accordingly, for one thing, deep conventions incorporate and specify widespread values, which shape their contents without determining them. In that respect, deep conventions are less general and abstract than the essential needs and broad interests they respond to. For another thing, deep conventions provide a complex background that enables surface conventions to form, while giving these conventions their rationale. Surface conventions, then, often exist against the shared normative background constituted by deep conventions, of which they are specific instantiations.

This general theory of conventions carries direct implications for our understanding of law. Law, Marmor argues, is best understood as a practice at once social and conventional.[11] The distinctively conventional structure of law is something that Marmor secures on three bases. First, he conceptualizes some legal norms – those introduced in order to address recurrent coordination problems – as coordinative conventions. Furthermore, Marmor relies on his general view of conventions to reinterpret Hart's notion of a rule of recognition, which fundamentally contributes to shaping the bare bones of law. In Marmor's conventionalist framework, rules of recognition are understood as constitutive conventions. Insofar as this is the case we can make two claims: that law rests

---

[11] This statement neatly distinguishes Marmor's legal theory from the conception of law as a shared activity. For, whereas both Marmor and the advocates of the latter conceive of law as a social practice, only for Marmor the specific nature of the social practice defining the law is inherently conventional. By contrast, those who theorize the conception of law as a shared activity are not committed to the conventionalist quality of law. True, at least on occasions, Jules Coleman – one of the torchbearers of the conception of law as a shared activity – establishes a connection between conventionalism and legal positivism – the broader tradition the conception of law as a shared activity aligns itself with and contributes to (see, for instance, J. Coleman, 'Incorporationism, Conventionality, and the Practical Difference Thesis', in J. Coleman (ed.), *Hart's Postscript* (Oxford, Oxford University Press, 2001), pp. 99–147; and J. Coleman, *The Practice of Principle* (Oxford, Oxford University Press, 2001), p. 68). However, on the one hand, in his work Coleman offers no systematic treatment of the notion of convention, which therefore he hardly distinguishes from the generic ideas of 'social practice'. As a consequence, conventions do not seem to play any central and distinctive explanatory role in Coleman's theoretical construction, which is instead deeply characterized by the non-necessarily conventional notion of a shared cooperative activity. On the other hand, far from structuring his theory of law around the concept of convention, the other leading figure in the camp of the conception of law as a shared activity – Scott Shapiro – refrains from presenting a joint action as a conventional practice. That is, Shapiro's idea of law as a 'massively shared agency with authority' hardly entails the conclusion that the quality of law is necessarily conventional.

on conventional foundations, and that all legal contents can be traced to those foundations.[12] Hence, as much as conventions do not fix all the contents of law by themselves – there is more to law than its conventional foundations – the conventional nature of law can hardly be overlooked, since even the features of a legal system that do not owe their existence directly to surface conventions (of either the coordination or the constitutive type) become part of the system precisely by virtue of their bearing some relation to a master rule the quality of which is conventional in the constitutive sense.

Finally, law is associated with deep conventions, too. Within law, deep conventions correspond to what we would ordinarily call legal traditions, which trace back to (but are not determined by) the basic needs and interests the law responds to. Legal traditions, in other words, are best understood as free-standing conventions that set the boundaries within which the surface conventions of law unfold. Underneath the layer of surface conventions, then, law is shaped by a deeper conventional layer. The picture that emerges from this account, therefore, is one in which law is deeply structured by, and mainly organized around, a set of conventional social practices unfolding at different levels: at its foundation lies a conventional practice, which, on the one hand, identifies and validates certain conventional coordinative rules, and, on the other hand, is associated with an even deeper layer of practices that are themselves conventional.

Importantly, as already mentioned, conventions are understood by Marmor as norms: far from being just socially effective patterns of behaviour or regularities, conventions are normative practices, or standards that guide the behaviour of those who are subject to them by instructing them to act in one way or another, or otherwise holding up a model in the light of which to choose how to act. By their very nature, then, conventions provide reasons for action: they point the way for us in shaping and justifying our practical undertakings. The remaining question then is: how can conventions, qua normative reasons embedded in a social structure, and so law, qua practice that is grounded in and identified by conventions, engender legal obligations?

---

[12] A connection can be established between legal contents and the constitutive foundations of law (however indirect it may be) insofar as those contents derive from the sources of law, which in turn are conventionally established. Legal contents thus bear some indirect connection with the conventional foundations of law via their common relation to the sources of law.

To address the obligatory dimension of law as a conventional practice, Marmor start out with a reason-shaped definition of obligation he borrows from Joseph Raz.[13] In order for an obligation to come into being, for Marmor there need to exist practical reasons of a specific kind: 'protected reasons for action'. By this phrase, following Raz, Marmor means an arrangement of first-order reasons for acting in the prescribed way and second-order reasons not to act on the basis of (certain types of) conflicting standards.

This conception of obligation, which is organized around the idea of a normative, or justificatory, reason (we have an obligation insofar as justificatory reasons of a particular kind apply to us), is revealing of the deep nature of Marmor's account.[14] Indeed, the reliance on normative reasons to elucidate legal obligation justifies the understanding of Marmor's view of legal obligation as a reason account, by thus also making it irreducible to the social practice model. Marmor's view should, more specifically, be characterized as a minimalist, or thin, variant of the reason account.[15] Marmor's minimalism is owed to a distinction he draws between two broad classes of obligations – external obligations and internal obligations – and to his appeal to the latter to conceptualize the obligations produced by the law.[16]

To elaborate, *external obligations* are defined by Marmor as statements of the protected reasons to participate in a given practice. Typically the reasons constituting external obligations are extra-institutional considerations; so, usually their quality is not conventional. That is to say, external obligations support one's following the practice they underpin, but they are not (characteristically) engendered by that practice, nor are they dependent on its conventional dimension. The kind of obligation so grounded is qualified as 'external', since it is primarily supported by considerations, based on practical rationality, that appeal to certain

---

[13] See especially J. Raz, *Practical Reason and Norms* (London, Hutchinson, 1990; 1st ed. 1975), pp. 49–84.

[14] This claim is made in A. Marmor, 'Conventions Revisited: A Reply to Critics', *Jurisprudence*, 2 (2011), pp. 496–7, for instance.

[15] The fact that on Marmor's theory no legal obligation can be divorced from certain convention-generated normative reasons that back it up if it is to count as a requirement carrying binding force legitimizes the understanding of Marmor's theory as the missing link between the social practice account (in its pure instantiation) and the uncompromising variants of the reason account of legal obligation, which in this work will be discussed in Chapters 6 and 9.

[16] This distinction is anticipated in Marmor, *Positive Law and Objective Values*, pp. 25–34, and further developed in Marmor, *Social Conventions*, pp. 168–71.

basic needs, interests and values originating outside the practice they are associated with and pre-existing that practice (at least in the conceptual sense).

In contrast to external obligations are *internal obligations*, which are the protected reasons instructing someone how to act within the relevant practice, on (and against the background of) the assumption that such a person has some independent reason to take part in that practice. Far from establishing the reasons one has to join in a certain enterprise, internal obligations (contribute to) determine the way in which one goes about participating in that enterprise. Internal obligations, in other terms, are (merely) intra-institutional demands. And, insofar as the institutional framework they refer to is conventional, they may well be considerations whose nature is entirely conventional – this is indeed paradigmatically the case with law and legal obligations, Marmor claims. Relatedly, internal obligations, qua intra-institutional demands, set out merely presumptive requirements the nature of which is conditional. Marmor characterizes internal obligations as conditional in consideration of the fact that their binding force depends on (namely, is conditional on) the existence of the external reasons one has to participate in the obligation-generating practice – which reasons, as already mentioned, find their sources outside the relevant practice and so normally are of non-conventional quality even when they refer to a conventional practice.

This distinction between external obligations and internal ones is used by Marmor to shed light on the nature of the obligations engendered by the law. Law is a conventional practice; and conventions, Marmor believes, do not generate *external* obligations, that is, they do not by virtue of their existence alone produce duties for someone to adhere to them. Accordingly, the conventions associated with the existence of law, be they of the coordinative type, the constitutive type, or the deep type, are structurally unable to provide protected reasons for one to engage in the legal practice they define and regulate. That is, whether or not one has an external obligation to abide by the law as a practice grounded in convention is a matter that cannot be settled on the basis of conventional considerations and can only be settled by the moral and political considerations that justify our having a legal system in the first place.

In Marmor's framework, the claim just made – that the conventions in which law is grounded cannot themselves engender an obligation to participate in the practices constitutive of law – combines with another claim: the thesis that once we have a reason to participate in the legal enterprise, we possibly have obligations generated by the conventions the law consists of. That is to say, while conventions are not equipped to generate external obligations, they do have the resources to engender *internal* obligations. For the conventions underpinning the law at once define and regulate a practice, by thus setting out requirements for those who engage in that practice. Therefore, once we have reasons for committing to the law – that is, once for whatever reason we become members of the social group governed by some system of laws – we will thereby come under a legal obligation to act as the conventions constitutive of that system require.

The specific mechanism through which constitutive conventions can generate legal obligations, qua internal obligations, is elucidated by Marmor by analogizing law to games. A game (say, chess) comes into existence by virtue of the set of conventions by which it is constituted. And, once we have a reason for playing the game, we are also under the obligation to behave as the game prescribes, making only the permitted moves. Likewise, the law is framed by certain social conventions that bring the legal practice into existence. And, once we have reasons to participate in the legal practice as legal subjects – as players in the 'game' of law, so to speak – we come under an obligation to act as the law requires or allows us to act. Just as a player's obligation to play chess in accordance with the rules of the game is grounded in the conventions constitutive of that game, so a legal subject's obligation to follow the rules of law is given by the social conventions constitutive of the legal practice.

This analogy has also the effect of shedding light onto the conditional quality of legal obligations. Not unlike the obligations engendered by games, legal obligations, qua internal protected reasons, have a conditional binding force – the binding force of legal obligation being conditional on the extralegal considerations that make one's participation in the legal enterprise intelligible and valuable. On Marmor's view, then, legal obligations do not hold necessarily, since their bindingness is dependent on one's having a reason to participate in the legal system: it is only on the condition that one is committed to a legal system that the conventional standards essentially shaping the law give them an obligation to act in conformity with the requirements in force within a given system of laws.

Now, since legal obligations, as they are established by certain conventional standards, are conditioned on one's having a reason for being a legal subject, no requirement to participate in a legal practice can be explained by reference to conventions alone. That is to say, the requirement to play the 'legal game', is not a requirement determined by the conventions that constitute the law as an independent and distinctive domain. It is, instead, an external requirement shaped by the considerations – moral and political in nature – which justify our having a system of laws in the first place. To that extent, the obligation to be a legal subject, if it exists, is an external obligation, to wit, a moral obligation or a political obligation, as opposed to a conventionally established obligation. Marmor's conventionalist reason account, in other words, provides an explanation of the internal legal 'ought' – the obligation to follow the requirements set by a legal system the participants in that system have – whilst remaining silent over the external legal 'ought' – the primary obligation to be part of a legal system or have a legal system to begin with.

In sum, legal obligations are defined by Marmor as internal, or intra-institutional, duties, which are further characterized as presumptive and conditional protected reasons for action of a conventional nature, as opposed to a moral nature. For Marmor, therefore, a legal obligation exists insofar as a legal system succeeds in establishing conditional requirements for one to act as the standards validated by the basic conventions of that system demand.

5.3 A Modest Objection to the Conventionalist Reason Account of Legal Obligation

In the previous section, I claimed that Marmor conceives of legal obligation as an *internal* obligation. For him the bindingness of a legal obligation is accordingly conditional on the existence of some external reason(s) to commit to the legal practice engendering the obligations in question. In turn, legal obligations, qua instantiations of what is obligatory, are *genuine* practical requirements: they rationally bind us qua agents living under the jurisdiction of law. It is my view that in Marmor's theoretical framework this combination of tenets stands on less than solid grounds. For, as I will argue in this section, from Marmor's conceptual analysis it only follows that the obligations engendered by the law *may* be genuinely binding, not that they *necessarily* are so. In Marmor's construction, in other terms, legal obligations, qua internal reasons whose normativity is conditional on external considerations legal theorists need not be concerned with, do not unavoidably make practically rational claims on us (though they may indeed make such claims). And this means that Marmor does not succeed in showing that legal obligations of necessity are at one and the same time *internal* requirements and *practically rational* standards or, to state it otherwise, obligations proper.

To elaborate on this introductory statement, I should first reiterate that for Marmor legal obligations are intra-institutional requirements, whose genuine bindingness is both presumptive and conditional on one's (non-institutional, or external) reasons to commit to the conventional practice producing legal obligations. In my understanding, there is nothing amiss in the claim that legal obligations are presumptive and conditional reasons for action. As to the presumptive quality, any obligation – whether internal or external – can be either prima facie or conclusive. This quality impacts on the overall 'weight' the requirement in question has on practical reasoning, but it does not affect the practically rational dimension of such requirement.[17] Marmor's assertion that legal obligation has conditional character is also unobjectionable, or so I think. Marmor is committed to the thesis that the genuine bindingness of legal obligation is dependent on one's having some reason(s) to participate in the legal system. On this view, baked into legal obligation is an if-clause (which usually remains unexpressed) such that legal requirements bind us only if we have reasons to be subject to the jurisdiction of law. This claim is perfectly in order, as it keeps legal obligation distinct from another kind of obligation – call it *inescapable* obligation – without calling its genuine character into question.[18] That is, insofar as we take

---

[17] Conclusive obligations are binding in the (stronger) sense that they determine how one ought to behave all things considered: the demands they make are accordingly of *decisive* practical relevance. Presumptive obligations are likewise binding in a practically rational sense, but their genuine bindingness is attenuated: they do not have the resources to conclusively settle which conduct one ought to perform; so they merely provide pro tanto support to the course of conduct they demand. Crucially, attenuated obligatoriness is hardly less-than-genuine. Accordingly, far from lacking practically rational significance, thus falling short of a genuine requirement, what is presumptively obligatory only fails to have a decisive, or conclusive, impact on our conduct, whilst still affecting our practical deliberation as rational agents living in a legal system.

[18] As the name suggests, an inescapable obligation is an obligation that binds everyone in a class, the inclusion in which is unavoidable, and so an inescapable obligation necessarily applies to everyone who has inexorable reasons to be a member of the class of people the obligation specifically addresses. Inescapable obligations, which thus contain no if-clause, are associated with practices the memberships in which one cannot opt out or 'unsubscribe' – if one could do that, then the obligation at issue would thereby implicitly revert to a conditional obligation carrying an if-clause of the form 'you are under obligation X if you have no reason to opt out of practice Y'. Correspondingly, whenever one's inclusion in the enterprise engendering certain obligations is optional, the obligations at stake

Marmor's conceptual analysis, with its insistence on the dependence of legal obligations on the obtaining of some external considerations justifying one's membership in a legal institution, to be functional to the conclusion that legal obligation is not inescapable in quality, Marmor's characterization is fully tenable. Legal subjects – the addressees of legal obligations – do have the chance to opt out of a system of laws, because the reasons supporting their membership in, and commitment to, the legal system can be disregarded and even rejected. Ergo, legal obligations are conditional, qua non-inescapable.[19]

---

should be regarded as conditional; in contrast, whenever an obligation is associated with the existence of (and derives from) social activities that are practically necessary (because there are unavoidable reasons for being committed to them), that obligation is inescapable. The existence of practically necessary binding standards and, relatedly, inescapable obligations is acknowledged by at least some theories of practical rationality. Prominent among these is constitutivism – an internally differentiated position defended in different forms in A. Gewirth, *Reason and Morality* (Chicago, University of Chicago Press, 1978), pp. 21–42; C. Korsgaard, *The Sources of Normativity* (Cambridge, Cambridge University Press, 1996), pp. 90–130; C. Korsgaard, *Self-Constitution* (Oxford, Oxford University Press, 2009); T. Schapiro, 'What Is a Child', *Ethics*, 109 (1999), pp. 715–38; D. Velleman, *The Possibility of Practical Reason* (Oxford, Oxford University Press, 2000), pp. 123–43 and 170–99; D. Velleman, *How We Get Along* (New York, Cambridge University Press, 2009); L. Ferrero, 'Constitutivism and the Inescapability of Agency', *Oxford Studies in Metaethics*, 2 (2009), pp. 303–33; S. Bertea, 'Constitutivism and Normativity: A Qualified Defence', *Philosophical Explorations*, 16 (2013), pp. 81–95; and P. Katsafanas, *Agency and the Foundations of Ethics: Nietzschean Constitutivism* (Oxford, Oxford University Press, 2013), among others (for an introduction to this debate, see S. Bertea, 'Normativity, Human Constitution and Legal Theory', in B. Brozeck and J. Stelmark (eds.), *Studies in the Philosophy of Law, Vol. VI: The Normativity of Law* (Krakow, Copernicus Center Press, 2011), pp. 99–126; and P. Katsafanas,. 'Constitutivism about Practical Reason', in D. Star (ed.), *The Oxford Handbook of Reasons and Normativity* (Oxford, Oxford University Press, 2018)). Important critiques of constitutivism can be found in P. Railton, *Facts, Values and Norms* (Cambridge, Cambridge University Press, 2003); D. Enoch, 'Agency, Schmagency: Why Normativity Won't Come from What Is Constitutive of Action', *Philosophical Review*, 115 (2006), pp. 169–98; A. Tubert, 'Korsgaard's Constitutive Arguments and the Principles of Practical Reason', *Philosophical Quarterly*, 61 (2011), pp. 343–62; M. Silverstein, 'Inescapability and Normativity', *Journal of Ethics and Social Philosophy*, 6 (2012), pp. 1–26; and E. Tiffany, 'Why Be an Agent?', *Australasian Journal of Philosophy*, 90 (2012), pp. 223–33.

[19] To briefly elaborate, the legal domain is widespread and pervasive, but we need not necessarily be legal subjects, at least not in the sense in which and to the same extent that we are necessarily agents (if constitutivism is correct). Because law may reach into many facets of our lives, our legal subjectivity may feel cumbersome. Furthermore, the jurisdiction of law may stretch across entire nations or continents: indeed, there seems to be almost no corner of the earth that does not fall under some jurisdiction. But this is not the same thing as saying that there is no way to escape a system of laws. Unlike agency, from which we cannot free ourselves, we do have the practical possibility of freeing ourselves

What, by contrast, I find flawed in the picture Marmor offers is the twofold claim that, on the one hand, legal obligations are genuinely binding internal requirements and, on the other hand, we, as legal theorists in search of a comprehensive account of legal obligation, should be unconcerned with the (external) reasons supporting those requirements. The problem with this set of claims can be formulated as follows. By construction, internal requirements have no independent genuine binding force: their genuine obligatoriness is entirely owed to the external reasons associated with them. Therefore, (exclusively) insofar as the external reasons underlying an internal demand can be regarded as sources of practically rational claims on us, the bindingness of that internal demand (and so of legal obligation qua internal demand) will have to be considered practically rational. By contrast, an internal requirement conditioned on external reasons that lack the practically rational dimension can hardly be regarded as genuinely binding. Stated otherwise, internal obligations are practically rational requirements, when they are so, in a derivative sense only, since they import and borrow their practically rational dimension from the outside: whether or not the obligatoriness of an internal requirement is genuine will be established, not by that internal requirement itself, but by the external considerations legitimizing the conclusion that certain individuals ought to treat given institutional demands as practically rational and so binding on their conduct. Likewise, legal obligations qua internal demands cannot be said to constitutively have a genuine, or practically rational, binding character, for such character only obtains in legal obligations accompanied by external considerations bestowed with a practically rational dimension. Hence, considered in isolation from the external underlying reasons, legal requirements are devoid of any practically rational relevance. From this, it follows that for Marmor legal obligations, qua considerations whose obligatoriness is secured by the external

---

from our status as individuals subject to a legal system by moving from one jurisdiction to another or even by finding some remote, lawless land. As can be appreciated, neither option is ordinarily perceived as easy – for one must overcome procedural and bureaucratic hurdles in the former case and commit to a less than ordinary life in the latter. However, it is still a proposition that stands a chance of being realized. We can thus forfeit our legal subjectivity to an extent that is not possible with our agential status. From this, it follows that legal obligations are to be understood as practically avoidable and so conditional rather than inescapable.

reasons we have to participate in the obligation-generating practice, *may* but need not have genuine binding force.

Now, in principle there is nothing that can be held against this conclusion, since it does not call into question the genuine bindingness of legal obligations as such – it does not entail that a legal obligation, as Marmor conceives of it, necessarily is not genuinely binding; it rather emphasizes the fact that by construction the practical rationality of legal obligations is dependent on considerations external to those obligations. In order to make the case that a legal obligation is (of necessity) genuinely binding, all one has to do to is show that the facts or practices to which such obligation ultimately owes its obligatoriness essentially are instantiations of practical rationality and so that those facts or practices necessarily issue requirements which contribute to determining the conduct we rationally ought to perform (even if such a determination is only presumptive). And here is where the difficulty with Marmor's theory lies. For this further step – showing that the considerations on which a legal obligation, as an internal obligation, is conditional are constitutively justified in the practically rational way – is not explored in that theory.

In fact, this further step is explicitly ruled out by Marmor as irrelevant for a specifically legal-theoretical investigation of legal obligation. This means that Marmor's conceptual analysis systematically lacks the resources to establish the genuine obligatoriness of legal obligation: within the limits of Marmor's conceptual framework, the claim that legal obligation necessarily is at one and the same time an internal requirement and a practically rational requirement cannot be justified. Insofar as Marmor fails to engage with the external reasons supporting one's legal obligations, then, his thesis that legal obligations are internal duties and his thesis that legal obligations have a practically rational quality do not support each other, at least not necessarily. From which it follows that legal obligations, qua internal reasons insulated from external reasons (this is how Marmor conceptualizes them), do not respond to Marmor's own characterization of them as requirements at once internal and equipped with genuine binding force. On this basis, the conceptual framework associated with Marmor's conventionalist reason account should be considered theoretically unsatisfactory to anyone who regards legal obligation as a normative standard being of necessity *genuinely binding*.

To rephrase this point and bringing my first criticism to its conclusion, the preceding remarks support the statement that Marmor's characterization of legal obligation as an internal duty makes the practical normativity of legal obligations *possibly* but not necessarily genuine. It is true that there is no mutual incompatibility between Marmor's claims of the internal character of legal obligations and his claim of the practical rationality of legal obligations, since it is hardly a conceptual impossibility for an internal requirement to be obligatory in a genuine sense, as Marmor argues legal obligations to be. But, this is far from a necessity either: internal demands may well make no practically rational claim on us, for their binding force is grounded in outside factors and so such force is genuine only insofar as those outside factors possess a rationally practical dimension.

To summarize, in Marmor's theoretical framework whether or not a legal obligation, qua internal duty, is genuinely binding – whether or not it constitutes a practically rational demand and so makes a claim on one's rational agency – depends on whether it can be demonstrated that the interests, needs, and values justifying the establishment and perpetuation of a given legal system – namely, the external reasons conceptually associated with legal obligations – are practically rational. For, only insofar as the law is grounded in external considerations that can be argued to hold valid within the practically rational domain, can the demands set out by the law be considered practically rational claims, as opposed to being less than genuine requirements. This means that, absent a specific treatment of the external reasons we have to participate in the legal enterprise and absent an argument showing that we do have external reasons to commit to the legal practice to the effect that legal systems are institutions which can be rationally justified, legal obligations, as they are conceptualized by Marmor, cannot be qualified as necessarily genuine duties. Couple this statement with the fact that programmatically Marmor offers no argument supporting the practical rationality of the legal enterprise – indeed, he explicitly considers such an argument beyond the scope of any jurisprudential account of legal obligation.[20] From this combination, it follows that the practically rational quality and associated genuine bindingness of legal obligation find no support in Marmor's theoretical treatment of legal obligation. Such treatment is therefore conceptually compatible with the conclusion that legal obligations are not practically rational demands, or demands binding in a genuine sense. Which demand, insofar as it fails to amount

---

[20] Paradigmatic in this sense are the claims defended in Marmor, *Positive Law and Objective Values*, pp. 24–34.

to a practical requirement, can hardly be conceptualized as obligation without calling into question the widespread concept of obligation introduced in Chapter 1.

5.4 An Objection

To this critique showing that legal obligation, as Marmor conceives of it, *may* but need not (turn out to) be genuinely binding one may reply that the conclusion I am dissatisfied with is made inevitable by the conditional character of legal obligations. Conditional obligations, it may be claimed, are such that their bindingness is constitutively *contingent*, being derivative on the obligatoriness of the external reasons underlying the practice to which conditional obligations owe their capacity to make claims on us. My critique can accordingly be said to overshoot its target in two related senses. First, it may be taken to mean that no conditional obligation can ever necessarily have *any* genuine binding force. Which would be a startling claim for one to make, since conditional obligations generally encompass a whole variety of obligations proper, by so also binding us in a genuine sense. Second, my critique seems to entail that *no* theory (rather than just Marmor's) can explain the necessarily practically rational quality of legal obligations – their genuine bindingness – unless it defines legal obligation as an inescapable, or unconditional, obligation.

In reply to this hypothetical objection, I should emphasize that what I argued to be problematic is not Marmor's claim that legal obligations are both conditional and equipped with genuine binding character (a claim that seems to me to be undeniable once we set it in a different conceptual framework), but rather the combination of the following theses about legal obligation into a single theory (as is the case with Marmor's theory): (a) legal obligation is an internal demand, to the effect that its bindingness is conditional on the external reasons one has to live under the jurisdiction of a legal system; (b) our external reasons for participating in a legal system need not be addressed by a theoretically sound and comprehensive account of legal obligation, since our engagement with those reasons constitutively lies outside the scope of such an account (indeed it inherently lies outside the whole discipline – jurisprudence – to which the account is meant to contribute); and (c) legal obligation, qua an instance of what is obligatory, has genuine binding character. This whole package – and not the notion of a conditional obligation, when it is understood as a genuine requirement – is the target of my critique as it was set out earlier.

What I object to Marmor, thus, is that, insofar as he does not take pains to elucidate (and so to programmatically engage with) the external considerations on which legal obligations are conditional (claim (b)), the thesis that legal obligation is an internal obligation and so an obligation whose bindingness is derivative on those external considerations (claim (a)) does not secure the genuine obligatoriness of the demands arising out of the law (claim (c)). So the edifice built by packaging together the theses framing Marmor's theory rests on a shaky foundation: the thesis that legal obligation is at once internal and, qua an instantiation of obligation as such, genuinely binding cannot be validated unless we show that the external reasons grounding the normativity of legal obligation, qua internal duty, lend genuine obligatoriness to it – genuine obligatoriness that is far from necessarily inscribed in, or intrinsic to, internal demands. However, Marmor's theory is unconcerned with the external reasons that ground the obligatoriness of law. On this basis, such theory can be argued to be constitutively unable to explain the genuine normativity of the external reasons legal obligations are shaped by and, relatedly, the genuine bindingness of legal obligation. Hence my dissatisfaction with that theory.

To further expand on this thought, the objection made in Section 5.3 was not directed at Marmor's claim that legal obligation is conditional. The objection was instead directed at Marmor's coupling such assertion with the statement that it is not the business of a theory of legal obligation to state what the nature of these reasons is, and in particular what makes them normative. That is, in my view the qualification of legal obligation as a conditional requirement is tenable, provided that it goes hand in hand with the recognition of the theoretical importance of determining the specific normativity attached to the (external) reasons on which that requirement is conditioned. Indeed, whenever one claims that legal obligation is a conditional standard and the existence conditions of legal obligation – namely, the external reasons to commit to the institution issuing legal obligations – are irrelevant from within legal theory (as distinct of political philosophy, or moral philosophy, or other disciplines), we are left with an account unable to settle the issue as to whether or not legal obligation is a genuinely normative demand. It is, therefore, reasonable to expect that those who accept the conditional structure of legal obligation closely engage with the (external) considerations that secure the bindingness of legal obligation. For, in a theoretical framework shaped by the thesis that legal obligation, qua genuine demand, is a conditional requirement, any disengagement from external reasons results into the impossibility to establish the genuine normativity of legal obligation on firm grounds. Namely, once we endorse the statement that legal obligation is conditional, we need to provide a systematic account of the external considerations on which the bindingness of legal obligation is conditioned; otherwise we would be condemned to a conceptualization of legal obligation as a non-necessarily genuine demand.

That such conceptualization is, in turn, fundamentally flawed can also be appreciated by considering a further dimension of legal obligation. It is widely and ordinarily acknowledged that, in determining the course of action we ought to take in any given situation, we look to legal obligations as much as to the (likewise presumptive) requirements set out by other instantiations of practical rationality, such as morality. Namely, the different sources of obligation – law, morality, etc. – are commonly presented as *concurrent*, not as mutually exclusive. A theory of legal obligation can therefore legitimately be expected to explain, vis-à-vis to do away with, this dimension of legal obligation. And this it can only do by finding a firm basis on which to rest the genuine obligatoriness of law (presumptive and conditional though it may be). A theory of legal obligation, in other words, should tell us why it is conceptually necessary that legal demands be treated as practically rational requirements and so as genuinely binding directives. That is precisely what Marmor's account fails to do: by framing legal obligations as *internal* obligations, it explains the presumptive and conditional force of legal demands, but by disregarding the (external) considerations on which legal demands are based, it casts the genuine obligatoriness of those demands as a mere possibility.

In conclusion, unless a theory of legal obligation as a requirement that is internal to the law comes with an account of the external reasons to comply with the law, the resulting picture of legal obligation will be that of a demand that may not be genuinely binding. Marmor's conceptual analysis is silent in precisely that respect: it refrains from discussing the external reasons and considerations that can give rise to legal obligation as an internal and conditional requirement. As a consequence, Marmor's account ends up justifying the conclusion that legal obligation need not partake of any genuine normativity. Otherwise stated, since on Marmor's account a legal requirement can make a genuine claim on us *just in case* the external considerations that legal requirement is based on inhabit the practically rational domain and so transmit their genuine normativity to that legal requirement, the discussion of the external considerations should be regarded as part and parcel of his theory of legal obligation, qua genuine demand, vis-à-vis a mere accessory component of such theory as instead Marmor claims. For, without an argument showing that the external reasons to commit to the institution engendering legal obligations are genuinely normative, any legal requirement dependent on them is less than genuinely binding. Namely, insofar as we recognize that certain external considerations lend (their own) rational force to the requirements of the law, by thus turning these requirements into genuine obligations specifically engendered by the law, the study of those considerations is to be understood as integral to a theory of legal obligation. Marmor's account fails to secure any genuine normativity for the external reasons on which the bindingness of legal obligation is conditioned is far from secured – indeed, that construction is shaped by the thesis that legal theorists are legitimated to show no interest in those reasons and so ultimately in the question as to whether or not legal obligations are practically normative demands. And this disengagement with the external considerations on which the genuine bindingness of legal obligation is conditioned means that in Marmor's theory there is no assurance that legal obligation is a genuine reason for action. Or, to put it the other way round, Marmor's conceptualization allows for the *possibility* that legal obligations make no genuine normative claim on their addressees. For, whenever the external reasons supporting a legal requirement prove to be practically rational inert, so that legal requirement will.

In this context, one cannot overemphasize the circumscribed tenor of this critique of Marmor's theory of legal obligation. My claim here is *not* that in Marmor's conventionalist reason account legal obligations are conceptually prevented from instantiating genuinely binding duties. Rather, the problem I see with the conventionalist reason account is that, while Marmor makes room for the *possibility* that legal obligations amount to practically rational requirements, his conceptualization lacks the resources to show that legal obligations are *necessarily* rational demands and so have *of necessity* a genuine binding quality, since he bans the discussion of the external reasons attached to legal obligations from legal theory. As much as this shortcoming can be acknowledged to be limited – indeed, I have not showed that for Marmor legal obligation necessarily is less than genuinely binding – I take it sufficient to support the conclusion that Marmor's construction is theoretically defective. A satisfactory and encompassing account of the obligations generated by the law should explain how the requirements deriving from legal practices genuinely bind us; it is not enough for such an account to simply make room for the mere possibility that legal obligations are practically normative in a genuine sense.

My concern with Marmor's construction – the reason why I find it theoretically inadequate and problematic – in sum, is that it is compatible with the conclusion that legal requirements may not make *any* genuine normative claim on us at all, not even a presumptive and defeasible claim. This conclusion is objectionable, I believe, as it means that, for Marmor, a legal obligation may well be a duty that does not compete with practically rational directives in determining the course of action we ought to take, thus occupying a territory not inhabited by considerations of practical rationality.

5.5 Are Marmor's Internal Obligations Genuinely Binding at All?

I just argued, in the last section, that on Marmor's account legal obligations may end up making no practically rational claim on us. In this section I will radicalize that line of criticism by illustrating another conclusion that can be extracted from Marmor's theory, namely, that the binding force of legal obligations is necessarily non-genuine, in that legal obligations (as framed in Marmor's theory) are conceptually unable to have any role in rationally determining (even presumptively) the conduct we ought to perform.

This dimension can be best appreciated if one considers the nature of legal obligations, qua internal obligations, as this nature is presented by Marmor. So far I have assumed that Marmor conceives of legal obligations qua internal duties as presumptive and conditional requirements. Admittedly, there is no conceptual obstacle that prevents a presumptive and conditional requirement from instantiating a genuine duty (despite the fact that, as I argued in Sections 5.3 and 5.4, the thesis that legal obligation has genuine binding force is not granted with the force of necessity by the account Marmor defends). In this section, I tentatively question the assumption, which has underpinned the discussion so far, that Marmor can ultimately accommodate the genuine bindingness of legal obligation. In embracing that assumption I may, in fact, have adopted a too charitable approach, by so overlooking an alternative conceivable reading of Marmor's project. For, on a possible understanding, Marmor's account can be argued to defend a *perspectivized view of legal obligation*. And this reading would commit Marmor's conception of legal obligation to a far more serious problem than the one I emphasized in the preceding sections.

In fairness, before I begin, it should be noted that nowhere in his work does Marmor explicitly define a legal obligation as a duty that holds in the perspectivized sense. Yet some central claims Marmor defends can plausibly be understood as implicit statements that legal obligation is a perspectivized requirement. What this means is that Marmor can be understood to construct legal obligation as a requirement that binds us only from the standpoint of the practices constitutive of law, which is the standpoint taken by those who have reasons to commit to legal practices (and to hold on to that commitment).

One can start to appreciate the plausibility of this interpretation by restating Marmor's notion of legal obligation as the internal duty to do what a given practice presumptively demands of those who have external reasons to be part of the same practice. That restatement can be formulated as follows:

> Insofar as there is an external reason for you to participate in practice X, you have a pro tanto internal obligation to do Y, which is what practice X requires (call this statement IO, short for 'internal obligation').

In the context of law, this reads:

> Insofar as there is an external reason for you to participate in the legal practice, you have a pro tanto legal obligation to do Y, which is what the underlying legal practice requires (call this statement IOL, short for 'internal obligation within law').

IO and IOL should be interpreted in light of Marmor's general characterization of internal obligations and his characterization of legal obligations, qua internal obligations. For Marmor the binding force of internal obligations, and so of legal obligations, is conditional on the obtaining of certain considerations external to the obligation-generating practice. These considerations provide participants with reasons to engage in that practice, meaning that participants can analyse and evaluate the practice on the basis of those considerations.

Such engagement with these external considerations is in turn regarded by Marmor as beyond the scope of the study of legal obligation, as this study is carried out within the limits of jurisprudence. As far as a legal-theoretical account of the obligations engendered by the law is concerned, therefore, the quality of the considerations on which legal obligations, qua internal obligations, are conditional is simply assumed as a given – a datum that lies beyond the boundaries of the discipline which that account is meant to contribute to. Accordingly, Marmor's jurisprudential account of legal obligation proceeds on the *assumptions* that certain external facts obtain, those facts stand in a direct relation to legal obligations, and those facts have the resources needed to explain the obligatory force of law.

That is to say, in Marmor's framework an internal obligation – whose standard formulation reads, 'insofar as there is an external reason for you to participate in practice X, you have a pro tanto internal obligation to do Y, which is what practice X requires', as per IO – is both semantically and conceptually equivalent to the following formulation:

> On the assumption that there is an external reason for you to participate in practice X, you have a pro tanto internal obligation to do Y, which is what practice X requires (call this statement IO').

The legal counterpart to this statement reads,

> On the assumption that there is an extralegal reason for you to participate in the legal practice, you have a pro tanto legal obligation to do Y, which is what the underlying legal practice requires (this I will call IOL').

Internal obligations and legal obligations thus bind us on the assumption that we put ourselves in the position of someone who has reasons to value the obligation-generating practice. Crucially, within the discourse on internal obligations (as well as on legal obligations) the assumption at issue cannot be modified. To that extent, the assumptions stated in IO' and IOL' describe an unavoidable framework, or fixed perspective, from which the entire discourse on internal obligations and legal obligations unfolds. On Marmor's conception, in other terms, the binding force of internal obligations and legal obligations is understood as dependent on, and granted by, the existence of a given standpoint. This means that the obligations the relevant practice generates are binding only in a 'specialized' sense, that is, they are binding only on condition that we have reasons to endorse the fixed perspective with which those obligations are associated.

Now, this last formulation strikes me as a paradigmatic statement of a *perspectivized* obligation – an obligation that binds *from a certain point of view*. That is, in the context of Marmor's work, IO' does not just account for an internal obligation, which as such can well (although need not) have genuine bindingness; it instead accounts for an internal obligation in the perspectivized sense. Correspondingly, within Marmor's conceptual framework, IOL' means that we have an obligation to do what a legal practice demands from us only insofar as we have reasons to take up the standpoint of someone who is a committed to participate in that practice, and so only from the specialized outlook of a legal subject.

The perspectivized stance that IO′ and IOL′ lay out is apparent from the fact that in the context of Marmor's conception they can be reformulated, without any loss of meaning and conceptual distortion, as follows:

> From the point of view of someone who has reasons to be committed to the practice X, you have a pro tanto internal obligation to do Y, which is what practice X requires (which formulation can be named IO″).

Correspondingly, a legal obligation can be formulated thus:

> From the point of view of someone who has reasons to be committed to the legal system, you have a pro tanto legal obligation to do Y, which is what the underlying the legal practice requires (call this statement IOL″).

IO″ and IOL″ enable us to immediately appreciate the perspectivized quality that internal obligations and legal obligations respectively incorporate in Marmor's framework of thought. Insofar as IOL and IOL″ are conceptually equivalent, therefore, legal obligation can be claimed to be understood by Marmor not only as a conditional and presumptive obligation but also as a perspectivized one. Namely, at least on one possible interpretation, Marmor's account can be said to present legal obligation as a perspectivized demand.

So far in this section I have argued that Marmor's project can be understood to characterize legal obligation as a specialized and perspectivized kind of obligation. On this reading, a legal obligation is an internal obligation that binds those who take the perspective of a legal system, as this perspective is defined and instantiated by those who have reasons to be committed participants in that system. Accordingly, Marmor's account of legal obligation can plausibly be interpreted as committed to the claim that the duties engendered by the law are not protected reasons for action one presumptively has (call them 'straight' presumptive practical reasons) but rather protected reasons for action one presumptively has by virtue of occupying a certain perspective (let us call them 'perspectivized' presumptive practical reasons).

Now, insofar as legal obligation is constructed as an obligation in the perspectivized sense, it falls short of setting out a normative standard. This statement finds support in the argument used in Chapter 3 to criticize the account of legal obligation defended by the advocates of the conception of law as a shared activity. In my critique there, I argued that the perspectivized meaning renders a legal obligation normatively inert. Here, I intend to make a similar point with respect to Marmor's account. In Marmor's view, as reconstructed in this section, legal obligations are not an ordinary species of presumptive obligations – or reasons setting out defeasible practical demands with genuine binding force – but are instead perspectivized presumptive obligations of a sort.

Let us elaborate on this point by spelling out the distinction between presumptive standards and perspectivized ones in further detail. A *presumptive standard* is an ordinary practical standard – one that comes with genuine normative force – but it is justified only pro tanto, as opposed to being justified all things considered. Such a standard is a practically rational norm that may be defeated and so does not of necessity conclusively establish the course of conduct one ought to perform. Hence, presumptive standards are action-guiding, but, as merely presumptive directives, they may occasionally be defeated (in which case they will fail to dictate the course of conduct one ought to undertake all things considered). Far from being a requirement unsupported by any rational justification, and so devoid of genuinely normative force in the practical domain, a defeasible standard is binding on rational agents even though its binding force may on occasion be weakened or even defeated, when a stronger requirement applies that is equally justified as a normative standard. Therefore, an account that conceptualizes legal obligation as a presumptive protected reason is hardly objectionable: as presumptive reasons in principle come with a genuine justification attached to them, defeasible legal obligations will be genuinely binding, whenever the law succeeds in establishing a reason for action. And this means that a theory which presents legal obligation as a presumptive standard has the conceptual resources needed to shape a theoretically insightful account of legal obligation.

Unlike presumptive standards, which generate defeasible reasons and so can well be associated with the existence of a presumptive obligation with genuine bindingness, *perspectivized standards* do not belong to the normative realm. Perspectivized standards are considerations that favour a given conduct only from a certain standpoint. So, by their own construction, they hold only within the context of their formulation, rather than holding as normative standards of practical rationality at large. Relatedly, they do not connect with straight presumptive practical reasons (at least not directly) by thus failing to establish normative standards, not even defeasible ones. That is to say, while presumptive obligations are genuinely (albeit inconclusively) binding – they are normative standards – perspectivized obligations can only be framed as non-normative statements and so statements that have no direct impact on what one ought to do.

Since the perspectivized statement of an obligation hardly connects with the 'practical ought', and so has no bearing on the issue of the way one should act – it fails to make any normative claim on us – perspectivized statements of obligations have no genuine binding quality, namely, they are obligations in name only. Accordingly, an account that conceptualizes legal obligation as a perspectivized protected reason for action falls short of framing the obligations generated by the law as duties with built-in genuine bindingness: to conceptualize legal obligation as a perspectivized statement is to condemn the norms of law to normative irrelevance for anyone who does not identify with the point of view of the legal system, namely, potentially for everyone apart from self-identified legal officials. The claim that law sets up perspectivized legal requirements therefore forces on us the unpalatable conclusion that law does not guide action – it does not perform its distinctively normative and practical function – through the obligations it sets forth.

I find this conclusion objectionable. For, whereas generating obligations may well not be the only way for the law to provide practical guidance, it is certainly an essential way. We therefore cannot explain legal obligations as reasons of a special kind and with a special structure unless we also theorize them as requirements with genuine binding force. And this is why the reasons that (contribute to) define legal obligations cannot be characterized as perspectivized presumptive practical reasons, as that would be tantamount to characterizing them as requirements lacking the normative force of an obligation.

In sum, on the interpretation I have introduced and discussed in this section, Marmor explains legal obligation as a perspectivized reason. By defining legal obligations as perspectivized duties, Marmor theorizes an account of standards that do not have binding force. Relatedly, legal obligations, as constructed by Marmor, cannot shape the practical deliberation we engage in as rational agents deciding how we ought to act. Obligations can be shown to have any genuine normative quality only when defined in terms of *straight* (presumptive) practical reasons. By contrast, Marmor can be interpreted as explaining legal obligations in terms of *perspectivized* (presumptive) practical reasons. Marmor's conceptual framework is therefore constitutively incapable of establishing legal obligations as standards that genuinely bind us, namely, as authentically practical norms that concur with the demands originating in (other domains of) practical rationality in determining what we ought to do. For, insofar as the duties generated by the law are understood as perspectivized presumptive practical reasons, they do not constitute normative statements, not even presumptive ones. Likewise, they lack the resources needed to guide our conduct: they cannot tell us how we ought to behave.

5.6 Conclusion

In this chapter I looked at Marmor's conventionalist reason account of legal obligation, discussing some unresolved issues the account is arguably plagued by. As much as it should be acknowledged that Marmor's conceptual framework for the study of legal obligation is valuable and theoretically sophisticated, since it takes a step in the right direction when it abandons the social practice paradigm and interpretivist approach, and replaces them with a reason account, his theory is vulnerable to a twofold critique.

First, Marmor claims that legal obligation is a kind of internal duty that is genuinely binding. But the combination of these qualifications in Marmor's theory of legal obligation is problematic: insofar as an obligation is qualified as internal, its genuine bindingness (however presumptive it may be) cannot be taken for granted. The point made in this context is not that in Marmor's conceptual framework internal obligations necessarily fall short of providing practical guidance. The point is rather more modest: I merely offered the negative argument that Marmor's theory cannot secure the genuine binding force of legal obligations. And, insofar as the bindingness of internal obligations does not have genuine force, even legal obligations (which on Marmor's conception are internal) cannot be explained as duties that constitutively concur in establishing the conduct one ought to perform.

Secondly, I argued that, at least on a conceivable interpretation, Marmor's account of legal obligation is even more questionable than that. Marmor's statement of the conditional nature of legal obligation can plausibly be taken to embrace a perspectivized view of legal obligations. Perspectivized obligations, however, do not occupy the same conceptual space as practical requirements, since they inherently lack any genuine binding force. Therefore, Marmor's theory (at least on one conceivable interpretation) not only lacks the conceptual resources needed to explain how the obligatoriness of law must *necessarily* be genuine, but also fails to account for the very *possibility* that legal obligations are genuinely binding: as perspectivized statements, legal obligations are intrinsically unable to (contribute to) establish which courses of conduct one ought to perform. As a result, Marmor's theory departs from the ordinary understanding of legal obligations as standards that play a role in settling the course of conduct one ought to perform.

The twofold argument I developed in this chapter shows that Marmor's failure to provide a comprehensive and entirely sound explanation of legal obligation is not owed to the overall strategy behind his theory, which is the strategy distinctive to the reason account of legal obligation in its many variants. In fact, it was noticed that, far from being objectionable, Marmor's strategic choice – his aligning with the research programme based on the claim that legal obligation is best explained in terms of normative practical reasons – enables him to contribute significantly to our understanding of the nature of legal obligation by insightfully presenting legal obligation as a justificatory practical reason (of a certain kind and with a specific structure). Marmor's failure instead comes down to his reluctance to fully embrace the reason paradigm in the study of legal obligation. For Marmor takes a *minimalist* reason approach.[21] And by taking that narrow approach – on which legal obligation is such only in the internal sense and so we are legitimized to programmatically abstain from addressing the nature of the external reasons on which the normative force of legal obligations is conditional – Marmor ends up being unable to explain the genuine bindingness of legal obligation. His theory therefore fails to explain the *intrinsic* practically rational relevance of the obligations generated by the law. For that relevance can be appreciated only by systematically engaging with the external reasons that justify the law.

In conclusion, Marmor rightly claims that legal obligations are best defined as reasons for action having some special structure, but his minimalism prevents him from appreciating the theoretical need to further specify, and elaborate on, this claim, which is still insufficiently detailed to serve as a basis on which to attempt a sound comprehensive conceptualization of the obligations set forth by the law. It is therefore Marmor's minimalism – not his endorsement of the reason approach – that in my view prevents him from acknowledging the built-in genuine bindingness of legal obligations. On this basis, I conclude that a sound and comprehensive conceptualization of legal obligation needs to go

---

[21] The minimalism of Marmor's reason account can be appreciated in particular in his claim that the obligatory force of legal obligations is conditional on external reasons that we need not further explore or characterize in any detail.

beyond Marmor's minimalist reason account, while remaining within the reason camp to which that account belongs. And here it also lays the groundwork for any critical engagement with another, less modest reason account of legal obligation, which will be presented in the following chapter.

6

The Exclusionary Reason Account

6.1 Introduction

The failure of the *conventionalist reason account* does not disqualify the reason paradigm for the study of legal obligation in its entirety. There are other variants of that paradigm offered in the literature and they may well prove to be more successful, since they combine the promising claim that the notion of a practical reason is fundamental to explaining the nature of legal obligation with a less minimalist definition of that notion. This combination has the potential to be theoretically insightful, since the root cause of the shortcomings of Marmor's account of legal obligation has been argued to be (not his endorsement of the reason paradigm as such but rather) his minimalism about reasons, from which descend Marmor's objectionable statement that legal obligations are internal reasons associated with the existence of a system of laws.

This reading justifies my choice to discuss another variant of reason account: the *exclusionary reason account*, which will be the subject matter of this chapter. In engaging with the exclusionary version of the reason account of legal obligation, I will be almost exclusively concerned with the work of John Finnis, who in *Natural Law and Natural Rights* (especially in Chapter 11) and a number of subsequent works sets out a comprehensive and sophisticated conception of legal obligation. In this chapter, I will first introduce Finnis's theory of legal obligation and then critically assess it. In my critical assessment, I will argue that Finnis's treatment of legal obligation marks a significant advance over the accounts discussed in the previous chapters in consideration of the fact that it defends the views that legal obligation (a) has genuine practical force, (b) is ultimately grounded in rational considerations, to the effect that (c) is best understood as a kind of rational necessity, and (d) is not entirely will-dependent. Those views sound unobjectionable to me: no theory of legal obligation, I think, can afford to disregard them.

By contrast, two other important, and closely interlinked, claims forming part of Finnis's account of law and legal obligation can be argued to be problematic. The first of these claims is the statement that the force of legal obligation is invariant. Contrary to that view, in this chapter I will argue that the obligations arising out of the law are defeasible requirements, and that as such they have variable force. Accordingly, legal obligation cannot be regarded as a strict demand unaffected by non-legal considerations and subject to no extralegal exception. The second, and related, tenet Finnis supports and I will argue to be questionable is the thesis that legal obligation can be adequately characterized in terms of the notion of an exclusionary reason. Here I will maintain that it cannot, since legal obligation stands in a dialectical (or inclusionary, as opposed to exclusionary) relation to the fundamental demands of practical rationality. The two objections are closely interlinked: it is because legal obligation is not informed by an exclusionary logic that its force is variable, and it is because legal obligation is a defeasible requirement, whose force can vary in different contexts, that the notion of an exclusionary reason is ill-suited to account for what a legal obligation is and how it works.

6.2 Finnis on Legal Obligation

Finnis conceives of legal obligation as a particular species of a broader genus, obligation *simpliciter*. Obligation *simpliciter* is, in his view, a requirement of practical rationality: it is a form of rational necessity that ultimately originates in a demand of conscience and results in some claim on the action we ought to carry out.[1] For Finnis, thus, an obligation singles out the courses of action that we ought to do, in that it would be wrong, or even shameful, for us to act otherwise.[2]

---

[1] Obligations are defined by John Finnis as 'requirements of practical *reasonableness*' (J. Finnis, *Natural Law and Natural Rights* (Oxford, Oxford University Press, 2nd ed. with a Postscript, 2011; 1st ed. 1980), p. 297; emphasis added). In that definition Finnis does not exactly refer to the notion of practical rationality. However, the distinction between practical reasonableness as understood by Finnis and practical rationality as this term is used in this book is merely terminological and so conceptually impalpable. Considering that my argument throughout this book is cast in terms of the notion of practical rationality, it makes sense to do the same here, if only to maintain some terminological consistency throughout and make the presentation clear. Finnis's position will accordingly be reframed here in terms of practical rationality, which I take to be the conceptual equivalent of practical reasonableness, as Finnis understands the latter.

[2] These claims are made in Finnis, *Natural Law and Natural Rights*, pp. 297–8.

Since in Finnis's theoretical framework legal obligation is a species of obligation in general, it is claimed to reproduce the features of the latter. Nonetheless, it can take up four distinct senses. First, legal obligation may be understood as an 'empirical liability to be subjected to sanction in event of non-compliance'.[3] Secondly, legal obligation may indicate a requirement set by the law, in turn conceived as a system of practical reasoning insulated, and so partially autonomous, from other forms of practical deliberation. Something is legally obligatory in this second sense – referred to by Finnis as the 'intra-systemic' sense of legal obligation, or legal obligation 'in the legal sense', or in 'contemplation of law' – if it is required by the law, understood as a posited set of norms shaping an independent sphere of practical reasoning. That is the lawyers' sense of legal obligation, namely, the kind of legal duty that ordinarily concerns legal practitioners and scholars embarking on a doctrinal study of law. Thirdly, legal obligation can be interpreted in a *moral* sense, referring to the presumptive duty we have to obey the law. Legal obligation in the moral sense is something that is morally required – there are good moral reasons for doing it – if law says that we are to so act. Legal obligation so understood (in the moral sense) is 'a unique kind of moral obligation which obtains only as a property of, or resultant from, *positive* law'.[4] Finally, in its fourth meaning, the obligation to obey the law consists in a moral obligation to comply with legal standards even if their contents turn out to be morally unsavoury.

Of these meanings of legal obligation, two play a central role in Finnis's discussion: legal obligation in the legal sense (this is the second meaning just mentioned) and legal obligation in the moral sense (this is the third meaning mentioned).[5] In order to explain legal obligation in the two main senses just introduced, Finnis builds on an idea we are all familiar with, referring to an obligation we experience as a matter of

---

[3] Finnis, *Natural Law and Natural Rights*, p. 354.
[4] J. Finnis, *Philosophy of Law: Collected Essays Volume IV* (Oxford, Oxford University Press, 2011), p. 125; original emphasis.
[5] It is hardly surprising that legal obligation in these two senses should be central to Finnis's understanding of legal obligation, considering his claim that legal obligation is derivative on obligation in general, which in turn is understood as a form of rational necessity. For, on the one hand, the first meaning of legal obligation – legal obligation as empirical liability to sanction – is by definition primarily an empirical matter, rather than a rational one; on the other hand, the fourth meaning is expressly introduced as a *collateral* sense of legal obligation and thus, like any sense that can be qualified as collateral, it should be considered ancillary to, and derivative on, some other primitive, primary, or central sense.

course in our daily affairs with others. This is the obligation we come under when making a promise.[6] Finnis call this a promissory obligation and offers three levels of explanation for it. Each of these levels builds on the previous explanatory level, so that only on the third level we have a comprehensive account of the relevant type of legal obligation – here promissory obligation. The first level explains promissory obligation as a requirement deriving from a given social practice, namely, the widespread practice of promising; the second explanatory level connects the binding force of promissory obligations to prudential considerations, arguing that keeping one's promises is obligatory because it can be shown to be in our own best interest, in that those who fail to do so run the risk of losing the trust of others; finally, the third level of explanation locates obligation as the conclusion of a train of practical reasoning about what is necessary as demanded by, and grounded in, the common good. For Finnis, the common good refers to 'the good of individuals, living together and depending upon one another in ways that favour the wellbeing of each'.[7] The obligatory force of a promissory obligation – its being a rational demand – thus derives from its being functional to securing the common good, which in turn is something everyone has a reason to value as a matter of practical rationality.

The third explanatory level offers, as anticipated, an elucidation of promissory obligation that is theoretically superior and so preferable to the ones provided on the previous two levels. For the first explanatory level 'fails to give an account of the role of the notion of obligation in the practical reasonings both of the persons under that obligation and of those other persons who take his being under an obligation as giving good (justifying) reason for their demands, pressure, criticisms, etc.'.[8] An explanation of promissory obligation that primarily relies on considerations stemming from an agent's personal interests – the second explanatory level – is equally unsatisfactory for a different set of considerations: it only accounts for the prudential 'ought' and, additionally, it does not explain why we are under an obligation even when the risk we run of losing trust is remote or even negligible. Therefore, it is only by establishing a connection between promissory obligation and practical reasoning aimed at pursuing the common good that we can arrive at a correct understanding of what an obligation is and how it binds us.

[6] See Finnis, *Natural Law and Natural Rights*, pp. 298–308.
[7] Finnis, *Natural Law and Natural Rights*, p. 305.
[8] Finnis, *Natural Law and Natural Rights*, p. 301.

This conclusion, Finnis believes, applies not just to promissory obligations but also to any kind of obligation, including legal obligation. If we are to appreciate the fundamental traits of the obligations generated by the law, we have to bring the third level of explanation to bear on *both* of the main senses in which a legal obligation can be understood, namely, the legal sense and the moral sense. Crucially, it is Finnis's view that some of the fundamental traits of obligation, as they emerge on the third level of explanation, characterize legal obligation in whatever sense it is understood, whilst other fundamental traits singled out on the third level of explanation specifically distinguish legal obligation in the legal sense from legal obligation in the moral sense.

The traits that, on Finnis's account, are shared by all the senses of legal obligation can be summarized as follows. Legal obligation figures as an element of an individual's practical reasoning and so contributes to one's deliberation concerning which action one ought to perform in a given circumstance. On this basis, legal obligation is defined as a requirement that provides reasons for action. The reasons for action that are specifically associated with a legal obligation have compulsory force: they make it *necessary* for an agent to perform the action identified in the content of the obligation. The kind of necessity at stake here is *rational*: legal obligation is conceived by Finnis as a demand of practical rationality requiring that certain actions be carried out on the ground that those actions are acknowledged to be indispensable means to valuable ends.[9] The value that is relevant in this context is *moral*. That is to say, the necessity of legal obligation is neither that of a prudential 'ought' nor that of a technical 'ought'. Related to this, a course of conduct that is made legally obligatory is supported by moral considerations: it singles out a moral 'ought', which in turn is ultimately aimed at the pursuit of the common good. This statement secures a primary connection between legal obligations, on the one hand, and the establishment or the consolidation of a morally valuable normative framework of mutual coexistence and coordination within a community, on the other. For this reason, whilst the content of a legal obligation is set by some expression of will – typically that of lawmaking authorities – this will-based component constitutes not the source of legal obligation but rather a (necessary) element of legal obligation.[10]

---

[9] These arguments are made in Finnis, *Natural Law and Natural Rights*, pp. 307–8.

[10] The relations between obligation and will are discussed at length in Finnis, *Natural Law and Natural Rights*, pp. 330–43.

To elaborate on this point, the will of lawmakers is regarded by Finnis as the main determinant of the *content* of legal obligation: legal obligation does not come into being unless some voluntary and intentional act is done (hence the necessary role allotted to the will in defining legal obligation). However, a voluntary and intentional act is only one of the several conditions that need to be in place for a legal obligation to emerge. It is true that these conditions are essential, since no legal obligation could obtain without them. But, those conditions are not the ultimate determinants, or grounds, of legal obligation. For, whilst legal obligation arises from the lawmakers' expressions of will – their decisions – it is not their will per se that gives rise to such obligation, as to that end there needs to also be a morally valuable normative framework in the background. The force of legal obligation, then, cannot be explained in terms of a decision-making act. The obligatoriness of law rather results from the interplay of some rational element – the demands of practical rationality – with some decision taken by those who are competent to make choices on behalf of the legal community as a whole.[11]

Even though legal obligation in the legal sense and legal obligation in the moral sense share many fundamental traits, they are not reducible to each other. Indeed, there is at least one distinctive element that sets them clearly apart: the nature of their force. Legal obligation in the moral sense is an obligation of variable force, its bindingness being affected, and even outweighed, by extralegal valuative considerations. As a result, a change in circumstances may well release us from certain legal obligations when they are understood in the moral sense. This makes legal obligation in the moral sense a *defeasible* requirement to act in accordance with the law. That is hardly the case with legal obligation in the legal sense. The force of legal obligation in contemplation of law is *invariant*: it is the same in every case, to the efffect that obligation in the legal sense does not come in 'degrees' of obligatoriness. Finnis thus qualifies legal obligation in the legal sense as positing a black-and-white requirement, rather that a defeasible one. Once it is established that a case falls within the scope

---

[11] This point is central to Finnis's theory, which is deeply shaped by the Aristotelian tradition, especially as filtered through Aquinas. Hence, Finnis states that 'Aquinas describes human positive law as made by will (that is, by a choice to adopt one reasonable scheme in preference to another or others). But when speaking precisely, he contends that law is a matter of reason rather than will; obligation is a matter of means required for serving and respecting practical reason's ends and principles; the *imperium* by which in executing one's choices, one directs oneself (or, analogously, as ruler directs one's community) belongs to reason rather than will' (Finnis, *Philosophy of Law*, p. 161).

of a legal obligation in the legal sense, the relevant matter should be deemed legally *settled*, and no extralegal consideration can be introduced to modify our legal obligations in contemplation of law.[12] This characterization establishes a direct link between Finnis's account of legal obligation in the legal sense and the notion of an exclusionary reason for action.

The notion of an exclusionary reason for action was originally introduced in the legal-theoretical debate (not by Finnis but) by Joseph Raz, who makes it central to his theory of practical reasoning and norms.[13] We can fully understand the idea of an exclusionary reason by looking at the place it occupies in the scheme that Raz uses to account for practical reasoning, which he structures on two levels: a basic level, where we reason on action, and a higher metalevel where we reason on reasoning itself. Inhabiting the practical sphere, then, are not only (first-order) reasons for action but also (second-order) reasons for acting for a reason.[14] Second-order reasons can be positive (reasons to act for some reason), or they can be negative (reasons *not* to act for some reason). It is in this latter slot that we can fit 'exclusionary reasons', which are accordingly defined as negative second-order practical reasons. This picture of practical reasoning figures as a basic premise in Raz's definition of an obligation-imposing norm, which is explained as a practical reason of a particular type, namely, a protected reason for action. A protected reason is a first-order reason combined with an exclusionary reason, resulting in a directive that instructs us to both (a) behave in a certain way and (b) disregard certain reasons to act otherwise. There is, then, an exclusionary force built into an obligation-imposing norm.[15] This exclusionary component makes it so that obligation-imposing norms enjoy 'a relative independence from the reasons which justify them' and can be regarded as 'complete reasons in their own right'.[16] In this sense,

---

[12] These claims are introduced and defended in Finnis, *Natural Law and Natural Rights*, pp. 308–14.

[13] In fact, it is Finnis himself who explicitly establishes a direct connection between his own view of legal obligation and Raz's account of exclusionary reasons (Finnis, *Natural Law and Natural Rights*, p. 255).

[14] See J. Raz, *Practical Reason and Norms* (London, Hutchinson, 1990; 1st ed. 1975), pp. 39–40.

[15] As Raz puts it, an obligation-imposing norm 'is taken not merely as a reason for performing its norm act but also as resolving practical conflicts by excluding conflicting reasons' (Raz, *Practical Reason and Norms*, p. 73). This feature is further elaborated on in Raz, *Practical Reason and Norms*, pp. 190–4.

[16] Raz, *Practical Reason and Norms*, p. 79.

obligation-imposing norms crystallize a given balance between practical reasons and apply it directly in an unreflective fashion whenever the relevant conditions obtain.

Finnis relies on this component of Raz's account of practical reasoning to explain the crucial dimension that sets legal obligation in the legal sense apart from legal obligation in the moral sense. The former, but not the latter, singles out a legal requirement that is rescued from, and so is made independent of, the flow of general, or extralegal, practical reasoning. Accordingly, a legal obligation in the legal sense cannot be overridden, outweighed, diminished, or modified by extralegal considerations. So, while legal obligation in the legal sense inhabits the practical sphere (and in this respect is just like legal obligation in the moral sense), it does not occupy the same level of practical reasoning as other requirements of practical rationality. Legal obligation in the legal sense is instead sealed off, or insulated, from other departments of practical rationality and contiguous domains of practical reasoning.

On this (Razian) basis Finnis proceeds (a) to claim that the force of legal obligation in the legal sense – as a practical requirement impermeable to extralegal considerations – has invariant force, as well as (b) to characterize the type of reasoning involved in establishing legal obligation in the legal sense as 'means-ends practical reasoning'.[17] This form of reasoning is practical through and through, as it ultimately yields a directive telling us what we ought to do; yet it cannot be qualified as a complete form of practical reasoning, for it is not concerned with the *ends* of action. So, while in Finnis's framework, general practical reasoning also encompasses the ends of action, practical ends fall beyond the scope of deliberation where legal obligation in the legal sense is concerned.

This trait of legal obligation in the legal sense – its invariant obligatory force – accounts for the 'inflexibility' of law. A system of laws can be qualified as inflexible insofar as it does not, as a normative framework, allow an unrestricted feedback of morally significant evaluations and policy considerations from the justificatory level of practical rationality (which largely consists of extralegal considerations) back into the level of legal practice and reasoning. A legal system is inflexible, then, since it 'systematically restricts such feedback by establishing institutions, such as courts, arbitrators, and legislatures, and then requiring that any shifting

---

[17] Finnis, *Natural Law and Natural Rights*, p. 473.

of the obligations imposed by existing rules and subsisting arrangements shall be authorized only by those institutions'.[18] This means that even though law, as a system for regulating conduct, is ultimately grounded in practical rationality, it is at the same time self-sufficient and autonomous from practical reasoning. This inflexibility of law is owed to the nature of legal obligations, at least those in contemplation of law, in that here we have to do with demands that provide exclusionary reasons for action and so are insensitive to extralegal considerations (except in cases where those considerations are explicitly allowed to be counted in by the law itself, in accordance with specifically defined procedures and within certain limits set by the law itself).

In sum, Finnis understands legal obligation to have two main senses – a legal one and a moral one. Those two senses share several defining traits and yet importantly differ as far as their force is concerned, which is variable in the former sense and invariable in the latter. But the defining traits that legal obligation in the legal sense shares with legal obligation in the moral sense are no less important than their differences. Indeed, it is more than just an occasional set of similarities that the two senses share. For those similarities secure a single common ground for both the claim that we have a presumptive moral obligation to obey the law – or that there exists a legal obligation in the moral sense – and the claim that legal obligations in contemplation of law are sealed off from the unrestricted flow of practical reasoning – and hence that legal obligation in the legal sense has an invariant force. The ability of law to impose obligations (in any of the two relevant senses), in other words, has a common foundation in Finnis's account.

More specifically, the argument Finnis deploys to vindicate the obligation-imposing capacity of law has its starting point in his conception of obligation in general as a requirement that issues from a necessarily valuable normative framework. In turn, in order for a normative framework to be *intrinsically* and *unquestionably* valuable, it must be conducive to the pursuit of the values and principles of practical reasoning that Finnis argues to be basic, and so fundamental, for beings like us.[19] These basic values and fundamental principles are to be considered intrinsically and unquestionably valuable because they are essential to any meaningful individual or community life. As far as a community is

---

[18] Finnis, *Natural Law and Natural Rights*, p. 312.
[19] The argument for the fundamental status of certain principles and values is developed in Finnis, *Natural Law and Natural Rights*, pp. 59-99.

concerned, there is an arrangement of the basic values and principles of practical reasoning that defines the common good. This means that any normative framework governing social interactions can be regarded as intrinsically and unquestionably valuable (and so capable of generating obligations) only if it promotes the common good.

Now, and this is where the law crucially enters the stage, the methods for securing the common good are limited in number. Finnis claims in particular that ultimately they are reducible to just two: unanimity and authority. Unanimity defines a method in accordance with which the people concerned seek a collective agreement that is functional to the pursuit of what they all come to perceive as the good of the community they are part of. However, in complex societies, where people have different worldviews, deontological standpoints, and conceptions of which specific combination of fundamental values and principles makes life worthwhile, recourse to unanimous solutions to practical problems is not a realistic option.[20] Therefore, the only viable option for working out common concerns is by appeal to authority. This means that authority is a practical necessity for any community seeking to secure the common good.

Whilst authoritative institutions can take different shapes, only the law can legitimately be qualified as a general, and not patchy, 'fair method of relating benefits to burdens, and persons to persons, over an immensely wide, complex, and lasting, though shifting, set of persons and transactions'.[21] This is to say that the law, vis-à-vis other authoritative arrangements, is an indispensable instrument for pursuing a state of affairs in which individuals are enabled to participate in all the basic practical values and principles that, in combination, contribute to defining what is good for a community. This is a role the law can play by virtue of its unique capacity to work as an institution offering solutions for a community's coordination problems: it can do so by bringing definition, specificity, clarity, and predictability to human interactions.[22]

---

[20] This critique of unanimity as a method for dealing with social issues is set out in Finnis, *Natural Law and Natural Rights*, pp. 231–3.

[21] Finnis, *Philosophy of Law*, pp. 72–3; see also Finnis, *Philosophy of Law*, pp. 61–6.

[22] The argument is offered in Finnis, *Natural Law and Natural Rights*, pp. 266–70. A caveat should be added here. Finnis understands 'coordination problems' in a broad, non-technical sense as the 'problems of united action'. In this respect, too, he follows the Aristotelian and Thomist tradition in practical philosophy, thus rejecting the narrow way in which coordination problems are conceived by game theorists, among others. On this aspect, see Finnis, *Philosophy of Law*, pp. 69–71.

Finnis's claim that the law is a normative framework essential to achieving the common good supports his claim that the law can give rise to obligations. For, just as any necessary means to an intrinsically valuable end is obligatory – it is a means we necessarily ought to take – so the law, as a necessary means to the common good, ought to be complied with. This is why certain obligations we experience in our practical existence can properly be qualified as *legal* obligations, namely, as requirements which are imposed by the law and which thus make it necessary for us to act in certain ways. Hence the two claims that (a) legal obligations, as practical requirements, contribute to shaping our practical domain by specifically entering into our deliberations about how we ought to act, and, at the same time, (b) we need to comply with the law in order to realize the common good.

These two claims are strictly connected. We ought to comply with the requirement issued by the law, thus acting as the law demands, whenever there is an obligation-setting legal norm that governs the case at hand. And this is why we should accept that legal norms should enter into our practical deliberation, thus playing a role in settling what we ought to do in any given circumstance where the common good is involved and a legal issue is at stake. Those subject to the law therefore ought to take legal demands into account: inherent in the legal world is the requirement that individuals restrict the occasions on which they act on their own evaluations about what is good for them (or for the whole society) and instead act on the prescriptions issued by the law.[23]

This demand of self-restraint is owed to the systemic nature of law. Law is conceived by Finnis as a seamless web that holds together or collapses as a whole. Unless a legal system is accepted and complied with in its entirety, it dissolves into a disparate bunch of norms, turning into a different entity. As soon as this happens, the order essential to realizing the common good breaks up. Therefore, unless legal subjects treat law as an indivisible package and defer to *all* its norms – abstaining from the practice of 'picking and choosing' which obligation-imposing norms of law they should comply with and which they may legitimately depart from – law loses its capacity to foster the common good. On these grounds, Finnis concludes that it is obligatory for us to act as law prescribes: at least from the perspective of someone who cares for the common good, generalized obedience is a necessity, since any alternative

---

[23] These points are made in Finnis, *Natural Law and Natural Rights*, pp. 314–20.

form of legal compliance – selective and subject to personal critical assessment – would be incompatible with the existence of law as a seamless web, and so it would jeopardize our very ability to pursue the common good, something we would not be able to do without relying on law as a seamless normative framework. In Finnis's theoretical construction, then, 'an individual acts most appropriately for the common good not by trying to estimate the needs of the community "at large" nor by second-guessing the judgements of those who *are* directly responsible for the common good, but by performing his particular undertakings and fulfilling his other responsibilities to the ascertained individuals who have contractual or other rights correlative to his duties'.[24]

Now, as we saw, the claim that certain legal provisions are obligatory and we must therefore comply with them can be interpreted in two different ways, depending on whether legal obligation is understood in the legal sense or in the moral sense. And it is at this point that the distinction becomes relevant, considering that the argument takes different directions according as it supports the possibility of legal obligation in one sense or the other. More to the point, if we are arguing for the possibility of legal obligation in the *legal* sense, the claim that we need to follow the law in order to realize the common good should be taken as a 'postulate', or something that is completely isolated from, and unassailable by, the unrestricted flow of practical reasoning. Insofar as this claim is treated as a postulate, and so cannot be challenged by appeal to the general principles of practical rationality, the reasoning undertaken within law is impermeable to, and distinct from, other deliberations about what we ought to do. Relatedly, not all obligation-stipulating norms of law can be weighed or played off against one another. From this perspective it is the law itself that forbids any feedback from extralegal sources, to the effect that the general (indeed the moral) values that underpin the law are completely irrelevant to determining what legal obligations we have in the legal sense. This framework of thought justifies Finnis's thesis that legal obligation, when understood in the legal sense, has an invariant force and is governed by an exclusionary logic – a thesis that also excludes the role of any extralegal consideration in the practical deliberation we embark on from a strictly legal perspective. In other words, calling a legal obligation in the legal sense into question on extralegal grounds is not an option we can exercise as legal subjects,

---

[24] Finnis, *Natural Law and Natural Rights*, p. 474.

since legal obligation is part of a frame of reference – law – which by construction is impervious to, and independent from, morality. On this basis, Finnis concludes that legal obligation in the legal sense should be 'sharply distinguished from all those moral (or other) obligations which would subsist apart from or in the absence of the law'.[25]

When legal obligation is instead understood in the *moral* sense, the separation between legality and morality is mitigated. This is because, from the standpoint of someone who engages in practical reasoning at large, the claim that we need to be law-abiding subjects in order to realize the common good is not treated as an unchallengeable principle, or 'postulate'. As a consequence, in this context legal reasoning and moral reasoning stand in a relation of continuity and merely provisional distinction, rather than of mutual exclusion. Likewise, legal obligation in the moral sense does not connect with exclusionary practical reasons and so may well be weighed against non-legal obligations. This does not mean that legal obligations in the moral sense and non-legal obligations stand on the same footing. As noted, the legal enterprise as construed by Finnis can serve the common good only if individuals restrict the occasions on which they judge the weight of their legal obligations in light of their individual evaluations.[26] Even from the moral perspective, then, obeying the law is at least *presumptively* what one ought to do. So, on the one hand, the force of legal obligation in the moral sense is variable, but, on the other hand, there is a (weighty) presumptive obligation to obey the law, in that legal subjects are not free to depart from legal requirements unless there are countervailing general practical considerations sufficiently strong to defeat the presumption that legal obedience is morally required. And this is why, morally speaking, generalized legal obedience should be considered the default position, albeit not an irreversible one.

6.3 Legal Obligation and the Seamless Web of Practical Reasoning

Central to Finnis's treatment of legal obligation, as we saw, is the distinction between legal obligation in the legal sense and legal obligation in the moral sense. The terms of this distinction make good intuitive sense. Finnis is certainly not the only theorist to think it important to

---

[25] Finnis, *Natural Law and Natural Rights*, pp. 319–20.
[26] This claim is defended in Finnis, *Philosophy of Law*, pp. 48–52 and pp. 69–74, for instance.

keep a purely legal sense of obligation apart from obligation in the moral sense. In its traditional version, the distinction between the legal sense and the moral sense of legal obligation has made it possible to account for the possibility of conflicts between the demands that law and morality make on us. This sort of conflict is indeed part and parcel of the experience of legal professionals and lay people alike: it is far from exceptional for, say, a judge to assert that from a strictly legal perspective they are under a duty to decide a case in a certain way even though there are morally compelling reasons to settle the matter otherwise, such that their decision, though legally unobjectionable, lacks full moral justification. However, in Finnis's theoretical framework the distinction between an intra-systemic sense and a moral sense of legal obligation incorporates features that are peculiar to that framework, and that distinction is therefore not reducible to similar distinctions defended in the legal-theoretical literature, such as Hans Kelsen's and Joseph Raz's.[27] One of these features lies in the practical source that legal obligation is argued to have in either sense. This is unique to Finnis's legal theory. And it is also conceptually puzzling when read in the context of his study of law. Let me explain.

Even a superficial reading of Finnis's work shows that legal obligation in the legal sense, as Finnis depicts it, is an ordinary practical requirement in every respect except that it owes its distinctiveness to the way its

---

[27] For ease of reference let me concisely introduce the distinctions between a technical sense of legal obligation and a moral sense that have been put forward by Hans Kelsen and Joseph Raz. Kelsen claims that one has a legal obligation to perform a given action 'in so far as the contradictory of that behaviour appears in the legal norm as the condition of a compulsive act, described as the penalty (consequence of tort)' (H. Kelsen, 'The Pure Theory of Law', *Law Quarterly Review*, 50 (1934), p. 495). This is a purely formal characterization of legal obligation, which, unlike moral obligation, does not, in Kelsen's work, have any practical implication and is understood as the formal counterpart to a norm empowering certain individuals – legal officials – to impose sanctions depending on whether or not a course of conduct specified in a legal text is performed. In a critical study of Kelsen's legal theory, Raz introduces the notion of the legal point of view – that of the 'legal man' – to enable one to understand central legal notions, including legal obligation, in a hypothetical sense, or from a detached perspective. A detached statement of legal obligation would inform us on how we ought to behave in accordance with the law. But that is not a first-person practical statement about the way *we* ought to act: it is rather a hypothetical statement about the way one ought to act *if* one accepted the law as an action-guiding institution. Legal obligation, then, can be understood in either a detached sense or a practical one, the former being purely technical and hypothetical, the latter being typically moral. This distinction is discussed at some length in J. Raz, *The Authority of Law* (Oxford, Oxford University Press, 2009, 2nd ed.; 1st ed. 1979), pp. 122–45 and pp. 293–312.

contents are established, namely, by legal institutions rather than by practical rationality at large. Legal obligation in the legal sense, in other words, is genuinely practical – indeed, its nature is *moral*, as it is grounded in a moral value, namely, the common good – and it can be distinguished from other types of geuinely practical (and moral) requirements only on the ground that it would not exist without a legal system that brings it into being. This means that Finnis's distinction does not really set apart (i) a legal provision that, as a moral requirement, is truly practical and so plays a role in shaping one's practical reasoning (legal obligation in the moral sense) from (ii) a purely legal requirement, and so a requirement that is merely internal to a normative system – it is merely intra-systemic – and as such has no impact beyond that system, on one's practical reasoning in general (legal obligation in the legal sense). For Finnis's notion of legal obligation in the legal sense cannot be equated with either of the ideas that are conceptually most akin to it: either the notion of an intra-systemic legal obligation, as theorized by Kelsen, or the detached statement of one's obligations under the law, in Raz's sense. Both of those notions – Kelsen's and Raz's – refer to a meaning of legal obligation that is practically inert, since it is meant to grasp the specific perspective of a lawyer claiming that acting in accordance with the law occasionally requires one to do what all things considered ought *not* to be done. By contrast, in Finnis's legal theory – which is deeply shaped by the view that law is a component of practical rationality and so is an institution that by its very constitution affects one's practical deliberation at large – even legal obligation in the legal sense (and not just legal obligation in the moral sense) has a genuinely practical role to play. In that respect, legal obligations in the legal sense play the same role in our deliberation as legal obligations in the moral sense, in that both are practical through and through.

But now – and this is where the peculiarity of Finnis's distinction looks conceptually puzzling – we can ask whether the original point of the distinction as traditionally drawn by legal theorists (in particular by Kelsen and Raz) is lost in Finnis's alternative framework of thought. The distinction between the two types of obligation pertaining to the law – legal obligation in an intra-systemic sense and moral obligation generated by the law – carries theoretical weight as long as we are seeking to distinguish (a) obligations that are institutionalized through a legal system and have a practical bearing from (b) obligations that exist in law but are practically inert (obligations in an intra-systemic legal sense). This is not Finnis's theoretical objective, though, since in Finnis's legal theory both legal obligation in the legal sense and legal obligation in the moral sense are determinants of practical reasoning. However, insofar as legal obligations in the legal sense and in the moral sense both concur in shaping our practical experience, any distinction between them seems to lack deep theoretical justification. For what is the justification for differentiating between legal obligation in the legal sense and legal obligation in the moral sense once it is claimed that they have the same nature, in that both are practical, and that they have the same scope, in that both concern our (practical) deliberation?

Finnis might reply here that the deep theoretical justification for the distinction lies in the distinctive ways in which the two types of practical requirements have force, which is invariant in one case and variable in the other. Yet this reply would be to no avail, since the distinctive criterion it appeals to does not sit easily with other central claims of Finnis's legal theory. To elaborate, Finnis states that, not unlike moral reasoning, legal reasoning (including legal reasoning that involves obligations) 'derives from and participates in practical reasonableness'.[28] Therefore, in Finnis's framework of thought, practical rationality forms an unbroken normative network, where practical concerns originating in different sources (legal institutions, social practices, morality, etc.) all contribute to determining the conduct that ought to be had all things considered. This means that Finnis's legal theory is premised on the continuity of practical rationality and its requirements, which are understood to constitute the seamless web within which practical deliberation is carried out.[29] On this basis, in Finnis's framework, all three types of 'ought' – prudential, technical, and moral – stand in a relation of continuity that secures their mutual influence and interaction.

Now, it is not clear how this conclusion can be reconciled with what I will be referring to as the 'thesis of the exclusionary nature of legal

---

[28] Finnis, *Philosophy of Law*, p. 215.

[29] Statements of this position can be found at several places in Finnis's work. Paradigmatic in this sense is Finnis's claim that 'both legal philosophy and political philosophy are parts of aspects of a wider enterprise, no part of which can safely be pursued without some attention to the others and to the character of the whole. That wider enterprise can be characterized as Aristotle does: "philosophy of public affairs". Or, more pointedly, as Aquinas does: the study of human action as self-determined and self-determining' (Finnis, *Philosophy of Law*, p. 111). In a similar vein is Finnis's statement that 'the principles of practical reasonableness and their requirements form one unit of inquiry that can be subdivided into "moral", "political", and "jurisprudential" only for a pedagogical or expository convenience' (Finnis, *Natural Law and Natural Rights*, p. 359).

obligation', which on the premise of the invariant force of legal obligation in the legal sense argues that legal obligation in that sense operates in the same fashion as an exclusionary reason. The thesis of the exclusionary nature of legal obligation means that legal obligation in the legal sense is protected from the force of countervailing and potentially conflicting demands arising from other branches of practical rationality – that is the ultimate justification for the invariant force of legal obligation in the legal sense. Which view in turn frames general practical reasoning as a compartmentalized domain consisting in subsets that are *not continuous* with one another, in that each different instantiation of practical rationality has its own sphere of competence, where it exclusively shapes practical reasoning without interference, thus blocking, or excluding, considerations coming from other subsets of practical rationality.

Apparently, this conception of practical rationality – on which each specific instantiation of practical rationality has its own scope, within which it has exclusive jurisdiction – is far from theoretically meaningless. Still, in the context of Finnis's legal theory, it proves to be a problematic claim, for it seems inconsistent with Finnis's view that practical rationality is continuous and that practical deliberation at large is internally unbroken. Namely, insofar as we accept that different branches of practical rationality govern discrete domains and those domains are insulated from one another (as per Finnis's thesis of the exclusionary nature of legal obligation), we end up with a conceptual framework in which practical rationality is *not* a seamless whole. Indeed, on the construction built around the thesis of the exclusionary nature of legal obligation, practical rationality is a fragmented territory, whose requirements– namely, the claims made by the different instances of practical rationality – are mutually independent: each of them governs a different sphere, such that any possible conflict between them is unreal and can be dissolved simply by switching from one perspective, or point of view, to another. Which conclusion is in effect a straightforward denial of the thesis of the continuity of practical rationality.

To put it the other way around, if legal obligation in the legal sense is an ordinary practical requirement – its only peculiarity consisting in its being engendered by the law (which in turn is a particular instantiation of general practical rationality) – it should be regarded as a form of obligation that occupies the same practically deliberative space that is inhabited by all other practically rational requirements. Accordingly, all the forms of practically rational deliberation involving legal obligation are to be understood as making up a single undifferentiated domain, namely, a continuous and seamless web: practical reasoning. On this ground, they should all legitimately be expected to shape practical deliberation in the same fashion. Which means that legal obligations in the legal sense cannot be insulated from the unrestricted flow of practical reasoning.

What can be objected to Finnis's treatment of legal obligation, therefore, is that it tries to weave together two views that, at a foundational level, can hardly be shown to be compatible. On the one hand, Finnis is committed to the view that legal obligations in the legal sense and the obligations generated by other instantiations of practical rationality (and so legal obligation in the moral sense, too) both involve our deliberation on how we ought to act: the various obligations we experience are part of the same landscape, as it were – that of practical reasoning – and so are distinguished for expository convenience only. On the other hand, Finnis sets legal obligation in the legal sense radically apart from the obligations set out by other instantiations of practical rationality, prominent among which is legal obligation in the moral sense. From this construction he derives the view of the invariant force and exclusionary character of legal obligation in the legal sense. But this view makes legal obligation in the legal sense heterogeneous when compared to other types of practical requirements and obligations, since the logic by which one is governed is incompatible with the logic by which the others are governed. Which leaves us with an unstable combination of views, since one element of the combination is grounded in an assertion of the continuity of practical rationality, while the other is justified only if we argue for a clear-cut distinction – and so a radical discontinuity, not just an internal differentiation – between the subsets practical rationality internally consists of.

The two views therefore cannot be simultaneously endorsed without making their combination unstable, for if we theorize legal obligation in the legal sense and legal obligation in the moral sense to be radically distinct kinds – as Finnis does when he characterizes the former as having invariant force and the latter as an obligation of variable force – we wind up ultimately charging them with governing two distinct and discrete subdomains of practical rationality. Accordingly, practical rationality cannot be presented as a unitary realm, as Finnis's statement of the continuity of practical rationality instead suggests. For Finnis's account of legal obligation in the legal sense can be argued to feed into a picture that decouples legal reasoning from general practical reasoning. Which picture is at odds with his claim of the continuity of practical rationality, a claim that in this way ends up being replaced by a framework making legal thought and reasoning impermeable, autonomous, and isolated from other forms of practical thought and reasoning.

Thus far I have suggested that Finnis's theoretical framework is shaped by claims that presuppose mutually incompatible pictures of practical reasoning. This conclusion may be taken to suggest that a sound explanation of legal obligation can be secured by giving up either of the two basic claims Finnis defends. This suggestion, however, is too quick, as it does not take into careful account the argument that Finnis deploys to ground the ability of law to impose obligations. That argument is revealing of the fact that the statement of the continuity of practical rationality is more fundamental than the thesis of the exclusionary nature of legal obligation, and so that it cannot be abandoned without calling for a deep revision of Finnis's theoretical framework. The argument thus seems to force us to abandon the claim that legal obligation in the legal sense has invariant force and is shaped in accordance with the paradigm of exclusionary reasons.

To elaborate on this point, recall that law is understood by Finnis as an institution that can impose obligations by virtue of its being functional to the achievement of the common good. In the absence of law, Finnis claims, the members of a community could not coordinate their efforts, and as a result they would be unable to effectively pursue the common good. Since the common good should, in this context, be understood as a moral value, it follows that in Finnis's legal thought the obligatory force of law stands on moral foundations. At the core of Finnis's legal construction, then, we find the idea that the capacity of law to generate obligations (in the legal and moral sense alike) is ultimately owed to sources that are moral. Likewise, morality and its requirements can be claimed to occupy the ground layer of Finnis's overall legal-theoretical construction. But then, how can one who accepts these theoretical premises support the conclusion that legal obligation in the legal sense is insulated from the general flow of practical reasoning, a central component of which is moral reasoning? Insofar as the ability of law to impose obligations is ultimately grounded in moral considerations, legal obligation in *any* of its senses must be recognized to be at bottom moral. We accordingly need to abandon the claim that legal obligation in the legal sense is a morally neutralized kind of obligation, namely, an obligation whose force is invariant and, within its scope, insensitive to any countervailing moral consideration. The thesis of the exclusionary nature of legal obligation thus proves to be untenable. Which conclusion is justified by an argument that can be summarized as follows: moral considerations provide the foundation for the obligation-generating capacity of law (as conceived by Finnis); ergo, legal obligation cannot be considered impermeable to moral considerations, since by construction – namely, by virtue of their foundational role in Finnis's framework – moral considerations are always in a position to feed back into a legal obligation, and even to displace it if it should turn out to be morally unwarranted.

The conclusion that legal obligation (even in the legal sense) is intrinsically open to moral considerations can be so rephrased. Finnis claims that legal obligation in the legal sense is governed by the logic of exclusionary reasons, and thus is separate from the unrestricted flow of practical reasoning. However, in his framework, the conceptual independence that legal obligation in the legal sense enjoys from legal obligation in the moral sense, and so from the unrestricted flow of practical reasoning, is ultimately supported by moral considerations. What makes the insulation of legal obligation in the legal sense necessary – what explains its ability to necessarily prevent the unrestricted flow of practical reasoning from filtering in – is its moral purpose. From which it follows that the capacity of law to impose obligations owes its rationale and its justification to the moral aim to which law is functional. In this picture, the value of law is measured by the value of the moral ends it helps us achieve, since law would not have any *raison d'être* but for the ultimate moral goal it serves, and its obligation-imposing quality would be unjustified but for the essential service it *alone* offers in enabling us to achieve this goal. This feature makes law closely dependent on the moral end to which it is instrumental. Finnis's reasoning, in other terms, frames the law as a merely intermediate good, which as such is only partly autonomous from the moral aim it is meant to (contribute to) achieve. Because law and its requirements are dependent on practical values and principles having a more fundamental status – these are the values and principles constitutive of the common good – law and the obligations deriving from it (including legal obligations in the legal sense) cannot be claimed to enjoy any absolute independence from those basic practical values and principles.

Therefore, if we understand law as a necessary condition for the achievement of the common good, as Finnis does, we will have to acknowledge that legal obligation in the legal sense has only a limited autonomy from the practical values and principles forming the core of the law. As a product of the law – which is framed by Finnis as a means to an intrinsic moral value, namely, the common good – legal obligation in the legal sense is only partially independent and partly separate from the moral considerations that define the common good. Just like any other means – which can always be checked against their justificatory ends, on which they constitutively depend – the requirements of law remain open to clarification, revision, and fine-tuning in light of the moral values and principles that supply the foundation for law's obligation-imposing capacity. That is to say, the instrumental status of the law ultimately delimits as well the autonomy of its obligation-setting provisions and makes these constitutively open to influence from the intrinsically valuable standards that justify them. And that is why legal obligation – even when understood in the legal sense – can never gain complete independence from the moral considerations that justify the establishment of a legal system as an obligation-imposing institution. Having no justification in itself, legal obligation in the legal sense cannot but retain some connection with the moral values and principles in which the obligatory dimension of law is grounded. So legal obligations in the legal sense are only *to some extent* independent from the substantive principles and values law programmatically supports. Stated otherwise, as long as law cannot claim any intrinsic value and borrows its value from the ability to promote the common good, its obligation-imposing norms will not be able to exclude extralegal considerations at large from practical deliberation, at least not *entirely* and *definitively*. It will only be able to sum them up. And it will be able to do so only provisionally and temporarily, since obligation-imposing legal directives retain, at a deep and essential level, an intimate connection with their underlying moral justification. By the same token, there are moral considerations that, owing to their intrinsic value, can at any time be resurrected and used in support of, or against, the claims the law makes on us. Relatedly, there is no way that we can completely divorce obligation in the legal sense from the underlying extralegal considerations (most notably the moral considerations) that give point and substance to the ability of law to impose obligations.

The thesis that legal obligation in the legal sense is radically independent from moral considerations, such that the two are mutually opaque, therefore, remains unwarranted. This thesis requires an argument showing that legal requirements are ends in themselves. But this argument cannot be coherently provided in Finnis's framework. To put it the other way around, the requirements of law cannot conclusively be argued to have an absolute insulation from extralegal considerations, unless those requirements can be shown to have an original value that does not derive from such moral considerations and is not dependent on them. Because Finnis understands the law as having a derivative value – its value being dependent on law's capacity to foster the common good – then, there is no conclusive argument that he can use to secure the fundamental independence of the requirements issued by the law. As a result, Finnis only justifies the conclusion that legal obligation in the legal sense is *relatively* and *functionally* independent – rather than absolutely and categorically independent – from the moral principles and values that define the common good by thus also grounding the ability of law to impose obligations. Which is why Finnis's attempt at rescuing legal obligation in the legal sense from the influence of extralegal considerations – such that legal obligation in the legal sense is completely insulated from other demands of practical rationality in general and from the demands of morality in particular – is unsuccessful.

In sum, the limited separation of law from non-law that Finnis's approach can establish lacks the resources needed to support the thesis that legal obligation in the legal sense operates in the same way as exclusionary reasons do. The logic of exclusion presupposes a radical separation of law from non-law. However, in Finnis's jurisprudence the separation of law and non-law as well as the distinction between legal obligation in the legal sense and the moral considerations that ground the ability of law to give rise to obligations is no more than partial. Which is why the relation between these two types of standards cannot be exclusionary: it is instead dialectical. Dialectical relations hold between entities that are distinct but intermingled, meaning that they can neither be fully equated nor radically insulated. A dialectical relation presupposes a mutual permeability of standards, that is, the possibility of communication and interchange among standards. The relationship between legal obligation in the legal sense and extralegal considerations is precisely a dialectical one of permeability and interchange. Therefore, Finnis's appeal to the logic of exclusion is ill-placed in such a context and should yield to a reliance on dialectics.

Crucially, this conclusion should not be taken to mean that the use of obligation-imposing legal norms *requires* making reference to moral considerations. Quite the opposite: norms that set legal obligations can very well be occasionally used *without* recourse to moral considerations. But this possibility – of using obligation-imposing legal norms without invoking any underlying moral justification – should not be taken to mean that the two standards (obligation-imposing legal norms and moral principles) are fully cut off from each other: they are not. What it means is that obligation-imposing legal norms are *relatively* opaque to moral justifications, as well as *partly* independent from them and *partly* autonomous. Communication therefore does take place between the two standards, which is exactly what the dialectical approach counts on and what sets it apart from the exclusionary approach: while dialectics has no need to deny that the different standards of practical reasoning enjoy some autonomy, the exclusionary logic turns this possibility into a requirement – not simply *allowing* a use of obligation-imposing legal norms that is independent of moral considerations, but *requiring* such a use.

6.4 A Reply to My Criticism

In reply to the point just made – that legal obligation in the legal sense cannot be rigidly cut off from legal obligation in the moral sense, as both are species of a single kind – it might be argued that autonomy from other systems of social governance is essential where law is concerned. There are at least two ways that this argument might be made. First, one may want to deploy an argument designed to show that law is *conceptually* separated from other normative frameworks originating in practical rationality, including morality.[30] Here, the dichotomy between law and legal obligation in the legal sense, on the one hand, and morality and legal obligation in the moral sense, on the other, is introduced as an essential element of the conceptual specificity of both law and the obligations it gives rise to. On this view, it is the very concept of law that dictates the distinction between the legal and the moral sense of legal obligation. But this argumentative strategy can be ruled out straightaway in this context because Finnis's legal-theoretical project is incompatible with the conceptual separation of law, on the one hand, and morality and practical rationality, on the other. For Finnis theorizes a concept of law that explicitly incorporates moral considerations, in the form of an appeal to the common good, thereby conceiving law, at least in its central case, as a morally coloured institution.[31] And this is why Finnis cannot avail himself of this argument.

---

[30] This argument has been explored in detail by the exclusive strand of legal positivism. See, for instance, J. Raz, *Ethics in the Public Domain: Essays in the Morality of Law and Politics* (Oxford, Clarendon, 1994), pp. 199–204.

[31] See, for instance, Finnis, *Natural Law and Natural Rights*, pp. 276–81.

The second way in which one might reply to my criticism is on the basis of a *moral* argument, using moral considerations to support the autonomy of law and the strict separation of legal obligation in the legal sense from legal obligation in the moral sense. On this argument, the isolation of law from non-law is not a function of the *concepts* needed to correctly understand the legal domain: it is rather primarily a *morally* justified thesis. This argumentative strategy is coherent with Finnis's legal thought, and so it needs to be explicitly addressed in this section, where I provide a concise statement of the moral argument for the separation of law from non-law (in one of the versions the argument can take) and then present a counterargument.[32]

The argument stresses that legal systems play an essential role in society in that they are uniquely suited to providing stable mechanisms for social coordination, which should in turn be regarded as a valuable state of affairs. The point thus made is twofold. On the one hand, social coordination is deemed essential as a precondition for pursuing objectives that can be achieved only by collective effort – it is in particular the common good of a community that cannot be achieved without social coordination. On the other hand, law is the normative framework that more efficiently and fairly than any other mechanism can advance the purpose of promoting social coordination, thus enabling a community to pursue its common good. However, the argument continues, this feature of law – its being uniquely functional to social coordination as a precondition for achieving the common good – is owed to traits that are specific to law itself, namely, the positivity, determinacy, conclusiveness, and ease of identification of legal provisions. This is to say that law is distinctively positioned to secure social coordination and so is genuinely functional to the achievement of the common good, but only so long as the contents of law can be traced to predetermined and easily identifiable practical norms – statements about courses of conduct that may or may not or must or must not be performed – and only on condition that these statements are issued by lawmaking institutions and are consistently enforced, if necessary by recourse to coercive measures. In turn, the only way legal norms can have these traits – positivity, determinacy, conclusiveness, and ease of identification – is if

---

[32] The version of the argument presented here is derived from the remarks on Finnis's thesis of the isolation of law offered in M. Köpcke Tinturé, 'Finnis on Legal and Moral Obligation', in J. Keown and R. George (eds.), *Reason, Morality, and Law* (Oxford, Oxford University Press, 2013), pp. 384–9.

law and its requirements are radically separated from extralegal domains and from the ensuing obligations.

In other words, if law were not autonomous from practical rationality in general and morality in particular, each of those traits would be in jeopardy: (a) the positivity of law would be weakened, since rational principles and moral considerations do not necessarily result in human acts, stipulations, and social practices; (b) the determinacy of legal norms would be undermined, especially if practical rationality and morality are conceived as sets of general principles and values that cannot be made operative unless they undergo some process of specification, which cannot be completely fixed in advance; (c) it would not be easy to identify the contents of law, because practical rationality and morality are highly controversial and debatable practices; (d) finally, those contents could not be conclusive, for the outcome of practical reasoning and moral deliberation are structurally revisable and so constitutively *inconclusive*.

Therefore, the argument concludes, if we value the function law plays in fostering social coordination, thus enabling a community to pursue its common good, law should be kept rigidly apart from non-law. For the same reason, obligation-setting legal norms should be understood in terms of exclusionary reasons for action, namely, requirements that, in contemplation of law, cannot be outweighed or otherwise defeated by extralegal considerations. On this basis, the black-and-white, or invariant, force of legal obligation in the legal sense can be said to be demanded by the very role law is entrusted with in society, a role that by stipulation is moral.

To this argument I would object that it is premised on an artificial and ultimately untenable radicalization of the distinction between law and non-law: the argument turns the distinction between the legal domain and the extralegal realm into a downright separation between radically heterogeneous entities, whereas that distinction, I submit, is best rendered as one of degree as we move between subsets within the continuous whole which is practical rationality. Before I substantiate this claim, however, I should like to acknowledge the good sense of the argument I am reacting to.

It is hardly deniable, I believe, that social coordination (and so the pursuit of the common good) is significantly furthered by a reliance on a stable normative framework. Also sensible is the claim, defended by the proponents of the argument at issue, that in complex societies inhabited by individuals who do not necessarily share worldviews and life projects, the introduction of some institutionalized normative arrangement for governing social interactions is not just valuable but indeed essential. But two points need to be made here, and this is where my disagreement begins. For one thing, we should not overstress the degree of positivity, determinacy, conclusiveness, and ease of identification that is required for such an institutionalized normative arrangement to perform its essential function. And, for another thing, even a radical separation of law and non-law cannot secure an absolute (or quasi-absolute) degree of positivity, determinacy, conclusiveness, and ease of identification of the obligation-setting norms of law, as the advocates of separation seem to imply.

As to the first point, it is true that, other things being equal, the more positive, determinate, conclusive, and easily identifiable a normative framework is, the more stability, predictability, and certainty it can secure. And a maximally stable, predictable, and certain arrangement is well suited to reinforcing social expectations, which in turn can help social coordination. But social coordination can be achieved even without a maximum degree of stability, predictability, and certainty. Likewise, even less-than-absolute stability, predictability, and certainty are compatible with a sound system of social interactions. In fact, acting under conditions of uncertainty is a condition humans ordinarily experience and accommodate, considering that much of their practical existence cannot be predetermined, or fixed in advance. And yet, despite that fact, human beings manage not only to act as individuals but also to coordinate action as members of social groups that are variable in their composition, indeterminate in their scope, and open-ended in their objectives. That is to say, most humans have an ability to navigate conditions of uncertainty and deal with instability and unpredictable states of affairs, both as individuals and as members of a community. Which is why social interaction is not only possible but can also flourish under conditions of uncertainty. So while law – as a system of positive, determinate, conclusive, and easily identifiable norms – may be able to advance social cooperation, this capacity is neither exclusively nor mainly owed to its capacity to contribute to stability, predictability, and uncertainty in the practical domain.

As to the second point, even when law is completely isolated from morality, it can hardly be understood as a maximally stable normative framework for ensuring full predictability and complete certainty in social relations. Controversies are far from exceptional under a system of law: even legal officials and practitioners genuinely disagree about the contents of legal norms and the way disputes ought to be legally settled.

The determinacy of law may be comparatively higher than that of rationality and morality, at least in certain areas, but it is neither absolute nor quasi-absolute. Similarly, in some areas, it is more myth than fact that law can be identified with ease.[33] Legal systems face complex social challenges in a rapidly changing world, and as a result they are not of necessity structurally able to provide straightforward and clear-cut practical instructions in all cases. For this reason, even experienced legal professionals may be at a loss to find the one right answer to a legal issue. Accordingly, while we can all agree that the effort to identify a morally correct answer to practical dilemmas more often than not ends up in controversy, it is likewise unrealistic to depict law as a normative framework consisting in a set of easily identifiable norms giving conclusive answers to practical disputes. The differences between legal systems and moral systems can thus be radicalized only at the cost of seriously misrepresenting the ordinary functioning of law.

These remarks, taken together, are meant to put into perspective the role that the positivity, determinacy, conclusiveness, and ease of identification of legal provisions plays in social coordination. The law is certainly characterized by a *significant* degree of positivity, determinacy, conclusiveness, and ease of identification, and these features all play some part in enabling the law to serve as a device for the collective pursuit of the common good. But whether legal arrangements can secure social coordination, and hence the common good, is not predicated on law's possession of a *maximum* degree of positivity, determinacy, conclusiveness, and ease of identification. Indeed, on the one hand, social coordination can be achieved even without an absolutely determinate and conclusive system of easily identifiable positive norms, and, on the other hand, even when law is kept strictly separated from non-law, it could not be adequately described as such a system. This calls into doubt the proposition that law can secure social coordination only so long as it is kept rigidly apart from non-law.

In addition to these general considerations in support of the view that law and non-law need not be rigidly separated in order for law to be able to play its distinctive role in promoting social coordination, there is also a specific reason for rejecting the radical insulation of law. This is a reason closely related to Finnis's framework of legal thought. So far I have

---

[33] Examples of this phenomenon abound in (certain subfields of) private international law, which originates in different domestic legal systems and may also contain provisions issued by international lawmaking or rule-making bodies.

emphasized the effectiveness of law as a means to the common good. But effectiveness is far from the only criterion that matters in that regard. As Finnis himself acknowledges, the law is not merely an *effective* means through which we can pursue an intrinsically valuable end – the common good – but also a *fair* method that can be used to that end, in that the law minimizes the role that arbitrary and partisan considerations can play in our pursuit of valuable ends.[34] If, in seeking to foster social coordination and pursue the common good, we value the law over other devices (such as propaganda or manipulation of the social environment), we do so in large part because, unlike propaganda or manipulation of the social environment, the law can be understood as a fair or just method of governing social interaction. It is the perceived fairness or justice of law, and not merely its effectiveness, that makes it a valuable, and indeed indispensable, mechanism for pursuing the common good.

Now, it seems to me that this dimension – fairness or justice – can wind up being drastically compressed, or even altogether annihilated, if we embrace a rigid separation of law and non-law. For however justice may be specifically defined, the idea of justice is essentially built around moral principles: basic moral standards or notions of the good are constitutive of the very idea of justice and help to define it. But, insofar as a rigid separation is maintained between law and non-law, the latter of which includes morality, law will be isolated from the basic moral values that contribute to the justice of a legal arrangement. As a result, regardless of how effective law may prove to be in the pursuit of the common good, the value of law as a *justified* and essential means to an intrinsically valuable end – the common good – is severely diminished. At the same time, we lose the distinction between law and other possible means of social coordination, at least in part.

True, one should not overstate this point. The relation between law, morality, and fairness is complex and may go in different directions. To some extent, the very elements that may be argued to mark out law as distinct from non-law – namely, positivity, determinacy, conclusiveness, and ease of identification – also contribute to the justice of a system of laws. After all, the fairness of a system of social governance can be constrained (even considerably) by its lack of stability, predictability, and certainty. To some extent, then, stability, predictability, and certainty

---

[34] See, for instance, Finnis, *Philosophy of Law*, pp. 62–6, where it is explicitly claimed that in communities made up of a vast and complex set of individuals and transactions, only a system of laws can promise a *fair* method for dealing with issues of social coordination.

can be argued to be essential elements of fairness, since an unstable, unpredictable, and uncertain normative system is at least presumptively unfair. But that is not to say that the justice of a normative system can be reduced to its stability, predictability, and certainty: that would come at the cost of drastically impoverishing the notions of fairness and justice. Indeed, a normative framework that should constantly prioritize stability, predictability, and certainty over any other demand and aspiration would almost unavoidably end up failing to meet fundamental criteria of justice. This is because, in order for a normative system to be stable, predictable, and certain, it has to largely rely on general norms. And general norms are constitutively both over- and underinclusive when assessed against an ideal of justice.

So, on the one hand, general norms tend to cover too much ground – this is the overinclusivity of such norms – thus setting out normative standards that may well prove to be unjustified in particular cases. Take, for example, a general rule that dogs are not admitted into restaurants, so as to ensure a quiet or formal dining environment. As sensible as this rule may be on the whole, it would be overinclusive if it meant that even guide dogs are barred from access with their owners, in which case it would also be unjust.[35] On the other hand, general norms may also fail to cover cases that are relevantly similar to those they explicitly govern. In this circumstance the norm may be considered underinclusive, thus generating unjustifiable discriminations among cases that bear a strong analogy. For example, a legal norm prohibiting people from driving vehicles in a park may be argued to be defective in this sense, for it fails to prohibit other equally annoying or dangerous activities from taking place in the same area.[36]

In sum, the complexity and peculiarity of specific cases that may render general norms either overinclusive or underinclusive are such that a reliance on such norms is constitutively incapable of securing justice. So, insofar as we consistently prioritize the stability, predictability, and certainty of the legal system, as those are secured by the reliance on general norms, we end up compromising its fairness, at least to some extent. Correspondingly, because no legal system can really be described

---

[35] I borrow this example from F. Schauer, *Playing by the Rules* (Oxford, Clarendon, 1991), pp. 17–37, where it is discussed at some length in connection with the generalizing dimension of certain standards.

[36] A variant of this norm has been famously introduced in the legal-theoretical debate in L. Fuller, 'Positivism and Fidelity to Law', *Harvard Law Review*, 71 (1958), pp. 661–4.

as fair unless it agrees with moral standards (these standards, in other words, figure as defining elements of the idea of justice), the moment we radically dissociate law from non-law and legal obligation in the legal sense from legal obligation in the moral sense, we have thereby undermined the ability of a system to count as a fair method for securing social coordination and as a just device for the achievement of the common good. Especially in Finnis's legal thought, we can hardly overemphasize the important role that considerations of justice play in shaping the identity and the boundaries of the legal domain. The thesis that legal obligation in the legal sense cannot be unqualifiedly separated from legal obligation in the moral sense therefore finds solid support in the claim that if law is to play the essential role Finnis acknowledges it to play in a distinctive, specifically legal fashion, it needs to be not only stable, predictable, and certain but also just. And justice is not a value that can be sought unless moral principles are taken into account and incorporated into the legal system.

The previous remarks should not be taken to mean that it is pointless to keep law and legal obligation apart from non-law and non-legal obligation. It *is* useful to distinguish legal obligation in the legal sense from legal obligation in the moral sense, but not for the purpose of arguing that rational and moral requirements have nothing to do with legal requirements. However, that is precisely the radical separation that Finnis draws, and this is where I disagree with his project. For, as I would argue, Finnis unwarrantedly radicalizes what are otherwise undeniable differences between rational and legal obligations. As much as these two kinds of obligation may be distinct, they bear a relation of interchange, permeability, and continuity; that is, they stand in a dialectical relation, and so a relation that is neither one of identification nor one rigid separation in an exclusionary sense. This applies as well to the relation between what Finnis calls legal obligation in the legal sense and legal obligation in the moral sense. They *are* distinct, to be sure, but as different *species* of a single kind, rather than as fully independent *kinds* (as Finnis instead claims).

This last point can also be stated in positive terms. From the argument just offered, it follows that the relation between legal and non-legal obligation (the latter inclusive of rational obligation and moral obligation, too) should be qualified dialogical and 'non-deferential'. By this I mean that extralegal considerations bear on the force of legal obligation even when legal obligation is understood in the legal sense. In acknowledging a legal obligation, we are not *necessarily* or *invariably* bound to do what is demanded by a set of legal norms. The claims the law makes on those who are subject to it cannot be taken lightly, to be sure; but this is not to say that we are thereby prevented from considering their moral soundness. A dialogical and non-deferential model of legal obligation, vis-à-vis an exclusionary model, enables us to judge legal requirements in light of the basic non-legal, or generally practical, principles that justify recourse to the law in the first place. On this model, our practical reasoning as legal subjects relies on the judgement of others – those who hold legal authority. But such reliance is not complete and so does not amount to blind deference; it rather comes with a critical attitude: a willingness to evaluate the reasons in support of the authoritative judgements we are subject to.[37] In other words, legal obligation remains defeasible even when understood in a strictly legal sense; and just because it is legal in that sense, it does not follow that we must thereby relinquish all moral judgement once and for all. Subjecting ourselves to a legal obligation simply means that we temporarily suspend our moral judgement and accept the authoritative judgement of law. In so doing, we relate to legal obligation in such a way as to retain an ability to monitor the soundness of legal requirements in light of extralegal considerations.

This statement may seem blunt, and so a final caveat is in order. The account I have sketched out should be rephrased as follows. Only as a systemic artifice – a seamless web, in Finnis's words – can the law serve the function of ensuring social cooperation, thus furthering the common good. So it is in a distinctive way that legal obligations affect our practical reasoning. In contrast to exclusionary requirements, which keep out extralegal considerations, legal obligations come with built-in reasons for action which are rooted in their origin in an authoritative source, and which gain supplemental strength in virtue of that source. Hence, legal obligations cannot be equated with exclusionary commands, for they do not force exclusion. Rather, the operation of legal obligations is akin to that of specifically legal reasons, in that they carry more weight than non-legal obligations and reasons, respectively: they both enjoy a prima facie priority over extralegal considerations.

The justification for this modus operandi in turn lies in the fact that legal obligations differ, not in kind, but only in species from obligations originating in non-legal practices shaped by practical rationality.

---

[37] The dialogical model of legal obligation finds a counterpart in the non-deferential model of authority theorized, for instance, in J. Cunliffe, and A. Reeve, 'Dialogic Authority', *Oxford Journal of Legal Studies*, 19 (1999), pp. 453–65.

Legal obligation is therefore different from but *continuous with* non-legal obligation, for it shapes our practical deliberation, not by restricting the flow of general practical reasoning, but rather by competing with practical reasons originating in non-legal practices from a position of presumptive priority, or prima facie advantage. There is a systematic bias at play here: legal obligations provide reinforced practical reasons that by virtue of their source – the law – will generally outbalance any other reasons that would otherwise apply. So the legal demands will ordinarily as a matter of fact prevail over conflicting non-legal demands. They will do so most of the time, but not always, though. For there will be cases in which the additional strength built into legal obligation will not enable it to outweigh conflicting extralegal considerations, not even within its own sphere of competence. In these cases we have to act contrary to the legal requirements. Clearly, however, the departure will be possible only under very special circumstances. Which is to say that a really strong case will have to be made in order to strike down a legal obligation.

These remarks also show that the force of legal obligations in part depends on their merit. Legal obligations doubtless owe their special force to their source, not to their content: the special binding force of legal obligations comes from the fact that legal obligations are issued by a competent lawmaking body. So merit-related issues will be immaterial most of the time in the ordinary functioning of the law. But none of this should suggest that extralegal considerations are entirely displaced by legal obligation. Even when legal obligation is understood in Finnis's legal sense, it retains a relation to extralegal considerations; so these considerations are never ruled out a priori in an exclusionary fashion. They are always in the background and can at any time be reintroduced and brought to bear directly on the practical reasoning by which we engage with legal obligation. So we can never cut extralegal considerations off, for that would deprive legal obligation of its basis, which is extralegal. By contrast, legal obligation *needs* this basis, for otherwise it would lose its normative anchorage and binding force.

In summary, the positive conclusion supported by the argument presented in this section is that our subjection to a legal obligation is compatible with our use of practical reflection and judgement under that obligation. And this reinforces the point, central to the reason paradigm for the study of legal obligation, that there is a deep connection between obligation (including legal obligation) and the practice of exchanging justificatory, or normative, reasons. The upshot of this construction, then, is that the functioning of legal obligation (even in the legal sense) needs to be framed as a *discursive* relation between law as an obligation-imposing practice and its rational foundations. In this way, legal obligation (even in the legal sense) can be recognized as the outcome of a dialogue, or a dialectical relation, between law and non-law.

6.5 Conclusion

In this chapter, I discussed Finnis's exclusionary legal account of legal obligation, noting that Finnis identifies and radically separates two main senses of legal obligation: a moral sense and a legal sense. Legal obligation in the former sense is a *moral* obligation generated by the law, and its moral foundation is such that it functions as a *defeasible* and *presumptive* requirement to obey the law. What ultimately makes it a *legal* obligation (despite its moral foundation) is that it would not exist to begin with but for the legal system that brought it into being. Legal obligation in the moral sense is then marked by its *variable* force, which cannot be fixed in advance and independently of the context of application. In that also lies its main distinction from legal obligation in the legal sense, which by contrast is either binding or not binding: its force is neither presumptive nor defeasible. At least in contemplation of law, having a legal obligation simply means that one ought to act in accordance with the rules contained in a legal system.

In my discussion I took issue in particular with Finnis's conception of legal obligation in the legal sense, arguing that this notion involves a distortion. Indeed, Finnis recognizes that law is a species of practical rationality and that practical rationality forms a *continuum* (its manifold species differing by degree rather than by kind). As long as law and legal reasoning are conceived as *kinds* of practical rationality and practical reasoning, respectively, any distinction between the requirements issued by the law and those stemming from other instances of practical rationality, such as morality and extralegal practices in general, is to be understood as limited and merely superficial. Whilst this element of legal obligation is clearly acknowledged in Finnis's conception of legal obligation in the *moral* sense, it is completely abandoned when Finnis turns to legal obligation in the *legal* sense. And that is where the distortion comes in. For, in treating legal obligation in the legal sense, Finnis sketches a picture where the separation between legal directives and moral considerations is unbridgeable. This conclusion, I argued, sits poorly with the fundamental claim, explicitly endorsed by Finnis, of the continuity of practical rationality – a domain that comprises both law and morality. As a result, Finnis not only inscribes a fundamental tension into his legal theory but also provides us with a dualistic view of legal obligation. Like any form of dualism, Finnis's dichotomous picture is potentially unstable, since the same idea – legal obligation – is not only given two different interpretations but is also shaped by logics that cannot be harmonized: a dialectical logic, applying to legal obligation in the moral sense, and an exclusionary logic, applying to legal obligation in the legal sense.

My suggestion, throughout this chapter, has been that this tension internal to Finnis's dichotomy can be resolved by giving up the notion of legal obligation in the legal sense. That would make it possible to arrive at a unified view of legal obligation, marking a clear advance over the other accounts championed by contemporary legal theorists. For, by abandoning Finnis's characterization of legal obligation in the legal sense, we can salvage his conception of legal obligation as a kind of obligation *simpliciter*, and hence as a demand that introduces some rational necessity into our legal experience. By combining this element with the emphasis that Finnis places on the relation between legal obligation and practical deliberation – a legal obligation is understood by Finnis as having a role in shaping our deliberation concerning how we ought to act – we can qualify Finnis's conception as a paradigmatic instantiation of the reason account. Moreover, in Finnis's rendering of the reason account, legal obligation is presented as a practical requirement associated with, and indeed grounded in, the existence of a rationally valuable normative framework – law. At the same time, the contents of law are acknowledged to be largely dependent on the will expressed by certain individuals holding institutional positions. Which means that the rationalist component of legal obligation and its voluntarist component both find a place in Finnis's theoretical framework. All these claims are, I think, substantially tenable: any adequate theory of legal obligation should make room for them, and indeed should put them front and centre. Hence, there is much to learn from Finnis's study of legal obligation. Still, as has been argued here, if Finnis's account is to wholly fulfill its theoretical value, it must let go of its flawed conception of legal obligation in the legal sense, along with three related claims that (a) legal obligation embraces two mutually irreducible notions; (b) legal obligation – at least in one of its two senses, namely, the legal sense – is impermeable to considerations originating in other branches of practical rationality and so can be defined in terms of exclusionary reasons; and (c) the force of legal obligation in the legal sense is invariant.[38] And that is precisely what I intend to do in Chapter 7, where I will put forward my own conception of legal obligation, a conception that, whilst indebted to Finnis's view, and to some extent continuous with it, is distinctively shaped by a rejection of his central claims as just introduced.

---

[38] Incidentally, by abandoning this third claim, we will also have to abandon the claim that 'there are no overlapping and conflicting legal duties' (Finnis, *Natural Law and Natural Rights*, p. 311). As Finnis points out, insofar as 'any such overlap would oblige the lawyer to weigh one obligation against the other and to declare the weightier obligation to be the more binding', this claim is strictly connected to the thesis of the 'invariability in the formal force of every legal obligation' (Finnis, *Natural Law and Natural Rights*, p. 311). These claims strike me as controversial and indeed ideological, considering that in legal practice legal obligations occasionally do conflict and overlap. It seems to me, therefore, that it makes sense to abandon these claims. Which would also be a welcome implication of the approach defended in this chapter.

7

A Revisionary Kantian Conception

7.1 Introduction

In this chapter, I intend to provide the outline of a conception of legal obligation that is irreducible to the accounts of the kind of obligation engendered by the law theorized within contemporary legal philosophy. In my effort aimed at constructing a conception that is alternative to the theories of legal obligation currently on offer I will mainly draw on the theses I argued for in the previous chapters. That is to say, the theory of legal obligation set forth in what follows constitutes both a specific instantiation of the general concept of obligation *simpliciter* (as this concept was introduced in Chapter 1) and an attempt to improve upon the views of legal obligation criticized in Chapters 3–6. I will thus start out from a concept of obligation understood as a normative claim in virtue of which we are bound to take some course of action, such that to fail to do so would be to commit a wrong. With this concept in hand – summarizing how a competent user of the term *obligation* would understand the relative concept at its most basic level – I will proceed to specify it into a conception of *legal* obligation, using the *concept* of obligation as the ballast with which to ensure coherence for the conception of legal obligation, while drawing on the critiques offered of the four standard accounts discussed in what precedes and treating the problems detected in them as focus points for identifying the fundamental traits of legal obligation.

In moving towards a comprehensive conceptualization of legal obligation I will then take it to be the case that any sound conception of legal obligation will have to sidestep the shortcomings and avoid the mistakes I argued to plague the contemporary jurisprudential theories of legal obligation discussed in chapters 3 to 6. In a nutshell, therefore, this chapter is meant to substantiate the working hypothesis that a conception of legal obligation can only aspire to be conceptually sound and theoretically adequate if (i) it specifies the basic tenets defining obligation as a concept and, at the same time, (ii) it does not reproduce the mistakes made by the social practice account, interpretivist account, conventionalist reason account, and exclusionary reason account. To put it otherwise, the combination of claims I argued for, in the positive, when defining the concept of obligation and, in the negative, when rebutting the main contemporary theories of legal obligation, constitutes the materials from which in this chapter I intend to construct an alternative conceptualization of legal obligation, which for reasons to be introduced in detail in Chapter 8 is best qualified as a revisionary Kantian conception. The theoretical account I purport to so structure is meant to make explicit the basic traits and presuppositions underpinning the learned understanding of obligation as well as to provide an interpretation of these ideas and presuppositions while arranging them into a coherent framework that applies to the legal domain.

This means that a legal obligation will, among other things, have to be understood as (a) an intrinsically rational demand, (b) equipped with general practical justification, the force of which (c) is variable and (d) constitutively binds every legal subjects in a genuine sense. As the reader will remember, each of these traits that I take here to both provide guidance to and supply constraints on my conception of legal obligation was argued to be an essential component of the idea of obligation engendered by the law in my critical discussions of the accounts theorized in contemporary jurisprudence. The intrinsic rationality of legal obligation (a) was defended in Chapter 5 as against the view, central to Marmor's conventionalist reason account, that legal obligations are merely internal requirements and so possibly, but not necessarily, practically rational demands. The claim that legal obligation is equipped with general practical justification (b) was argued, in Chapter 4, to be theoretically more insightful than the view, championed by the interpretivist account, that grounds legal obligation on the standards defining the political morality of the relevant legal community and so on particular, vis-à-vis general, practical standards of rationality. The thesis that legal obligation has variable force (c) was established in Chapter 6 as against Finnis's exclusionary reason account in accordance to which, by contrast, legal obligation has invariant force, since it is shaped by an exclusionary logic. Finally, the statement that legal obligation constitutively binds every legal subject in a genuine sense (d) was shown in Chapter 3 to be an improvement upon the less than satisfactory picture of legal obligation as a requirement that may well bind just legal officials whilst applying to the rest of the populace in a merely perspectivized sense – a picture that is drawn by the advocates of the social practice account.

Before I engage in this exercise leading to an original conception of legal obligation, a caveat is in order. In the constructive exercise I am about to embark – an exercise that will be shaped by a methodology I call presuppositional interpretation that will be laid out in detail in Chapter 10 – I will enter a partly uncharted territory where theoretical considerations informed by potentially controversial assumptions and claims need be introduced and defended. In contrast to the framework set out in my study of the concept of obligation, then, the approach I will be taking in this chapter is thick and theoretically demanding. That is, it reflects philosophical preferences that, however much they may be rigorously argued and clearly set out, cannot be supported by any logical or otherwise watertight argument. So I neither assert nor expect that the following argument will be found uncontroversial, command general consensus, or reflect the ordinary understanding of legal obligation, as this understanding emerges from the views of legal practitioners and laypeople alike. After all, theoretical statements are by nature highly contentious, and my account of legal obligation is unlikely to be an exception. With this caveat in place, let us proceed in the construction of (what I regard as) a theoretically sound conception of legal obligation.

7.2 Obligation and Reasons

In Chapter 1, I claimed that obligation is widely regarded as a practical and normative notion. Describing obligation as a normative notion, thus locating it within the broader normative domain, means that it will not suffice to frame legal obligation as something that guides conduct. By contrast, the obligations engendered by legal institutions will have to provide guidance in a specific way: by instantiating *reasons* for us to behave as they instruct. This statement is rooted in, and buttressed by, an established approach to the study of normative issues: the approach shaped by what one of its critics refers to as the 'discovery of reasons'.[1] The gist of this approach is summarized in Joseph Raz's claim that 'the normativity of all that is normative consists in the way it is, or

---

[1] J. Broome, 'Reasons', in R. J. Wallace, P. Pettit, S. Scheffler, and M. Smith (eds.), *Reason and Value* (Oxford, Clarendon, 2004), p. 28.

provides, or is otherwise related to reasons'.² On this approach, something is normative in as much as, and because, it provides reasons. Hence the justification of the thesis that the notion of a reason is crucial to our understanding of normativity in general and specific normative notions in particular.

In the context of my study of legal obligation this idea can be worked into a more definite thesis, which I will be calling the 'reasons thesis'. The reasons thesis stands for the claim that reasons are essential to normativity in a constitutive sense, in that they fundamentally establish what it means for something to be normative. In the conceptual framework shaped by the reasons thesis the normative discourse *essentially* consists in reasons given in support of this or that course of conduct. Likewise, a reason is the *fundamental normative concept*, the concept to which any other notion inhering in the normative dimension of human experience must be traced, and in terms of which any other normative notion can ultimately be captured. That is to say, the notion of a reason is not only essential to any adequate conceptualization of what is normative but it is also the basic building block of any normative idea. For all normative concepts can be constructed in terms of the notion of a reason, namely, as a reason of some specific type or as a combination of reasons (possibly of different kinds). By contrast, the notion of a reason cannot be defined in terms of any other normative concept, or combination of normative ideas, since there is no known way of exhaustively characterizing a reason by appeal to other normative concepts or relations. On this basis, a reason is considered the most flexible and normatively basic tool one can resort to in order to define all normative notions. From this theoretical perspective the idea of a reason is normatively basic, or primitive, since it instantiates the simplest, or most elemental and fundamental, normative concept we have experience of.³ This means that,

---

² J. Raz, *Engaging Reason* (Oxford, Oxford University Press, 1999), p. 67.

³ As Thomas Scanlon puts it, a reason is a fundamental notion, since 'any attempt to explain what it is to be a reason for something seems to me to lead back to the same idea: a consideration that counts in favour of it. "Counts in favour how?" one might ask. "By providing a reason for it" seems to be the only answer' (T. Scanlon, *What We Owe to Each Other* (Cambridge (MA), Harvard University Press, 1998), p. 17). Sophisticated arguments for this thesis can be found in Raz, *Engaging Reason*, esp. pp. 67–89; J. Raz, 'Reasons: Explanatory and Normative', in C. Sandis (ed.), *New Essays on the Explanation of Action* (Basingstoke, Palgrave, 2009), pp. 184–202; J. Raz, *From Normativity to Responsibility* (Oxford, Oxford University Press, 2011), pp. 13–101; Scanlon, *What We Owe to Each Other*, pp. 17–77; T. Scanlon, *Being Realistic about Reasons* (Oxford, Oxford University Press, 2014), pp. 1–15, J. Dancy, *Ethics without Principles* (Oxford, Oxford University

for one thing, a reason is not analysable in terms of, or reducible to, other normative concepts – it is a notion that cannot be explained through an eliminative definition – for another, the notion of a reason can be used not only to account for, and shed light on, the other concepts inhabiting the normative domain but also to make all those concepts commensurable by providing a sort of common metric, or basic currency, within the normative sphere.[4]

The endorsement of the reasons thesis carries direct implications for the study of obligation. If we accept that obligation is a practical and normative concept, and that, as such, it belongs to the realm of practical normativity – a realm where nothing becomes normative except through the use of practical reasons (this is the reasons thesis, or rather, its practical instantiation) – then we should be able to conclude that obligations themselves (be they moral obligations, legal obligations, social obligations or else) are essentially practical reasons of some distinctive type.[5] The acceptance of the reasons thesis has, thus, a direct consequence for the conceptualization of legal obligation.[6] Those who endorse

---

Press, 2004), pp. 15–37; J. Dancy, 'Reasons and Rationality', in S. Robertson (ed.), *Spheres of Reasons* (Oxford, Oxford University Press, 2009), pp. 93–112; and D. Parfit, *On What Matters* (Oxford, Oxford University Press, 2011), pp. 31–8. A critic of the reasons thesis is John Broome (J. Broome, 'Normative Requirements', *Ratio*, 12 (1999), pp. 398–419; J. Broome, 'Reasons'), who, by contrast, claims that (a) normativity incorporates features reasons cannot fully account for (his main reference here is the idea of 'normative requirement'), to the effect that our concern with reasons is at least partially distracting; and (b) a reason is a complex, vis-à-vis primitive, notion.

[4] On these points, see also Raz, 'Reasons: Explanatory and Normative', pp. 13–35. This set of claims should not be taken to suggest that a reason stands for a straightforward and non-controversial idea. In contemporary philosophy we find a vast variety of theories of a reason and they offer even radically different accounts of the metaphysical dimension, epistemological nature, and semantic component of what is here referred to as a reason. The implication of what precedes is that the fundamental normative notion is an idea devising a full conception of which is a demanding and potentially divisive task. That is to say, for those who, like me, turn to reasons to explain normativity, the normative is fundamentally shaped by, and can be conceptualized in terms of, a notion that is at one and the same time basic and controversial. What ultimately justifies my acceptance of the reasons thesis, thus, is (not the belief that conceptualizing the notion of a reason is a comparatively uncomplicated job, but rather) the belief that taking any other concept or relation as the elemental and fundamental normative unit would secure us a merely partial, unilluminating, inadequate, or even mystifying picture of the normative realm.

[5] As far as obligation *simpliciter* is concerned, this point is clearly stated in M. Gilbert, *On Social Facts* (Princeton (NJ), Princeton University Press, 1992), pp. 27–30.

[6] I would like to thank Marcus Willaschek for discussing this point with me and providing most valuable insights. If there is any error or shortcoming in this discussion, however, I am entirely responsible for it.

the reasons thesis are committed to acknowledge a conceptually necessary link between legal obligation and practical reasons, to the effect that something can be regarded as legally obligatory only by virtue of its being a reason for action of a distinctive kind. That is, legal obligation rests in an essential way on the use of reasons and it cannot be fully understood unless its indispensable and essential reliance on practical reasons is made apparent.[7] Legal obligation is thus best conceived as an intrinsically rational binding standard: it is a demand that ultimately originates in, and stems from, practical and rational considerations. This statement, as it is derived from the reasons thesis, does not mean that all the legal obligations we experience coincide in content with the requirements of practical rationality, to be sure. It more modestly means that legal obligation deals in rationality and so is affected by concerns that are both practical and rational.[8]

Once we take the reasons thesis as pivotal to our study of the kind of obligation engendered by the law, a correct understanding of the meaning of a practical reason is of paramount importance to the construction of a sound theory of legal obligation. So, also in consideration of the fact that contemporary philosophy offers a range of disparate and often conflicting views of what a practical reason stands for, here it is important to further specify what I mean by practical reason in this work – namely, to indicate how I conceive of a practical reason. In doing so, I will not offer a complete overview of the panoply of existing conceptions of a practical reason, though, because that would take me too far from the immediate task of devising a conception of legal obligation. So instead of taking in the full landscape, I will elaborate on my understanding of the reasons thesis by specifically focusing on the *meaning* of a practical reason, as this meaning is largely fixed by the role practical reasons play in our normative discourse. The treatment that follows can accordingly be described as an introduction to the semantics of a

---

[7] The acceptance of the reasons thesis and its application to the legal domain makes me a 'legal rationalist', in Christopher Essert's jargon, namely, someone 'who holds the view that the law's normativity is to be explained in terms of the law's effect on the reasons of its subjects' (C. Essert, 'Legal Obligation and Reasons', *Legal Theory*, 19 (2013), p. 63 ft. 4).

[8] The claim about legal obligation that the reasons thesis supports is, accordingly, thin, since the reasons thesis alone does not establish which contents legal obligations may have or not have. That is, the reasons thesis is a purely conceptual claim in accordance to which the nature of legal obligation is shaped by practical reasons and so bears the mark of practical rationality.

practical reason. It is therefore a circumscribed introduction to, not a full explanation of, a practical reason.[9] Nonetheless, I take it to be sufficient to the limited purposes of the argument deployed later in this chapter.

By a practical reason, in the current debate, is generally meant any consideration that supports, or counts in favour of, some course of action. Such a supporting, or favouring, consideration can in turn be understood in any of three ways, namely, as something that attempts to (a) *justify* some act, that is, rationalize it or show why it is a good action or the right or proper thing to do; or (b) *motivate*, or drive, someone to do something; or (c) *explain* why somebody did, or would do, something. Practical reasons, then, can be grouped into three classes, depending on whether they are meant to serve as justifications, as motivations, or as explanations.[10] Let us briefly consider these three classes in turn.

(a) Practical Reasons as Justifications

A practical reason can stand for a consideration that *justifies* a course of action, that is, it can say why we ought to act that way and not in another way, thus endorsing one line of conduct. A reason so understood is both practical and evaluative. It is practical in the sense that, as Raz frames the idea, it 'gives a point or a purpose to one's action', which accordingly 'is undertaken for the sake of or in pursuit of that point

---

[9] The limited scope of my engagement can be appreciated by considering that different conceptions of a practical reason may well agree on a certain meaning of a practical reason – on its semantics – while diverging in significant, even irreconcilable, ways on its metaphysics and epistemology.

[10] The three classes just mentioned are often reduced to two in the literature: there are (a) reasons that justify, which are referred to as justificatory, justifying, prescriptive, normative, or grounding reasons; and (b) reasons that explain, which are referred to as motivating or explanatory reasons. We can see this, for instance, in J. Dancy, *Practical Reality* (Oxford, Oxford University Press, 2000), pp. 1–25. However, Maria Alvarez has compellingly argued that this twofold distinction arbitrarily conflates reasons that motivate with reasons that explain: this is arbitrary because, as much as a motivating reason may go some way towards explaining someone's behaviour, it is but one ingredient in such an explanation, and so cannot be the explanation itself (see M. Alvarez, *Kinds of Reasons* (Oxford, Oxford University Press, 2010), pp. 33–9). We should not therefore conclude that to show what motivates one to action is what explains that action. Motivating reasons ought to accordingly be kept distinct from explanatory reasons. This enriched threefold taxonomy of action can also be found in P. Hieronymi, 'Reasons for Action', *Proceedings of the Aristotelian Society*, 111 (2011), pp. 409–14. For an introduction to the various kinds of practical reasons, see J. Lenman, 'Reasons for Action: Justification vs. Explanation', in E. N. Zalta (ed.), *The Stanford Encyclopedia of Philosophy* (Spring 2010 ed.), http://plato.stanford.edu/archives/spr2010/entries/reasons-just-vs-expl/.

or purpose'.[11] However, the relevant point, or purpose, is not just *any* point or purpose, but a point, or purpose, understood to have inherent value. And it is in this sense that a justificatory reason also carries evaluative meaning. The point – that is, the reason why we ought to behave as indicated – is understood to be right, valuable, appropriate, or otherwise reasonable. So it carries with it a value judgement introducing the relevant behaviour as sound. A justificatory reason does that by offering a standard of evaluation and correctness, that is, a criterion in light of which we can judge a course of action as having those qualities (its being right, valuable, appropriate, reasonable, and so on) and by virtue of which that course of action can be grounded, or rationalized, that is, shown to be the reasonable, or the right, thing to do, or otherwise shown to be the correct way to conduct ourselves.

(b) Practical Reasons as Motivations

A practical reason can also be understood as meaning what ultimately *drives* action, or what brings us to act in one way rather than another when pondering the question what to do. The interest here is not in justifying a course of action but rather in showing why that course of action was in fact taken or what motivated that course of action. The task at hand is part hermeneutical, part psychological. It is hermeneutical in the sense that we have to interpret agents so as to understand what meaning they themselves attribute to their own practical decisions and ensuing conduct. It is psychological because, from the point of view of the agent we want to interpret, it is a psychological force that ultimately 'tips the scales' in moving one to action. For it is that agent's psychology that makes those reasons operative. So the work we do in providing motivating reasons is twofold: in making sense of an agent's conduct (an interpretive task), we have to step into the agent's shoes to see what it is that holds sway on the agent in driving action (and this must be shown to have psychological force).

(c) Practical Reasons as Explanations

As it is the case with motivating reasons, the purpose of explanatory reasons is not to justify, or ground, a course of action so that one may see that as the reasonable, or the right, thing to do, but rather to inquire into why it is that someone did something. There is however a

---

[11] Raz, 'Reasons: Explanatory and Normative', p. 184.

significant line that separates motivating reasons from explanatory ones. The difference lies in the mode of inquiry: whereas motivating reasons are arrived at through a hermeneutical and psychological investigation aimed at making sense of an agent's performances – meaning that we have to reason from the agent's own perspective and worldview – explanatory reasons are formulated from an outside point of view: that of the inquiring observer who investigates why one would act in a certain way in this or that circumstance. So, unlike a motivating reason, which lays out a sort of narrative by which to make sense of someone's behaviour and see what it was that prompted the agent to so behave, an explanatory reason looks at that behaviour as an *explanandum*: something to be explained in a lawlike manner by pointing out in the *explanans* why people do certain things when certain conditions obtain.

One consequence of this distinction is that an explanatory reason may account for an agent's behaviour by singling out factors the agent may not have been aware of. Which cannot be the case with a motivating reason, whose point is to figure out what the agent was going through, or experiencing, or otherwise how agents explain their own actions to themselves. An explanatory reason can in this sense be said to offer a causal account of action, and since such causes need not be something an agent actually contemplates in deciding what to do – they need not be part of an agent's motivating process – they may include the unconscious forces acting on the agent. So, unlike a motivating reason, which for its accuracy depends on our ability to capture an agent's internal discourse, or flow of consciousness, an explanatory reason will have to take a broader range of factors into account. This may well include the agent's own narrative, but it may equally contradict such narrative by revealing causal forces working in the background unbeknownst to the agent called on to make a practical decision.

7.3 Stringent Quality

I have thus far claimed that practical normativity and so legal obligation, when understood as a specific kind inhabiting the practical and normative domain, rest essentially on the existence of practical reasons and that practical reasons fall into three broad classes as justificatory, motivating, or explanatory considerations. It is now time to take another step forward in clarifying which of the classes, or meanings, of practical reasons can specifically be used to define legal obligation. For not all such classes can be used to that end.

A preliminary move in my argumentative strategy aimed at establishing which of the three meanings of a practical reason singles out the specific part of the normative dimension that is inhabited by legal obligations consists in specifying the kind of normative pressure associated with the existence of an obligation. In conceptualizing obligation *simpliciter*, I argued that the normative pressure attached to obligations is non-trivial, tangible, or noticeable, albeit far from inexorable. Here I will qualify this kind of normative pressure as 'stringent'. And my suggestion is that by looking at the idea of stringency, as this idea is associated with the existence of a legal obligation, we can lay the groundwork for determining which meaning of a practical reason constitutes what is legally obligatory. The question that will be addressed in this section will therefore be: how should the notion of stringency be unambiguously cashed out when applied to legal obligation? This question is important to a theory of legal obligation because stringency is a generic idea that can be inflected and instantiated in different ways in different contexts. Therefore, knowing what precisely is meant by *stringency* (when stringency is applied to the legally obligatory) is a key passage of a sustained argument aimed at establishing how legal obligation ought to be properly conceived.

Now, on the basis of the remarks introduced thus far in this work, certain meanings of *stringency* can be ruled out as inappropriate in connection with the normative pressure associated with legal obligation (even if those meanings are perfectly sound in other contexts). To begin with, when stringency concerns the normative pressure of what is obligatory, it cannot mean that we are thereby left without any practical alternative. Obligations, legal or otherwise, are normative requirements and so, qua normative standards, they may be disregarded as a matter of fact – they do not act as inexorable constraints on action. When we have an obligation to do something, in other words, we are faced not with a practical impossibility to do otherwise, nor even with an ontological or metaphysical impossibility, but with a normative one. For the point of legal obligation – or of obligation *simpliciter*, for that matter – is precisely to make a demand on someone to act in some way *given the practical possibility of their* not *taking the prescribed course of action*. That is, a legal obligation, as a normative demand, can only make sense against a background in which those who are subject to it can choose to violate it.

Without that option, the obligation loses its normative status: it can no longer be recognized as an obligation; it simply becomes the only available course of action, in a conceptual space in which it thereby sheds its stringency.

Nor does stringency, on this conception, mean that legal obligation will always trump other (non-obligatory) normative standards designed to guide practical action. These may well prevail over legal obligations depending on the force of the reasons by which they are backed up. Just as the stringency of an obligation (legal or otherwise) conceptually rules out the practical impossibility of acting in ways other than what the obligation itself requires, so it cannot be equated with the notion of overridingness. In case of normative conflicts, legal obligations neither necessarily nor automatically prevail over non-obligatory standards providing guidance in the practical domain. In ordinary circumstances it may well be legitimate to depart from what is legally obligatory, should such departure be supported by normative considerations of other, non-obligatory, kinds that are strong and important enough to defeat the legal obligation at stake. That is to say, overridingness is not a feature inscribed into the idea of legal obligation as a stringent standard applying a normative kind of compulsion on us: it is not a conceptual property of what is legally obligatory to command absolute allegiance in the sense that performing an act in breach of what an obligation requires, in order to abide by another, non-obligatory, standard, is never justified. Likewise, the totality of legal considerations does not always and necessarily favour one's acting in accordance with what a legal obligation demands. True, certain legal obligations can be assumed to be so important that on most occasions they override other normative considerations incorporated in a legal order. But there may also be circumstances in which the non-obligatory normative standards of law prevail over the obligatory ones, since legal obligation is not constitutively supreme. In sum, because one's having a legal obligation, qua a stringently compelling normative principle, does not mean that acting against such obligation, by thus performing some alternative course of action favoured by non-obligatory standards of law, is necessarily an illegitimate move, stringency, as it concerns legal obligation, cannot stand for overridingness.[12]

---

[12] It follows from the foregoing, by way of corollary, that stringency cannot be interpreted as conclusiveness, since legal obligations can be both conclusive, or all-things-considered, requirements and merely presumptive, or prima facie, demands. That is, whilst all legal obligations can be claimed to be stringent, not all legal obligations can be said to be

Nor should the stringency of a legal obligation be understood to mean that failure to comply with it must necessarily be a matter of serious or grave concern. In fact, the law can obligate us to do or abstain from doing things of limited practical import. So one may at least occasionally have a legal obligation to perform, or abstain from performing, something of menial importance, to the effect that the resulting action – by itself an infringement of a legal obligation – should be qualified as a less than serious misconduct. Consider trespass, or the obligation not to enter someone's land without the owner's permission: the doctrine behind this prohibition has a long history – its roots going deep into the currently dominant political ideology of Western societies, namely, liberalism. Yet entering someone's land without the owner's permission, by thus infringing on the legal obligation not to trespass, does not necessarily amount to a fundamental misbehaviour. This is attested, for instance, by the circumstance that trespassing may be instrumental, or even necessary, to rescue a toddler who unwisely and inadvertently happened to crawl there, by so possibly preventing that toddler from suffering harm. And breaching a legal obligation in order to protect a vulnerable being from possible harm can hardly count as a grave transgression of the law, or as a stern legal misconduct. So the obligations that issue from the rule on trespass retain their stringency even if the gravity of the behaviour they seek to prevent can be mild. From which it follows that stringency cannot be taken to be a property that describes the severity of infringing on certain normative requirements – those qualified as obligations.

That, in summary, is what stringency does *not* mean: when a legal obligation is stringent this does *not* mean that it is (i) inviolable (we always have the practical option to act otherwise), (ii) overriding (it may be defeated by other normative standards), or (iii) conclusive (what it prescribes may ultimately not turn out to be obligatory). Nor does it mean that (iv) violations of it are necessarily serious (they may be illegal yet justified on other grounds). Having gone through that list of exclusions, we can now consider what obligation does mean. Here it will be observed that nothing can count as obligatory unless it enjoys some kind of independence from our individual goals, desires, interests, and projects. Accordingly, it can be claimed that the idea of stringency, as it applies to the normative pressure of legal obligation, is to be spelled out in terms of the independence of a certain class of requirements from the

conclusive; therefore, stringency as it applies to obligation is not equivalent to conclusiveness.

subjective states of the individual agents to which those requirements apply. I will thus say that a legal obligation is stringent insofar as what it requires of us is non-hypothetical, or categorical, in the following distinctive sense: obligation binds us regardless of whether we have a personal stake in it, and so it applies to us unconditionally, whether we like it or not.[13]

To briefly expand on this point, stringency qua categoricality, or non-hypotheticalness, is such that a practical requirement qualifies as an obligation if the reason why we should act accordingly is not essentially connected with what we happen to personally prefer, or what we might be naturally inclined to do (for instance, as a matter of particular habit or subjective disposition or by virtue of our individual psychological make-up), or what we might have a personal interest in doing.[14] Accordingly, a categorical requirement is resistant to, and insulated from, the inner states of the specific individuals subject to such requirement. A legal obligation should be considered stringent qua categorical in quality, since the moment we are under an obligation generated by the law we are expected to comply with it – an obligation is a demand bound to be conformed – whether or not doing so comports with or advances our individual plans, objectives, and projects.[15] This means that in the presence of legal obligation we have before us a practical requirement we cannot opt out of for reasons that only apply to us specifically. This idea can be reformulated by saying that our complying with a legal obligation

---

[13] Categoricality, so conceived as a form of non-hypotheticalness, is a notion I borrow from P. Railton, *Facts, Values and Norms* (Cambridge, Cambridge University Press, 2003), pp. 120–3. Categoricality can be described as a humanized and revisited variant of the Kantian idea of the Categorical Imperative.

[14] On this point, see Gilbert, *On Social Facts*, pp. 30–1. A similar claim is made in K. E. Himma, 'The Ties That Bind: An Analysis of the Concept of Obligation', *Ratio Juris*, 26 (2013), pp. 26–30, where this trait of obligation is referred to by the term 'exclusionary'. Despite the different terminologies in use, Kenneth Einar Himma's characterization of legal obligation as exclusionary does not differ from my qualification of legal obligation as a categorical, or non-hypothetical, standard, since for Himma when an exclusionary directive is at stake an agent (A)'s 'desires and prudential interests are generally irrelevant with respect to whether A should perform an act required by a mandatory prescription' (Himma, 'Ties That Bind', p. 27). See also Essert, 'Legal Obligation and Reasons', p. 68 ft. 22), where it is claimed that 'obligation is also generally thought to be categorical such that an agent's being obligated to φ does not depend on her own projects or goals'.

[15] On this aspect of obligation, see also K. Baier, 'Moral Obligation', *American Philosophical Quarterly*, 3 (1966), p. 216; and J. Gardner and T. MacKlem, 'Reasons', in J. Coleman and S. Shapiro (eds.), *The Oxford Handbook of Jurisprudence and Philosophy of Law* (Oxford, Oxford University Press, 2002), pp. 464–70.

is a question of objective necessity and has little to do with what we like or dislike doing: a legally obligatory act is one we are (prima facie) normatively required to do as a matter of practical rationality, no matter what we desire, wish or are inclined to do or are actually committed to doing. Likewise, the specific perspective one has as an individual agent does not exhaust the framework within which legal obligation finds its proper place.[16]

7.4 Obligation and Justification

Once we see legal obligation in this way – namely, as a practical reason enjoying some degree of independence from its addressees' personal preferences, wishes, interests, and plans – it is possible to further specify which class of practical reasons defines legal obligation. For what it means for a reason-like requirement to be obligatory – namely, a stringent qua categorical demand – depends on the degree of independence from individual states that the reason supporting that requirement has.

---

[16] The preceding remarks should not be taken to mean that a legal obligation, with the categorical claim it makes on us, must be acted on, since that would take us to what is *conclusively* binding, vis-à-vis *categorically* binding. What it means to me for a requirement to be stringent qua categorical is not that it must be acted on, regardless of any consideration, but that we cannot 'undo' our obligation for reasons of personal preference or interest. The categorical bindingness of legal obligation may well be presumptive, not final, to be sure. Therefore, an important caveat in thinking about the categoricality of legal obligation is that this idea should not be mixed up with the distinct notion of what is conclusively binding all things considered. This caveat is important especially in the context of a study of obligation informed by a Kantian outlook. For, in Kant's philosophy both the conclusive character of a requirement and its independence of an agent's personal, or contingent, features are grouped under the notion of categoricality. In that respect, therefore, the conception theorized in this chapter departs from Kant's, since, on my view, a practical demand is non-hypothetical if we cannot opt out of it for personal reasons; it is conclusive if it is backed by reasons that on balance trump all other reasons – or can be shown to do so in the course of practical reasoning – and we are therefore expected to comply no matter what. That is to say, in my view (but not on Kant's) a legal obligation can apply to us categorically and still be inconclusive: what makes it categorical is a criterion different from that which makes it conclusive. This means, incidentally, that whereas a categorical demand need not be conclusive, the converse is not also true: a conclusive obligation is thereby also categorical, not only in the sense that we must reason with it from a normative standpoint but also in the more stringent sense that we must comply, as a matter of practical rationality, since the reasons that make it conclusive must be recognized as valid in such a way as to support a proposition we are unconditionally bound to commit to not only in thought but also in action. I thank Marcus Willaschek for bringing this point to my attention. Needless to say, I am entirely responsible for any error or failing in this interpretation of Kant's position.

Hence, it is only insofar as a class of a practical reason can be characterized in terms of its independence – as a class comprising of, and inhabited by, standards of stringent qua categorical character – that one can use a practical reason to define legal obligation (which, to reiterate, stands not just for any requirement but for a categorical demand).

This remark has deep implications, since there are classes of reasons that are established by, or are directly related to, subjective states, contingent personal ends, and undertakings of the relevant agent. As a result, not all kinds of practical reasons partake of the categorical quality. In fact, to begin with, there is a strong presumption that motivating reasons, as personal and psychological considerations, do not have what it takes to make a practical reason non-hypothetical and, hence, unconditionally binding. To see this, we have to critically engage with Jonathan Dancy's contrary claim that at least some motivating reasons are not psychological states.[17] This is relevant because the moment we unhinge motivating reasons from psychological states, we have thereby opened the possibility of making these reasons non-hypothetical, by thus also making them an essential part of obligatoriness. That is, if we identify a motivating reason with something other than a psychological state – for instance, with a fact or a state of affairs – we are in the position to establish a conceptual link between obligation and the class of motivating reason. By contrast, if a motivating reason is identified with a psychological state, it is then impossible to characterize a motivating reason as a reason with categorical force and so as an obligatory standard. For in this case we will not be able to show that such a class can provide support on a non-hypothetical and non-contingent basis. Accordingly, one can define legal obligation in terms of motivating reasons only as long these reasons are predicated not on an agent's psychology (which is contingent) but on certain facts, or states of affairs, having inherent normativity.

But the argument showing how a motivating reason can be anything other than a psychological state looks unconvincing, because there is simply no such thing as a fact, or state of affairs – a non-psychological condition existing out there in the world – that can be pointed out as a motivating reason for action, however obvious or self-evident it may be as such a reason. The point is that this fact, or state of affairs, however straightforward it may be as a motivating reason for action, does not

---

[17] See Dancy, *Practical Reality*, pp. 14–15.

become such a reason until we complete the thought by showing how an agent is to take that fact, or state of affairs, namely, until we spell out the kinds of beliefs and desires needed to act on that fact, or state of affairs, and the frame of mind through which to relate to it. It is therefore fair to say that an agent's beliefs, psychological features, attitudes, interests, and frames of mind play an unavoidable mediating role in establishing what ultimately counts as a motivating reason for action. This mediating role rules out the possibility that a motivating reason can hold categorically. From which it follows that motivating reasons – as reasons whose point would be defeated if they were decoupled from the psychology of action and whose basis lies in a personal view of what is valuable in life – cannot bear any *essential*, or constitutive, relation to legal obligation, at least not when legal obligation is acknowledged to be a stringent qua non-hypothetical requirement.

This conclusion leaves us with only two candidates for the role of a defining element of legal obligation: justificatory reasons and explanatory reasons. However, explanatory reasons can be ruled out straightaway as a defining element of legal obligation, since these reasons are concerned with the *causes* of action – with why an action *is* performed, and not with why a course of conduct *ought to* be engaged in. And the discourse concerned to explain why agents behave the way they behave has little to do with legal obligation, since that kind of discourse is not normative. Accordingly, it is as far removed from the 'ought' of action, which instead is distinctive of what is obligatory, as one can imagine when contemplating action.

From this it follows that the core of legal obligation, qua practical and normative notion, is provided by justificatory reasons. Only justificatory reasons (a) can make something distinctly normative and (b) can do so in such a way as to make it stringent qua categorically binding. Motivating reasons may in some sense succeed in that first role (a), by prompting agents to act in one way or another when faced with a practical decision. But they definitely fail in the second role (b), because that decision cannot be divorced from an agent's psychological make-up and unique system of beliefs and so is contingent, even when felicitously congruent with what turns out to be the normatively validated course of action.

To restate this point, since motivating reasons are reasons which reveal an agent's psychology, personal character, and individual inclinations, they are not specifically designed to bind us regardless of how well we may be disposed towards it or how we may feel in contemplating it. Explanatory reasons, for their part, fail on both counts, for they neither

(a) say how we ought to act nor (b) do they concern themselves with determining whether someone's actions were non-hypothetically right, correct, commendable, appropriate, demandable, reasonable, or what have you. Only justificatory reasons fill both of those seats, which are central to the definition of obligation understood as a practical, normative and stringent qua categorical requirement. For justificatory reasons are the reasons that make an agent's performance acceptable when measured up against certain standards of *correctness*: they are conceptually connected to notions – justification, evaluation, and grounded criticism – that are constitutively normative, as opposed to being cause-shaped and descriptive in the fashion of explanatory reasons. In addition, justificatory reasons grant the possibility that specific instances of practical normativity bind *non-hypothetically*, since justificatory reasons do not make psychology-related features essential to determining what they support as, instead, motivating reasons do. Accordingly, the reference to justificatory reasons has the potential to account for the central aspects of what is (legally) obligatory: its distinctiveness from what is descriptive and its categorical quality.

This argument ultimately grounds the conclusion that legal obligation need be conceptualized as a specific class of reasons – justificatory reasons. Legal obligation, in other terms, is essentially defined by *justificatory* reasons, not motivating or explanatory ones. Namely, the obligatory dimension of certain legal demands depends on the existence of justificatory reasons – the reasons which (have the potential to) make it the case that someone non-hypothetically ought to perform certain actions and refrain from doing something else. This is also how reasons will be understood in the rest of the discussion, where the unqualified term 'reasons' will designate neither motivating reasons nor explanatory reasons but justificatory ones. This is because, as I hope to have illustrated, only justificatory reasons can have any categorical normative force in discourse involving that which ought to be done (that is, in any normative and practical discourse).[18]

---

[18] For remarks supporting the terminological stipulation just made, see P. Greenspan, 'Asymmetrical Practical Reasons', in M. E. Reicher and J. C. Marek (eds.), *Experience and Analysis: Proceedings of the 27th International Wittgenstein Symposium, 8–14 August 2004, Kirchberg Am Wechsel* (Vienna, ÖBV & HPT, 2005), pp. 387–94 and R. J. Wallace, *Normativity and the Will* (Oxford, Clarendon, 2006), pp. 63–70. To generalize the stance, the account of practical normativity that I am putting forward might be called 'normativity as justification'. As Patricia Greenspan has expressed this point, 'rather than

In summary, the argument offered in this section has shown that legal obligation should be understood as inextricably bound up with justification, in that it fundamentally revolves around *justificatory* reasons (as against motivating reasons or explanatory reasons). A conceptual link can thus be said to exist between legal obligation and justification, a link by virtue of which these two notions are to be regarded as intimately, or conceptually, connected. When viewed as a notion pertaining to the sphere of practical normativity, then, legal obligation is essentially defined by justificatory reasons. Since in this context practical reasons are to be understood as *justificatory* reasons, not as motivating or explanatory ones, legal obligation is fundamentally and primarily a matter of justification. This means that, because legal obligation as a practical notion would make no sense but for the reason-giving practice through which it comes into being – the practice of offering *justificatory* reasons for action – the proper domain of legal obligation is going to find its main focus in the ideas of answerability, or standard-relatedness, and legitimate criticism. The foregoing argument, therefore, takes us to the conclusion that legal obligation is best conceptualized by locating it in the domain of justification, where it is shaped through the activity of giving (justificatory) reasons, an activity by virtue of which the action identified as the object of an obligation can be rationally justified.[19]

---

picturing normativity as an influence on choice ... we should understand it as a logical or justificatory relation' involving agents and actions – a logical relation in the sense just mentioned of framing a standard, without seeking to make the standard look attractive so as to enjoin compliance (Greenspan, 'Asymmetrical Practical Reasons', p. 391). On this account, it is only on the basis of an argument conducted through a giving or exchanging of reasons that something (a course or plan of action) can be justified. Yet not all classes of reasons are meant to justify what we do or plan to do. Some reasons are meant to motivate us, others to explain why something was or is done. And we must be careful to distinguish these areas of interest and discourse. True, a normative consideration (i.e., a justificatory reason) can carry motivational force, that is, it can prompt one to act accordingly. But this is not what justification is *essentially* meant to do (nor does the happy coincidence mean that a motivating reason can justify): justification – the core of practical normativity – is no more concerned with motivating us to do the right thing than logic is with motivating us to think and act consistently.

[19] Support for this conclusion can also be found in H. A. Prichard, *Moral Obligation* (Oxford, Clarendon, 1949), pp. 142–52, and P. M. S. Hacker, 'Sanction Theories of Duty', in A. W. B. Simpson (ed.), *Oxford Essays in Jurisprudence* (Oxford, Oxford University Press, 1973), pp. 142–8.

7.5 Legal Obligation as Intersubjective Reason

I have just argued that there can be no legal obligation without justificatory reasons for acting as prescribed. What we are looking at, therefore, is a necessary, conceptual connection between legal obligation and justification, or between legal obligation and the practical reasons adduced in justifying a claim that we must act in this way or that. But what kinds of justificatory reasons is legal obligation defined by, and what theoretical implications does such a definition carry? These questions can be answered by introducing a distinction that can be recognized as fundamental in practical discourse, especially in the legal domain – a distinction between two basic stances one can take to the practical ought, and between two corresponding ways of supporting a course of action: this is the distinction between reasons that, for lack of better words, I would call *subjective*, on the one hand, and *intersubjective*, on the other.

To anticipate the argument that I intend to deploy in this section, the distinction between subjective reasons and intersubjective reasons is crucial to conceptualizing legal obligation, because it brings into focus the specific force that different types of justificatory reasons have as well as the particular role that that force plays in a theoretically illuminating account of legal obligation. For, whereas both subjective reasons and intersubjective reasons provide support to certain undertakings – they both justify the performance of a given conduct – subjective reasons and intersubjective reasons justify action in different ways. Subjective reasons typically secure practical justification by showing that some courses of conduct are advisable, or recommendable, qua the sensible thing for an agent to do. Hence, subjective reasons routinely come with the force of that which is recommended or held up as good in giving practical guidance. Intersubjective reasons, by contrast, play their justificatory role largely (although non-exclusively) by establishing that certain undertakings can be demanded to, or required from, an acting subject, since those undertakings are singled out as the right thing for someone to do. As a result, intersubjective reasons characteristically have the force of that which is necessitated. I regard this force-related difference as fundamental in the context of the study of legal obligation, since, as noticed in Chapter 1, the domain of obligation is the realm of what is demandable qua right, not the sphere of what is advisable qua sensible: obligations prescribe, require, necessitate, or mandate, as opposed to advising or recommending. From which it follows that legal obligation, as an instantiation of the obligatory, specifically pertains to the camp of intersubjective justificatory reasons, as distinct of the ambit of subjective justificatory reasons.[20]

To expand upon this initial statement of my argument, let us have a closer look at subjective reasons first. When an agent appeals to a subjective reason to justify their performance we are presented with the claim that such agent ought to do, or avoid doing, something because that would be detrimental to such agent's own interests or personal stance. Subjective reasons, as I understand this kind of reasons, are, thus, self-regarding considerations: they purport to secure practical justification by making appeal to the preferences, evaluative orientations, and needs of the subject who performs the relevant piece of conduct – which is also why I call this kind of reasons 'subjective'. The standard against which the value of the conduct supported is measured, then, consists in the criterion of comparative advantage of the acting individual: that individual would be better off or worse off than they are now as a result of pursuing or not pursuing the course of action at issue. Conversely, subjective reasons are statements that need not account for anything else than the agent's private gain, own advantage, or personal interest.

To rephrase the point, when one acts on subjective reasons, they guide their action by the measure of personal advantage and, hence, they adduce their own preferences, aspirations, ends, and desires in justifying the undertaking they carry on. What I define as subjective reasons, hence, are purely agent-centred and self-referential considerations, namely, considerations that solely cater to the needs of the acting self, by thus neglecting, or at least failing to grant the same importance to, the concerns of others. And insofar as this is the case – subjective reasons essentially appeal to the personal interests of the agent – those reasons subordinate the claims of other subjects to the needs of the acting self.

On this basis, subjective reasons can be taken to paradigmatically define the realm of what is prudentially ought and so they can be taken to be standards constitutive of prudential rationality, as such rationality applies to action. An example of this kind of practical reasoning – practical reasoning informed to subjective reasons – might help to clarify the prudential quality of subjective reasons. A standard instance of

---

[20] I should like to thank Aldo Schiavello for discussing this point with me and providing most valuable insights into the relation between subjective reasons and recommendatory force, on the one hand, and intersubjective reasons and mandatory force, on the other. If there is any error or failing in the discussion carried out in this section I am entirely responsible for it.

reasoning shaped by subjective reasons is at play in the following pattern: one should opt for a vegetarian diet, since refraining from eating meat supposedly constitutes a healthy option and unless one sticks to a healthy diet one is at risk for a variety of medical conditions. The reasoning carried out in this scenario can be described as prudential practical thinking. It is practical because it involves deliberating about what to do – it concerns action; it is prudential, because its essence lies in hypothetical means-end reasoning where the ends need only be consistent with the value inherent in the idea of that which is in the agent's best interest, however construed.

A distinctive trait concerning the force of subjective reasons, once so defined and characterized, is of particular significance in the context of the study of legal obligation as the study is undertaken in this work. The range of practical considerations we formulate in pointing out a subjective reason for action is associated with a given kind of force: *recommendatory* force. This is the case, since anything done contrary to a subjective reason will be amenable to criticism as either inadvisable, or insensible, or unwise, or ineligible, or even foolish, qua not in accordance with the agent's self-interest. Recommendatory force is attractive in quality: a course of conduct is justified in the recommendatory sense as long as it is found appealing to the agent – which is why considerations with recommendatory force (as subjective reasons inherently are) can be said to justify by means of exercising some attraction to the supported performance – to the effect that carrying out such course of conduct should be regarded as reasonable, qua advisable.

I find this conclusion of utmost theoretical significance in the context of a conceptualization of legal obligation, since the force of what is ordinarily deemed to be obligatory is irreducible to, and qualitatively distinct when compared with, recommendatory force. An obligatory standard does not *recommend* an agent to take a given course of action; it rather *prescribes* that agent to act in a certain way – an obligation is a demand, or requirement, vis-à-vis a piece of advice, or recommendation.[21] The force of legal obligation, therefore, cannot be equated to the force with which subjective reasons justify the undertaking they support. Whilst subjective reasons can explain the recommendatory force of law, the specific force associated with what is legally obligatory is not advisory – obligations set out demands, as opposed to issue recommendations.

---

[21] This trait of what is obligatory, the reader may well remember, depends on the very concept of obligation as this concept was set out in Chapter 1.

Which means that we cannot rely on subjective reasons to conceptualize legal obligation.[22]

This is why in our search for a theoretically sound account of legal obligation we should turn our attention to the other sort of justificatory reasons for action that I singled out as likewise fundamental: intersubjective reasons. Intersubjective reasons point something out as being correct – the thing that ought to be done – regardless of whether realizing the correctness in question gives the agent any 'edge', or any advantage paradigmatically construed in terms of self-interest, over other individuals directly or indirectly influenced by the agent's conduct. That is to say, in contrast to subjective reasons, which are purely self-regarding and so exclusively concerned with the interests of the agent, intersubjective reasons are not merely self-promoting in so that they take into account not just the concerns of the acting self but also the values and necessities of other individuals who are affected or may be affected by the action carried out by an agent. Moreover, intersubjective reasons, as I define them here, incorporate and refer to interests and value-orientations that may not be associated with any specific individual as they should be ascribed (not to persons but rather) to social groups, non-human sentient animals, and states of affair instrumental to the welfare of current as well as future sentient beings – call them impersonal concerns.[23] Intersubjective reasons, in other terms, grant their support to action by showing that the course of conduct one is justified to undertake matches with concerns that account for, but are not limited to and so go beyond, the comparative advantages of the individual subject who acts, by thus also embracing the claims of a wider set of beings and states of affairs.

More specifically, from the outlook shaped by intersubjective reasons, the necessities of everyone concerned count equally. This means that one uses intersubjective reasons to take into account the needs of each subject impartially, give full weight to each need, and make each need matter in practical deliberation. Thus, going back to the diet example, an agent may opt for eating vegetarian because that agent believes it to be healthier

---

[22] The differences between the force of advice and the force of requirement are discussed at length in T. Pink, 'Normativity and Reason', *Journal of Moral Philosophy*, 4 (2007), pp. 416–23. See also T. Pink, 'Moral Obligation', in A. O'Hear (ed.), *Modern Moral Philosophy* (Cambridge, Cambridge University Press, 2004), pp. 159–85.

[23] What I have in mind here are our concerns with the protection of public goods, such as the environment and the interests of future generations (and so of beings yet to be born), among many others.

than an omnivorous diet, in which case they would be said to act out of subjective reasons and to act prudentially; but it may be that the agent chooses to so act because they believe that, as a matter of principle or in the interest of the community at large that agent is part of, it is wrong to kill animals (tasty as their meat may be experienced by the agent), and in that case the agent can be said to act out of intersubjective reasons.

Intersubjective reasons, as they have been characterized here, encompass considerations that build on, and widen, the narrower set of concerns taken into account by subjective reasons. Intersubjective reasons thus have a broader scope than subjective ones, since they factor in the needs of others as well as the first-person needs of the acting self. This means that first-person, self-regarding considerations play a role in the practical reasoning shaped by intersubjective reasons, but only alongside other-regarding considerations. This also means that the distinction between subjective and intersubjective reasons should not be understood as an oppositional dichotomy. True, there may well be occasions on which a course of action is justified by intersubjective reasons while lacking any support in subjective reasons. But this should not be taken to mean that intersubjective reasons are fundamentally inconsistent with subjective ones, or *necessarily* in conflict with them. In fact, intersubjective reasons, as just defined, do not disregard the agent's interests, as those interests are supported by subjective reasons. Hence, any discrepancy that may emerge when subjective and intersubjective reasons are at play is not due to some necessary or built-in contrast between the claims an agent makes from a first-person perspective and the claims made taking into account the interests of others. The discrepancy, then, is not inherent in the distinction between subjective and intersubjective reasons, in that intersubjective reasons demand that we broaden the range of our practical reasoning in the manner just described, by appreciating the need to justify our position to others whenever our own claims, interests, and concerns may be in conflict with theirs. And this means giving reasons that others may accept, in such a way that our claims, interests, and concerns do not necessarily take precedence over those of others but stand on an equal footing with them. It is our ability to make this shift from a self-interested perspective to an inclusive one that explains any discrepancy that may arise between subjective and intersubjective reasons.

By way of a restatement, intersubjective reasons require one to recognize the claims, interests, and concerns of all the parties affected by some course of action. This means proffering reasons in a public space filled by all those concerned, and to do so is to justify oneself to others. This process is at once constraining and embracing. It is constraining because to enter a public space is to restrict the range of reasons that can be offered in support of a proposed course of conduct. It is embracing because in this space our interests cannot be accorded any more weight than those of others: all interests count equally, and we are therefore forced to broaden our perspective so as to include a range of viewpoints that are not limited to our own. The space of intersubjective reasons, then, is the space of practical justification in which the justificatory process is not complete until all interests and viewpoints have been taken into account, especially when they diverge from our own. This is also the space of the right, as opposed to the good, understood as that which is advisable, recommendable, prudential, or advantageous from the standpoint of the single agent engaged in practical reasoning without considering the interests of others.

Ultimately, intersubjective reasons owe their justificatory significance to the proposition that statements appealing to an agent's personal concerns do not necessarily outweigh the considerations based on the interests of the other affected parties, which too should accordingly be entitled to have a say in the justificatory procedure. Which is also why practical justification needs to factor in both an agent's preferences and the purports of anyone else influenced by the relevant performance: unless a justificatory process pays the interests of all those involved their due and grants those interests proper weight, to the effect that each concern counts as much as the claims of the others and everyone's preferences are made to matter equally in the justificatory process, the process itself is to be considered incomplete and so the conclusions reached by way of it cannot be regarded as genuinely, or practical-rationality-wise, justified. That is to say, the rationale of appealing to intersubjective reasons, vis-à-vis subjective reasons, is that of securing that in practical justification the reasons based on the agent's claims do not count more than the reasons shaped by everyone else's claims.

Precisely in consideration of the fact that a broader and more inclusive perspective defines the camp of intersubjective reasons – intersubjective reasons are deferential to both the agent's personal stance and the other parties' concerns – intersubjective reasons have the potential to point out what can be argued to be not merely advisable, qua prudentially recommendable, but rather *right*. Likewise, departing from what is justified by intersubjective reasons will not necessarily be considered unwise or foolish – a course of conduct that is less than sensible and hence one has a personal interest in avoiding it. It will rather be considered *wrong* and so amenable to criticism as being an instance of wrongdoing.

The form of criticism that is appropriate when one departs from practical patterns justified by intersubjective considerations is, hence, qualitatively different from the form of criticism attached to an act performed against a subjective reason for action. Deviance from what is supported by intersubjective reasons is qualified as, and is criticized for being, wrong when compared to a set of interpersonal standards – it is something that ought not to be done even if it turned out to be in the interest of the agent and so less than unwise. The departure from intersubjective reasons, therefore, legitimizes the specific accusation of incorrectness, qua wrongness, which, when contrasted with the accusation of inadvisability, or lack of wisdom, is a distinct reason-based criticism.

This element associated with the existence of intersubjective reasons – peculiarity of criticism – means that intersubjective reasons possess distinctive kinds of justificatory strength and so kinds of justificatory strength that cannot be found in association with subjective reasons. More analytically, the force associated with intersubjective reasons branches out into two directions: (a) they are reasons that demand something from an agent – intersubjective reasons can thus be claimed to have *mandatory* force; (b) they are reasons that allow an agent to perform a generally valued piece of conduct despite the fact that it is neither required nor prudentially sensible and so advisable from the standpoint defined by that agent's personal interests considered in isolation from the concerns of other affected parties – intersubjective reasons can then be taken to single out something that is valuable, praiseworthy, virtuous, or honourable by thus having *supererogatory* strength. Hence, intersubjective reasons can justify performances in two ways: they can show that certain performances are *due* as a matter of everyone's interest or they can show that those performances are *praiseworthy* and yet not (strictly) required from an all-encompassing perspective – those performances are more than what is due.

Now, the latter kind of force – supererogatory strength – takes us outside what is prudentially rational, qua advisable, since what comes with such force is optional and valuable in a non-prudential sense. But it also takes us off the domain of what is demanded as a matter of practical rationality, since what is justified as a supererogatory act is not *due* practical-rationality-wise. Accordingly, the relevance of the supererogatory force of intersubjective reasons to the conceptualization of legal obligation is only limited and indirect. By contrast, mandatory force, as one of the specific kinds of force that distinctively accompany intersubjective reasons, plays a central role in establishing obligation. For mandatory force is binding and compulsive: an action is supported in the mandatory sense as long as it is demanded and exactable, to the effect that the agent is neither simply advised to perform it nor praiseworthy for doing it; rather the agent is bound to act that way. Therefore, action supported by practical reasons with mandatory force is justified in the strong sense of being required, or necessitated.

In this context, it cannot be overemphasized that it is because a course of conduct supported by the intersubjective reasons is neither merely advisable nor simply praiseworthy and yet non-demandable, but indeed it is mandatory and required, that deviating from it can be criticized as a wrong decision. Hence, a relation of mutual interdependence can be established between intersubjective quality of a practical reason, its mandatory force and the practical criticism expressed in terms of wrongness. This makes the link between intersubjective reasons, mandatory force, and wrongness definitional, or constitutive: an act is supported by intersubjective reasons insofar as it is backed by practical reasons that have mandatory force and so can justify the criticism of the deviant conduct as wrongful.

This conclusion is key in the context of a study of obligation. For obligation has the force of a demand and a directive, namely, the force of a mandatory requirement, as opposed to the force of a recommendation or the force of something that is just valuable in an optional sense. In addition, action performed in breach of an obligation is at least presumptively neither inadvisable nor praiseworthy and optional; by contrast, it is wrong – something that ought not to be done. This means that obligation is conceptually and distinctively associated with intersubjective reasons, as opposed to subjective reasons. One has an obligation to act so and so by virtue of the fact that the relevant course of conduct is favoured by intersubjective reasons (in one of their possible fundamental instantiations), since only when practical reasons come with mandatory force – the force which is distinctive of intersubjective reasons (in one of their possible fundamental instantiations) – and single out a wrongdoing – as intersubjective reasons characteristically have the potential to do – an obligation arises. That is, having an obligation can hardly be equated to having a practical reason recommending one to act in a certain way, as it is the case when subjective reasons apply. Unless the reason supporting a certain conduct possesses the force of a requirement no obligation can be said to arise. And only intersubjective reasons (in one of their possible fundamental instantiations) can have such force. Which is why obligation links up conceptually with a specific subset of practical reasons – intersubjective reasons – by so singling out a narrow division within that which is rationally justified and secured from criticism.[24]

This conclusion applies as well to legal obligation by virtue of the fact that the latter is a garden-variety kind of obligation. Because not everything that is supported by practical reasons in their justificatory mode is made obligatory, not practical reasons whatsoever but rather practical reasons the nature of which is intersubjective can be claimed to give rise to legal obligations. From which it follows that legal obligation is best conceptualized as a practical reason endowed with some enhanced force – mandatory force – to the effect that the supported action is compellingly justified (and indeed demanded) as a matter of intersubjective reasons.

7.6 Taking Stock: The Bare Bones of Legal Obligation

Central to the conception I have put forward in this chapter is the idea of legal obligation as having a constitutive connection with intersubjective reasons for action and mandatory force. In this section I am going to further elaborate on this idea by bringing together the main points made in the foregoing discussion. What I am going to claim, in a nutshell, is that by virtue of the conceptual link which ties legal obligation to intersubjective reasons, on the one hand, and to mandatory force, on the other, legal obligation at once acquires non-prudential justificatory force and sets itself up as a rationally binding practical standard. In their combination, these axes frame legal obligation as a (i) demand that is (ii) intersubjectively (iii) justifiable, and (iv) rational. This definition of legal obligation can in turn be understood as the outcome of two theses: (a) the thesis that obligation is shaped by intersubjective reasons, such that no obligation can arise unless the conduct it upholds is non-prudentially and rationally justifiable – hence the rational, intersubjective, and justificatory component in the definition of legal obligation – coupled with (b) the thesis that obligation carries a distinctively mandatory force – hence the imperative, or demandingness-related, component of the definition. It is only the interplay of intersubjective

---

[24] Remarks supporting this conclusion can also be found in S. Darwall, 'Moral Obligation: Form and Substance', *Proceedings of the Aristotelian Society*, Supplementary Volume 110 (2009), pp. 31–6.

and rational justification with imperativeness that gives us a full picture of legal obligation. If we should leave either one of these two dimensions out of the picture – as by defining legal obligation exclusively in terms of intersubjective and rational justification or exclusively in terms of requirements – we will therefore have a *partial* account, one that chooses to bring out some features of legal obligation without fully acknowledging other essential traits of what is obligatory.

7.6.1 Legal Obligation as an Intersubjective and Rational Justificatory Standard

Obligation is a practical normative notion; practical normativity can be defined in terms of reasons for action of a certain kind (*intersubjective reasons*);[25] and reasons for action can in turn be defined as justifications for acting in one way rather than another. These are the premises from which I have argued that legal obligation bears a conceptual connection to non-prudential and rational justification, such that nothing can be regarded as obligatory unless it is justifiable in light of non-prudential rational considerations.

It should be noted here that intersubjective and rational justification figures in the definition of obligation as a necessary but not a sufficient condition for a legal obligation to exist. The obtaining of intersubjective reasons is *necessary* for a legal obligation to arise, since other kinds of reasons – and subjective reasons in particular – do not have the resources to constitute obligatory standards. While we need intersubjective reasons to exist for a legal obligation to hold, however, intersubjective reasons may well fail to produce obligations and so they are not a *sufficient* condition for the existence of legal obligation. Indeed, a course of action does not become legally obligatory just by virtue of its being non-prudentially and rationally justifiable. This is attested by the fact that, in addition to intersubjective reasons with mandatory force – the kind of

---

[25] As indicated in the previous paragraph, the qualification 'intersubjective' has been understood in an extended sense. For, on the one hand, intersubjective reasons have been taken to be considerations that account for the interests and values of the agent too – they are not exclusively oriented to other subjects by thus lacking any consideration, or deference, to the perspective of the acting subject. On the other hand, intersubjective reasons cater for what can be considered impersonal values and interests, namely, values and concerns that are not exclusively borne by sentient beings – the agent themselves or other individuals – but also by communities and states of affairs instrumental to the well-being of individuals and social groups.

intersubjective reasons engendering obligations – there are intersubjective reasons with supererogatory force and so reasons supporting the performance of valuable but optional (and so non-obligatory) courses of conduct. That is, the existence of intersubjective reasons is not by itself sufficient to the issuance of a legal obligation, since on occasions it is rather associated with the emergence of supererogatory standards. So, many courses of action exist that are intersubjectively and rationally justifiable and yet are not obligatory. Stated otherwise, in order for a course of action to become legally obligatory, it need be non-prudentially and rationally justifiable, but its being non-prudentially and rationally justifiable does not make it *ipso facto* legally obligatory. This is ultimately because (on my conception) intersubjective and rational justification is only one of the elements constitutive of legal obligation and so cannot alone account for the whole legal obligation.

Although non-prudential and rational justification does not make up the whole of legal obligation, it does figure centrally in any adequate account of legal obligation. In fact, one can hardly overstress the role intersubjective and rational justification plays in defining legal obligation, for if one underrates that role one will inevitably wind up with a partial, or one-sided, account of legal obligation that blows its imperative element out of proportion, defining legal obligation only in terms of what is required by law. This point finds a clear statement in Kurt Baier's work on obligation (in general), where it is observed that 'in having an obligation to do x, one *necessarily* has a good reason for doing x'.[26] Similarly, Baier asserts: '"N has an obligation to do x" entails that "N is justified in doing x and *not justified* in not doing x".'[27] In making these claims Baier perspicuously points out that an obligation cannot arise from the mere fact that a given action has been demanded or required. Nor can an obligation consist simply in what is called for under the rules of any social practice we subscribe to. For both of those approaches fail to show what it is that non-prudentially and rationally justifies the relevant practical requirement.[28] The same conclusion applies with reference to legal obligation, to the study of which Baier's remarks can be extended.

---

[26] Baier, 'Moral Obligation', p. 214; original emphasis.
[27] Baier, 'Moral Obligation', p. 214; original emphasis.
[28] So, where an obligation exists, intersubjective and rational justification for it must also exist. This, in turn, means that what one has an obligation to do is necessarily linked to some state of affairs that rationally ought to be pursued and realized. Accordingly, incorporated in the claim that one has an obligation to act in a certain way is the claim that this course of action is valuable, in the specific sense pointed out by the

The link between legal obligation and intersubjective justificatory reasons can also be appealed to shed light on the relationship between legal obligation and compulsion. Indeed, it was argued, just as it would be a mistake to separate legal obligation from justificatory practical reasons, so it would be a mistake to view legal obligation as something falling short of a demand – what is obligatory can be *exacted* from us: it identifies a requirement. So it is only if we are somehow *compelled* by the law to do something that we can be said to have a legal obligation in regard to that thing.[29] However, there are different ways in which someone can be compelled to do something, and not all of them can be reconciled with the idea of legal obligation. That is to say, it is not compulsion as such that figures as an essential element of legal obligation, but compulsion for which some kind of justification is available, and in particular a justification involving the proffering of intersubjective reasons counting in favour of that which is claimed to be legally obligatory. What makes an action legally obligatory, in other terms, is not the mere fact that some sanction will follow or is likely to follow if we fail to comply. Something is legally obligatory only if the sanction that accompanies, or is likely to accompany, the non-compliant behaviour can be argued to be justifiable, or legitimate.

So, on the one hand, legal obligation cannot be separated from the force of what is *required*;[30] but, on the other hand, any element of compulsion built into the notion of legal obligation is hardly independent of the essential justificatory component that characterizes and defines what is legally obligatory. Namely, the mere existence of a sanction does not entail the existence of a legal obligation: you have a legal obligation to do what you can be *justifiably* required to do, not what you can be compelled to do. Or, again, a legal obligation is not just something you can be coerced or threatened into doing – on the reasoning that you might not like the consequences of non-compliance; it is rather a legal requirement that becomes compulsory by virtue of its being correct or justifiable (by virtue of its being backed by normative reasons).

---

intersubjective practical reasons adduced in pointing that action out as something required of us. This aspect is discussed in R. Brandt, 'The Concepts of Obligation and Duty', *Mind*, 73 (1964), pp. 389-93.

[29] On this point, see M. Forrester 'Some Remarks on Obligation, Permission, and Supererogation', *Ethics*, 85 (1975), pp. 219-22, among others. In the emphasis on the coercive element of obligation lies the core contained in the now widely discredited 'sanction theory' of obligation.

[30] This is clearly stated in Brandt, 'Concepts of Obligation and Duty', pp. 389-93.

And, insofar as it is not the *likelihood* of sanction that makes something obligatory but the *justification* on which basis that sanction (regardless of how likely it is) can be set forth and enforced, legal obligations are more than mere requirements with sanctions attached to them.

7.6.2 Legal Obligation as a Requirement

In the foregoing I have also defended the claim that a legal obligation should be understood as a categorical requirement. The force of legal obligation is binding and non-hypothetically demanding. This conclusion can be further specified by introducing the companion idea of the sense in which the bindingness of legal obligation makes something a practical requirement: it does so by setting up a sort of necessitation that is neither physical nor psychological. In contrast to the kind of necessity associated with legal obligation, the other two sources of necessitation – namely, the physical and the psychological – can be described as empirical, in that the force they exert is material. Physical force is material in a coercive way proper; psychological force is material in a dispositional way, for it inclines and even pushes us to act in certain ways in certain circumstances. Both forces offer resistance to our ability to make practical choices, and must in this sense be qualified as non-normative.

We can see what this means where physical force is concerned. Our being physically coerced into something entails that there is no way for us to act otherwise. We saw earlier that, by contrast, the normative is precisely the sphere of possibility, the sphere of that which might be other than it is. Normativity, thus, requires practical freedom as a basic presupposition. The moment we take that freedom away (and with it an agent's ability to make choices), we take away any possibility of justifying a course of action and subjecting it to critical scrutiny. This applies to the normative in general as it does to that part of the normative where legal obligation has its place. Just as normativity cannot live in the space of physical constraint so legal obligation is fundamentally incompatible with there being but one practical possibility of action. Just as there is nothing normative about our being forced to do something at gunpoint, there is nothing legally obligatory about it, either. Legal obligation cannot make sense without the possibility of its being violated: it presupposes an ability to do something different from what it prescribes; namely, it presupposes a view of agency as that which can be freely chosen, and so practical freedom.

This leads us to the second source of necessitation, the kind exerted by psychological promptings. Legal obligation cannot be equated to the psychological form of compulsion either. Having a legal obligation differs from the psychological state of believing or feeling to be bound to carry out a given action. True, there may well be certain psychological states either typically or frequently associated with the existence of a legal obligation and with one's doing or not doing what is legally obligatory. For instance, ordinarily an obligation is believed to be a requirement adhering to which may well be felt as entailing sacrifice and renunciation. Moreover, performing courses of conduct that are in contrast with what is regarded as obligatory is commonly associated with feelings of blameworthiness and guilt: an act performed in breach of an obligation is typically believed to be blameworthy and the agent who performs it may feel culpable. But, no matter how often legal obligation, on the one hand, and certain beliefs and feelings, on the other, coexist, a distinction remains between the psychological states of 'believing to have a legal obligation' and 'feeling to have a legal obligation', on the one hand, and the condition of 'having a legal obligation', on the other. For no particular internal state is required for the latter to obtain. An agent can well have a legal obligation, as I have conceptualized it in this chapter, without believing or feeling that they have one: the beliefs, feelings, and other internal states of the agent are not essential to determining their legal obligations. Therefore, there is a crucial distinction at conceptual level between the force of a legal obligation and the psychological kind of compulsion. That is because legal obligation is not an internal state of the agent (be it cognitive or volitional), and so it cannot be equated with such a state any more than justification can be equated with the motivating reason one may have for doing what is justified. Just as a proposition is justified not by the way we feel about it but by the justificatory argument on which it rests, so a legal obligation comes into being not through any accompanying feeling or beliefs of the agent but through the justification on which basis the legal obligation is validated.

In fact, there is a common source of the failures of both physical force and psychological force to account for the kind of binding force conceptually associated with legal obligation: neither of the two forces – physical force and psychological force – is normative; by contrast, legal obligation individuates a requirement that unfolds in the normative territory. It is because legal obligation is normative that it directs the agent to certain performance but it neither pushes the agent nor goads them to act in a way rather than another. The connection obtaining between normativity and legal obligation, thus, does not establish and characterize exclusively the justification-related component of legal obligation; it also determines the specific sense in which legal obligation is a mandatory force requiring one to act in a certain way. As it occupies the normative space, legal obligation can be conceptualized as neither a psychological force nor a physical one. The force of legal obligation is a distinctive kind of necessitation, the nature of which is practical and normative, as opposed to empirical (be it physical or psychological). And it is precisely because legal obligation belongs with the normative that a conceptual distinction should be maintained between 'having a legal obligation', 'being coerced', 'believing to be under a legal obligation', and 'feeling to be under a legal obligation'. For, only the first expression relates to a condition that cannot be described, and categorized, in exclusively empirical terms. The normative, or non-empirical, character of legal obligation, therefore, secures its own distinctiveness by making sure that the mandatory force associated to the existence of legal obligation is not confused with either the physically compelling force of coercion or the psychology of being compelled to act in the demanded way.

7.7 Closing Remarks

Legal obligation, I argued in this chapter, is not a simple notion but a multilayered notion that presents distinct normative levels, or components: intersubjective and rational justification, stringent qua categorical quality, and demandingness, or requiredness. Rational justification is constitutive of the concept of legal obligation by virtue of the fact that legal obligation has a normative quality, and normativity, being defined in terms of justificatory reasons, is conceptually continuous with rational justification. But legal obligation does not demark what is rationally justifiable qua eligible, or advisable. Legal obligation, instead, individuates, in the realm of the normative, that which is required, or demanded, by the law. Legal obligation is, then, conceptually associated with the idea of intersubjectively justifiable requirement, or demandingness (in some stringent and non-trivial meaning of this term). In this context, the idea of requirement is to be interpreted as referring to a distinctive normative strength of a practical reason, a strength that is exclusively associated with intersubjective practical reasons, vis-à-vis subjective ones. Legal obligation, as a result, is to be understood as a practical reason incorporating a peculiar kind of force – binding force – and this force is conceptually linked to intersubjective and non-merely-prudential justification.

Hence, the idea of legal obligation as a intersubjective and rational justificatory force.

Legal obligation, I also argued, takes up a further dimension that characterizes certain normative phenomena: stringent qua *categorical, or non-hypothetical*, demandingness. By this it is meant that legal obligations exert their mandatory force independently of the purposes and ends contingently given to the agents they apply to. A legally obligatory course of conduct is non-hypothetically demanded, since its obligatory status holds for any agent no matter which their subjective preferences, individual projects, particular inclinations and personal goals are. This, I claimed, also explains why legal obligation delimits a distinctive kind of compelling force that is irreducible to any powerlike relationship, the nature of which is empirical, and is instead to be characterized in terms of a non-empirical sort of necessitation.

In a nutshell, then, in this chapter I arrived at a conception of legal obligation as an *intersubjectively* and *rationally justifiable* statement of law with *categorically mandatory force*. This is, it may be readily appreciated, a composite definition of legal obligation – the main components of the definition being the rational dimension of intersubjective justification and the constrain-centred dimension of categorical mandatory force, or requirement. This account I will henceforth refer to as the '*revisionary Kantian conception*' of legal obligation. As I will argue in Section 8.4, the conception put forward here can be described as *Kantian* because it preserves two insights I take to be central to, and fundamentally constitutive of, Kant's treatment of obligation, namely, the thesis of the oneness of obligation across different practical domains and the thesis of obligation as something necessitated by practical rationality. At the same time, the account can be qualified as *revisionary*, because it does not offer a faithful rendition of Kant's conception of legal obligation but rather recasts it, while still preserving its spirit and essential contentions.

Likewise importantly, the components around which the revisionary Kantian conception of legal obligation can be organized makes such conception irreducible to alternative, partial, and one-sided accounts equating legal obligation to either a rational component (where reason-relatedness is taken to be the sole fundamental constituent of legal obligation) or a constraining component (where compulsion alone is understood as summarizing the core of legal obligation). As a result, on my conception legal obligation is a notion that resists any reductive attempt, be it a rationalistic version of reductionism dissolving legal obligation into the force of practical reasons, or a realist version of reductionism whereby legal obligation is depicted as what has the power to coerce to the effect that the legally obligatory and the legally enforceable are one and the same thing. For, on the one hand, legal obligation can hardly be described as a purely rational force, since central components of what is legally obligatory – including most contents of the duties engendered by the law – depend on the will of those in power and thus are neither predominantly fixed by nor mainly dependent on rational considerations. On the other hand, legal obligations can improperly be reduced to requirements that certain legal officials and institutions issue, since those requirements can be regarded as obligatory only insofar as they are backed by justificatory reasons and so incorporate a distinctively rational, vis-à-vis voluntarist, dimension.

This set of statements buttresses the conclusion that legal obligation is to be understood as a notion in its own right and indeed a notion owing its distinctiveness to the internal complexity, or multilayered quality, which steers it away from both pure instantiations of practical rationality and sheer manifestations of political power. However, in presenting legal obligation as a compound concept that cannot be reduced to a pure instantiation of practical rationality or to a sheer manifestation of political power I should like to stress the weight of the rationalist component in my conceptualization of legal obligation. True, any reductivist reason approach is as ill-equipped as the will-theory to account for the nature of legal obligation. Likewise, one should reject the thesis that legal obligation is best conceived as, or even is essentially defined in terms of, just an unqualified practical reason. But rationalism, once understood in a qualified sense, has some edge over voluntarism and realism in accounting for what is legally obligatory.

To elaborate on this point, also by way of concluding the exposition of the revisionary Kantian conception of legal obligation, let me summarily characterize rationalism, in connection with obligation, as the broad view that 'it makes sense to do something because you are under an obligation to do it only in so far as this obligation constitutes a reason to do it and/or a reason for you to deliberate about whether to do it in a certain way'.[31] As long as this characterization is not interpreted in the

---

[31] D. Owens, 'Rationalism about Obligation', *European Journal of Philosophy*, 16 (2008), p. 404. Of course, this definition of rationalism about obligation is neither analytic nor robustly informative, especially considering that a theory of obligation based on this premise can be moulded in a range of ways, depending on the different interpretations we bring to it in stating what it means to have a reason to do something and to be compelled

reductivist fashion, it constitutes, I believe, a solid and potentially illuminating point of departure for one's exploration of legal obligation. This is not to say that any variant of non-reductivist rationalism would do. As I argued at some length in this chapter, a credible and theoretically sound reason account of legal obligation builds a number of fundamental qualifications into the claim that legal obligation is a practical reason generated by legal norms and systems. Relatedly, we need a discerning and non-reductive rationalist theoretical perspective explicitly acknowledging that legal obligation is a reason for action of a very distinct sort – for instance, in the conception specifically theorized here, a categorical, justificatory, and intersubjective reason for action.

Yet, once it is understood in an appropriately restricted sense, rationalism about obligation is an insightful theoretical approach to the study of legal obligation, since we cannot legitimately aspire at comprehensively elucidating the nature of legal obligation whilst failing to acknowledge the rational dimension as (partially but intrinsically) constitutive of what is legally obligatory. Insofar this is the case, therefore, rationalism about obligation should be considered an illuminating approach to the study of what is legally obligatory. Which is why in this work I allowed the core claims defining rationalism about obligation to shape my revisionary Kantian conception of legal obligation. Indeed the picture of legal obligation emerging from what precedes stands in a relation of conceptual continuity with non-reductivist rationalism about obligation. That is to say, my revisionary Kantian conception takes as privileged reference point for the study of legal obligation the (vast and internally differentiated) theoretical perspective defined by the view that 'we are living in the age of law and reasons', as Christopher Essert has pithily put it.[32] In more detail, this view is shaped by, and based on, the assumption that 'the task of explaining the normativity of law' is 'a central part of the project of jurisprudence'.[33] Once this assumption is combined with the further tenets that (a) obligation, legal or otherwise, is a normative concept, (b) the core of a complete explanation of the normativity of law

---

to accept that reason. Nor are all of these interpretations necessarily compatible. But this open-endedness is in fact a virtue. For the definition not only locates this conception within a broad philosophical tradition in the study of obligation (the rationalist tradition) but also, and more importantly, it enables us to coherently develop the revised Kantian conception of legal obligation.

[32] C. Essert, 'From Raz's *Nexus* to Legal Normativity', *Canadian Journal of Law and Jurisprudence*, 25 (2012), p. 465.

[33] Essert, 'From Raz's *Nexus* to Legal Normativity', p. 465.

will be in terms of reasons – elucidating the normativity of law fundamentally means clarifying the relationships between law and reasons, since 'the explanation of normativity is the explanation of reasons'[34] and reasons are 'the key normative phenomenon'[35] – despite the fact that a complete explanation of the normativity of law requires one to engage with a number of (normative) concepts as they are at play in the legal domain, and (c) the notion of a reason is a basic normative notion, or at least a notion one cannot explain through an eliminative definition (but only by setting out its interrelations with other normative concepts) – this is a reformulation of the reasons thesis introduced in Section 7.2 – we are in the presence of a general theoretical framework, the quality of which is distinctly rationalist, which has the potential to significantly advance our understanding of legal obligation, or so I argued in this chapter.

It should also be clear, however, that in explaining the normativity of law by pointing to the central role of reasons in justifying law and its prescriptions – in a way that makes possible a general, comprehensive account of legal obligation – the revisionary Kantian conception of legal obligation should not be understood as a strict form of legal rationalism. In fact, the rationalist tradition to which this Kantian conception belongs is wide-ranging, accommodating a number of ways of understanding rationalism about obligation. So, while the revisionary Kantian conception takes the view that it is impossible to explain legal obligation without recourse to considerations justifying the conduct the law makes obligatory, and it additionally argues that these considerations require a basis in practical rationality – for otherwise obligation becomes arbitrary and subjective, whereas its force needs to be shown to be intersubjective – this does not amount to saying that what practical rationality dictates should necessarily coincide with what is legally obligatory, or that what can be shown to be in agreement with practical rationality is *ipso facto* legally obligatory.[36] Hence, my position is not correctly understood as a contribution to legal rationalism qua philosophical tradition asserting that practical rationality establishes some supreme principle, or set of supreme principles, of both morality and legality. Nor do I endorse the

---

[34] Raz, *From Normativity to Responsibility*, p. 5.
[35] Raz, *From Normativity to Responsibility*, p. 11.
[36] This point will be further elaborated on in Chapter 8, where we will look at a more ambitious and sweeping variant of the rationalist tradition in the study of legal obligation: the robust reason account of legal obligation.

claim that practical rationality alone can determine what is legally right, to the effect that what is legally obligatory is exhaustively established by what is practically rational. This philosophical approach to law and its obligation, which comprises the panoply of legal doctrines identified under the labels of 'ethical rationalism' and 'legal idealism', refers to ambitious variants of rationalism that have only some elements in common with, and thus cannot be equated to, my own reason account of legal obligation. While rationalist, then, the account of legal obligation I am advancing here should not be understood as an instance of either ethical rationalism or legal idealism.[37]

---

[37] For a recent introduction to the rationalist tradition in philosophy, and how it breaks down into ethical rationalism and legal idealism, see P. Capps and S. Pattinson, 'Introduction', in P. Capps and S. Pattison (eds.), *Ethical Rationalism and the Law* (Oxford, Bloomsbury, 2017), pp. 1–16.

8

Further Dimensions of the Revisionary Kantian Conception

8.1 Introduction

Having laid out in the last chapter a distinct account of legal obligation – the revisionary Kantian conception – I will now expand on three of its components: its recourse to a specific type of a practical reason for legal obligation (intersubjective reasons), its inclusion of mandatory force in defining what can count as legal obligation, and its Kantian underpinnings. These components are addressed in the following three sections.

Section 8.2 takes a deeper look at intersubjective reasons by fully working out the implications of their contrast with subjective ones. This will make it possible to bring into focus the nature of intersubjective reasons as moral reasons (in a given sense of the term). For both intersubjective reasons, as I define them in this work, and moral reasons are widely understood as practical standards holding categorically and accounting not only for the interests of the agent but also for the concerns of the others who are potentially affected by the course of conduct those reasons justify. A direct consequence of this statement is, I will claim, that legal obligation, being conceptualized in terms of intersubjective reasons, has a distinctively moral, vis-à-vis prudential, quality.

Next I will return to the conceptualization of legal obligation as a requirement, vis-à-vis a recommendation, namely, as a standard with compulsive, vis-à-vis attractive, strength. I will argue that such conceptualization frames legal obligation as a practical reason with a distinctive kind of *force*. Accordingly, the revisionary Kantian conception is committed to the statement that what is distinctive of a legally obligatory pattern of conduct is the specific kind of strength with which that pattern is buttressed. This statement means that I understand legal obligation as a given force which (just) some practical reasons the law engenders have. This places the revisionary Kantian conception of legal obligation within the so-called *force model* of obligation, as against the *feature model*, on which obligation is conceived as a feature of action, rather than being identified by the force of the reasons on which basis a course of action is justified.

Finally, Section 8.4 will elaborate on the asserted Kantian quality of the theoretical account of legal obligation introduced in this work. First I will notice that the conception theorized in the previous chapter was not meant to consolidate Kant's *original* view of legal obligation by supporting it with new arguments. That is to say, not only is my conception far from a restatement of Kant's own position but also it departs from Kant's original stance in a number of respects. Nonetheless, I will claim, my conception of legal obligation should be understood as Kantian in spirit, since, for one thing, it incorporates the basic insight, as it can be found in Kant's body of work, that obligation is a practically rational necessitation, for another thing, as it is the case with Kant's, my conception of legal obligation draws on the idea of obligation in general and yet is not committed to the view that legal obligations are either directly derivable from or coincident with other forms of obligation. My account of legal obligation, therefore, is deeply indebted to Kant's philosophy, even if it incorporates a revisionary character in so that it fashions Kant's own ideas about legal obligation in new terms and calls for a partial revisit of Kant's original framework of thought.

With that overview of this chapter, we can enter into its contents in greater depth, bearing in mind that a variety of issues will be discussed and those issues are not necessarily related. But the discussion finds its cohesiveness in virtue of the fact that these issues all pertain to the three components of the revised account previously mentioned: the discussion therefore builds on Chapter 7 (where the account was presented), and in emphasizing three components of it will enable us to see in what ways this revised account departs from Kant's original conception whilst keeping a close connection with it.

8.2 The Moral Nature of Legal Obligation

As noted, central to the revisionary Kantian account is the thesis that legal obligation cannot be reduced to a coercive constraint to do what the law requires: there must always be a *reason* for so acting, and this reason must be of a particular kind, that is, it must be intersubjective. This is significant because it makes legal obligation a requirement the nature of which is inherently moral. To elaborate on this point, not all reasons for action qualify as moral reasons, since some of them are exclusively designed to advance an agent's own interests and are accordingly prudential, removing them from the realm of the moral. The moral sphere is widely (although far from indisputably) viewed as a territory inhabited by practical standards that (a) can be *categorically justified* and (b) constitutively factor in the *concerns of others*, which are thus made to count as much as the interests of the agent. Thus:

1. Morality is *categorical*, in the sense that the force of moral principles is independent of an individual agent's preferences, dispositions, and inclinations. As a result, morality constrains the pursuance of an agent's individual purports and personal plans, such that acting morally may occasionally require us to act even against our self-interest, or at least may require us to act in ways we would otherwise choose not to. This is because moral commitments do not necessarily agree with our preferences and desires.
2. In addition, morality needs to have an *intersubjective* basis, since it requires agents not to act in their exclusive self-interest but to consider the stance of everyone else who may be affected by a proposed course of conduct. Morality, in other words, requires an impartial attitude in making decisions, taking everyone's claims into account without necessarily neglecting one's own interests and point of view. Only when everyone's interests receive equal weight, then, can we be said to be acting within a moral space.

Now, insofar as this is the case, a necessary, or conceptual, connection can be argued to exist between moral reasons and intersubjective reasons. Indeed, moral reasons and intersubjective reasons alike are impartial considerations, the justificatory force of which is categorical. That is to say, both moral reasons and intersubjective considerations need to take into account the interests and concerns of all the agents who stand to be affected by the proposed course of action, and they must give equal consideration to all such interests and concerns, that is, they must satisfy a criterion of impartiality which subjective moral reasons need not satisfy, and which takes them away from the realm of the prudential, where a practical move need not be justified to others and so can proceed solely from the first-person perspective on which an agent's own values and interests can be given normative priority over those of others.

On these grounds, the appeal to intersubjective reasons is best understood as a form of moral deliberation, in so that, in the reasoning leading to establish which course of conduct one ought to take, the stance of the agent enjoys no normative priority over the claims of all the others affected by the relevant conduct. That is to say, morality is an inherently intersubjective practice necessitating one to cater for the values and interests of each person directly or indirectly affected by the undertaking under consideration. Which is why agents relying on intersubjective reasons and so taking the perspective of others into account partake of a moral practice. Likewise, the moral discourse is structured by, and organized around, intersubjective reasons.

Insofar as this is the case – both moral considerations and intersubjective reasons occupy a territory in which taking a non-self-centred stance is of essence – the thesis that legal obligation is specifically defined by intersubjective reasons means that legal obligation has a distinctively moral quality. Otherwise stated, the nature of legal obligation is moral (vis-à-vis prudential), because what is legally obligatory is defined by what is morally justified in the sense of being supported by intersubjective reasons, not by subjective reasons – the latter being prudential, vis-à-vis moral, considerations. Therefore, despite the fact that a legal obligation can originate in different kinds of concerns and situations and despite the fact that the contents of the obligations generated by the law can depart from what any given substantive moral code may require, the nature of legal obligation should be acknowledged to be distinctively and intrinsically moral.[1]

In making this claim it does not escape me that intersubjective reasons may be viewed by some practical philosophers as considerations that do not map exactly onto moral reasons. This would be, for instance, the position of someone conceiving of moral reasons not merely as categorical and intersubjective standards but also as overriding considerations. By overridingness it is generally meant the property, which some ascribe to morality and moral standards, of taking precedence over other practical perspectives, concerns, and reasons, to the effect that what is owed as a matter of morality is what an agent ought to conclusively do. Insofar

---

[1] See K. Baier, 'Moral Obligation', *American Philosophical Quarterly*, 3 (1966), pp. 211–13, for an additional argument supporting this conclusion. The same conclusion has recently been drawn by researchers who follow different argumentative strategies and rely on distinct theoretical perspective. Among them one can find, M. Greenberg, 'The Moral Impact Theory of Law', *Yale Law Journal*, 123 (2014), pp. 1288–342; S. Hershovitz, 'The End of Jurisprudence', *Yale Law Journal*, 124 (2015), pp. 1160–204; and K. E. Himma, 'Is the Concept of Obligation Moralized?', *Law and Philosophy*, 37 (2018), pp. 203–27.

as one considers moral reasons overriding in this sense, a conceptual discontinuity emerges between moral reasons and intersubjective reasons. For intersubjective reasons, as I have characterized them, cannot be claimed to necessarily have supreme authority in the broader practical domain.

The main theoretical implication I draw from this remark is that the claim concerning the moral, vis-à-vis prudential, quality of legal obligation, qua standard constituted by intersubjective (not subjective) reasons, should be qualified. That is, the nature of legal obligation can be argued to be moral specifically (and exclusively) in the sense that legal obligation is a standard shaped by intersubjective, categorical, and not-necessarily-overriding considerations. Only as long as the moral domain is equated to the realm of what is intersubjective, categorical, and possibly non-overriding is it possible to characterize legal obligation as a moral requirement. The same qualification – presenting legal obligation as a moral standard – does not apply, instead, once morality is defined otherwise and, in particular, once overridingness is taken to be an essential feature of what is moral. Since I am inclined to define morality and moral reasons in the distinctive sense just introduced – namely, as a set of intersubjective, categorical, and possibly non-overriding considerations – I am prepared to subscribe to the conclusion that legal obligation is a requirement the nature of which is not just generically practically rational but also specifically moral.

The claims that legal obligation is constituted by intersubjective reasons and, relatedly, the quality of what is legally obligatory is moral (in the sense just introduced) have two further implications that I consider of some theoretical significance. First, the acceptance of the revisionary Kantian conception leads one to assert that there is no conceptual space for anything like a 'prudential (legal) obligation'. Prudential reasons, qua subjective and so exclusively agent-centred justifications, cannot result in any obligation to carry out given courses of action, since we cannot be said to be under a legal obligation unless intersubjective reasons apply to us. Likewise, whereas subjective reasons, and so purely prudential considerations, may justify one's action, the force of the justifications based on prudence cannot be qualified as obligatory. Stated otherwise, self-interest cannot take us into the realm of legal obligation: legal obligations are constitutively grounded in moral considerations, not in prudence, and, related to this, obligation-generating reasons are necessarily intersubjective reasons – and so moral reasons qua not merely self-regarding, subjective, and prudential, reasons.[2] Similarly, the nature of legal obligation can be claimed to be moral by virtue of the conceptual connection between legal obligation and intersubjective reasons for action. At its core, therefore, legal obligation is a moral construct, to the effect that the very idea of 'prudential legal obligation' should ultimately be regarded as a meaningless phrase.

The second implication of the revisionary Kantian conception on which I would like to draw the reader's attention can be so formulated. The thesis that legal obligations are a *subclass* of intersubjective practical reasons and the assertion of the moral quality of legal obligation means that the nature of the obligations arising out of law is not conventional. Conventional practices, especially when they are understood along the lines of Marmor's perceptive variant of legal conventionalism, have the conceptual capacity to provide subjects with justificatory reasons for action. A sophisticated conventionalist legal approach is, therefore, perfectly able to explain the constitutive link existing between legal obligations and justificatory practical reasons. By the same token, however, even Marmor's insightful conventionalist approach lacks the resources to secure the more specific connection obtaining between legal obligations and intersubjective reasons justifying one's action, since such approach programmatically allows for the possibility that the obligations the law engenders, qua generically practical and rational requirements issued by conventional practices, are grounded in subjective reasons for action, as opposed to intersubjective reasons associated with a domain – morality – that is constitutively non-conventional in nature. The conclusion that the nature of legal obligation can be conventional, vis-à-vis moral – a conclusion I argued to be misleading – depends on the fact that contemporary legal conventionalism amounts to a minimalist statement of the connection between practical reasons and legal obligation. This minimalism prevents the champions of legal conventionalism from further qualifying the essential connection between practical reasons and legal obligation as a linkage between intersubjective, or moral, reasons and legal obligation.

Importantly, once the essential connection between moral reasons, qua intersubjective and categorical justifications, and legal obligation is granted, we are also in the position to characterize legal obligation as a standard genuinely binding on its subjects, as opposed to taking it to be a

---

[2] In Prichard's words, 'conduciveness to our advantage is simply irrelevant to the question whether it is a duty to do some action' (H. A. Prichard, *Moral Obligation* (Oxford, Clarendon, 1949), p. 97).

generically internal constraint and so possibly a less than genuine constraint (which is what instead legal conventionalists entail). A theoretical implication of acknowledging the moral quality of legal obligation, therefore, is the claim that legal obligation is inaccurately accounted for in terms of a generically internal, practical, and rational requirement the genuine bindingness of which is ultimately conditioned on the existence of extra-institutional, or external, reasons one may have to participate in the obligation-engendering practice. Far from being a generically rational demand, possibly supported by subjective considerations, legal obligation is buttressed by a specific kind of non-merely-prudential reasons. To put it the other way around, in stating that the quality of the obligations engendered by the law is moral, the revisionary Kantian conception goes beyond the assertion, associated with legal conventionalism, that legal obligation is a (generic) reason for action. For, once it is conceptualized as a requirement the nature of which is moral qua intersubjective, legal obligation is best understood as a distinctive kind of constraint on our practical deliberation and ensuing conduct – indeed as a constraint that is conceptually discontinuous with at least some of the types of directions conventional practices impart. The statement of the moral quality of legal obligation, hence, supports the conclusion that the obligations produced by the law are requirements specifically anchored in a kind of considerations – intersubjective reasons – that conventionalist enterprises may well fail to establish.

8.3 The Force Model

A distinctive claim framing the revisionary Kantian conception is the thesis that in the presence of a legal obligation action is justified in the twofold sense that (a) it is required, not just recommended; and (b) departing from it lacks justification in the specific sense of being wrong qua unsupported by intersubjective considerations, not just prudentially inadvisable. This thesis has a significant implication insofar as it ultimately conceptualizes legal obligation as a practical reason with a distinctive kind of justificatory *force*. For, in order to be understood as (the source of) a legal obligation, a practical reason need count in favour of an action in the specific sense of justifying it with the force of a requirement. Accordingly, in my framework of thought, what distinguishes a pattern of conduct that is legally obligatory from one that is not so is the specific kind of strength with which that pattern is buttressed: the practical reasons legal obligation consists in are compelling and binding practical reasons – reasons with mandatory justificatory strength – vis-à-vis enticing practical reasons – reasons with recommendatory strength. What is legally obligatory, in other terms, is legally required, or demanded, by which – requirement or demandingness – it is meant what is practically justified with a given type of force.

This thesis is revealing of the fact that my conception of legal obligation is organized around the idea of a distinctive force that (just) some practical reasons – intersubjective reasons – have. And this is the intuition underpinning the accounts of obligation that, in Thomas Pink's terminology, instantiate the 'force model' of obligation.[3] The force model is to be contrasted with the 'feature model' of obligation – which is substantiated, instead, by the theories characterizing obligation as a specific trait of action. A concise introduction to those contrasting models of obligation may contribute to clarify and contextualize the conception of legal obligation that I am defending here.

On the force model, an obligation is owed to the strength of the underlying reason on which basis an action is justified: this underlying reason is a justificatory reason carrying a distinctive validating force which it lends to the conduct it backs up.[4] The force model, then, conceives of obligation as a reason with a peculiar strength – mandatory strength – which is, to reiterate, the kind of force (a given subclass of) intersubjective reasons distinctively come with. Relatedly, on the force model, there is no single feature that all and only obligatory actions have – single feature that is what ultimately makes them obligatory. Which is why obligation stands for a specific force, not property, that certain practical reasons carry with them, namely, a distinctive kind of support that only some reasons provide to action. Anything that counts as obligation will, then, be associated with a given sort of justificatory strength attached to certain reasons for action.

On the feature model, obligation is an equally distinctive notion. But instead of analysing its nature through its underlying rationale, we analyse it as a feature, or property, of action.[5] In other words, instead of asking 'What is the rational basis that morally binds us to certain lines of

---

[3] See T. Pink, 'Moral Obligation', in A. O'Hear (ed.), *Modern Moral Philosophy* (Cambridge, Cambridge University Press, 2004), pp. 159–85; and T. Pink, 'Normativity and Reason', *Journal of Moral Philosophy*, 4 (2007), pp. 406–31.

[4] On this model and its implications, see Pink, 'Moral Obligation', pp. 169–85; and Pink, 'Normativity and Reason', pp. 416–31.

[5] On the feature model, see Pink, 'Moral Obligation', pp. 161–9; and Pink, 'Normativity and Reason', pp. 409–16.

action?', we ask 'What outward property of action makes some conduct mandatory and others not?'. If we can identify that property – an independent element shared by all mandatory actions – we will have singled out the class of actions that qualify as obligatory. In this model, then, if a conduct exhibits a certain property A, then it is obligatory (this contrasts with the force model, which concerns itself not so much with the objective, observable properties of action as with the justification of action).

I set up this contrast between the force model and the feature model not only because it brings into sharp focus the account of legal obligation I am supporting, but also because it shows that the revisionary Kantian conception is incompatible with any theory of (legal) obligation that is best understood as an instance of the feature model. And examples of the feature model abound in English-language practical philosophy and legal theory from the early modern period onward (and they come from some authoritative sources, too). Here I will confine myself to briefly refer to three of those examples, all of which have been very influential, and widely discussed, in jurisprudence.

Let us first consider the account of obligation devised in the work of John Stuart Mill, whose conception is in one respect similar to the one I am putting forward but in another respect markedly different from it. For, on the one hand, Mill views obligation as a matter of right and wrong (rather than placing it in the camp of what is advisable or inadvisable, like I do); but, on the other hand, he brings that idea into correlation with that of a penalty or sanction. For Mill claims that 'we do not call anything wrong, unless we mean to imply that a person ought to be punished in some way or other for doing it'.[6] Therefore, for Mill 'it is part of the notion of Duty in every one of its forms, that a person may rightfully be compelled to fulfil it. Duty is a thing which may be *exacted* from a person, as one exacts a debt.'[7] So what Mill does is to single out a feature of certain actions – their being enforceable – as a trait by virtue of which it becomes our duty to perform any action falling within that class, meaning that those actions are obligatory (obligation being for Mill a concept coextensive with that of duty, as it is for me). The reasoning, then, is essentially as follows: if coercion can be used to enforce an action or punish its non-performance (an independent property of action), then that action is obligatory.

---

[6] J. S. Mill, *Utilitarianism* (Indianapolis (IN), Hackett, 2002; or. ed. 1861), p. 45.
[7] Mill, *Utilitarianism*, p. 45; original emphasis.

Even before Mill, the same view was set out by Jeremy Bentham, who specifically looked at obligation in law as well as morality and argued that actions in these two areas are obligatory if there are consequences which can be made to follow or which are likely to follow as a result of not performing those actions (or as a result of performing an action contrary to what is prohibited). Bentham specifically gauges this idea to legal obligation by arguing that laws are obligatory to the extent that they are provided with a specific kind of sanction he calls 'political', namely, a sanction set forth in the laws themselves, and which officials will carry out in accordance with forms and procedures likewise set forth in law.[8] He then goes on to argue on this basis that obligation in law is conceptually linked to a specific *feature* of law: its ability to set forth and impose sanctions, or the likelihood that when the law is broken, sanctions will follow. And this view of Bentham was later taken up by John Austin in putting forward his own influential model of law as a command issued by the sovereign and backed by the threat of force.

Interestingly, even Hart – who felt that Austin's account was fundamentally misconceived and so that a theory was needed to make up for its failings – proceeded to build such a theory working from within the very feature model of obligation that framed Austin's thinking, too. Hart criticizes Austin's account of obligation as inadequate in that the account frames the problem from the external point of view of an observer.[9] By contrast, Hart argues, if we are to understand legal obligation, we have to look at the law from an internal point of view as members of a group following a social practice governed by rules we ourselves subscribe to by taking these rules to be legitimate standards of behaviour. This is a theory of legal obligation shaped by the idea of a social practice-rule, an idea aptly summarized by Leslie Green in his restatement of Hart's view that a social practice-rule exists insofar as we have before us a 'regularity of behaviour, deviations from which are criticised, such criticism is regarded as legitimate, and at least some people treat the regularity as a standard for guiding and appraising behaviour'.[10] By so replacing the

---

[8] See J. Bentham, *An Introduction to the Principles of Morals and Legislation* (Kila (MT), Kessinger, 2010; or. ed. 1789), pp. 8–23.

[9] See H. L. A. Hart, 'Legal and Moral Obligation', in A. Melden (ed.), *Essays in Moral Philosophy* (Seattle (WA), University of Washington Press, 1958), pp. 82–107; and H. L. A. Hart, *Concept of Law* (with a Postscript, Oxford, Clarendon, 1994; or. ed. 1961), pp. 79–91.

[10] L. Green 'Law and Obligations', in J. Coleman and S. Shapiro (eds.), *The Oxford Handbook of Jurisprudence and Philosophy of Law* (Oxford, Oxford University Press, 2002), pp. 514–47.

sanction-based account of legal obligation with a rule-based one, Hart succeeds in explaining what it is that makes obligation different from a mere habit, or a convergence of behaviour. He does so by framing legal obligation as an ought arising from (a) the existence of a social practice, in combination with (b) an endorsement of that practice from an internal point of view.

This might be taken to suggest that Hart espouses a force model of obligation, since he frames obligation from the standpoint of self-identified participants sharing a special attitude to the practice they engage in, that is, they relate to that practice from an internal point of view that consists in a willingness to regard the rules governing the same practice as binding reasons – reasons bestowed with binding force, that is – to act accordingly. But in fact what Hart offers is a feature model of obligation. We can appreciate as much by noticing that the practical reasons we have for accepting a social practice cannot be divorced from that practice. They cannot exist without the corresponding practice, just as the practice cannot exist without those reasons. By setting up this double bind, Hart is essentially saying that the reason why we subscribe to a practice is that we accept the rules governing that practice. This in turn amounts to the view that actions are obligatory insofar as they are prescribed by a social practice-rule. So, just as Austin singles out the use of sanctions as a feature of certain actions by virtue of which those actions become obligatory, Hart singles out the demands of social practice-rules as a feature of a certain class of actions that in virtue of that feature – their being demanded by those rules – likewise become obligatory. Hart is therefore working from within the feature model of obligation.

8.4 The Kantian Quality of the Account

The account of legal obligation put forward in this work was described in Chapter 7 as Kantian, since I take it to be anchored in Kant's theory of what is obligatory. The account was, more specifically, presented as a *revisionary* Kantian conception because, as much as it draws on Kant's practical philosophy and approach to obligation, my account is not intended as an accurate restatement of Kant's views.[11] In consideration

---

[11] Here it should be reiterated that the aims of this research are not hermeneutical, exegetical, or reconstructive, but rather systematic. So, even if it turns out that the proposed theory of legal obligation is not fully coherent with Kant's views, that should

of the fact that the original insights underpinning my account of legal obligation come from Kant's practical philosophy, it seems only appropriate to trace that genealogy, lest any misunderstanding should arise in casting a theory of legal obligation in a Kantian mould.

In this context, to begin with, it should be noted that the main *substantive insight* shaping my conception of legal obligation is characteristically Kantian. For I conceptualize legal obligation as a kind of necessitation imposed by practical rationality. And such conceptualization owes much to Kant's idea of obligation as 'the necessity of a free action under a categorical imperative of reason'.[12] Indeed, in both frameworks – Kant's and mine – the basis of obligation is not metaphysical, logical, or empirical: obligation rests on practical rationality, whose principles make it normatively (as opposed to metaphysically, logically, or empirically) necessary to act accordingly even in the face of contrary inclinations, interests, and dispositions.[13] That is to say, the general idea from which I derive my conception of *legal* obligation as a categorical constraint on action based on practical rationality and issued by law is distinctively Kantian in so that it maps onto Kant's view of *obligation* as a rational necessitation.

No less important in this context is the fundamental premise I relied on to arrive at the conceptualization of legal obligation as a rational requirement. I started out in the investigation from a general *concept* of *obligation* (obligation simpliater) as a construct within which to specify a *conception* of *legal* obligation. In this move lies a significant point of contact between my construction of legal obligation and Kant's approach to what is obligatory. For the process that has us move from a concept of obligation to a conception of legal obligation as a specific instantiation of such concept is rooted in, and ultimately justified by, Kant's fundamental thesis that there is 'only one obligation'. This thesis finds an emphatic statement in the preliminary draft of Kant's *Metaphysics of*

---

not prevent one from being able to judge this theory on its own merits, namely, from assessing whether the theory is internally coherent and comprehensive, while also offering an accurate and insightful account of legal obligation.

[12] I. Kant, *The Metaphysics of Morals*, AK 6:222-3 (Cambridge, Cambridge University Press, 1996).

[13] *Principles*, or 'laws', in Kant's terminology, are *objective* standards of conduct based on practical rationality, and so standards that any clear-thinking person should acknowledge. They can be contrasted with *maxims*, which instead are general standards that not everyone can be expected to embrace or find sensible, and whose force is therefore that of *subjective* guidelines. On this distinction, see Kant, *Metaphysics of Morals*, AK 6:225.

Morals, where it is claimed that 'there are various duties though only one obligation overall in regard to the totality of duty. This latter has no plural.'[14]

The centrality of this insight – call it the oneness-of-obligation thesis – in Kant's practical philosophy can be made to emerge by looking at Kant's legal-philosophical project, especially as it is carried out in *The Metaphysics of Morals*. *The Metaphysics of Morals* has been described as 'a very difficult book, partly because of the difficult nature of the issues dealt with, but partly also because of obscurities and inconsistencies, real or apparent'.[15] And, in fact, even the basic claims defended in it have been interpreted in different ways by Kantian scholars. But for all these disagreements, there can be little doubt that there Kant does theorize a conceptual continuity among the obligations set forth by different departments of practical rationality, such as law and morality among others. To appreciate the precise meaning of this claim it will help to highlight its contrast with mainstream contemporary jurisprudence, where the question as to whether law and morality are conceptually connected or separate is typically discussed by treating them as two discrete and self-standing domains, each amenable to investigation in isolation from other systems by which to regulate action. In treating that same question, Kant takes a radically different approach, by introducing an overarching element, namely, practical rationality, which he refers to as *Sittlichkeit*, *Sitten*, or *moralis*, and can be translated into English also as 'morals'. Practical rationality, or morals, is understood by Kant as encompassing both law (*Recht*, or *ius*) and morality (*Ethik*, *ethica* or *moralitas*). That is, practical rationality, on this account, singles out the arrangement of action-related standards, norms, and requirements based on, or derivable from, reason alone, and thus holding for everyone unconditionally.[16] Accordingly, in *The Metaphysics of Morals* practical rationality is introduced as a thin and overreaching constraint on reasoning on practical matters (be they legal issues or concerns pertaining to morality).

---

[14] I. Kant, *Draft for Metaphysics of Morals*, AK 23:250 (Berlin, de Gruyter, 1968).
[15] M. Willaschek, 'Why the *Doctrine of Right* does not belong in the *Metaphysics of Morals*', *Jarbuch für Recht und Ethik*, 5 (1997), p. 205.
[16] See Kant, *Metaphysics of Morals*, AK 6:216. For a thorough discussion of these terms and how they relate to one another, see Willaschek, 'Why the *Doctrine of Right* does not belong in the *Metaphysics of Morals*'.

So where most contemporary legal theory only works with two concepts (law and morality, which thus is not distinguished from morals), in *The Metaphysics of Morals* Kant has three distinct concepts (practical rationality, or morals, morality, and law). Namely, Kant's architecture of the practical distinctively includes a wide-encompassing idea – practical rationality qua morals (*Sitten*) – which is specifically understood as a standard of action that governs the whole of the practical sphere. Related to this, the practical sphere is claimed to include, and be distinguishable in, both law (*Recht*) and morality (*Ethik*).[17] Namely, in Kant's framework of thought as it emerges in *The Metaphysics of Morals*, on the one hand, law (*Recht*) and morality (*Ethik*) are each a subset, or department, of practical rationality (*Sitten*); and, on the other hand, they are both continuous with practical rationality, drawing on practical rationality in framing their own rules and principles of action.

This philosophical framework enables one to address the problem of the relation between the requirements issued by law and morality in a fashion that has no direct counterpart within the main schools of legal thought defended in contemporary jurisprudence. That is to say, we should not think that Kant's theory of morals qua practical rationality (*Sitten*) applies directly to the problem of the relation between law and morality, as the problem is addressed by legal theorists today. Indeed in Kant's philosophy morality is exclusively concerned with that part of the practical domain which revolves around the Categorical Imperative. So it would be a mistake to lump morality together with morals qua practical rationality (*Sitten*), where the Categorical Imperative sits next to other kinds of fundamental principles and basic demands of reason in its practical use.

---

[17] A terminological caveat should be added here. Traditionally, Kantian scholars use the term 'Right', as opposed to 'law', to refer to the juridical domain. The main reason supporting this terminological choice is that in Kant's philosophical framework 'laws' do not stand for provisions the quality of which is specifically juridical but rather, as indicated in footnote 13, for ethical standards of conduct that, being objective, should be differentiated from 'maxims'. Whilst using the term 'Right' to refer to juridical systems and norms is well supported in the context of studies specifically devoted to the understanding of Kant's body of work, adhering to this terminological use would be more confusing than insightful here, since in the rest of this work I conformed to the standard practice among legal theorists to indicate juridical systems and juridical norms by the term 'law', while using 'right' to exclusively refer to subjective claims, as they are recognized by a juridical order. This is the reason why in this chapter I will depart from the general terminology in use among Kantians and stick to the practice of jurisprudes, a practice that has informed the rest of this book.

A closely related point to keep in mind, in any effort to bring a Kantian philosophical approach to bear on the jurisprudential problem of the relation between law and morality, is that to this end the problem needs to be specifically reframed consistently with Kant's tripartite architecture as just outlined. That is to say, the relation we properly need to figure out is not the one between law and morals qua practical rationality (*Sitten*), but the one between law (*Recht*) and morality (*Ethik*) understood as two instantiations of practical rationality. Crucially, in this context practical rationality is not understood as a merely contentless placeholder; it rather stands for the set of principles that fundamentally govern and basically justify action and so for normative standards engendered by, and constitutive of, our deliberative capacity as it applies to the practical domain in its different declinations (such as the moral realm, the legal sphere, the political space, and so on). Practical rationality is, hence, defined and delimited by our capacity for addressing through reflection issues concerning the courses of conduct that ought to be undertaken. Which statement is in turn premised on the thesis that deliberation is a rational process and, qua rational process, at a fundamental level it is regulated by the norms that make the very activity of deliberating both possible and distinctive. That is to say, the content of practical rationality is settled by the arrangement of fundamental principles and basic norms of action, among which they prominently figure not only the universalization requirement and the instrumental principle but also the standards that secure an acting self a degree of unity, wholeness, coherence over time, control, and self-mastery minimally sufficient to constitute such self as the author of its own action by thus differentiating it from a mere heap of inclinations and wishes – call those standards the 'norms of authorship' for short.[18] Practical rationality, in sum, is taken to mean, and granted content by, all the wide-ranging and all-encompassing action-related requirements and entitlements (such as the universalization requirement, the instrumental principle, and the norms of authorship I have just mentioned) that are based on rationality and, accordingly, bind us categorically.[19] Now, by bringing a third mediating term – practical rationality – into the dualistic picture now in wide use among contemporary jurisprudes, Kant's practical philosophy can differentiate legal obligation and moral obligation while also showing them to be

---

[18] or a sophisticated argument defending a similar characterization of practical rationality I refer the reader to C. Korsgaard, *Self-Constitution* (Oxford, Oxford University Press, 2009).
[19] Here 'categorically the term' is used in the sense introduced in Chapter 7.

continuous. And this in turn makes it possible to support the thesis of the oneness of obligation I referred to earlier in this section. But let us unpack this argument and its theoretical implications, so as to provide a sense of Kant's legal project, while also illustrating in what way the conception of legal obligation put forward here ought to be understood as Kantian (however much revisionary it may be in that respect).

As my brief introduction to Kant's distinctive philosophical vocabulary and associated conceptual constructions reveals, a number of adjustments are required for those wishing to rely on Kant's practical philosophy when joining in the contemporary jurisprudential debate. Two of those adjustments are of particular significance in the context of this study. To begin with, we should take care not to equivocate Kant's claims about morals (qua practical rationality – *Sitten*) with his views about morality (qua *Ethik*). Failing to do so may lead one to conclude that Kant's theory of practical rationality (*Sitten*) directly applies to the discussion about the relation between law and morality, as this discussion is carried out in jurisprudence today. Doing so would indeed be revealing of a conceptual confusion ultimately inducing one to mistaken (what today we would call) Kant's account of practical rationality with his view of morality, by thus confounding the positions that Kant defends in relation to the whole of practical rationality with the views that Kant theorizes about just one subset of it – morality. Related to this, those wishing to benefit from, and appeal to, Kant's contribution when dealing with today's jurisprudential puzzle concerning the conceptual relation between law and morality need to be aware that in Kantian parlance the puzzle has to be reframed as the issue of whether or not the *legal* instantiations of practical rationality – namely, the legal instantiations of morals qua *Sitten*, vis-à-vis morality qua *Ethik* – stand in a relation of conceptual continuity with the *moral* instantiations of the same overarching domain (with the adjective 'moral' referring to morality, qua *Ethik*, not to morals, qua *Sitten*).

Secondly, it should be appreciated that the addition of a third term – practical rationality – to the dualistic picture in wide use among contemporary legal theorists is crucial to understanding the overall project that Kant specifically undertakes. For in Kant's philosophical construction, as I understand it, practical rationality is functional to securing the differentiation of legal obligation and moral obligation, whilst also granting their continuity, which would otherwise be unconceivable. This structure in turn vindicates Kant's thesis of the oneness of obligation. This statement requires further elaboration, since some additional groundwork needs to be done before the full theoretical implications of Kant's specific framework of thought can be adequately grasped. So let me expand on this point, which is also key to the qualification of my conception of legal obligation as (revisionary) Kantian.

Once practical rationality, as distinct of morality – is brought into the picture, law cannot be reduced to a mere emanation, or specific application, of morality and its constitutive principles without substantially departing from Kant's legal project. Likewise, in Kant's philosophy the contents of law cannot be claimed to flow from the standards constitutive of morality. Nor can the binding quality of law either be borrowed from considerations stemming from morality or be made to depend on those considerations.[20] At the same time those endorsing Kant's conceptual framework cannot radicalize the distinction between law and morality as well as the differentiation in kind of the requirements issued by each of them either, since that would obscure the relations of continuity that in Kant's practical philosophy hold together law and morality, once they both are constructed as specific instantiations of a common genre – practical rationality.[21] It is in light of this understanding of the relation that obtains among practical rationality, law, and morality, I submit, that the continuity between law and morality (and the relative obligations) is best understood, with the deep role that practical rationality plays in shaping law and morality alike and explaining their difference within their unity.

Notice that it would be questionable to interpret that continuity as warranting the derivability, and so the conceptual subordination, of one domain in respect to the other, as some Kantians nonetheless try to do: in Kant's picture law and its fundamental principles, notions, structure, and contents can hardly be derived from, and are not subordinate to, morality, the Categorical Imperative, and other essential notions, mechanisms, and contents pertaining to the realm of morality.[22] Interpreting the

---

[20] A convincing argument for this statement can be found in M. Willaschek, 'Right and Coercion: Can Kant's Conception of Right Be Derived from His Moral Theory?', *International Journal of Philosophical Studies*, 17 (2009), pp. 49–70. See also M. Willaschek, 'The Non-Derivability of Kantian Right from the Categorical Imperative: A Response to Nance', *International Journal of Philosophical Studies*, 20 (2012), pp. 557–64.

[21] This interpretation of Kant's project finds a clear statement in Willaschek, 'Right and Coercion'; and S. Bacin, '"Only One Obligation": Kant on the Distinction and the Normative Continuity of Ethics and Right', *Studi Kantiani*, 29 (2016), pp. 49–62.

[22] In fact, this dimension of Kant's work is the subject matter of a long-standing controversy among Kantians. The two main competing views here are the so-called Dependence Thesis and Independence Thesis. The champions of those theses disagree over the way in which Kant conceives of the conceptual relation between the legal domain and legal

continuity of law and morality that way would indeed force one to call into question claims that figure centrally in Kant's architectonics of practical thought, or even abandon altogether Kant's overall approach to practical philosophy in fundamental respects.[23] But, likewise objectionable from the Kantian standpoint, as I read it, is the statement of the radical separation and mutual independence of law and morality, as this statement is theorized by the champions of certain contemporary schools of legal thought, notably by legal positivists. For Kant's philosophical construction secures a deep conceptual dependence and an essential connection between law and morality through the mediating role played

obligation, on the one hand, and the moral realm and moral obligation, on the other. Likewise they disagree over the way in which Kant conceptualizes the relation between practical rationality and obligation in general, on the one hand, and the two pairs formed by law–legal obligation and morality–moral obligation, on the other. In a nutshell, the Dependence Thesis, which is the traditional, or 'official', view, has it that the legal realm is conceptually connected to the moral domain, from which ultimately both fundamental legal notions and legal contents are derived. On this reading, Kant treats legal obligation as a direct emanation of moral obligation and, hence, he ends up theorizing the dependence of legal obligation on moral obligation. The consequence of this construction is that legal obligation is to be regarded as grounded on moral obligations and the contents of the obligations engendered by the law are ultimately derived from, and fixed by, the fundamental moral principles. As a reaction to this view, another interpretation of Kant's treatment of legal obligation, as it relates to other kinds of obligation, has been put forward by contemporary Kantian scholars, such as Thomas Pogge (see T. Pogge, 'Is Kant's Rechtslehre a "Comprehensive Liberalism"?' in M. Timmons (ed.), *Kant's Metaphysics of Morals: Interpretive Essays* (Oxford, Oxford University Press, 2002), pp. 133–58), Allen Wood (see A. Wood, 'The Final Form of Kant's Practical Philosophy', in M. Timmons (ed.), *Kant's Metaphysics of Morals: Interpretive Essays* (Oxford, Oxford University Press, 2002), pp. 1–21; and A. Wood, 'The Independence of Right from Ethics', in *The Free Development of Each* (Oxford, Oxford University Press, 2014), pp. 70–89), and Arthur Ripstein (see A. Ripstein, 'Authority and Coercion', *Philosophy and Public Affairs*, 32 (2004), pp. 2–35; and A. Ripstein, *Force and Freedom* (Cambridge (MA), Harvard University Press, 2009), who are among the advocates of the so-called Independence Thesis. In accordance to this alternative interpretation, law and legal obligation constitute autonomous departments that bear no fundamental connection with, and are not derivable from, morality and moral obligation. Likewise, the fundamental principles structuring the legal domain and constituting what is legally obligatory are irreducible to the basic standards of morality, as morality is conceived by Kant. This also means that Kant's legal theory is not a direct emanation of his moral theory. As Marcus Willaschek shows in detail in his systematic engagement with the legal doctrine Kant puts forward in *The Metaphysics of Morals*, both the Dependence Thesis and Independence Thesis can be claimed to find support in (different) passages of Kant's texts (Willaschek, 'Why the *Doctrine of Right* does not belong in the *Metaphysics of Morals*').

[23] This point is convincingly and systematically made throughout Ripstein, *Force and Freedom*.

by practical rationality. That is to say, in Kant's theoretical framework practical rationality – its constitutive norms and notions – can be claimed to profoundly and fundamentally shape both law – its basic standards, concepts, and structure – and morality – its fundamental principles, notions, and edifice. Accordingly, law and morality are *distinct* realms that nonetheless should be acknowledged as *closely related* and *interdependent* at a conceptual level by virtue of their common participation in practical rationality. Hence, Kant's tripartite construction theorizes the existence of a special relation between law and morality, relation that is best understood as a form of 'unity-within-difference'.[24] In other terms, law and morality are constructed by Kant as distinct departments of one unifying genre – practical rationality qua

---

[24] The treatment offered in this part of my argument also indicates that there is no straightforward way to enlist Kant as a champion of either legal positivism or legal naturalism. Clearly, this is not the place to engage with the broad discussion as to whether Kant's legal theory is positivist or non-positivist in quality, since doing so would distract from the main topic I am considering in this chapter. However, it may be worth mentioning that, on the one hand, Kant's legal theory can hardly be presented as a version of legal positivism for a decisive reason, among many others that will not be introduced here: whereas Kant's practical philosophy denies the autonomy of law, understood as an obligation-generating practice, the thesis of the autonomy of law is defended by the torchbearers for legal positivism (and indeed such thesis can be regarded as one of the distinctive and fundamental tenets associated with legal positivism). For, as I will elaborate, Kant is committed to the claim that the law derives its obligatory character from elsewhere (namely, from practical rationality); which claim, in turn, is incompatible with the thesis of the autonomy of law, as this thesis is theorized within legal positivism. Relatedly, for Kant a system of (merely) posited laws constitutively fails to be authoritative; and this is a conclusion that few legal positivists would be comfortable with. On the other hand, Kant's legal theory can hardly be qualified as a standard form of legal naturalism for at least the following reason, among many others that emerge from my discussion of the conceptual distinction of law and morality, as this discussion is carried out later in this section. Traditionally legal naturalism has insisted on the existence of a deep-seated connection between law and morality. In this context, the assumption widespread among legal naturalists has been that such connection is *direct*. That is to say, law has been claimed by legal naturalists to necessarily incorporate certain traits and features that (contribute to) define morality, to which law is then argued to be conceptually connected. By contrast, I notice here, Kant establishes a conceptual connection between law and morality – and more specifically between the obligatory dimensions of the two realms – *indirectly*, namely, via practical rationality. Accordingly, the argumentative strategy Kant relies on in his treatment of the conceptual connection between law and morality is irreducible to the arguments traditionally deployed by legal naturalists to vindicate such connection.

Sitten – namely, as realms sharing a generic unity, or continuity, which still makes room for specific differences among them.[25]

Crucially, to anticipate the interpretation of Kant's position about legal obligation defended in what follows, for Kant the conceptual relation between the two domains – law and morality – specifically amounts to the claim that neither the bindingness of the requirements set out by law nor the obligatoriness of the claims made by morality are self-standing; rather they are both borrowed from practical rationality. That is, the continuity of law and morality, as it is secured by their common belonging to the wider sphere of what is practically rational, specifically consists in the fact that the obligatory quality of both what is binding in law and what is binding in morality is owed to, and warranted by, the standards constitutive of practical rationality. As far as the obligatory force is concerned, thus, the (otherwise distinct realms of) law and morality are claimed by Kant to be at one – continuous or undistinguishable – in so that there is no systematic separation between law and morality, as far as the grounds of their authority are concerned, since the obligatory force of legal standards and the binding quality of moral principles alike have their sources in practical rationality. In what follows I will pass to substantiate this assertion by paying attention to Kant's claims about law and morality, as they can be found in *The Metaphysics of Morals*.

In *The Metaphysics of Morals*, Kant draws a distinction between law as being concerned with the *external* component of freedom and morality as being concerned with the *internal* one. Indeed, as Kant observes, law 'has to do ... only with the external and indeed practical relation of one person to another, insofar as their actions, as deeds, can have (direct or indirect) influence on each other'.[26] This stands in contrast to morality, understood as an agent's 'capacity for self-constraint not by means of other inclinations but by pure practical reason (which scorns such intermediaries)'.[27] That is to say, law is designed to protect our *external freedom* from the constraint that other people place on our range of action through their decisions. To this effect law is legitimized to make

---

[25] Incidentally, on this basis it is tempting to conclude that the Dependence Thesis and Independence Thesis can be both misleading. For, in stressing the closeness of law and morality, the Dependence Thesis obscures their distinctiveness and mutual autonomy; by contrast, in emphasizing the separation of law and morality, the Independence Thesis seems to miss their common root, which lies in practical rationality.
[26] Kant, *Metaphysics of Morals*, AK 6:230.
[27] Kant, *Metaphysics of Morals*, AK 6:396.

use of coercion.[28] Accordingly, a constitutive link is claimed to obtain between law, external freedom, and coercion. In turn, such link contributes decisively to determine not only the fundamental principle of law – the so-called Universal Principle of Right – but also the substance of law.[29] In contrast to law, which is so understood by Kant as a system functional to protecting our external freedom, morality is exclusively concerned with our *internal* freedom. In Kant's framework, internal freedom singles out an agent's independence from the hindrances of their own sensuous dispositions, or non-rational influences. Since morality sets out the rational standards that need to be followed for an agent to make proper use of their internal freedom, ultimately Kant conceives of morality as a set of practical principles upholding one's rational agency.

The different functions of law – preserving external freedom – and morality – enabling us to correctly exercise internal freedom – explain why the distinction of the two domains theorized by Kant runs deep. To begin with, law is governed by a fundamental principle – the Universal Principle of Right – that is irreducible to, and cannot be derived from, the fundamental principle of morality – the Categorical Imperative.[30] Secondly, coercion, which is justified in law as a means for protecting the external freedom of everyone, is not legitimate in moral affairs, since in the context of Kant's practical thought coerced rational agency should be acknowledged as a conceptual impossibility. Related to this, the motives one has to conform to the law are irrelevant, for the purpose of upholding the external freedom of those subject to the law is served just by the fact that legal subjects abide by the rules of law, no matter what the motives underpinning their obedience are.[31] By contrast, for Kant the motive is constitutive of moral obedience, since we do not fulfil our rational agency and so make an improper usage of our internal freedom, unless we follow the standards of morality because of rational

---

[28] On coercion and law, see Kant, *Metaphysics of Morals*, AK 6:231–3.
[29] A systematic treatment of Kant's legal conception can be found in Ripstein, *Force and Freedom*, where the relations between law and morality, as they are conceptualized by Kant, are discussed in great detail.
[30] This at least is the view that some scholars impute to Kant, *Metaphysics of Morals*, AK 6:231–2. See, for instance, Ripstein, *Force and Freedom*, pp. 30–56 and 355–88. For a contrary view, see P. Guyer, 'Kant's Deductions of the Principles of Rights', in M. Timmons (ed.), *Kant's Metaphysics of Morals: Interpretive Essays* (Oxford, Oxford University Press, 2002), pp. 23–64.
[31] On this aspect, see Kant, *Metaphysics of Morals*, AK 6:220–1.

considerations, or out of the 'incentive of duty', as Kant puts it.[32] Finally, in consideration of the fact that the requirements associated with the protection of freedom in its external instantiations do not necessarily coincide with the demands arising from the need of properly exercising internal freedom, law and morality incorporate substantive requirements that do not necessarily match and may well overlap only in part.[33]

Despite these plentiful and far from insignificant differences, law and morality are not conceptualized by Kant as realms radically apart one from another. Notably, in my understanding of Kant's philosophical construction, the continuity of the two domains is due to their objects.[34] Those objects, whilst diversified, are not irremediably heterogeneous, as they both insist on (different dimensions of) one and the same notion: freedom, which is understood by Kant as independence from non-rational constraints (be those hindrances external or internal).[35] Once it is so understood, freedom is conceptually associated with the idea of

---

[32] Kant, *Metaphysics of Morals*, AK 6:219.

[33] For further elaboration on these differences and their conceptual implications see Ripstein, *Force and Freedom*.

[34] This reading of Kant's project is based on a twofold belief. First, I embrace the view that 'Kant draws a series of sharp divisions between Right and ethics. Ethical conduct depends upon the maxim on which an action is done; rightful conduct depends only on the outer form of interaction between persons. The inner nature of ethical conduct means that the only incentive consistent with the autonomy at the heart of morality must be morality itself; rightful conduct can be induced by incentives provided by others. Other persons are entitled to enforce duties of right, but not duties of ethics' (Ripstein, *Force and Freedom*, pp. 11–12). Importantly, 'each of these differences precludes any direct appeal to the Categorical Imperative' (Ripstein, *Force and Freedom*, p. 12) when legal issues are at stake. Therefore, the legal domain cannot be understood as some form of applied morality – or a direct emanation of the standards of morality – without abandoning Kant's own distinctive project. Secondly (and here my interpretation of Kant's legal and political philosophy arguably departs from Ripstein's influential reading (cf. Ripstein, *Force and Freedom*, pp. 355–88)), I think that in Kant's philosophical framework, despite their conceptual distinction and contentual divergences, law and morality are both rooted in practical rationality. As a result, I am committed to the view that practical rationality secures a deep continuity between law and morality, which should both be regarded as (different and mutually irreducible) instantiations of practical rationality. In my reading of Kant's practical philosophy, then, whilst the basic standards of law cannot be derived from the fundamental principles of morality – law is not properly understood as applied ethics – practical rationality does set the limits of law (as well as the limits of morality). Law, in other words, is not a self-confined independent domain but rather a particular declination and a peculiar extension of what is practically rational. Relatedly, law is best understood as a sphere that conceptually connects with, fundamentally responds to, and is ultimately rooted in, practical rationality.

[35] This definition of freedom can be found, for instance, in I. Kant, *Critique of Pure Reason*, AK 4:A534/B562 (Cambridge, Cambridge University Press, 1998).

autonomy. For in Kant's philosophy, on the one hand, being free means to be bounded by principles of one's making (vis-à-vis being subject to no principle and so having the opportunity to act whimsically); on the other hand, autonomy stands for the capacity for rational self-legislation.[36] This statement is revealing of the fact that for Kant freedom is also closely linked to practical rationality and, more specifically, it singles out the domain where practical rationality, as Kant conceives it, unfolds. On this basis, it should be concluded that in Kant's theorization *freedom*, *autonomy*, and *practical rationality* form a conceptually tightly knit unit, as *autonomy* is the capacity that enables agents to make good use of their *freedom* by subjecting them to the standards of *practical rationality*. Or, to rephrase the same idea, appropriately exercising one's freedom means for one to conform to the standards of practical rationality by thus enjoying autonomy. So, ultimately, acting autonomously, making proper use of freedom, and following the standards of practical rationality are conceptually inseparable states. And this means in turn that the fundamental standards of practical rationality set the limits of our freedom by grounding the normativity of any principle of action through which we, qua autonomous creatures, aptly exercise freedom.

Now, insofar as in Kant's philosophical framework both law and morality are concerned with freedom, which is essentially connected to both autonomy and rationality in its practical use, the fundamental principles of practical rationality find their way, and directly apply, to law (and morality). More specifically, the role those principles play is that of grounding the normative authority law (and morality) can legitimately claim in relation to autonomous and free agents. Law (and morality) should be acknowledged to make claim on us, qua autonomous and free acting subjects, only to the extent in which law (and morality) can be anchored in the principles constitutive of practical rationality. This reasoning applies not only to law and morality but also to legal obligation and moral duty: both types of requirements are grounded in the principles of practical rationality, absent which there can be no suitable exercise of freedom – freedom that is the domain both law and morality are concerned with. This is to say that the principles of practical rationality constitute the sources of practical requirements in the sphere of law and in the realm of morality alike.

---

[36] Autonomy is defined in these terms in I. Kant, *Groundwork of the Metaphysics of Morals*, AK 4:440 (Cambridge, Cambridge University Press, 2012).

To rephrase the idea, legal obligations and moral duties can be considered obligatory only insofar as they are functional to the freedom of the agents to whom they apply. And this freedom is rooted in the practical rationality of agents qua self-legislating creatures, namely, qua selves whose action is subjected to rational constraints. That is, freedom is only appropriately used as a result of one's adherence to the fundamental standards of practical rationality. Which is why legal obligation and moral obligation have a common source in practical rationality. Hence, by virtue of their intrinsic link with freedom (which in its different declinations – external and internal respectively – is the object of both law and morality), the principles defining practical rationality establish the binding force of the requirements of both law and morality. From which it follows that the ground of the obligatoriness of law and morality is one and the same: practical rationality, understood as a precondition of one's exercise of freedom as well as a necessary dimension of autonomy. In Kant's philosophical framework, therefore, the quality of the bindingness of law and morality is acknowledged to be homogeneous, or undifferentiated, in kind.

The upshot of this reading of Kant's philosophical project, in sum, is that law is neither derivable from morality nor separate from it, in that both law and morality are grounded in practical rationality.[37] For the standards of law and morality are considered by Kant essential to an agent's exercise of freedom and, thus, autonomy, or rational determination qua independence of the hindrances coming from the influences (which in Kant's construction are likewise heteronomous) of others (law) and one's own sensuous self (morality).[38] In this framework, the fact that law and morality have to do with two distinct dimensions of freedom – external and internal – makes it possible to explain why law and morality cannot be reduced to each other, whilst the fact that both law and morality are concerned with freedom – however much in different dimensions – makes it possible to explain the one and the same obligatoriness – rational obligatoriness – that each claims in its own dimension. And this takes us back to the original idea, namely, that legal obligation and moral duty are both grounded in the principles of practical

---

[37] As Willaschek puts it, 'it is important to see that denying that the Kantian conception of Right can be derived from Kant's moral theory does not force us to deny that the universal principle of Right is an expression of rational autonomy' (Willaschek, 'Right and Coercion', pp. 65–6).

[38] See Kant, *Metaphysics of Morals*, AK 6:214.

rationality; and, relatedly, that practical rationality is the source of the binding force of law and morality alike.[39] Which conclusion in turn supports the oneness-of-obligation thesis.

Having taken time to unpack Kant's account of legal obligation, explaining how it fits into his broader architecture of practical philosophy, by way of concluding this section, I should just stress here the two main insights I draw from the Kantian account. The first of these consists in the *process* of investigation, on which legal obligation is recognized to be a species of an all-encompassing genus covering the whole of obligation, thus making it necessary to start out from a preliminary theory of obligation as such (obligation per se) before we can develop a conception of *legal* obligation. This is the main premise for the oneness-of-obligation thesis, on which obligation is construed as a unified concept encompassing both legal and moral obligation. This in turn takes us to the other main insight – which is a *substantive* insight – since this unified concept of obligation was constructed as a requirement necessitated by practical rationality, serving as common ground for obligation in law and morality alike. For, in taking the principles of practical rationality as a basis for specifying the meaning of obligation in both law and morality, I could emphasize that, on the one hand, an underlying symmetry is at work that makes legal and moral obligation normatively homogeneous, but, on the other hand, neither can be derived from the other.

8.5 Concluding Remarks

In this chapter I brought critically into focus three aspects of the revisionary Kantian conception of legal obligation laid out in Chapter 7: (i) the constitutive connection between legal obligation and intersubjective reasons; (ii) the idea of legal obligation as carrying a specific kind of *force* (rather than as being described by a set of features); and (iii) the Kantian quality of the account as a whole. This critical discussion made it possible to clinch some points that are central to legal obligation as construed in this work, and they can be summarized as follows.

---

[39] For a similar reading of Kant's project, see Willaschek, 'Right and Coercion'; B. Laurence, 'Juridical Laws as Moral Laws in Kant's *The Doctrine of Right*', in G. Pavlakos and V. Rodriguez-Blanco (eds.), *Reasons and Intentions in Law and Practical Agency* (Cambridge, Cambridge University Press, 2015), pp. 205–27; and Bacin, '"Only One Obligation"'.

The engagement with the intersubjective dimension of the reasons constituting what is obligatory in law gave me the opportunity to point out that the quality of those reasons is moral, since they account for the concerns of all the potentially affected parties and hold categorically. This means, in turn, that embracing the revisionary Kantian conception commits us to conceive of legal obligation as an inherently non-merely-prudential standard of behaviour that, whilst far from necessarily overriding, binds its addressees no matter whether they are subjectively prepared to accept it. Discussing the claim that legal obligation is associated with a specific force, which is mandatory as opposed to recommendatory, allowed me to align the revisionary Kantian conception to a particular theoretical model for the study of legal obligation – the model instantiated by the conceptions that take legal obligation to be a specific force intrinsically attached to certain reasons, vis-à-vis a property of the action supported by those reasons. That way, the revisionary Kantian conception was also conceptually distinguished from any feature model of obligation defended in the philosophical literature, such as Bentham's, Mill's, and Hart's. So, I claimed, any substantive convergence one may register between the revisionary Kantian conception and the theories conceiving of legal obligation as a trait of action should be understood as merely superficial and, hence, as an agreement occurring in the context of far deeper and more fundamental dissimilarities. Finally, I considered the overall quality of the account of legal obligation resulting from the claims defended in the rest of this book and noticed that, despite the possible existence of some (mostly superficial) discrepancies between Kant's original theory and my own conception of legal obligation, the latter is best understood as a Kantian account, since, it upholds the most fundamental theses underpinning Kant's thought about legal obligation and, related to this, creatively contributes to the Kantian tradition for the study of the obligatory dimension of human experience.

All the claims so introduced are as constitutive of the revisionary Kantian conception I constructed in this work as those argued for in the previous chapter. Accordingly, the effort I embarked into in the last two chapters consisted in bringing together the critical remarks made in Chapters 3–6 and building on that material with a view to arrive at a sufficiently detailed, sophisticated, and ambitious account of the kind of obligation engendered by the law. Whether such account, in addition to having those characters, is also authentically original and irreducible to a family of existing accounts is a matter that needs a separate discussion, which will be carried out in the next chapter.

9

The Robust Reason Account

9.1 Introduction

In Chapters 7 and 8, I theorized the revisionary Kantian conception, which conceptualizes legal obligation as a law-sourced reason categorically requiring certain courses of conduct to be carried out as a matter of intersubjective considerations. This concise formulation can be more analytically spelled out in the following terms. Firstly, legal obligation, as the revisionary Kantian conception conceives of it, describes a *normative* kind of *necessitation* – a standard *demanding*, as opposed to simply recommending, that those who are subject to the law act in the prescribed way. Secondly, complying with legal obligations should *presumptively* be understood as the *right* thing to do, whereas departing from what a legal obligation prescribes is legitimately regarded as pro tanto wrong. Relatedly, legal obligation holds *categorically*, such that the subjective states and personal interests of those placed under a legal obligation do not affect its bindingness. As a result, for one thing, legal obligations bind us in a *genuine* sense, as opposed to a merely perspectivized one, and, for another, they operate as *rational* requirements, vis-à-vis instantiating a social 'ought' or a technical 'ought'. In addition, the distinctive kind of 'ought' attached to legal obligation has a *defeasible*, or variable, force, as distinct from an exclusionary, or invariant, force. Finally, legal obligations are best understood as reasons addressing the *generality* of legal subjects, namely, the legal community as a whole, rather than just a subclass of it, such as the legal officials, meaning those who occupy certain institutional roles, or those who otherwise commit to, accept, or take an internal point of view to, the legal enterprise.

In this chapter I intend to firm up this picture of legal obligation. This I will do by, on the one hand, clarifying the relation between that picture and a specific family of views of legal obligation – the robust reason account – and, on the other hand, emphasizing the distinctively legal dimension of the kind of requirement just described. This chapter is accordingly devoted to two purposes, corresponding to its two main sections. In the next section, I will deal with the conceptual links that hold between the revisionary Kantian conception and the robust reason account. As mentioned in Chapter 2, the robust reason account of legal obligation is defined by the thesis that, as much as legal obligation and moral obligation may differ in important respects, they share the same foundation, origin, nature, and force as well as, to a large extent, the same contents. Contrary to the other versions of the family of reason accounts, the robust reason account comes as close to identifying legal obligation with moral obligation as one can possibly think. Among the views of legal obligation theorized in contemporary jurisprudence, the robust reason account is the position conceptually most akin to the revisionary Kantian conception, since the substantive conclusions the two approaches draw differ only in part: while the paradigmatic versions of the robust reason account endorse different conceptual premises, are shaped by different philosophical assumptions, follow different argumentative strategies, and address different theoretical concerns than the revisionary Kantian conception I defend, the conclusions they arrive at and the resulting picture of legal obligation they offer are in important respects conceptually continuous or at least compatible with the claims I make about legal obligation. For this reason, by engaging with the robust reason account I have the opportunity to further clarify the theoretical status and conceptual implications of the revisionary Kantian conception. And this is the justification for my critical discussion of the robust reason account in Section 9.2, where I will focus on two variants of that account – Antony Duff's, on the one hand, and Deryk Beyleveld and Roger Brownsword's, on the other – which bear some similarity with my view of legal obligation.

Having made this comparative analysis, by thus precisely establishing the place my theory of legal obligation occupies within contemporary jurisprudence, I will move on, in Section 9.3, and elucidate the sense in which the revisionary Kantian conception of legal obligation is specifically tailored to the law, and so it is designed to explain the distinctive kind of obligation set forth by the law, as distinguished from moral obligation and obligation as it is engendered by practical rationality. In this context, I will show that, on the revisionary Kantian conception, legal obligation can be distinguished from other kinds of obligation (especially the kind of legal obligation associated with rational morality), since in several ways and circumstances the contents of legal obligation, as I understand it, may well diverge from the contents of the moral demands arising out of the principles constitutive of practical rationality. In my theoretical framework, then, as much as the obligation-generating statements of law may reproduce the directives of practical rationality, they are primarily meant to serve different sorts of functions. It is on this different basis that law and the obligations it generates can be argued to make a difference in our deliberation about what we ought to do. So, while the *nature* of legal obligation, as I conceive it, is rational, its *contents* – what the (rational) requirements established by legal institutions direct us to do – do not necessarily coincide with what the principles constitutive of practical rationality demand of us. As I will argue, there are circumstances in which law requires us to do things that practical rationality does not. This is so where the conduct in question is of a kind that practical rationality addresses only at a high level of abstraction, or is silent about, or is not concerned with, or fails to conclusively settle. In these cases, the law can issue requirements by setting forth obligations that do not coincide with the demands of practical rationality.

Crucially, the fact that the obligations engendered by the law need not have the same content as those of practical rationality does not mean that legal obligations forfeit their rational quality, for even when legal obligations do not coincide with the requirements of practical rationality as a matter of substance they complete and integrate practically rational standards, rather than clashing with or contradicting the latter. This means that law can set up obligations having no counterpart in the realm of practical rationality and yet still being practically rational. It also means that the revisionary Kantian conception of legal obligation is best understood as an account of the obligation distinctive to law, and that my conceptualization of legal obligation as a rational requirement does not make law redundant, namely, it does not make legal institutions and directives mere reproductions of the demands of practical rationality.

9.2 The Robust Reason Account of Legal Obligation

The revisionary Kantian conception of legal obligation establishes a close conceptual link between the obligations set out by the law on the one hand, and practical, rational, and intersubjective requirements, on the other. As noted in Chapter 8, I take this to mean that legal obligation is a practically rational demand grounded in morality, where morality is understood as a *rational* and intersubjective standard of conduct, as distinguished from an arrangement of practical principles that are customarily or socially accepted within a community. In contemporary jurisprudence a similar view of legal obligation is defended by some variants of the natural law theory. Contemporary natural law jurisprudence is a wide-ranging tradition of legal thought that has been defended by legal philosophers whose theoretical assumptions, philosophical backgrounds, and scholarly concerns vary significantly. Hence, not all natural lawyers come to the same conclusions about the nature of legal obligation. Even so, one can hardly deny that some instantiations of the natural law theory of legal obligation tends to converge with the revisionary Kantian conception of the obligations engendered by the law. This is especially true of the rationalist strand of contemporary legal naturalism, which shares the basic rationalist premise with the revisionary Kantian conception.

In the rationalist tradition of natural law theory, law is conceived as a rational standard for conduct.[1] On this view, by its very nature law is intended to provide 'a set of standards that rational agents should take as a guide to their conduct'.[2] We can thus appreciate a 'necessary continuity between law and the requirements of practical reasonableness'.[3] As a consequence, the standards of conduct that translate into the rules of law are understood to be rationally binding. The claim that the obligations associated with mandatory legal directives are practically rational is, thus, a view shared by the rationalist strand of legal naturalism and the conception introduced in this work.

However, the continuity between the two views of legal obligation need to be qualified in a couple of significant ways. First, if the convergence is to be possible, the core of the rationalist stream in contemporary natural law jurisprudence should not be understood as the claim that 'Φ-ing's being morally required is sufficient for Φ-ing's being legally required, or that Φ-ing's being independently morally required is necessary for Φ-ing's being legally required'.[4] On some interpretations, legal naturalism is conceptually linked to the view that the status of a statement as part of a system of rational morality is sufficient for it to be part of law as well. As a result, the contents of law are claimed to reflect

---

[1] This basic premise underpins the classical version of rationalist natural law theory developed by Aquinas, for whom law 'is nothing other than an ordinance of reason for the common good, issued by one who has care of the community, and promulgated' (T. Aquinas, *Summa Theologiae* (London, Blackfriars, 1964), Part: Ia, Question: IIae, Article number: 90, 4).

[2] M. Murphy, 'Natural Law Jurisprudence', *Legal Theory*, 9 (2003), p. 244.

[3] Murphy, 'Natural Law Jurisprudence', p. 244.

[4] Murphy, 'Natural Law Jurisprudence', p. 243 ft. 15, where this interpretation is introduced as a possible reading of the natural law theory before being criticized as an uncharitable and misleading interpretation.

rational morality, or in any event not to go beyond what is dictated by such morality. If the fundamental kernel of contemporary natural law theory, in its rationalist strand, is formulated in these terms, it will no longer be possible to record the existence of a conceptual continuity and theoretical convergence between the natural law theory of legal obligation and the revisionary Kantian conception of the same notion. For the revisionary Kantian conception is grounded in the view that the *quality* of legal obligation, as distinguished from its contents or *substance*, is intersubjective and, in this specific sense, moral. Accordingly, the revisionary Kantian conception allows for the possibility that the contents of law and of legal obligations depart from those of rational morality, moral obligations, and rational obligations. Such a possibility is, by contrast, incompatible with the interpretation of the (rationalist variant of the) natural law theory just introduced. In a nutshell, it is only in a qualified sense that the revisionary Kantian conception of legal obligation can be understood as continuous with the view of legal obligation supported by legal naturalism, since only in one of the interpretations that may be given of the rationalist variant of the natural law theory is the latter conceptually akin to the position I endorse.

Second, the revisionary Kantian conception of legal obligation does not collapse into the rationalist tradition in contemporary natural law theory even when the latter is qualified as just indicated. This is because of the special way in which natural law theorists understand practical rationality (or practical reasonableness, as they would say). In the naturalist tradition, practical rationality is predicated on a range of values that in combination constitute *the common good of a community* and thus define a *thick* ideal of conduct – one that can provide specific guidance across a whole spectrum of practical affairs. In other words, rationalism in contemporary natural law jurisprudence entails a full-fledged view of the good life. The idea of practical rationality underpinning the revisionary Kantian conception of legal obligation is remarkably different from that view. The account of legal obligation I theorize in this book partakes of the broader Kantian tradition in practical philosophy. In turn, this tradition, as I understand it, conceives of practical rationality as a standard that is highly abstract and so only sets out general principles of conduct making for a *thin* practical paradigm.[5] Indeed, the revisionary

---

[5] That the paradigm I embrace is likely to meet the criticism of contemporary rationalist natural law theorists emerges with clarity in J. Finnis, 'The Authority of Law in the Predicament of Contemporary Social Theory', *Notre Dame Journal of Law, Ethics and*

Kantian conception of legal obligation is based on the assumption, which I have not made explicit, that practical rationality is only concerned with comprehensive principles, principles that can be put into practice by means of different types of conduct sensitive to the context, situation, tradition, and culture in which one is acting.[6] On this view, practical rationality serves as a *foundation* in working out what we ought to do, but it does not necessarily (or even programmatically) tell us whether any specific course of action is right or wrong – precisely because, on a Kantian approach, the rational constraints on action are broad, abstract, and wide-ranging.

To expand on this point, the model of practical rationality that frames the revisionary Kantian conception of legal obligation is neatly distinguished from the idea of practical reasonableness found in the contemporary natural law theory. The former cannot be reduced to the latter for at least two related reasons. To begin with, unlike the idea of practical reasonableness associated with the rationalist version of the natural law theory, which instantiates a recognitional paradigm, the idea of practical rationality underpinning the revisionary Kantian conception is internal to a value-conferring, or constructivist, paradigm. Following Berys Gaut, one can qualify an account as *recognitional* if it proceeds from the assumption that there is out there such a thing as valuable, justified, or correct conduct which is independent of our exercise of the capacity to reason about what to do, and which we ought to accordingly choose as the appropriate course of action.[7] The role of practical rationality, on a recognitional account, then is to *discover* that which is independently valuable, justified, or correct. By contrast, on a *value-conferring* model, what is valuable, correct, or justified is not discovered but *constituted* by practical rationality, which turns something otherwise evaluatively inert and deontologically neutral into something bestowed with value, correctness, and justificatory force. On the value-conferring view, thus, nothing in nature is value-laden – nothing has the real property of being valuable – but for the working of practical rationality. Related to this, the notions of value, correctness, and justification are conceptually

---

Public Policy, 1 (1984), pp. 121–33 and J. Finnis, 'Foundations of Practical Reason Revisited', *American Journal of Jurisprudence*, 50 (2005), pp. 113–18.

[6] A similar approach finds a mature statement in O. O'Neill, 'Consistency in Action', in E. Millgram (ed.), *Varieties of Practical Reasoning* (Cambridge (MA), MIT Press, 2001), pp. 301–29.

[7] See B. Gaut, 'The Structure of Practical Reason', in G. Cullity and B. Gaut (eds.), *Ethics and Practical Reason* (Oxford, Oxford University Press, 1997), pp. 161–88.

dependent on our use of practical rationality, since it is through our capacity to reasoning in practical affairs that questions of value, correctness, and justification in the matter of action are settled. And rationality determines what has value, is correct, and is justified mainly by setting out practical principles, namely, by way of establishing norms that any action needs to satisfy if it is to be considered valuable, justified, or the right thing to do. Hence, ultimately it is only in relation to a standard framed by practical rationality that a course of action can acquire any normative significance in human experience.

Relatedly, on the value-conferring view I associate with the revisionary Kantian conception of legal obligation, the rational judgement put to use in agency offers a critical tool by which to select the ends and means that are appropriate to action as a reasoned-out construct within which to make choices in the practical sphere. By so reasoning on the principles of practical rationality and accordingly framing the ends and means of action, we can construct our very agency. In this sense, the conception of practical rationality associated with the revisionary Kantian conception being proposed here can be said to belong to the stream of theories known as ethical constructivism, and in particular it can be described as a critical rationalist, or Kantian, variant, which is organized around the threefold claim: (a) that an agent can construct a critical framework within which to reason about action, (b) that this framework can be designed with rational constraints built into it in order to reject some ends as irrational (accordingly to be avoided), and (c) that this framework can also point out some principles and ends of action as grounded beyond discussion.[8]

---

[8] The constructivist account is theorized in T. Hill, *Dignity and Practical Reason* (Ithaca (NY), Cornell University Press, 1992), pp. 123–46; O. O'Neill, *Constructions of Reason* (Cambridge, Cambridge University Press, 1990); O. O'Neill, *Bounds of Justice* (Cambridge, Cambridge University Press, 2000), pp. 11–28; C. Korsgaard, 'The Normativity of Instrumental Reason', in G. Cullity and B. Gaut (eds.), *Ethics and Practical Reason* (Oxford, Oxford University Press, 1997), pp. 215–54; and A. Reath, *Agency & Autonomy in Kant's Moral Theory* (Oxford, Oxford University Press, 2006), pp. 196–230, among others. The constructivist account can be set in contrast to the realist account of practical rationality, holding that practical rationality can guide us in the discovery of *intrinsically* valuable ends. Arguments for the realist account of practical rationality can be found, for instance, in P. Railton, 'Moral Realism', *Philosophical Review*, 45 (1986), pp. 163–207; D. Brink, *Moral Realism and the Foundations of Ethics* (Cambridge, Cambridge University Press, 1989); and T. Nagel, *The View from Nowhere* (Oxford, Oxford University Press, 1989). A comparative discussion of realism and constructivism is offered in C. Korsgaard, *The Sources of Normativity* (Cambridge, Cambridge University Press, 1996), pp. 28–48 and 90–130, with an argument in favour of the latter over the former.

In addition, the idea of practical rationality underlying the revisionary Kantian conception is irreducible to the one underpinning the rationalist variant of the contemporary natural law theory, since the revisionary Kantian conception is shaped by the thesis that practical rationality is *constitutive* of correct deliberation.[9] In a similar way, in the revisionary Kantian theoretical framework, justification is constrained by principles we should rationally will in a sense that cannot be contingent on one's personal preferences, circumstances, or utility: justified ends are not whatever it is that an agent desires or *wants* to do, or whatever an agent happens to light upon as a goal of action. That is to say, the rational principles by which action is constrained are determined by the overall structure of the self, which in turn is a structure understood to be *rational*. The ends we choose are justified not by our wishes but by our deliberation; they are accordingly justified when established through, and constrained by, a form of deliberation whose possible starting points are not intrinsically rational – such are our preferences, desires, personal commitments, social bonds, cultural influences, local identities, interiorized perspectives, unreflectively accepted values, and the like – but whose outcome (namely, the decisions we make about what to do) are reasoned out. Practical deliberation is thus conceptualized as an exercise in rationality whose starting points – the factors that go into our decision-making – are filtered by critical assessment.

This view of practical rationality and deliberation – which owes much to the contemporary Kantian scholarship, and to Christine Korsgaard's work in particular – is best understood as a 'humanization' of Kant's original conception.[10] In keeping with Korsgaard's philosophical perspective, when conceptualizing legal obligation I proceed from the idea that human agency is governed and described by constitutive standards which are distinctive to such agency and which play an essential role in shaping the boundaries of sound deliberation about what we ought to do and are justified in doing. Humanization means that the Kantian project

---

[9] For another formulation of this point, see A. Reath, 'Setting Ends for Oneself through Reason', in S. Robertson (ed.), *Spheres of Reasons* (Oxford, Oxford University Press, 2009), pp. 199–207.

[10] It is Christine Korsgaard, among others, who has influentially argued for the project of humanizing Kant's practical philosophy. See, for instance, Korsgaard, *Sources of Normativity*. As much as this project may be widely regarded as insightful, it is open to a number of objections. For a comprehensive critique of Korsgaard's project, see G. Cohen, 'Reason, Humanity, and the Moral Law', in C. Korsgaard, *The Sources of Normativity* (Cambridge, Cambridge University Press, 1996), pp. 167–88, for instance.

I am prepared to embrace Iays emphasis on human constitution. This approach accordingly revises and narrows down Kant's original views, which by contrast are centred on the more comprehensive notion of rational *agency*, as opposed to that of the *human* constitution. The basic idea behind the humanization of Kant's position is that practical deliberation – the process of (a) figuring out what we ought to do and (b) justifying our determinations in that regard – is shaped by the structure of the human constitution, understood as the complex of features we would all recognize as distinctively human. And, precisely because they are understood to describe human agency at large, those features are broad and general traits, namely, they refer to what we would *all* recognize as what it is to be human acting selves or to engage in action as human creatures. On this view, it is the human structure that supplies the necessary principles applying to, and governing, action. Accordingly, the fundamental forms of practical inference, along with the principles that regulate action, are derived from the structural elements acknowledged to be typically and distinctively human.[11]

The human constitution can be more specifically characterized as our reflective and autonomous structure, meaning a capacity for reflectivity and self-determination. This can be said because every normally functioning human agent either has these capacities or has the potential to acquire them, as well as because no human agent – whatever other interests, inclinations, desires, or affections they may have – can disown these capacities or the practical standards deriving from that constitution. The standards rooted in our distinctive constitution should therefore be understood to constrain our action in a general and necessary (or, non-contingent) way, because that constitution – our reflective and autonomous structure – is itself necessary and so cannot be ignored. In other words, if practical rational standards derive their authority and justification from some trait that is common to us all – the traits defining our human constitution – we have to each recognize them as inescapable regardless of our particular inclinations and interests.[12] So, because the standards of practical rationality do not depend on the contingent

---

[11] The conception is thus at once *distinctive* and *general*: distinctive because it uniquely identifies *human* action or *human* agency; general because it purports to encompass the *whole* of humanity, regardless of personal or cultural specificities.

[12] On this aspect, summarized by the so-called inescapability thesis, see D. Brink, 'Kantian Rationalism: Inescapability, Authority, and Supremacy', in G. Cullity and B. Gaut (eds.), *Ethics and Practical Reason* (Oxford, Oxford University Press, 1997), pp. 259–82.

characteristics, incentives, pressures, or circumstances that apply to this or that specific individual, they are to be regarded as universally and necessarily valid within the community of human agents at large.[13]

In light of the crucial differences just pointed out, we can appreciate that the convergence between the natural law theory and revisionary Kantian conception of legal obligation is only partial and superficial, for although both the revisionary Kantian conception with its humanized characterization of practical rationality and the account offered by the rationalist stream in the contemporary natural law jurisprudence proceed from the view that we should fundamentally rely on the use of *rationality* accounting for legal obligation, they work that premise in different ways and rely on different pictures of practical rationality. In order to further elaborate on the fundamental differences, while more accurately locating my conception of legal obligation within contemporary jurisprudence, I will devote the rest of the section to discuss two specific rationalist and naturalist accounts of legal obligation that in many respects fall close to my own.

9.2.1 Antony Duff's Theory of Legal Obligation

Duff's account of legal obligation shares more than just peripheral elements with the revisionary Kantian conception. Duff's account is premised on a legal theory that, unlike the dominant positivist paradigm, conceives of law as an essentially *legitimate* practice. Law, on this view, is an enterprise defined by a range of values that are vindicated by the rational standards that those who make up the legal community ought to regard as *justified*.[14] This is tantamount to theorizing a discriminating concept of law understood not as a generally and unqualifiedly normative framework, but as a normative framework justified by values that in their arrangement set up a conception of the common good appropriate to the governed community.

---

[13] I defend these claims in detail and contextualize them to the legal domain in S. Bertea, *The Normative Claim of Law* (Oxford, Hart, 2009), pp. 225–69; S. Bertea, 'Law and Obligation: Outlines of a Kantian Argument', in S. Bertea and G. Pavlakos (eds.), *New Essays on the Normativity of Law* (Oxford, Hart, 2011), pp. 199–218; and S. Bertea, 'Normativity, Human Constitution and Legal Theory', in B. Brozeck and J. Stelmark (eds.), *Studies in the Philosophy of Law, Vol. VI: The Normativity of Law* (Krakow, Copernicus Center Press, 2011), pp. 99–126.

[14] This conceptualization is argued for in A. Duff, *Trials and Punishments* (Cambridge, Cambridge University Press, 1986), pp. 79–86.

Key to this conceptualization of law is the view that there exists a common good shared by the legal community and that this common good acts as a benchmark against which to judge the activities of legal officials. The common good is in addition understood by Duff as a *moral* idea:[15] far from being defined in terms of a set of goals and principles that instantiate the interests and utility of a specific social group – say, the ruling class, the class of legal officials, or some other subset within the legal community – the common good is defined by an arrangement of concerns which *all* participants in the legal enterprise ought to acknowledge as rationally valuable.[16] Therefore, unless a legal system is geared towards, and informed by, a moral ideal, it will forfeit its legal status: an order in which legal officials only look after their own interests and are not prepared to justify their decisions by appeal to a reasonable conception of the common good is more appropriately conceptualized as a *perversion* of a legal system than as a *genuine* legal system.[17]

From this it follows that in a legal system properly so-called, the reasons provided for complying with the law are presented as moral reasons, as opposed to prudential ones. Specifically, legal reasons are considerations that offer justification by appealing to the common good, since for conceptual reasons the law does not make appeal to the self-interest of selected individuals or social groups. Accordingly, legal directives set forth obligations of a specific kind, namely, obligations grounded in a suitable conception of the common good, understood as a *moral* ideal, of the governed community. That is to say, since law programmatically aims to provide its addressees with *moral* reasons and is concerned with the interests an *entire* community can (or at least should) espouse, 'obligation-claims must be justified to those on whom they are allegedly binding, by reference to reasons which are independent of any sanctions which may be threatened in order to give them further incentives to do

---

[15] See A. Duff, 'Legal Obligation and the Moral Nature of Law', *Juridical Review*, 25 (1980), pp. 81-4, for instance.

[16] In Duff's words, 'a system of law cannot properly be founded on the self-interest of a particular group' (Duff, *Trials and Punishments*, p. 87). See also Duff, 'Legal Obligation and the Moral Nature of Law', p. 86, where it is claimed that 'the concept of law has an essential moral dimension, in that it is logically related to certain notions of value'.

[17] See Duff, 'Legal Obligation and the Moral Nature of Law', p. 82, where it is claimed that 'the idea of law contains within itself an ideal model of a legal system: as a system which is informed and structured by an adequate conception of the common good'.

what they ought to do'.[18] On this basis, Duff concludes that 'the logic of obligation-claims ... incorporates the moral demand that we should treat and address others as rational and autonomous agents'.[19] Legal obligations, in other terms, are not based on self-interested considerations of profit or convenience. And just as law is grounded in moral reasons and concerns, so are the obligations it brings into being. In sum, for Duff 'a law is morally binding' and legal obligation is 'a species of moral obligation', since 'to accept a legal obligation is to accept it as morally binding'.[20] More specifically, 'the obligations which the laws of my community impose on me are aspects of my moral obligation to care for the good of that community'.[21] As a result, in Duff's theoretical framework, to acknowledge a legal obligation is to recognize that we as legal subjects are being addressed with a *moral* demand grounded in the values that are constitutive of the *common good* (as distinguished from moral standards that do *not* take the common good into account).

The conceptual affinities that Duff's theory of legal obligation bears to my own conception are far from insignificant. Duff's insistence on the rational character of both the legal enterprise and the requirements it issues finds a parallel in my claim that the obligations engendered by the law are practically rational demands. In addition, for Duff too, the reasons associated with the law are not prudential, self-interested reasons but rather intersubjective considerations in favour of certain modes of conduct. From which it also follows that both Duff's theory and my own conception understand legal obligation as a specific kind of intersubjective reason.

Even with these core claims that the two accounts of legal obligation share, there is at least one thesis that radically sets them apart: namely, Duff's appeal to the common good in grounding the obligatory force of

---

[18] Duff, *Trials and Punishments*, p. 83. The moral nature of legal obligation finds a comprehensive formulation in Duff's statement that 'if I claim authority over someone (and not just the power to coerce him) I must claim that he is rationally bound to obey me, by reasons which he could and should (even if he does not) accept for himself: if I claim that he has an obligation to act in a certain way (and not just that he will be forced to act thus) I must claim that there is a rule or reason which requires him to act thus which he could and should (even if he does not) accept for himself. Claims to authority or obligation appeal to the rational assent of rational agents ... What is true of authority and obligation in general must equally be true of legal authority and obligation' (Duff, 'Legal Obligation and the Moral Nature of Law', p. 80).

[19] Duff, *Trials and Punishments*, p. 83.
[20] Duff, *Trials and Punishments*, p. 93.
[21] Duff, *Trials and Punishments*, p. 93.

law. For Duff anchors the binding force of law to a *particular subset* of intersubjective considerations: the subset comprising the moral values that define what a community ought to regard as collectively good. Law is thus presented as an institutional practice geared towards the pursuit of certain basic goods that the community of individuals living under the jurisdiction of law (should) acknowledge to be rationally justified. Relatedly, legal directives are meant to specify how a community ought to pursue certain objectives that are shared (or ought to be shared) by the generality of the community's members. For it is some conception of the common good – namely, of what is good for, or valued by, the relevant community – that provides the appropriate *raison d'être* of legal norms (including the legal norms that generate obligations).[22] By contrast, the idea of the common good plays no role in the revisionary Kantian conception of legal obligation, for I do not appeal to any shared set of values by which to define and ground the obligations generated by the law. This is a radical difference between the two approaches, since in underscoring the rational component of the law as an enterprise that addresses and recognizes legal subjects as rational and responsible agents – thus putting forward theses that overall comport with a Kantian picture of law and its obligations – Duff distinctively frames the idea of rationality through the values that are shared within a legal community and define interests the community members are said to have in common, vis-à-vis the features that define human constitution. Accordingly, for Duff the kinds of intersubjective reasons that can justify a system of laws and establish what is legally obligatory belong to a specific subset of intersubjective considerations: they are not *broad* intersubjective and rational claims but rather intersubjective and rational claims about the common good of the community.[23]

This takes me to the next point, which is that Duff's conception of the common good is sufficiently general, ecumenical, and flexible to accommodate different substantive moral theories, both teleological and

---

[22] On this aspect, see Duff, 'Legal Obligation and the Moral Nature of Law', pp. 79–86.
[23] To put it in Duff's words, the 'law must be justified to those whose obedience it claims by being shown to serve their common good; its officials must profess to direct their legislative and administrative activities towards that common good; and their activities, and the laws which they create and administer, must be critically assessed by reference to that common good. For the law claims authority over a whole community, and imposes sometimes arduous obligations on its members: only by reference to the community common good can the law's claim be justified to all its members' (Duff, *Trials and Punishments*, p. 89).

deontological. Nor, in framing his definition of the common good, does Duff necessarily exclude the interests of someone living outside the relevant legal community. In Duff's theoretical framework, the common good can accordingly be argued to be compatible with at least some universalist forms of legal rationalism. These qualifications, however, do not call into question the essential role the common good plays both in Duff's justification of legal practices and, relatedly, in his definition of law and its obligations, which can be legitimately imposed only insofar as they are designed and administered to serve the common good of the relevant legal community.[24]

Duff further elaborates on the relation between law and legal obligation, on the one hand, and the common good, on the other, in setting out his normative ideals about law. After criticizing the misleading picture on which legal subjects can be conceptualized as mere objects of the activity carried out by those in power – or at best as passive beneficiaries of that activity, namely, 'mere recipients of orders which they must obey under threat' – Duff claims that legal addressees should be understood as *participants*, even if merely subordinate ones, in the normative framework the law sets up, and so as individuals who 'can understand enough of [the normative discourse of law] to grasp and accept the binding reasons for action' the law claims to provide them with.[25] These claims mark a shift in the way law is pictured, a shift away from what, following Roger Cotterrell,[26] Duff calls 'the "*imperium*" model of law'.[27] This model 'portrays law as something imposed on a population by a distinct and separate sovereign' and takes the people as forming 'a distinct, and subordinate, category of "subjects" whom she must rule'.[28] This leads Duff to embrace a different normative paradigm of law. On this alternative paradigm – fashioned after the 'community' model Duff borrows from Cotterrell's legal theory – law is understood as a framework of norms 'belonging to the whole community', and so as a framework of norms shared by the governed people, who will then be able to regard law

---

[24] This view is defended in Duff, *Trials and Punishments*, pp. 90–1.
[25] A. Duff, 'Inclusion and Exclusion: Citizens, Subjects and Outlaws', in M. Freeman (ed.), *Current Legal Problems* (Oxford, Oxford University Press, 1998), p. 249.
[26] See R. Cotterrell, *Law's Community* (Oxford, Clarendon, 1995), pp. 221–48.
[27] Duff, 'Inclusion and Exclusion', p. 252.
[28] Duff, 'Inclusion and Exclusion', p. 252.

as a common enterprise embodying the 'shared values', as well as the 'shared understandings and way of life', of the whole community.[29]

The community model is not understood by Duff as a conceptual paradigm establishing what must be true of, or claimed for, a practice if it is to count as a system of law at all. The community model is instead meant to reconstruct and summarize general features that Duff takes to be crucial to a particular kind of legal system – the kind that is worthy of our respect as a system of law fit for the citizens of a democratic republic. But, even if those claims are recognized to be normative vis-à-vis conceptual, it is still essential, on Duff's account, to appeal to values 'embedded in the community's life', as opposed to the 'will of a distinct and alien legislator', if we are to have a proper understanding of law, whose voice 'is (or aspires to be) the voice of the community addressing itself and its members, the voice of all the citizens addressing each other and themselves'.[30] And, insofar as Duff's legal theory is shaped by the notion of common good, defined as a set of shared values embedded in the practices and convictions of a legal community, it is conceptually coherent with the endorsement of a communitarian political outlook. This outlook, in turn, is characterized as a civic republicanism, on which those living under a legal system should identify with the basic values underpinning the polity they inhabit, to the effect that, from a normative perspective, they are best conceived as fellow participants in an activity of self-government, and so as individuals who share a civic identity grounded in mutual respect and concern.[31]

This concise reconstruction can barely do justice to Duff's sophisticated legal theory and his view of the obligations the law generates. But it should nonetheless suffice to show that, despite some convergence when it comes to the substantive conclusions about legal obligation, the conceptual framework designed by Duff in his account of legal obligation is radically different from the revisionary Kantian conception I have set out to defend in this work. Accordingly, on the one hand, my conception of

---

[29] Duff, 'Inclusion and Exclusion', p. 253.
[30] Duff, 'Inclusion and Exclusion', pp. 254–5
[31] See A. Duff and S. Marshall, 'Criminal Responsibility and Public Reason', in M. Freeman and R. Harrison (eds.), *Law and Philosophy* (Oxford, Oxford University Press, 1998); and A. Duff and S. Marshall, 'Criminalization and Sharing Wrongs', *Canadian Journal of Law and Jurisprudence*, 11 (2007), pp. 7–22; as well as A. Duff, 'Blame, Moral Standing and the Legitimacy of the Criminal Trial', *Ratio*, 23 (2010), 123–40; and A. Duff, 'Responsibility, Citizenship and Criminal Law', in A. Duff and S. Green (eds.), *Philosophical Foundations of Criminal Law* (Oxford, Oxford University Press, 2011).

legal obligation is best understood as reinforcing a picture of legal obligation that Duff has arrived at from different routes; on the other, it should be understood to provide an original argument that consolidates and supports that view in an altogether new fashion, whilst at the same time refraining from establishing a direct connection between legal obligation and common good, as Duff conceives of it.

9.2.2 Deryck Beyleveld and Roger Brownsword's Theory of Legal Obligation

Some theses that are central to the revisionary Kantian conception of legal obligation can also be found in Beyleveld and Brownsword's account of the same notion. The latter is based on an ambitious and comprehensive conceptualization of the practical domain on which morality is understood as an umbrella concept divided into two classes: the legal and the purely moral. The two classes of morality share substance, origins, forms of administration, and sanctioning mechanisms. Law, along with everything that falls within the legal class, is thus conceived as a subclass of morality broadly understood, a class that can be distinguished from the purely moral only by its aspect.[32] This statement is based on, and entails, a rejection of the 'realist' view of law as a set of provisions that can be identified as legal by their empirically observable sources, that is, without any recourse to moral considerations.[33] Beyleveld and Brownsword's jurisprudence can thus be labelled a form of 'idealism', which in contrast to the realist legal tradition defines law not as socially organized power but as morally legitimate, or justified, power, that is, as a *moral* enterprise, or at least an enterprise that is not immoral. Similarly, legal validity is nothing like a morally neutral notion (for if it were, it would be an almost technical concept that can be of any relevance only to legal practitioners and students of law). By contrast, legal validity captures a special type of moral legitimacy and, more specifically, a subclass of moral legitimacy that differs in its aspect only

---

[32] These claims are defended in D. Beyleveld and R. Brownsword, *Law as a Moral Judgement* (London, Sweet & Maxwell, 1986), pp. 159-64.

[33] This definition of legal realism, as distinct from legal idealism, can be found in D. Beyleveld and R. Brownsword, 'Law as a Moral Judgement vs. Law as the Rules of the Powerful', *American Journal of Jurisprudence* 28 (1983), pp. 79-117, where Beyleveld and Brownsword's conception of legal idealism is also introduced and argued.

from what Beyleveld and Brownsword call 'the purely morally legitimate'.[34]

This construction carries direct implications for the theory of legal obligation. In accordance with the foundational claims underpinning Beyleveld and Brownsword's jurisprudence, legally valid rules are said to necessarily have moral weight, since they are produced by a morally justified scheme (or at least a scheme that is not immoral). This also applies to mandatory legal norms – the norms that generate legal obligations. And this means that legal obligations, as requirements issued by a morally legitimate (or non-illegitimate) set of mandatory norms, have a moral nature: 'the concept of legal obligation is necessarily and fully connected to the concept of moral obligation ... Being legally bound is being morally bound; having a legal reason for action is having a moral reason for action; appeals to legal obligation are appeals to moral obligation.'[35]

Building on this foundational claim, which depicts legal obligation as a kind of moral obligation – or, in Beyleveld and Brownsword's vocabulary, as a legal-moral obligation, in distinction from a purely moral obligation – Beyleveld and Brownsword further assert that legal obligations are typically generated by valid legal norms, which are morally legitimate (or non-immoral) directives. This view follows from the combined thesis that (a) law is part of the moral realm and that (b) legal validity is a form of moral legitimacy. However, on at least some occasions legal obligations can arise even without a valid legal claim, as when invalid legal rules have been issued by which one ought to abide in order to avert a greater moral evil. These cases – in which legal obligations arise not out of a valid legal proposition but out of a need to choose the lesser of two moral evils – are qualified by Beyleveld and Brownsword as 'collateral' legal obligations, which are thus distinguished from 'direct' legal obligations, the kind generated by valid legal statements.[36] The important distinction between direct obligation and collateral obligation does not, however, affect the nature of legal obligation, which in either case remains moral. Beyleveld and Brownsword thus put forward a

---

[34] This concept of legal validity is theorized in Beyleveld and Brownsword, *Law as a Moral Judgement*, pp. 326–8.

[35] Beyleveld and Brownsword, *Law as a Moral Judgement*, pp. 328–9. See also Beyleveld and Brownsword, *Law as a Moral Judgement*, pp. 352–3.

[36] On this distinction, see Beyleveld and Brownsword, *Law as a Moral Judgement*, pp. 328–37.

unified theory of legal obligation as a genuine practical requirement providing agents with moral reasons for acting as it directs.

The substantive conclusions about the character of legal obligation that Beyleveld and Brownsword derive from their conceptual framework differ only so much from the basic theses shaping the revisionary Kantian conception. For both approaches characterize legal obligation as a practically rational demand that binds its addressees on non-purely-prudential grounds. Still, the affinity between the two approaches to legal obligation should not be overstated, since not only is there discontinuity between the *arguments* supporting the qualification of legal obligations as practically rational requirements, but also, and no less importantly, there is a marked difference between the legal theoretical *frameworks* within which that qualification takes place. Let me elaborate on both of these divergences.

As to the argument supporting the conception of legal obligation as a practically rational requirement, Beyleveld and Brownsword rely on a foundational strategy, originally theorized by Alan Gewirth, that appeals to one supreme and all-encompassing practical standard, namely, the principle of generic consistency.[37] This principle states that everyone ought to act in accordance with the generic rights of others, as well as one's own generic rights. The truth of this principle is in turn established through a dialectically necessary method. That is, in order to show that an agent must necessarily act in accordance with the standards set by the principle of generic consistency, Beyleveld and Brownsword appeal to certain necessary practical presuppositions of purposive conduct. On this view, an agent is, as a matter of dialectical necessity, committed to the principle of generic consistency, irrespective of their practical purposes. Accordingly, any agent who should fail to meet the requirements directly or derivationally established by the principle of generic consistency will be caught in self-contradiction and thus found to be acting irrationally. On this basis, Beyleveld and Brownsword conclude that all the actions required by the principle of generic consistency are morally obligatory, while all the actions the principle of generic consistency disqualifies are morally wrong.

Importantly, the principle of generic consistency applies not only to individual action but also to action-governing collective practices. This means that, on pain of contradiction, any practice, institution, or joint

---

[37] See A. Gewirth, *Reason and Morality* (Chicago (IL), University of Chicago Press, 1978).

enterprise purporting to guide action ought to comply with the directives grounded in the principle of generic consistency. Law is a practice that subjects human conduct and social relationships to given standards; hence, on pain of issuing self-contradictory requirements, legal systems need to conform to the principle of generic consistency, as well as to any other requirement that can be derived from it. That is, as the supreme practical principle, the principle of generic consistency should be understood as the fundamental norm defining (a) what is legally *obligatory*, namely, any conduct required by the principle of generic consistency; (b) what is legally *prohibited*, namely, any action that conflicts with the principle of generic consistency; and (c) what is legally *permitted*, namely, any action that is compatible with, and does not violate, the principle of generic consistency.[38]

This argument commits Beyleveld and Brownsword to an extreme form of natural law theory. Insofar as the law is governed by the principle of generic consistency, which is not only a moral principle but also, by construction, the supreme principle of practical rationality, the law is most appropriately conceptualized as the rationally justified exercise of the power to subject human conduct to institutionally enacted rules. On this view, 'a legal order is a moral order' and, by the same token, any system of governance that cannot be justified under the principle of generic consistency will count as not only morally ungrounded but also illegal.[39] This proposition establishes a classifying connection between law and morality, to the effect that 'rules lack legal validity, lack status as laws, insofar as they are morally illegitimate in some specific way or ways'.[40] I understand this claim to entail a radical version of the natural law theory, since Beyleveld and Brownsword argue that if an institution or a standard is inconsistent with the supreme principle of morality, that institution or standard will be not just legally *defective* but legally *invalid*,

---

[38] The argument is set out in detail, and several objections to it are critically discussed and rebutted, in Beyleveld and Brownsword, *Law as a Moral Judgement*, pp. 120–45. For a restatement of the argument, see also D. Beyleveld, *The Dialectical Necessity of Morality* (Chicago (IL), Chicago University Press, 1991; and D. Beyleveld, 'Legal Theory and Dialectically Contingent Justifications for the Principle of Generic Consistency', *Ratio Juris*, 9 (1996), pp. 15–24.

[39] On this aspect of their theory, see Beyleveld and Brownsword, *Law as a Moral Judgement*, pp. 159–64.

[40] D. Beyleveld and R. Brownsword, 'The Practical Difference between Natural-Law Theory and Legal Positivism', *Oxford Journal of Legal Studies*, 5 (1985), p. 4. On the notion of a classifying, as against a qualifying, connection between law and morality, see R. Alexy, *The Argument from Injustice* (Oxford, Clarendon, 2002; or. ed. 1992), pp. 26–7.

that is, illegal.[41] This view, which constitutes the core of what Mark Murphy calls the strong natural law thesis,[42] underpins the most uncompromising versions of legal naturalism and should be kept distinct from the two other main contemporary (and milder) variants of the same theory: the moral-reading-of-the-natural-law thesis – namely, the claim that no law is morally obligatory unless it complies with certain fundamental principles of practical rationality – and the weak-natural-law thesis, or weak-reading-of-the-natural-law thesis, according to which legal statements that fall short of a standard of practical rationality should be regarded as legally defective and yet valid.[43]

These remarks concerning the argumentative strategy and legal-theoretical framework underlying Beyleveld and Brownsword's account of legal obligation should suffice to clarify the conceptual difference distinguishing that view from the revisionary Kantian conception of legal obligation introduced in this work. As much as the two accounts may share some conclusions about the moral, qua intersubjectively shaped, nature of legal obligation, I do not appeal to any supreme moral (or otherwise rational) principle in order to determine the nature of what is legally obligatory. The idea of rational morality behind my conception of legal obligation is fashioned by a belief in the multiplicity of basic practical principles and the possibility that they may come into conflict. Far from embracing some form of monism about values, thereby trying to reduce the plurality of basic values to a single overarching supreme principle, the revisionary Kantian conception allows for a multitude of practical principles. It is against the background of this recognition that the model of practical rationality at work in this book makes sense. This model is conceived as a compass-like device enabling one to navigate a domain populated by a variety of fundamental principles. Accordingly, the revisionary Kantian conception of legal obligation is not committed to a monistic view of practical reasoning as a process through which

---

[41] See Beyleveld and Brownsword, *Law as a Moral Judgement*, pp. 11–13. To put it in Beyleveld and Brownsword's words, 'no theory of law can qualify as an intelligible Natural-Law Theory unless it holds that inconsistency with an EMR [i.e., an Essential Moral Requirement] is fatal to legality' (Beyleveld and Brownsword, *Law as a Moral Judgement*, p. 13). See also Beyleveld, 'Legal Theory and Dialectically Contingent Justifications for the Principle of Generic Consistency', pp. 15–19.

[42] M. Murphy, 'Natural Law Theory', in M. Golding and W. Edmundson (eds.), *The Blackwell Guide to the Philosophy of Law and Legal Theory* (Oxford, Wiley-Blackwell, 2005), p. 19.

[43] See Murphy, 'Natural Law Theory', pp. 18–22.

specific practical directives are logically derived, or deduced, from a single general supreme principle governing the whole practical camp, as Beyleveld and Brownsword's view instead is.

To briefly elaborate, the understanding of practical rationality that shapes the revisionary Kantian conception of legal obligation can be summarized as follows. On the one hand, practical rationality is conceived as a tool with which to subject action to critical scrutiny on the basis of principles that agents set out on their own in their practical deliberation; on the other hand, in providing such guidelines, this capacity is not so powerful as to be able to mould the ends of action into actual courses of action for one to take. This means that, on the one hand, as a critical tool, practical rationality endows agents with the freedom they enjoy as autonomous, self-legislating individuals capable of acting in light of laws they themselves set out for themselves (and in this way they can lay out the bounds of rational aims and of the means by which to pursue such aims). On the other hand, in offering this guidance, and beyond the boundaries of this guidance, practical rationality cannot dictate or even suggest any specific course of action. In this sense, practical rationality acts more like a filter: it structures practical reasoning in such a way that agents know what is rational and necessary in action, as well as what is irrational and hence impossible or forbidden. But practical rationality so conceived is liberal and pluralistic too: it appreciates that different specific ends may be equally worthy of pursuit. It also allows for the possibility that specific ends, which are equally worthy, prove to be inconsistent and thus come into conflict, while also recognizing that it cannot itself do the job of weighing such ends and balancing them against one another (for this requires a kind of judgement that falls outside the purview of practical rationality itself, or a commitment to values that cannot be framed in the concrete on a rational basis alone).

A further important difference setting Beyleveld and Brownsword's account apart from the revisionary Kantian conception concerns the argumentative procedure through which I establish the character of legal obligation. Such argumentative procedure is not claimed to be capable of producing logically necessary conclusions, as the appeal to the principle of generic consistency and its direct conceptual implications are instead taken to be. As much as the methodological ideas shaping my conception of legal obligation is offered as a rigorous method for the study of legal notions (and of practical ideas in general), it cannot be presented as an exercise in logical derivation of certain conclusions from widely accepted premises. In that respect, the argumentative strategy underpinning my conception of legal obligation does not only differ in *substance* from the argument deployed by Beyleveld and Brownsword – I make no reference to the principle of generic consistency or to other core claims Gewirth defends in his body of work – but is also informed by a pluralist and constructivist *approach* to practical matters that cannot be reduced to the monist and deductivist approach embraced by Beyleveld and Brownsword.

Finally, my conception of legal obligation does not presuppose, and is not entailed by, the truth of the strong natural law thesis. True, nowhere in this work have I systematically addressed the debate between positivism and natural law theory. Even so, my conception has emerged from a critique of both positivist theories of legal obligation (such as Coleman's, Shapiro's, and Marmor's) and views of legal obligation conceptually associated with the natural law tradition (such as Finnis's) and with other forms of non-positivism (such as Dworkin's and Stavropoulos's). In fact, as I argued in Chapters 3–6, it seems to me that neither legal theories of positivist persuasion nor any variant of non-positivism have so far arrived at a sound comprehensive account of the obligations engendered by the law. On this basis, it seems to me that if we are to arrive at an insightful account of legal obligation, we have to move beyond the classic debates in jurisprudence and engage with theories, ideas, and discussions in practical philosophy at large. From this theoretical perspective Beyleveld and Brownsword's research programme looks fundamentally vitiated, for it unfolds within the theoretical boundaries that constrain the seemingly endless debate pitting positivism against non-positivism – a debate that, as I have just suggested, when it comes to the study of legal obligation is more distracting than enlightening.

9.3 The Practical Difference Law Can Make with Respect to Our Obligations

The conceptualization of legal obligation as a practically rational requirement the quality of which is inherently and distinctively intersubjective – a conceptualization that the revisionary Kantian conception shares with the robust reason account – may be thought to be vulnerable to a fundamental objection. This objection proceeds from the observation that legal statements make, or at least claim to make, a difference in our practical deliberation. Legal standards, in other words, must in principle be capable of making a relevant difference in either the structure or the content of our practical reasoning (or both) as we go about the task of working out what ought to be done and on what basis that determination might be justified. However, the purported practical guidance of law would be merely nominal and illusory, rather than real, if of all the things we do or are required to do as addressees of a legal system, none can be picked out that we would not already be doing outside the scope of such a system. This general feature of law – its ability to make a difference in our practical deliberation – extends to the obligations it engenders, which, too, must be capable of making such a practical difference. So, if legal obligations are to retain a distinctive function in the practical guidance they offer, they cannot merely reproduce the requirements one can extract from the standards constitutive of practical rationality in its intersubjective mode – call these kinds of requirement 'rational obligations', for ease of reference – but must show at least some degree of specificity and autonomy from those requirements.[44] For, insofar as legal obligations are collapsed into rational obligations, the law would be prevented from making any practical difference in our deliberation about the conduct we ought to have. On this basis, the revisionary Kantian conception could be claimed to be unable to explain what it is that makes legal obligation distinctive, offering instead an explanation of what one is *rationally* obligated to do, and so an explanation of the obligation generated by practical *rationality* and *rational morality* rather than by the law.

In this section, I intend to show that the revisionary Kantian conception does not conflate the two kinds of obligation. The main reason why it does not – and so why, in my conceptual framework, legal obligation exists in distinction to rational obligation and cannot be reduced to the latter – is, in a nutshell, that on the conception being proposed here legal obligations and rational obligations can take different *contents*. This can be appreciated by looking at some paradigmatic scenarios in which the contents of legal obligation (as I construe this notion) would typically differ from the contents of the requirements set forth by the principles defining practical rationality in its intersubjective mode. This argumentative strategy will also make it possible for me to spell out a key aspect of the revisionary Kantian conception, which is that the moral dimension

---

[44] By *rational obligation*, then, I mean the kind of obligation that is generated by the standards of rational morality; and *rational morality* I understand to be the set of principles that are constitutive of, and thus define, practical rationality in its appeal to intersubjective considerations.

I associate with legal obligation has to do with its *quality*, not with its content or substance. In other words, the view of legal obligation as a practically rational demand that binds us on intersubjective grounds should not be confused with the claim that the contents of legal obligations reflect, in a mirror-like fashion, the contents of rational obligations: while on my conception legal obligations are practically rational demands shaped by intersubjective considerations – that is, the quality of legal obligation is rational – what they prescribe (that is, their contents) does not necessarily coincide with the contents of the prescriptions deriving from the standards constitutive of practical rationality. Which in turn means that, on the one hand, there are circumstances where legal institutions can legitimately obligate us to do something that practical rationality does not exact from us, and, on the other hand, legal obligations are not *subordinated* to rational demands, but only conceptually connected with them. Likewise, whereas the law is grounded in practical rationality, its substantive contents – its permissions, prohibitions, and obligations – do not necessarily replicate the standards of rationality as it applies to action. The picture of legal obligation I defend thus recognizes that legal obligations may not coincide with the obligations of practical rationality, to the effect that it can make a difference whether our practical reasoning is carried out in compliance with legal standards, as opposed to being carried out by a direct appeal to practically rational standards.

The key difference I draw in this context, then, is between (a) the *contents* of legal obligations, which are distinct and independent of those of rational obligations, and (b) the *nature*, or status, of legal obligation, which instead is borrowed from practical rationality at large. This shows that the revisionary Kantian conception does not overestimate the resources of practical rationality. Practical rationality, as I understand it, performs an essential guidance function in the domain of action by setting out fundamental conduct-guiding principles. However, if practical rationality is taken in isolation from other practices and institutions programmatically meant to govern our conduct, it will turn out to lack the resources needed to offer comprehensive, sufficiently detailed, and conclusive practical guidance in all circumstances. In fact, from a Kantian perspective, the standards constitutive of practical rationality in its intersubjective mode are not only inherently abstract and incomplete – and hence typically inconclusive – but also possibly uncertain. The claims that practical rationality makes on us therefore call for, and need to be fleshed out by, directives associated with other action-guiding enterprises, among which the law figures prominently. Far from providing exhaustive direction, the action-guiding principles of rationality leave open a significant number of issues. And when we face issues we cannot work out in any definite way on the sole basis of practical rationality, we can legitimately turn to the guidance of institutional practices – such as the law – that accordingly may overstep the bounds of practical rationality. Precisely for this reason, these other practices, in carrying out their practical function, may generate obligations whose contents do not match those one would derive from the standards defining practical rationality. The same applies to legal obligations: Their contents do not necessarily coincide with the contents of the requirements set forth by practical rationality. Which is why legal obligation (as I conceive it) cannot be claimed to collapse into rational obligation.

The differences in content between the two kinds of obligation – legal obligation and rational obligation as well as any obligation rational morality engenders when the latter is understood as the kind of obligation generated by the standards constitutive of practical rationality in its intersubjective mode – can be more analytically stated by pointing out four features of the practical standards that belong to the latter category: in a number of circumstances these may well be abstract, incomplete, inconclusive, and uncertain. Let us consider these features in turn. To begin with, the practical guidance we can derive from rationality, as this idea is understood in the Kantian tradition of philosophy, is inherently *abstract*. Practical rationality sets out *general* principles of action, as opposed to specific immediately *actionable* directives. Accordingly, far from being concerned with the details of the course of action an agent ought to take in specific circumstances, practical rationality provides a blueprint for action while leaving the task of filling in the specifics to other practical devices. In fact, not only are the standards of practical rationality intrinsically general and therefore unsuited to determining how people ought to behave in any given instance or context, but specific guidance cannot always be simply deduced, or derived in a logical fashion, from abstract principles of practical rationality. This feature of practical rationality opens a space for action-governing practices – the law being one of them – that are meant to provide us with recommendations and requirements specifying the general and abstract directives we can derive from practical rationality.

Consider, for instance, either of these two practical provisions that for the sake of argument I ask the reader to regard as in agreement with practical rationality in its intersubjective mode: the requirement that a company pay a wage affording their employees a decent quality of living, and the requirement that, in exchange for some basic public services, citizens pay taxes proportional to their income. These directives would typically translate into specific legal obligations. At a point in time, there has been, for example, a legal obligation to pay workers an hourly wage of no less than £7.83 in the United Kingdom, or to pay taxes up to 43 per cent of one's annual gross income in Italy. But we can see that the contents of these legal obligations do not coincide with the contents of any rational obligation, since in both cases practical rationality provides at most generic guidance, perhaps by fixing some kind of threshold beyond which any imposition would be rationally indefensible. So whereas practical rationality arguably acknowledges a generic need for a living wage or for a progressive income tax, that prescription is not specific enough to say what the exact numbers ought to be in either of those two cases. This means that while at a given time one may have had a *legal* obligation to pay employees at least £7.83 an hour, for example, or to pay 43 per cent of their earned income in taxes, there is no corresponding *rational* obligation to do just that. The differing contents of legal obligations and rational obligations in these cases can thus be explained by noting that the principles set by practical rationality are abstract and so may fail to point out any specific course of action for us to take (whilst still giving some kind of guidance in the practical domain). Which is why in our societies there are usually mechanisms and institutions to deal with the abstractness of practical rationality so as to supply *specific* guidance in the practical sphere. Paradigmatic among these mechanisms and institutions are legal systems: their rules cover as well cases which practical rationality does not govern in any specific way, and they may (indeed they typically do) set out obligations applying to those cases.[45] These are cases where, by construction, the contents of legal obligation do not replicate those of any obligation grounded in practical rationality. Hence, legal obligation, as the revisionary Kantian conception construes it, does not coincide with rational obligation.

In addition to being constitutively general, and hence abstract, the standards issued by practical rationality, as I conceive it, are inherently *incomplete*. It is true that these standards cover vast areas of the practical realm, but not every legal issue can be resolved by recourse to

---

[45] For a thorough treatment of this aspect, see R. Alexy, 'My Philosophy of Law: The Institutionalisation of Reason', in L. J. Wintgens (ed.), *The Law in Philosophical Perspective* (Dordrecht, Kluwer, 1999), pp. 23–45.

considerations of practical rationality. True, practical rationality has a say on issues that are of concern to law too. This can be appreciated, for example, by considering cases involving a court having to decide whether two conjoined twins ought to be separated in order to save the life of the one with better prospects of life,[46] or whether a couple is entitled to damages for an unwanted pregnancy they claim to be a result of medical malpractice,[47] or whether terrorism suspects detained without due process have to be released even if this can jeopardize the security of other people or of the citizenry at large.[48] Nonetheless, there are a number of scenarios where practical rationality has little to say and yet they are not only ordinarily dealt with by the law but are also governed by specifically legal rights and duties. If we can agree that these cases fall outside the purview of practical rationality, it follows that there are no distinctly *rational* obligations that arise in that connection, but only legal obligations. As a constitutively incomplete basis of guidance, then, practical rationality faces cases where, for lack of resources, it cannot offer any counsel or directive that can be acted on. Or, stated otherwise, there are areas where the law applies but where the standards constitutive of practical rationality cannot be made to do the work of practical guidance proper: such areas are simply not covered by these standards, and so in these areas agents are free of practically rational constraints. Whatever choice one makes in situations of this kind, the outcome is not going to make any difference from the standpoint of practical rationality, for these are areas that practical rationality in its intersubjective mode cannot extend to. So in these cases the directives of a legal system simply *take over*, by thus *going beyond* the realm of what practical rationality can apply to. In these contexts, where the law operates in a sort of rational vacuum – an area falling beyond the bounds of practical rationality – the obligations the law can be claimed to impose do not reproduce the contents of the obligations grounded in practical rationality. In these gappy areas, therefore, legal obligations cannot be said to coincide with rational obligations.

---

[46] This was the practical matter at hand in *Re A (children)*, Court of Appeal (Civil Division) [2000] 3 FCR 577, for example.
[47] For a similar decision, see *McFarlane* v. *Tayside Health Board*, House of Lords [2000] 2 AC 59, and *Rees* v. *Darlington Memorial Hospital NHS Trust*, House of Lords [2004] 1 AC 309QB 20.
[48] This, for example, was the issue in *A and Others* v. *Secretary of State for the Home Department* 2004 (The Belmarsh Prison Case) [2004] UKHL 56.

A third reason why the contents of legal obligations may differ from those of rational obligations is that the standards of practical rationality may be *inconclusive*. Consider, for example, the rules of the road. Some of these rules are clearly dictated by considerations of practical rationality (drunk driving, for example, can be labelled a rationally indefensible behaviour). But other rules cover ground where practical rationality is underdetermined: although it does make rational sense that everyone should drive on one side of the road (as opposed to everyone being free to choose at will which side to drive on), there are no rational grounds on which to say that this has to be the right side or the left side, since in principle either option will be equally safe and efficient. When a choice is rationally indeterminate in this sense, agents are under no obligation engendered by practical rationality to choose one way or the other. Yet it is hardly deniable that there are compelling reasons to regulate road traffic, not least for the sake of public safety and ease of movement. This is where traffic regulation by law steps in as a sensible option. And this is why our conduct on the road is typically governed by legal obligations, requiring, for example, that we drive on the left (or the right) side of the road or that we stop when the stop light turns a given colour. These legal obligations do not coincide with any requirement of practical rationality, which as noted is inconclusive in the matter. In these contexts, as well as in countless other situations where practical rationality seems to provide no clear indication as to how we ought to act, we may have an obligation to act in accordance with the law, and typically we do have such an obligation, especially in areas where there are good reasons for everyone to follow the same rules, as on the road. On the revisionary Kantian conception, then, in rationally inconclusive situations legal obligations do not simply reiterate what we rationally ought to do: in these situations, law and its obligations perform the function of providing directives with which to fill the space of practical possibility which rationality leaves open, but which nonetheless needs to be normatively structured. That is, in some contexts, legal directives in general, and legal obligations in particular, impart a specific shape to otherwise inconclusive and indeterminate standards of practical rationality so as to turn them into actual directives that work 'on the ground' in everyone's best interest.

The fourth and final point is that, even when the matter covered is of rational concern and practical rationality in its intersubjective mode offers adequately concrete and conclusive requirements, these can remain *uncertain*, meaning that their addressees cannot gain any certain knowledge of them. In such cases, law and its statements can perform an essential epistemic function in our practical experience. The epistemic contribution specific to law finds a radical statement in the work of Heidi Hurd, where the authority of law is argued to be *theoretical* in nature, rather than practical, influential, or advisory.[49] For Hurd argues that legal forms and procedures are reliable heuristic guides by which to determine our (independent) rational and moral obligations. On this view, the forms and procedures typically associated with the law can help us discover and act on rational and moral obligations that, were it not for the law itself, might well remain hidden from us.[50]

In my conception of legal obligation I do not subscribe to Hurd's theory of legal authority, nor to her claim that, far from providing independent obligations, law simply gives us reasons to believe in the existence of obligations that are antecedently arrived at by moral reasoning. But my conception does acknowledge what I take to be one important insight of Hurd's legal theory, namely, that law may have an epistemic role to play in the practical domain. For it seems to me that, at least in liberal legal cultures, legal systems rely on deliberative procedures and decision-making processes that do contribute to determining the conduct we ought to rationally have, by making such choices less uncertain and the proper course of action easier to ascertain. I am thinking, for instance, of the (a) democratic institutions enabling us to gather together and treat equally the opinions, practical knowledge, and wealth of experience of all the affected parties, (b) formal devices through which those in charge can tabulate the preferences of the members of the governed community and then use those preferences in public deliberation, (c) set of general, transparent, and publicized beforehand rules about the concerns that can, or cannot, be admitted when issues of general interest need be settled, (d) principles, aimed at securing equal rights to all the parties involved, which fashion the forms in which legal proceedings in general, and trials in particular, are carried out, and so on. In combination, legal institutions, formalities, procedures, and principles contribute to making law a reliable epistemic guide to what is practically rational in the public domain. In this sense, law can be described as a tool

---

[49] See, in particular, H. Hurd, *Moral Combat* (Cambridge, Cambridge University Press, 1999), pp. 153–83.
[50] In Hurd's own words, 'the law is unique in its ability to provide us with information that is necessary to moral action', to the effect that 'as an empirical matter, individuals will effectively fulfil their moral obligations only if they attend to the epistemic ones generated by the law's unique abilities to reflect the content of morality' (Hurd, *Moral Combat*, p. 157).

within which to ascertain contents of practically rational requirements that might otherwise remain uncertain or unknowable.

In my view, the epistemic function of the law can be characterized as distinctively declaratory, not merely reiterative. When the claims of practical rationality are worked into a system of laws, they are publicly declared and so transformed into a hitherto inexistent common knowledge. The declaratory role played by the law is thus far from inert, since even when the law does not present us with independent demands – when its role is limited to ascertaining the claims of practical rationality – it contributes to consolidating those demands in the public domain by defining what practical rationality singles out as publicly wrong, thus establishing those demands as uncontroversially obligatory for the whole of society. In comparison to the standards and requirements of practical rationality, then, legal norms and obligations carry out the distinctive function of singling out certain types of conduct as *public* wrongs we ought to abstain from. On this basis, too, from the perspective endorsed in this work, the idea of legal obligation as a practically rational demand set on an intersubjective basis cannot be taken to mean that the law lacks any practical relevance, (also) because in the absence of the law we would not be able to rely on paradigmatic forms, mechanisms, and procedures for working out issues of public interest and we would not have the certainty we need to have about the contents of the obligations of rational morality.[51]

---

[51] A similar insight can be found in Duff's recent work on the role and purpose of criminal law in tolerably just societies and liberal democracies. Duff emphasizes the declaratory dimension of substantive criminal law, whose purpose is claimed to be not primarily 'prohibitory', since substantive criminal law 'does not offer us new normative reasons for refraining from the conduct it defines as criminal', to the effect that a definition of a wrong as a crime constitutes a declaration, as distinct of a prohibition (A. Duff, 'Relational Reasons and Criminal Law', *Oxford Studies in Philosophy of Law*, 2 (2013), p. 183). On this view, as I understand it, substantive criminal law does not have either the primary function, or even the power, to make some conduct wrongful and, relatedly, to issue obligations demanding that people refrain from embarking in such conduct. By contrast, the essential function of substantive criminal law consists in publicly declaring a given conduct as wrong and so making it salient that such course of action is wrong, or objectionable, on independent, extralegal, grounds. Likewise, substantive criminal law performs the essential role of holding those acting in breach of a legal obligation publicly accountable (typically) before a court. In my understanding, then, Duff's construction is aligned with Hurd's remarks in so that it too allows us to appreciate that even when the requirements of the (substantive criminal) law do not depart from the demands of extralegal standards (such as the standards constitutive of practical rationality) – namely, even when those requirements presuppose, as opposed to creating, the wrongfulness of

In summary, in the theoretical framework I am defending, legal obligation is to be treated differently from rational obligation, for although legal obligation is defined as a practically rational requirement ultimately grounded in intersubjective considerations, the contents of legal obligation and the contents of the obligations engendered by practical rationality are not the same. This is because, as discussed, practical rationality is not conceived as self-sufficient: the principles constitutive of practical rationality need to be coupled with other standards that contribute to determining what an agent has an obligation to do. Among these standards are those of the law. Therefore, as much as legal obligations may have a *rational* quality, they do not simply mirror or replicate the substance of the demands issued by practical rationality in its intersubjective mode: in addition to reinforcing moral directives independently framed on the basis of practical rationality, legal obligations specify, contextualize, complete, make conclusive, disclose, clarify, render salient, and make knowable the contents of the rational requirements. In these situations, the law as an institution does not merely reiterate and reinforce practically rational demands bestowed with moral force; it also supplements and completes rational morality by issuing binding practical directives applicable to cases that practical rationality fails to cover, since no independent and non-derivative moral obligation would have existed but for the law. Legal obligations, as the revisionary Kantian conception depicts them, thus, are not exclusively established by the standards of practical rationality. Even while retaining moral nature and practically rational status, legal obligations take shape in a way that is sensitive to the historically situated, socially contextualized, and institutional elements incorporated in legal systems.

Importantly, when legal obligations do more than just reproducing the requirements one can derive from the standards constitutive of practical rationality, their functions are interstitial. That is, even when legal obligations go beyond the propositions of practical rationality – so as to supply the missing element needed to round out the latter and make up for its abstract, incomplete, inconclusive, or uncertain guidance – they will not be able to bind us if they come into conflict with those propositions. That is because, as noted, legal obligation is *grounded in* practical

---

the conduct that they criminalizes – they do make a practical difference in our practical reasoning, for they decisively contribute to clarify and publicize the specific contents of those requirements and the consequences that breaking those requirements (should) have in the relevant polity.

rationality, which is what confers on it its binding force – binding force that is ultimately rational and so does not forsake its rational nature simply because its content does not coincide with that of the principles of practical rationality. The divergence that may arise between the content legal obligations and that of rational demands is therefore no basis to conclude that legal obligation lacks a rational status, since the considerations that justify introducing mechanisms and institutions capable of providing practical guidance where rationality is indeterminate are rational and intersubjective considerations. Thus, as long as legal obligations fulfil their integrative function, they are properly considered practically rational standards. The continuity of legal obligation and rational obligation that emerges from the revisionary Kantian conceptual framework, therefore, is rooted in the *nature* of those requirements: both sets of requirements are practically rational, but this is consistent with their differing in content. Hence the distinctive position that legal obligation occupies: on the one hand, it is a kind of obligation grounded in (the intersubjective instantiations of) practical rationality, but, on the other, its content diverges from that of rational obligation proper whenever the need arises to provide concrete directives that cannot be arrived at on the sole basis of practical rationality.

9.4 Conclusion

This chapter addressed two possible concerns that may arise out of the revisionary Kantian conception of legal obligation laid out in this book: the first of these concerns was how that conception might differ from others already defended in the literature; the second was that legal obligation as framed within the same conception might not be genuinely and distinctively legal.

In addressing the first concern, I noted that, whereas the revisionary Kantian conception fits into the family of the reason account of legal obligation and bears similarities in particular with the robust variant of that account, the differences between revisionary Kantian conception and the robust reason account of legal obligation are significant. I focused in particular on two instantiations of the robust reason account: the one put forward by Duff and the one theorized by Beyleveld and Brownsword. I observed that the revisionary Kantian conception shares with both accounts a view of legal obligation as a rational standard of conduct. But the three approaches frame that view in different ways – on the basis of distinct theoretical constructions, argumentative strategies, philosophical backgrounds, and conceptual presuppositions – and as a consequence they draw different conclusions about legal obligation. Thus, for example, the revisionary Kantian conception establishes no link between legal obligation and the common good – a link that instead is essential to Duff's construction. Nor does the revisionary Kantian conception make an appeal to some supreme moral principle or endorse the strong natural law thesis, which by contrast are central to Beyleveld and Brownsword's theory.

I then passed to discuss the second concern – the concern as to whether legal obligation can be characterized as a practically rational standard and yet still be understood as a distinctive kind of obligation in its own right. In response to that concern I emphasize the distinction between the *nature* of legal obligation and its *content*. This made it possible to appreciate that even if the practical rationality that provides a support for legal obligation is inflected as a justificatory *intersubjective* standard for reasoning in the practical sphere, it cannot *on its own* yield all the specific provisions the law needs to issue. In fact, we saw that the principles of practical rationality are not self-sufficient: they lack the requisite concreteness, completeness, conclusiveness, and determinacy, and hence cannot achieve the granularity needed to deal with the issues the law is concerned with. It follows that even if the principles of practical rationality function as a necessary foundation for legal provisions that impose obligations on the law's addressees, and even if the latter may not contradict the former, the two do not necessarily coincide. The contents of legal obligation, in other words, are not necessarily coextensive with the demands of practical rationality. Hence the distinctiveness of legal obligation as a body of legal requirements that – while sharing the same nature with practical rationality, in that both are built on a basis of intersubjective reasons for action – cannot be collapsed into this standard as far as their contents are concerned.

This thesis – that the *nature* which legal obligation shares with the requirements of practical rationality does not prevent the two from taking on different *contents* – can be rounded out by highlighting two further aspects of the relation between law and practical rationality and their respective demands. The first of these concerns Finnis's claim (discussed in Chapter 6) that the force of legal obligation is invariant: an obligation is either binding or it is not, and once it is established to be binding, it will defeat all non-legal reasons for action by taking them out of the picture, that is, by excluding them from consideration, thereby protecting legal obligations from non-legal considerations and securing their independence from the latter. The point to note here is that Finnis's thesis (framed within the exclusionary reason account of legal obligation) can be defended only on condition of positing between law and practical rationality (and their respective demands) a strict *discontinuity*. Thus it was argued in Chapter 6 that law and practical rationality are best understood to stand not in an exclusionary relation (as Finnis claims in agreement with Raz) but in a *dialectical* one, in which the two terms are distinct but transparent to each other and interconnected. Which in turn means that at a conceptual level those terms are not radically apart in an exclusionary fashion. For in that case there could be no communication between them to begin with. The communication and transparency characterizing dialectical relations, in other words, require (at least) two terms that are mutually *distinct* and *interconnected*. Now, the same applies to the relation between legal obligations and obligations engendered by practical rationality. Insofar as their relation is dialectical, they should be conceptualized as two distinct kinds (which, nonetheless, are not mutually exclusive and so are not radically separate). And this is exactly the kind of relation – non-exclusionary, or dialectical – that the thesis of the distinction of legal obligations from practically rational requirements I argued for in this chapter secures. On the position I espoused in this chapter, the substance of legal obligations does not dissolve into the contents of generically rational standards for action – we still have two distinct terms at play – and yet it is not radically disconnected from the latter. Indeed, on the view defended here, legal obligation is grounded in practical rationality; which enables the demands of law to be transparent to the requirements of practical rationality and to communicate with the latter in a dialectical way. At the same time, in order for their relation to be genuinely dialectical, legal obligations and practically rational requirements must also be acknowledged to *differ* from each other. And that is precisely the conception I put forward by arguing that their shared nature does not prevent legal obligations and claims made on us by practical rationality from taking different *contents*.

Hence, ultimately all those components of the revisionary Kantian conception of legal obligation come together in a full circle: it is because legal obligations have rational quality and yet their contents do not coincide with the substantive dimension of the demands of practical rationality – namely, there is a content-related distinction, vis-à-vis a relation of either identity or radical separation, between legal obligations and practically rational requirements – that we should embrace the claims that legal obligation (a) stands in a dialectical relation with rational obligation, (b) does not follow an exclusionary logic, for it is best understood as a non-exclusionary reason for action and so a directive possibly subject to extralegal exceptions – it is a defeasible norm – and (c) has variable force – namely, the law is hardly an inflexible standard of behaviour, as Finnis instead claims.

The second aspect of the relation between legal obligations and the requirements of practical rationality – as distinct but not separate areas of practical reasoning – can be brought into focus by further specifying the relation of continuity previously argued to exist between law and practical rationality. On this view, law is understood as an instantiation of, and so as continuous with, practical rationality.[52] From this 'continuity thesis' it follows that law and practical rationality are alike in that (a) they both serve a guidance function, (b) this function they serve by offering reasons for acting as directed, and (c) the guidance is in either case consistent with there being multiple values that the individuals concerned espouse. Both, in other words, are intersubjective to the extent that (i) the rules and principles they set forth apply in the *public* sphere – they address not one but *multiple* agents, who in this sphere are accordingly asked to renounce any personal value or interest that may be inconsistent with them – and (ii) they both purport to *justify* the courses of action they support to the generality of agents they address.[53]

Now, in keeping with the continuity thesis, the law needs to address its subjects as reasoning agents.[54] The subjects the law addresses, then, are conceived not as mere *subjects* to whom certain rules and principles apply, but as rational *agents* who will not submit to these rules and principles unless the reasons for them are made explicit, and unless these reasons make sense within a common framework of thought and interpretation, a framework that they themselves (as rational agents) are understood to have conceived or would otherwise recognize as valid.[55]

---

[52] As Steven Burton argues, the law 'can be understood to bear on practical deliberations by changing an addressee's reasons for action' (S. Burton, 'Law as Practical Reason', *Southern California Law Review*, 62 (1989), p. 768).

[53] For an initial treatment of the continuity thesis, see Burton, 'Law as Practical Reason', pp. 767–71.

[54] To put it in the words of Gerald Postema, law 'seeks to guide the behaviour of rational beings through rational means' (G. Postema, 'The Normativity of Law', in R. Gavison (ed.), *Issues in Contemporary Legal Philosophy* (Oxford, Clarendon, 1987), pp. 91–2).

[55] Here we can appreciate the dual nature of law as a system at once coercive and justifiable, that is, a system that, on the one hand, is backed by the threat of sanctions for non-compliant behaviour, while, on the other, claims not just the sheer power but the *authority*, or legitimate claim, to govern the terms on which basis individuals are to

In short, in much the same way as practical rationality understands acting selves as responsive to reasons and rational discourse, or as agents capable of reasoning critically about action and acting accordingly, so too does the law as an instantiation of practical rationality. The law, in other terms, would make no sense without this assumption in the background. And this is also why, in constraining action within a framework of rules and principles, the law speaks the normative language – the language of reasons – by thus engaging in the justificatory game.

A related final point needs to be stressed here in closing this discussion and full-circling it. I claimed that under the continuity thesis, the law is conceived as an instantiation of practical rationality and so as sharing with practical rationality a distinctive way of addressing those to whom it applies. That is, the law appeals to our capacity to understand the reasons for its rules, principles, and directives, while at the same time recognizing (in virtue of the same capacity) our need to appreciate those reasons as valid. But I also argued that the practical rationality governing this use of reasons is limited in its scope: the general principles of action are too sweeping as guides on which basis to lay out the shape of action in its every detail. And this means that on the view defended here, while the law is continuous with practical rationality, and so cannot be equated with the mere institutional enforcement of rules (for there is also a rational justificatory component to it), it cannot be collapsed into practical rationality, either. For the law needs to be fairly specific in its governing of social relationships, and to that extent it enjoys a degree of independence from the practical rationality of which it is an instantiation. Stated otherwise, the principles of practical rationality can place constraints on our deliberation in the practical affairs in which the law is concerned – it can set out a framework within which to reason about such matters – but there is only so much it can do to shape the law into

---

interact in society (on this dual quality of law see also R. Alexy, 'On the Concept and the Nature of Law', *Ratio Juris*, 21 (2008), pp. 281–99). But, going back to the point just made, law cannot claim this authority unless it takes a specific view of its addressees as endowed with a capacity for practical rationality. Very much in the same vein, Joseph Raz regards legal subjects as persons having the 'capacity to perceive and understand how things are, and what response is appropriate to them', as well as the 'ability to respond appropriately' to situations and inputs (J. Raz, *Engaging Reason* (Oxford, Oxford University Press, 1999), p. 67). Accordingly, the subjects of law are understood to be able to determine their lives 'in accordance with their appreciation of themselves and their environment, and of the reasons with which, given how they are, the world presents them' (Raz, *Engaging Reason*, p. 67).

the specific forms it needs to take in dealing with the matters it needs to work out. In virtue of its generality, practical rationality cannot *alone* fully determine how the law ought to be framed in different contexts and within specific traditions, or how the law can, or should, be justified in these contexts and within these traditions. Practical rationality can only lay out principles that cannot be violated in the domain of action, but it cannot exhaustively establish the particular forms of legal justification beyond that which any rational and reasonable person can be expected to accept. This also highlights the sense in which practical rationality is consistent with a plurality of ends and values. Therefore, on the one hand, the continuity thesis denies the complete autonomy of law, which accordingly is understood as an enterprise framed within the bounds of practical rationality; but, at the same time, in recognizing the limits of practical rationality itself, the continuity thesis also denies that law can be fully shaped on the basis of this capacity alone, or that the rules and principles of law are simply carried over from the rules and principles of practical rationality.

10

The Method of Presuppositional Interpretation

10.1 Introduction

The purpose of this chapter is to introduce the specific method that has shaped the theoretical exploration of legal obligation carried out in this book – a method I will refer to as 'presuppositional interpretation'. I intend to do so primarily by elucidating structure, quality, and rationale of presuppositional interpretation. In this context, I will also show that the method I rely on in my study of legal obligation builds on, and bears similarities to, more traditional methodological approaches that have been consistently used in philosophy.

To briefly introduce the main theses I will defend here the starting point of the proposed method will be claimed to be the concept of obligation – the features that the main contributors to the debate on the obligatory dimension of human practices have widely acknowledged to be constitutive of that dimension.[1] Of the concept of obligation presuppositional interpretation is purported to first determine the implicit conditions of intelligibility – this task corresponds to the 'presuppositional' component of the method shaping this study – and, second, to offer a theoretical characterization by giving a specific meaning both to the traits constitutive of the concept and to their conditions of intelligibility – a task corresponding to the 'interpretative' character of the method used in this work. This two-step procedure making up presuppositional interpretation – an analysis of the conditions under which obligation as a concept is thinkable coupled with an interpretation of those conditions in light of some explanatory hypotheses – has the potential to give us the fundamentals of a comprehensive and deep theoretical account of legal obligation – the very objective of this research work – or so I will argue. The end product of the presuppositional interpretation I undertake in this study is, therefore, a theory, or

---

[1] These features were set out in Chapter 1.

conception, or theoretical account, of legal obligation. By those terms ('theory', 'conception', and 'theoretical account' of something), which I use as synonyms, I mean a sufficiently rich, thick, and substantive characterization of the concept, or generic view, of the relevant something.

These introductory remarks indicate that presuppositional interpretation should be understood as a *syncretic* method of inquiry, which, on the one hand, is *derivative* upon a set of alternative methodologies of broad currency in philosophy and, on the other hand, is *irreducible* to those methodologies. This dimension of presuppositional interpretation will be specifically discussed in Section 10.4, where, in explaining the rationale behind my chosen method, I intend to also clarify the conceptual relations that obtain between presuppositional interpretation and some methodological alternatives, such as transcendental approach and conceptual analysis, which have been widely used in the theoretical study of practical issues. In comparing the methodological insights behind presuppositional interpretation with the methodological insights behind transcendental approach and conceptual analysis, I do not aspire to exhaustively account for all the methodological options potentially available to the study of legal obligation. The scope of my treatment is more limited, as I simply intend to show that presuppositional interpretation is conceptually continuous with and derivative upon, albeit irreducible to, some influential traditions of theoretical investigation. In this way, presuppositional interpretation will be shown to be a mixed method that is not fully identifiable with other philosophical methodologies in wide use. At the same time it will also be claimed to be not radically alien to some standard methodologies of inquiry relied on in practical philosophy. And this is why presuppositional interpretation can be found to be of significance in the philosophical discourse, while retaining a characteristic identity, lending it some distinctiveness and originality as a method for the theoretical account of legal obligation.

A caveat is in order before I begin setting out in detail the method I have applied in this work. The argument I have put forward in what precedes is almost exclusively concerned with the idea of legal obligation. Throughout the book, in other words, my main concern has been with determining the fundamental traits of what is legally obligatory, vis-à-vis the *method*, or procedure, through which those fundamental traits can, or should, be singled out. For this reason, in the previous chapters I have refrained from systematically engaging with methodological debates. Nonetheless, I am well aware of the fact that in jurisprudence substantive claims are in part dependent on, and to a degree settled by, the method one uses to arrive at them. Since the method used at least implicitly affects the substantive component of theoretical explorations, confronting methodological issues is an almost inescapable stage of legal-theoretical arguments. This combination of tenets – my primary interest in the substantive idea of legal obligation and vivid awareness of the significance of methodological concerns in theoretical studies – justifies the twofold decision of both introducing the method I rely on in my engagement with legal obligation only at a later stage of the discussion and devoting an ad hoc chapter to explicitly clarify that method.

To briefly expand on this point, on the one hand, I am mindful of the importance of the methodological component of theoretical arguments and believe that methodological concerns play an essential role in jurisprudence. Which is why I consider it important and appropriate to offer an *explicit, unambiguous,* and *structured* statement of the method I have used in this work, as opposed to let readers find out by themselves the procedure I have followed in order to arrive at the revisionary Kantian conception of legal obligation I have theorized in what precedes. On the other hand, in consideration of my specific interests in this book – interests, to reiterate, in the fundamental properties of legal obligation, vis-à-vis the methodology of jurisprudential inquiries into legal obligation – I am opting for discussing the method that underpins my conceptualization of legal obligation only after that conceptualization has been introduced and argued for in its essential details. This choice, which should not be interpreted as an indication of my scarce interest in the methodology underpinning substantive claims about legal obligation, is meant to unequivocally make the (partial) autonomy of my construction of legal obligation explicit, by thus emphasizing the mutual independence of substantive theses and methodological approach.[2] Indeed, despite its

---

[2] In my understanding, postponing the discussion of the methodological dimension of one's investigation should hardly be considered an indication of the limited interest of a theorist in the method underpinning their contribution. This statement finds support in Immanuel Kant's body of work. For, in all its three major *Critiques*, Kant, who can hardly be accused of failing to appreciate the significance of methodological concerns for the construction of philosophical theories, discusses the method underlying his philosophical theorizing in the conclusive part of his works, namely, only after, vis-à-vis before, he presents his substantive arguments. In this respect, then, my choice of dealing with the method that informs my treatment of legal obligation is not only a deliberate strategy that can be justified on independent grounds – as indicated in the text – but also a move mirroring Kant's own argumentative strategy and so a move coherent with the overall approach – Kantian,

inescapable (relative) method-dependence, my conceptualization of legal obligation can be assessed and discussed in its own terms, namely, separately from the consideration of the method used to produce it. In locating the methodological discussion in the conclusive part of my exploration, thus, I intended to preserve the continuity of the substantive component of my argument and to restate the fact that the proposed conception of legal obligation should be considered an achievement in its own.

10.2 The Structure of Presuppositional Interpretation

Taken in its literal meaning, presuppositional interpretation consists in a reflection aimed at making sense of both the fundamental features of the subject matter of inquiry and their basic conditions of intelligibility. Accordingly, a presuppositional interpretation of legal obligation is to be understood as a process by which the essential traits and conditions of conceivability of the kind of duty engendered by the law are identified and substantively characterized. This section, which is distinguished in three parts, is devoted to fleshing out this concise statement of presuppositional interpretation, as this method is used in my study of legal obligation.

10.2.1 Entry Point

In order to unpack the idea of presuppositional interpretation and to introduce its fundamental components, here I will elucidate the entry point, namely, the object, or subject matter, of that method. As anticipated, the starting point for the presuppositional interpretation undertaken in this work is the concept of obligation *simpliciter*. Such concept should not be understood as some objective and uninterpretable fact, since it would be futile to go looking for such a thing in the practical sphere. Nor should the entry point of my argument be reduced to any non-factual alternative that may seem likewise obvious as a candidate for the premise in constructing a theory of legal obligation. Two such candidates that bear at least some brief discussion are (a) commonsense beliefs about obligation and (b) the legal practitioners' unreflective implicit view of legal obligation. My presuppositional interpretation does

although in a revisionary sense – that structures my argument for a given conceptualization of legal obligation, as this argument has taken shape in this book.

not apply to either of those alternative sources of knowledge, since I regard both of them as epistemically less reliable than the concept of obligation. Let us see why.

(a) To begin with, it is essential that the concept of obligation, as I conceive it, be kept distinct from the ordinary notion, or common-sense understanding, of obligation that we might find in a pre-philosophical or folk theory of obligation. The concept of obligation I am referring to is rather fixed by a specialist subgroup – roughly stated: by mainstream practical philosophers and legal theorists – and in this sense it forms a distinctive category. It therefore should not be confused with a restatement of the opinions about obligation commonly held by laypeople.

To be sure, the concept of obligation, as it is developed by practical philosophers and legal theorists, is not unrelated to the ideas the broader community associates with obligation.[3] At the same time, however, a scholarly account of obligation neither merely maps onto the ordinary understanding of the concept nor simply records the folk view. I rather selectively *interpret* the ideas that form those understanding and view. And this necessarily means refashioning the ordinary idea of obligation. In anchoring the concept of obligation to the considered judgements of a specialist subgroup, then, the method of presuppositional interpretation I am using should be expected to depart from that common-sense account in at least some respects.

In turn, this strategic choice – to focus on the views and usages of a specialized subgroup – is grounded in some scepticism on the reliability of common-sense understanding. This scepticism is revealing of a broader methodological commitment: the commitment to the primacy of the theorist's understanding over the common-sense cognition, especially when complex and abstract notions are at stake. This commitment is not justified by some elitist preconception favouring the views of the few over those of the many. It is rather grounded in my confidence in the epistemic authority of the cognitive processes associated with systematic reflection and rational deliberation. It is my belief that, for all the limitations and inherent fallibility of a reflective and sustained engagement with a subject matter (as is a philosophical discussion of obligation), this

---

[3] The significance that common understanding and shared views of concepts have in theoretical disciplines has recently been argued for in N. Barber, 'The Significance of the Common Understanding in Legal Theory', *Oxford Journal of Legal Studies*, 35 (2015), 799–823, where both the value and the limitations of the appeal to common sense in theoretical enterprises, and especially in legal theory, are critically discussed.

practice proves to be a more trustworthy source of knowledge than what can be garnered from the unreflective, spontaneous, and often implicit engagement with obligation, legal or otherwise, that most of us have in ordinary lives.

That is not to deny that common sense is a valuable resource that on occasions may well protect us from conceptual misunderstanding and fundamental mistakes. It is rather to question the wisdom of either *exclusively* or *predominantly* relying on unconstrained exercises in common sense: the attitude of treating common sense as a sort of oracle, while at the same time shielding it from the critical scrutiny of those who rationally and systematically engage with the relevant subject matter. Hence, whereas I acknowledge that commonly held opinions do often incorporate more than a grain of truth and are ultimately revealing of a tacit wisdom that should be highly prized, I also believe that those opinions tend to take the form of a set of unsystematic, not necessarily integrated, possibly incoherent, and more often than not inchoate claims. For this reason, even when the folk view can be shown to be correct from a substantive point of view, it should be regarded as structurally inferior and presumptively less trustworthy than the considered judgements of those who, like practical philosophers and legal theorists, not only have special competence and expertise in the subject matter but also have put special effort into understanding the issues relating to the obligations engendered by our social practices. Which is why I take specialized knowledge, which proceeds from a systematic and sustained deliberative effort to come to understand the subject matter at issue, to be epistemically more authoritative than the conclusions we may come to by ordinary reflection.

My methodological commitment to the priority of the theorist's understanding of obligation over the folk view can therefore ultimately be traced back to the fact that the scholarly understanding of obligation is the outcome of a thorough, sustained, and intellectually rigorous cognitive process carried out by individuals who are both skilled and trained in the relevant field of inquiry. The outcome of such a process can legitimately be expected to be more trustworthy than that of the largely unreflective, implicit, and sporadic treatment that obligation receives in the community at large. This conclusion strikes me as reasonable especially when the object of inquiry is a highly speculative and abstract notion that does not necessarily bear a direct and immediate relation to everyday practices and ordinary experience. On this ground, I take the scholarly understanding of obligation, not the community view of it, as constitutive of the concept from which my presuppositional interpretation starts out.[4]

(b) The same attitude towards the reliability of pre-theoretical determinations, ordinary conceptualizations, and unreflective cognition (especially in relation to abstract and speculative problems) urges one to be cautious about the suggestion that the concept of obligation should be constructed on the basis of the legal practitioners' understanding of the obligations generated by the law. I will accordingly be taking the view that no notion of legal obligation becomes inherently correct simply by virtue of its corresponding to an opinion broadly shared among lawyers. On the same grounds I will also be proceeding from the background assumption that the lawyerly conception of legal obligation is not necessarily more reliable than a philosophical or jurisprudential one. Legal practitioners are skilled in the art and practice of litigation; and legal disputes often concern the *contents* of the obligations one has under a system of laws. At the same time, legal practitioners are generally not interested in conceptualizing legal obligation as a specific kind or, consequently, in reflecting on the *nature* and *structure* of such obligation. It thus seems reasonable to trust the considered judgements of legal practitioners when the issues at stake concern questions about the *contents* of the obligations we have under a specific legal system. When that is the problem, it would not make much sense to rely too heavily on the skills and expertise of practical philosophers and legal theorists, since they are most likely to lack the legal practitioner's substantive knowledge of the law. When, instead, we face issues concerning not the contents of legal obligation but its idea and nature – as is the case when attempting to explain what kind of obligations the law generates – the opposite seems to be true: we will want to give explanatory priority to the skills and knowledge of legal theorists and practical philosophers over those of legal

---

[4] The preceding remarks should also suggest that presuppositional interpretation, as I have used it here, is implicitly committed to the claim that, far from befogging our understanding of abstract concepts, the mediation of theory can help us arrive at a sound and comprehensive account of them. Or, to put it otherwise, 'innocent' views only minimally informed by theory cannot, even presumptively, be regarded as epistemically more authoritative than philosophically informed conceptions. Philosophical training and theoretical engagement with an issue, in other words, can hone our reasoning, analytical skills, and critical capacity, thus acting as a counterweight to the sloppiness that sometimes accompanies commonly held opinions. For arguments in support of this view, see H. Kornblith, 'Naturalism and Intuitions', *Grazer Philosophische Studien*, 74 (2007), 31–40; and T. Williamson, *The Philosophy of Philosophy* (Oxford, Blackwell, 2007), pp. 187–95.

practitioners. In this inquiry into the concept of obligation I will accordingly proceed not from the views that legal practitioners hold about the obligations associated with the existence of legal systems but from the understanding that mainstream practical philosophers and legal theorists can offer in that regard.

Now, it can be claimed that taking the mainstream experts' shared understanding of obligation as the entry point into the discussion of legal obligation is an objectionable move in at least four related respects.[5] First, to rely on the idea of obligation that is most widespread among practical philosophers and legal theorists means to presuppose the preliminary existence of independent criteria for distinguishing both specialists from non-specialists and the conventional view from outlying approaches. Second, the move may amount to writing the majority opinion right into the very concept of obligation, while at the same time discounting from the debate positions that may provide valuable insights into the obligatory dimension of human experience just because these positions are not shaped by generally held theses and so fail to conform to the dominant trend in the study of obligation. In this way, especially insofar as specialists are a self-identifying group, the proposed method may end up excluding, or at least marginalizing, those who disagree with the received view. Which may in turn favour conformism and groupthink, as dissent and independence of thought may end up being interpreted as failures to engage with the same issues as the ones mainstream accounts are concerned with. So, for one thing, numbers are accorded from the outset a significance they would not otherwise be entitled to have in theoretical arguments; and, for another, the work of the practical philosophers and legal theorists who do not endorse the standard approach is denied a fair chance to meaningfully join the debate. This is not only unfair but also objectionable – and this is the third possible line of criticism – especially considering that it arbitrarily and discretionally narrows down the material to which presuppositional interpretation applies: this material will not include all conceivable ideas about what is obligatory but will rather be reduced to a limited subset of the manifold constructions of obligation that have been put forward or could be put forward by those who systematically reflect on the obligatory dimension of human experience.

---

[5] This part of the discussion has benefited from an exchange with Nick Barber. The usual disclaimer applies here, as I remain solely responsible for the views expressed and the statements defended in this part of the argument.

Finally, choosing to sanction the specialist understanding of obligation requires us to devise a strategy for dealing with possible disagreements among experts. For it is reasonable to think that practical philosophers and legal theorists are likely to disagree even over the fundamental properties of obligation (general consensus being seldom the rule within either practical philosophy or legal theory). Without such a strategy, the inquiry inevitably proceeds from an arbitrary starting point, while failing to provide a stable reference for philosophical analysis.

I grant the force of these objections, but since I lack the space needed to address them systematically here, my defence of presuppositional interpretation will be limited to a 'partners in crime' argument. This argument I would set up by noting, to begin with, that no starting point is immune from the fourfold criticism just outlined: any point of entry is going to (a) presuppose an independent criterion on which basis to distinguish a mainstream or standard view (or indeed any other kind of view) of the object we set out to investigate; any point of entry is going to (b) exclude some views from consideration and thereby (c) restrict the scope of discussion; and any point of entry is going to (d) be a source of disagreement. In short, there is no safe house that one can retreat to in philosophy, hoping to find shelter.

We thus have to start from somewhere – from some place where we are going to be guilty as charged – and here I can only defend the choice previously made, the criterion used in making that choice, and its use in the presuppositional interpretation method. We thus ask, (i) why start out from the view of obligation that is most established among legal theorists and practical philosophers? (ii) what is the best criterion by which to identify that view, and (iii) how does that initial choice limit the range of possible outcomes? As to the first question, the choice we have to make in selecting a starting point is, do we start out from a common-sense understanding of obligation or from an expert view? I decided to start out from the expert view, but that is not because I am dismissing the common-sense understanding. In fact, I accept that this understanding can act as an essential check on the theory being put forward, by making sure that it comports with the thinking of those for whom the concept of obligation is to have any sense to begin with, regardless of whether they have specifically devoted time to its study. So the reason for starting out from the expert view – the view of those who do in fact make obligation an object of study – is not that this makes it possible to exclude all other views from the outset (quite the contrary) but that this expert view is more likely to be correct than the common-sense understanding, precisely because the experts have investigated the matter and are assumed to know what errors they should try to avoid, what the full range of opinions is, and what the objections and counter-objections are: this gives them a vantage point that the layperson (no matter how thoughtful they may be) cannot have.

This takes us to the second question, for we must now ask, how do we go about identifying this expert view? We want to cast as wide a net as possible, precisely because we do not want to be exclusionary, and we want the view to be as well established as possible, because any view that gains traction is likely to have something good in it simply on account of its wide reception. Thus I say that numbers do count: for how can one otherwise independently determine which view is most widespread and established, without bringing one's own bias to the selection and doing the least to exclude opinions?

Having made it clear that the point of making an initial selection is not to keep competing views of obligation out of the picture, we can turn to the third question and ask, how do we work that mainstream expert view into the theory and how does this affect the range of its substantive conclusions and hence its validity? Here I should stress that presuppositional interpretation is not an argument in defence of this or that view of legal obligation but a method for extracting the presuppositions behind whatever view is taken as a starting point so as to arrive at a deeper understanding of that view, all the while identifying any inconsistencies the same view may contain. So, much as the starting view (here the standard view most widely accepted among experts) may delimit the findings we arrive at through the investigation (it does so by forcing us to reason within its scheme), this does not preclude us from finding faults in the same view – in fact this is precisely what we should be encouraged to do: we want to subject the starting view to a 'stress test' that may bring out any aspects that might otherwise lie in concealment – nor does the method preclude us from taking any alternative view as a point of departure. Indeed, as noticed a moment ago, the method is not intended to be exclusionary: the idea behind it is not to rule out certain views as untenable from the outset so as to promote a certain conformism but, on the contrary, to test them, understand what is involved in asserting them, and in the process gain any valuable insights they may offer. As a method, then, presuppositional interpretation may limit its output in virtue of the initial input – thereby confining the validity of its findings within that range – but it does not limit the input itself and it is in this sense an input-agnostic method.

10.2.2 Procedure

I have thus far singled out the 'entry point' for the method of presuppositional interpretation that I used in this inquiry, namely, the concept of obligation. I have also singled out a 'base' for that entry point, noting that there are a couple of options – or a couple of angles from which to approach the concept we are interested in – that should not be accounted for – one of those options being the 'lay' view of legal obligation and the other the view (often implicitly) endorsed by legal practitioners. It is now time to have a closer look at what presuppositional interpretation does with that starting point, thus elucidating the procedure through which this method arrives at a theoretical account of obligation.

Here I will thus be devoted to expounding the idea of presuppositional interpretation as a method that proceeds from a set of premises to the conditions of conceivability of those premises, and then provides an interpretation, or substantive account, of both those premises and their conditions of intelligibility. That is, presuppositional interpretation is a two-step method of inquiry where we first (a) reflect on the often implicit conditions that make a selected starting point intelligible, and then (b) proceed to a hermeneutics of the subject matter at issue. So understood, presuppositional interpretation takes certain features for granted and proceeds in a non-trivial and non-mechanical way to lay out the preconditions, presuppositions, and assumptions that are necessary for us to account for those features.

As explained, in the presuppositional interpretation I have carried out in my study of legal obligation, the set of premises to which the method applies consists of the concept, or expert understanding, of obligation. By construction, at least within a given (broad) theoretical horizon this set of premises describes a notion that is widely accepted by, and uncontroversial among, those who systematically engage with the idea of legal obligation. The primary task of presuppositional interpretation then is to draw out the implicit presuppositions underlying that widely accepted base. So, in proceeding from a specialists' understanding of obligation, the presuppositional interpretation proposed in this study also (i) spells out the conditions of conceivability of that understanding and (ii) provides a substantive reading, reconstruction, or characterization, of it.

On a practical level, a presuppositional interpretation, as it applies to the conceptualization of legal obligation, is structured into a number of sub-activities. The preliminary step will be to describe a concept of obligation and establish what that concept presupposes. This step is aimed at unearthing and, thus, making explicit the essential features and conditions absent which obligation would not be conceivable. At this stage, one would also record any tension that there may be between those features and presuppositions and any conceptual quandary they may generate.

Building on these initial insights, through a critical engagement with the expert understanding of obligation, presuppositional interpretation will move on to interpret both the essential features defining our concept of obligation and the presuppositions that are constitutive of obligation, thereby proceeding to construct a theoretical account of legal obligation. In this way, presuppositional interpretation winds up embracing a thick philosophical characterization of the fundamental constituents of legal obligation, or of the general conditions needed to make obligation conceivable.

Presuppositional interpretation, as here described, thus enables us to transition from (a) what is stated in general terms and is widely accepted among those participating in the discussion at hand to (b) something that is more specifically inflected and so may be perceived as less obvious and occasionally even as more controversial than the general understanding. Otherwise put, presuppositional interpretation will enable one to move from a generic idea of obligation – a *concept* of obligation identifying a theoretically catholic and tolerant definition of *what is obligatory* – to a specific one – a *conception* of legal obligation understood as a theoretical construct designed to account for the fundamental features of *legal obligation* that can be derived from the basic traits of the broader concept delimiting the wide genre legal obligation is a species of. This means that through this method of inquiry one can arrive at a comprehensive and systematic conception of legal obligation emerging as the end result of a movement from the specialists' understanding of obligation to a philosophical one implicit in legal practices. By this combined process of unearthing and richly characterizing essential features and conditions of conceivability, presuppositional interpretation can help one single out and give substance to the defining traits of legal obligation. In its full statement the theory of legal obligation one arrives at by means of presuppositional interpretation will thus enable one to identify and substantively characterize the full range of conceptual properties associated with legal obligation.

In summary, presuppositional interpretation is to be understood as a peculiar procedure by which to critically reflect, at the most elemental level, on what it is for someone to take something to be legally obligatory. In keeping with this scheme, the presuppositional interpretation that has been carried out in this study has proceeded from a widely agreed starting point to an interpretation of the traits of legal obligation. This is a trajectory from what is apparent and immediately evident to certain unobvious and substantive truths about legal obligation – truths that, albeit less than self-evident, are nonetheless contained in the expert understanding, and so are derivable by means of a philosophical reflection from such an understanding. In this way, the presuppositional interpretation I have undertaken in my treatment of legal obligation is best understood as a procedure aimed at eliciting considered expert judgements, systematically isolating their conditions of intelligibility, reflecting on their relationships, and thus arriving at a conceptually perspicuous substantive characterization of legal obligation by way of a hermeneutical activity that addresses a widespread rational understanding.

10.2.3 Expected Outcome

A crucial dimension of presuppositional interpretation, as I conceive it, is that the theoretical account of legal obligation generated by this method cannot be reduced to the picture of the obligations engendered by the law shared by specialists. For that view is only the beginning of the process in which a full-scale presuppositional interpretation consists. The theoretical account of legal obligation yielded by presuppositional interpretation instead amounts to a substantive and potentially controversial characterization of the fundamental features of legal obligation. In bringing out the traits and preconditions of obligation, the presuppositional interpretation I have carried out in this study has been aimed at offering an explanation that digs beneath the surface elements of legal obligation to lay bare its deep structure.

That is to say, the theory generated by presuppositional interpretation programmatically transcends the specialists' shared understanding of obligation, which only plays an introductory role in the overall argument, thereby yielding an explanation of the deep nature of legal obligation. Relatedly, presuppositional interpretation should be expected to give us access to more than just the surface features defining the kind of obligation associated with law: presuppositional interpretation is instrumental to grasping the deep conceptual commitments underpinning the received view of obligation, and at the same time to securing a theoretically insightful understanding of the conventional picture and its inherent commitments. To that extent, presuppositional interpretation is best depicted as a method affording insight into the structure or distinctive logic of legal obligation by singling out and philosophically explaining the usually unthematized, conceptual presuppositions behind learned discourses about obligation. In that sense, the presuppositional interpretation of legal obligation I have carried out in what precedes was meant to help us to key in on, and critically scrutinize, those aspects of our engagement with legal obligation that have thus far largely remained unexpressed and have retained the status of an unreflectively accepted body of knowledge.[6]

As a result, embarking on a presuppositional interpretation of legal obligation can be equated to searching for a comprehensive explanation of what is conceptually implied in one's having a legal obligation. And the resulting theoretical account of legal obligation is best viewed as an attempt to reinterpret as well as to critically evaluate the standard view. That is, presuppositional interpretation directly engages with the received view but does not necessarily stick to that view: the ordinary understanding does not have the final say in determining the nature of legal obligation. Related to this, the conception produced by presuppositional interpretation may turn out to be more or less revisionary in comparison with the widespread learned view out of which it originates. Otherwise stated, whereas the specialists' acquired judgements provide the body of knowledge of which the theorist is tasked with identifying and characterizing the implicit presuppositions and necessary conditions of intelligibility, ultimately they are these presuppositions and conditions of intelligibility, as opposed to the learned understanding, that give us a conception of legal obligation. In this sense, the theoretical account of legal obligation resulting from the use of presuppositional interpretation can be described as deep: presuppositional interpretation is instrumental to identifying and elucidating the basic and almost hidden features of legal obligation, rather than to describing its most apparent traits as these

---

[6] Presuppositional interpretation, in other terms, has structured my reflection on the constituents of legal obligation that those who use the concept of obligation are already committed to. In this sense, presuppositional interpretation is primarily designed to explain ideas those who use the concept of obligation are familiar with and already handle, though not necessarily with an explicit degree of awareness.

can be discovered by means of a surface exploration of shared practices and uses of obligation.

Finally, the properties that presuppositional interpretation makes constitutive of the theory of legal obligation should be regarded as essential, or fundamental, in that these properties need to be presupposed in order for legal obligation to be thinkable, or to make sense, as a distinctive notion. Accordingly, the conception of legal obligation – the end product of presuppositional interpretation – consists in an elucidation of what is implied in, and intrinsically meant by, the standard concept of obligation: it is a theoretical explanation of what practical philosophers and legal theorists are of necessity committed to when a legal obligation is claimed to exist. In that respect, it can be claimed that presuppositional interpretation is concerned with laying out what might be called the defining logic and distinctive structure of legal obligation.

10.3 The Nature of Presuppositional Interpretation

In the preceding sections I introduced the basic structure – entry point, procedure, and expected outcome – of the presuppositional interpretation I have used to arrive at a comprehensive theory of legal obligation. In this section I will enrich the picture by emphasizing the quality, or nature, of presuppositional interpretation. This process will also give me an opportunity to go back to, and expand on, some of the issues introduced in Section 10.2. The main claim I will so defend in this section is that presuppositional interpretation can be characterized as a regressive, hermeneutical, explorational, and intra-categorial method for explaining the kind of obligation engendered by the law. Let me then elaborate on each of these qualifications.

10.3.1 Regressive

Presuppositional interpretation can be qualified as a regressive method of inquiry in that it takes as given something that is widely accepted and then reflects back on it in order to bring out and interpret the very conditions that one needs to presuppose for that widely accepted idea to be conceivable in the first place. The 'regressiveness' of this procedure lies in its backward-looking movement from an already acquired and widely assumed body of understanding to its hitherto unthematized preconditions of intelligibility. In order to appreciate the regressive nature of this component of the argumentative strategy based on presuppositional interpretation, it may be of some use to compare it to a forward-looking, or *progressive*, method of inquiry.

A method can be qualified as progressive insofar as it is aimed at expanding our knowledge by marching from a shared and uncontested set of notions to a set of theoretical consequences, or implications, not yet conceptually contained in, or presupposed by, that initial set. In stark contrast to this methodology, which invites us to look *outside* the consolidated view of the subject matter, presuppositional interpretation takes a step in precisely the opposite direction. It asks us to look at what lies *inside* the bulk of cognition we already possess, which is thus claimed to contain some important information, often implicitly formulated, about the notion we intend to characterize. In this sense, presuppositional interpretation leads us to ponder over the conceptual commitments underlying ideas we routinely manipulate, are familiar with, and consider trustworthy. Accordingly, the purpose of presuppositional interpretation, as a regressive method, consists in deepening our awareness of conceptual constructions and relations by unearthing elements of the acquired wisdom that had previously gone unnoticed.

Ultimately, I should add, the regressive dimension of presuppositional interpretation depends on the method incorporating a specifically presupposition-oriented component. Presupposition-oriented methods constitutively follow a trajectory from what is given to us – something that is often unreflectively assumed and treated as the received view – back to its necessary conditions of intelligibility. The presuppositional interpretation I advance in this study thus configures a rationally compelling regression from some explicit and widely accepted features of obligation to a set of claims about legal obligation that identify and substantively characterize the (mostly) implicit conditions necessary to make obligation conceivable.[7] Once introduced in these terms, presuppositional interpretation takes the form of an inference from some uncontroversial beliefs about a question to what is considered to be the best available explanation of that question: the method, in other words,

---

[7] This regressive feature of the method affords justification for the previously introduced claim that if we are to reject the theoretical account of legal obligation yielded by presuppositional interpretation, we must also be prepared to part ways with a constellation of ideas that are well established in the debate on legal obligation. For those who are not prepared to give up the received view, then, the outcome of my presuppositional interpretation will have to be regarded as compelling, yielding a conception that, within the boundaries of the framework delimited by the mainstream specialists' understanding of obligation, cannot be called into question.

supports a given conception of legal obligation by showing that this conception is more closely related to our concept of obligation – the wider genus legal obligation is an instantiation of – than alternative accounts.

10.3.2 Hermeneutical

In presuppositional interpretation the regressive dimension just outlined combines with a distinctive hermeneutical component offering a substantive reconstruction of the way legal obligation should be conceived in order to make sense of it as a practical notion in current use. This means that presuppositional interpretation is not primarily intended to describe, explain, or systematize what competent thinkers mean by legal obligation, but instead selects and elaborates on what may be deemed to be the essential features associated with the concept of legal obligation. The outcome of this method, then, is what I would call a *thick* account of legal obligation picking out the features of that notion which would make the most sense of it in light of the evidence available to us. In this respect, presuppositional interpretation can be characterized as a value-laden and to at least some extent normative approach aimed at bringing to light both meaning and significance of legal obligation. That is to say, even though presuppositional interpretation starts out from what is taken to be the understanding of an idea shared within the reference group, it is not intended as a descriptive or lexicographical account of that understanding, its point rather being to substantively reconstruct the essential features of that idea.

As such presuppositional interpretation offers a hermeneutics of both the convictions about obligation that competent thinkers widely share and the essential presuppositions governing the concept of obligation. Accordingly, the conception of legal obligation resulting from presuppositional interpretation summarizes the picture that fits with certain background assumptions and information concerning obligation as this is understood by the majority of those who systematically engage with the obligatory dimension of our practical existence. This intellectual effort asks us to reconstruct the structure of the broadly shared views and basic hypotheses we have about obligation. Which result is achieved by specifically engaging with the question: how should legal obligation be interpreted in order for us to arrive at a substantive explanation enabling us to make sense of the implicit presuppositions, standards, conditions of use, and inherent commitments underlying some basic widely shared beliefs about obligation?

10.3.3 Explorational

Another feature of presuppositional interpretation lies in its being 'explorational', in a sense that has gained some currency in the debate on transcendental arguments. Some theorists set up an opposition between two such kinds of arguments: *explorational* versus *retorsive*.[8] Explorational transcendental arguments 'are engaged in furthering the explanation of some known fact or judgement in order to expand our knowledge ... They start from a premise which is so minimal that it will not be questioned by a sceptic and draw out of it some a priori conclusions. They do so by looking for "necessary conditions for the possibility" of this premise to be true.'[9] Retorsive transcendental arguments, by contrast, are 'designed mainly to secure a judgement about something being the case', and so are 'employed in a straightforward anti-sceptical fashion'.[10] So, whereas retorsive transcendental arguments are intended to ground, or provide the foundations of, our knowledge, explorational transcendental arguments are intended to enrich our initial characterization of some knowledge.

Crucially, the presuppositional interpretation adopted in this study is at one with explorational transcendental arguments in its attempt to contribute to substantively reconstructing and enriching some known set of judgements: those that are constitutive of the concept of obligation. This concept only comprises a set of very basic and elemental features of obligation. In this sense, thus, the method of presuppositional interpretation I have advanced operates on a thin premise, which it seeks to expand by means of a rigorous argumentative procedure. Accordingly, in line with transcendental argumentative strategies that are explorational, presuppositional interpretation, as outlined here, takes us from a non-ambitious entry point – or at least an entry point that the vast majority of those who are part of the debate on legal obligation should be expected to regard as acceptable – to a thicker, more substantive, and potentially controversial conclusion, or what I earlier called a *conception* of legal obligation (as distinct from its concept). Which process is meant

---

[8] This terminology can be found, for instance, in C. Illies, *The Grounds of Ethical Judgements* (Oxford, Oxford University Press, 2003), pp. 30–63 and C. Roversi, 'On Constitutive Normativity', in S. Bertea and G. Pavlakos (eds.), *New Essays on the Normativity of Law* (Oxford, Hart, 2011), pp. 281–309.

[9] Illies, *Grounds of Ethical Judgements*, p. 31.

[10] Illies, *Grounds of Ethical Judgements*, p. 31.

to expand our existing understanding of legal obligation by clarifying and reinterpreting that concept.

What presuppositional interpretation instead does *not* purport to do is grounding or justifying legal obligation, by looking to shield it from sceptical doubt, as is the case with retorsive transcendental arguments. This is to say that the method I use in my treatment of legal obligation does not make any foundational attempt. For presuppositional interpretation is exhausted in a two-step procedure: it starts out from a weak and general understanding of obligation assumed to be accepted by everyone working from within a given theoretical tradition broadly understood; and then from that starting point it proceeds to extract certain features framed as conditions ignoring which the same initial understanding would not be conceivable. The outcome is a conception of legal obligation that, on the one hand, incorporates those features and, on the other, makes it possible to enrich those features with added theoretical content. The resulting conception is non-trivial, since it substantively reconstructs the premises of the argument, consisting in the conditions necessary for us to be able to make sense of obligation in the first place. But even though this endeavour – the presuppositional part of the method – identifies what are deemed to be conditions for the conceivability of obligation – it is not intended to *ground* the obligatory force of law. And this is the sense in which presuppositional interpretation is designed, not to explain why we should comply with the law or why legal obligation should exert a binding force or why it can exist in the first place, but rather to explore this force and hence spell out what the meaning of legal obligation is.

10.3.4 Intra-Categorial

Finally, presuppositional interpretation can be described as intra-categorial, in that the question it addresses is not whether it is possible for legal obligation to *exist*, but how it is possible to *conceive* of it. To elaborate, presuppositional interpretation is aimed at eliciting the basic connections between the major structural elements of our overarching conceptual framework for the understanding of the obligations generated by the law. In that respect, it is a concept-driven, or belief-oriented method, as opposed to an epistemic procedure aspiring to give us access to some mind-independent reality. The argument I have unpacked in this study, in other terms, addresses the question of what we ought to *believe* about certain premises that are widely accepted by those who take part in the debate. It then is meant to advance our knowledge of legal obligation by offering us a conceptual scheme that any clear-thinking person who subscribes the concept of obligation should be expected to accept. For this reason, presuppositional interpretation will be understood by some as modest in its ambitions. It can be qualified as modest for the conditions it sets out to uncover are not those subject to which legal obligation can *exist*, but those subject to which it becomes *conceivable*.[11]

Since presuppositional interpretation, as here outlined, is about things as they appear under the conditions of a widely shared conceptual framework – and so about the conditions for the possibility of thought, as well as about the fundamental connections between our thoughts – its scope is limited to determining how we ought to go about explaining our own understanding of legal obligation. It is thus limited in two ways, for (a) its object is a conceptual scheme (what can be assumed to be the scheme of thought through which we understand legal obligation), and (b) its work consists in pointing out that certain parts of this scheme are bound by conceptual links that are basic in that we cannot abandon them without calling into question the way we commonly think about obligation. As a result of its scope, then, presuppositional interpretation does not assume there to be any 'essence' of obligation that can be discovered independently of how we think about obligation: it only offers to lay out the conditions that enable us to think about it. Likewise, the account presuppositional interpretation yields tells us not about the 'reality' of legal obligation – the reality purportedly corresponding to our understanding of legal obligation – but about the way in which we *ought to* understand legal obligation if we are to make sense of it as a practical, non-arbitrary notion.

This quality of presuppositional interpretation is ultimately owed to the fact that the resulting account is worked out on a theoretical basis alone. And theory cannot on its own bridge the gap between thought and reality. In my argument, I have therefore not been concerned with the question of what legal obligation is *in fact* (that is, independently of the way it is *conceived* by us) or indeed with the question of whether the reality of legal obligation exists in the first place or with the question of whether it even makes sense to ask such questions. Those who are

---

[11] The usefulness of intra-categorial arguments emerges clearly from Robert Stern's thorough discussion of the power and limits of transcendental argumentation. See, for instance, R. Stern, *Transcendental Arguments: Answering the Question of Justification* (Oxford, Oxford University Press, 2000), pp. 66–125.

interested in such questions will need to answer them by way of an empirical inquiry that falls beyond the scope of the present investigation. In the absence of such empirical study, the theoretical account of legal obligation we can construct by the method of presuppositional interpretation is independent of any *reality* of legal obligation, or, on the flip side, is dependent of our way of conceiving of it (and this way of conceiving of legal obligation is inevitably going to reflect the context in which it is formed).

Even if presuppositional interpretation only offers (what some would qualify as) a modest outcome in its endeavour to clarify legal obligation, it is still powerful as a method for doing so, for the clarification it provides is illuminating: it is not confined to investigating how legal obligation is in fact conceived within a group but rather aims at determining how it must be conceived in light of the premises that most people belonging to that group are prepared to accept as part of their discourse on obligation. Presuppositional interpretation, then, is not merely concerned with accessory conditions of conceivability of legal obligation; it rather seeks an interpretation of a set of fundamental conditions of that sort. What it posits, in other words, is that insofar as we think coherently and clearly within given conceptual horizons, we cannot but have the specific conception of legal obligation that has been worked out in this study.

In sum, the claim that legal obligation should be conceived as the revisionary Kantian conception indicates is a concept-directed assertion about how we have to *think* about legal obligation and so how legal obligation has to appear to most of us. It is therefore weak by comparison with truth-directed claims about what legal obligation *is*. And yet the results achieved by presuppositional interpretation are far from insignificant, as they concern more than a merely arbitrary, or even idiosyncratic, understanding of the conceptual relations constitutive of legal obligation. And gaining a grasp of the non-arbitrary conditions for the conceivability of legal obligation should be generally acknowledged as an important theoretical result, in that it will force anyone thinking clearly and consistently within the relevant sphere of discourse to either embrace the resulting conception or reject the expert understanding of obligation. Related to this, since presuppositional interpretation reasons from what is taken to be the dominant conceptual scheme through which to understand obligation, the resulting theoretical account is designed to point out a way of thinking about obligation that cannot be done away with, precisely because it purports to set out the deep structure of our common framework of thought about legal obligation. So, by interpreting the conditions that are implicit in an expert understanding of obligation and are fundamental for that understanding to be conceivable, the conception of obligation we end up with acts as a constraint on our thinking about legal obligation.

The remarks just made also mean that the materials which presuppositional interpretation works from are unassailable from within the reference context. True, the concept of obligation may well be challenged and even replaced with some alternative construct by anyone who thinks that the standard understanding of obligation (or my interpretation of it) is misleading. Indeed, the concept of obligation – the current understanding of it that is widely, or even generally, embraced by the community of scholars – is not here regarded as universally compelling. In taking the concept of obligation as the starting point of my presuppositional interpretation, I thereby accept that the substantive conclusions deriving from my theoretical account of legal obligation are only as valid as the understanding of obligation currently held by mainstream experts in the matter. And insofar as this understanding is open to challenge, so is my theory of legal obligation.[12] Which is to say that because the theoretical account of legal obligation based on presuppositional interpretation starts out from a concept of obligation modelling what mainstream practical philosophers and legal theorists actually think about obligation, it is not entirely independent of the culture and norms specific to that source environment. At the same time, however, the theoretical account constructed out of that source material is not simply a description of what people in a chosen community think about obligation. Indeed, as mentioned, the method proposes to single out the conditions essential for that community view to make sense, and it interprets these conditions so as to arrive at a coherent account of legal obligation that

---

[12] We should not take it as disappointing that the conclusions derived from my theoretical exploration are open to challenge. From the history of ideas we learn that all forms of human knowledge are tentative. More realistic than attempting to arrive at necessary and universal truths, when constructing a theory, is to rigorously proceed from a reasonably reliable set of premises to conclusions that further expand our initial knowledge without smuggling in arbitrary assumptions. This is what in this book presuppositional interpretation was designed to do with respect to legal obligation. It has proceeded from what was taken to be a minimally controversial starting point, a domain-specific one situated within a widely shared understanding of obligation. On the basis of this set of premises presuppositional interpretation has rigorously derived a comprehensive theoretical account of legal obligation preserving the validity of those premises in its substantive conclusions.

removes from the corresponding concept all the preconceptions that can be identified by careful (presuppositional) analysis.

This statement takes me back to the main topic of this section. The method of presuppositional interpretation is concerned with legal obligation as an *idea*, or conceptual construct, and with its essential features as these are presupposed in, and derivable from, specialized discourses about obligation. Accordingly, the expected outcome of this enterprise is a general conceptual scheme, or framework of thought, designed to help us better understand legal obligation by clarifying and interpreting what is assumed or implied in having an obligation. In this process, no attempt is made to close the gap between our way of *conceptualizing* legal obligation and the *reality* of the obligations generated by the law. The method used in my treatment of legal obligation is thus exclusively concerned with concepts and beliefs, as distinct from facts and reality, its purpose being to help us explore legal obligation as a category of thought. So, as much as presuppositional interpretation does set out a certain fundamental way in which legal obligation ought to be conceived, it does so not by arguing that this is dictated by an 'ontology' or 'essence' of legal obligation but rather by showing that once a widely held conceptual framework is accepted as the standard view of obligation, then there will be no choice but to think about legal obligation in the specific way in which presuppositional interpretation accounts for it.

10.4 The Rationale behind Presuppositional Interpretation

I have so far considered presuppositional interpretation as a method for constructing a comprehensive theoretical account of legal obligation. In so doing I have highlighted the specificity of this method. But one might wonder why I have relied on this method to begin with, considering that it is largely untested and there are some tried and true methodologies in philosophy that one might turn to. For example, it was noted in Section 10.3 that presuppositional interpretation shares some central elements with at least some forms of transcendental argumentation, so why not use a chain of transcendental arguments in constructing a theory of legal obligation? In fact, why not go directly to the methodological principles originally defended by Immanuel Kant, who systematically relied on transcendental arguments to make his philosophical points? Or, again, given that my interests are conceptual – in this work I have intended to *conceptualize* legal obligation – would it have not made more sense to put forward a conceptual analysis of legal obligation? And could not the project have benefited from the method of reflective equilibrium, which a number of conceptual analysts, at least since John Rawls's influential contribution, have come to view as better suited when tackling issues in political theory and legal philosophy?

These are the concerns I will be answering in this section, explaining why we should want to rely on the method of presuppositional interpretation in a theoretical exploration of legal obligation when more established and consolidated methodologies are available for a philosophical study of practical questions. In offering this explanation, I will describe how presuppositional interpretation relates to some standard methodologies in philosophy, such as Kant's own method, transcendental argumentation, conceptual analysis, and reflective equilibrium. This will also make it possible to clarify the rationale behind the methodological choice in question. A caveat that should be added before we proceed is that the scope of this section is limited. For I am not going to take into account all of the methodologies that one might use as alternatives to presuppositional interpretation. I will instead restrict the scope of the discussion to the methods that are more akin to presuppositional interpretation, focusing on the main advantages that presuppositional interpretation can be claimed to have over them in making possible an arguably more comprehensive and deeper theoretical account of legal obligation.

10.4.1 *Presuppositional Interpretation and Transcendental Philosophy*

The conception of legal obligation being argued for in this book has been developed by reflecting on the presuppositions that need to be acknowledged in order for our discourses about obligation to make sense. In that respect one may wonder how my construction might differ from a transcendental argument for a given view of legal obligation. This question will be answered here by clarifying how presuppositional interpretation relates conceptually to the transcendental approach in philosophy, with a focus on two influential variants of that approach: the Kantian one (Section 10.4.1.1) and the one that has been advocated in analytic philosophy since the early 1950s (Section 10.4.1.2).

10.4.1.1 Presuppositional Interpretation and Kant's Analytic Method

The method of presuppositional interpretation on which basis I have investigated legal obligation in this work is deeply informed by Kant's insight that in philosophy we can deepen our knowledge of something by proceeding analytically 'from something already known to be dependable' to its 'sources, which are not yet known',[13] namely, from a body of cognition we already have and regard as trustworthy – something we can safely claim to know or be evident to us – to its principles, conditions of possibility, and sources. As far as practical philosophy is concerned, this methodological claim finds a paradigmatic statement and elaboration in the first two sections of the *Groundwork of the Metaphysics of Morals*, where Kant proceeds analytically from common knowledge about morality to the 'determination of its supreme principle'.[14] In such work, Kant relies on what he describes as an 'analytical' method, working from the 'common rational knowledge of morality' in order to arrive at the essential principles underpinning that knowledge.[15]

In his main contributions to philosophy, then, Kant uses a method of inquiry that can be characterized as analytic in the distinctive sense of taking a set of premises for granted and using them in an argument that singles out and interprets the fundamental principles by which those premises can be explained. In that respect, Kant's analytic method can be likened to my presuppositional interpretation in two basic ways, having to do with the *structure* and *purposes* of the method. First, as far as the *structure* is concerned, both methods proceed from a given body of cognition (understood to consist of the implications of certain constitutive principles) to the principles by which that body of cognition can be explained. Just as presuppositional interpretation is meant to extract the defining traits of legal obligation from knowledge that by consensus is regarded as reliable by those who engage with issues of obligation, Kant's analytic method can be understood as deriving principles from

---

[13] I. Kant, *Prolegomena to Any Future Metaphysics*, 4:275.
[14] I. Kant, *Groundwork of the Metaphysics of Morals*, 4:392.
[15] In Kant's time, the term *analysis* referred to a consolidated approach in modern philosophy where one assumes as true the very things that need be proved, and then looks for principles by which to explain those things. For an insightful discussion of Kant's analytical method, see G. Gava, 'Kant's Synthetic and Analytic Method in the Critique of Pure Reason and the Distinction between Philosophical and Mathematical Syntheses', *European Journal of Philosophy*, 23 (2013), pp. 728–49. After more than a century of intense analytical philosophy, the term *analytical* has now taken on another sense, which may be misleading, suggesting that a method is analytical in virtue of its aiming to isolate the simplest constituents of our conceptual constructs and identify the necessary and sufficient conditions by which those constructs are to be defined. But that is not the case with Kant's analytic method. For a helpful discussion of the differences between Kant's analytic method in practical philosophy and twentieth-century analytic philosophy, see A. Wood, *Kantian Ethics* (Cambridge, Cambridge University Press, 2008), pp. 43–65.

convictions that are widely shared. The two methods can also be described as consistent in virtue of their *purposes* (at least in spirit), since both set out to offer an *interpretation* of the object of investigation designed to bring out the essential features commonly associated with it: presuppositional interpretation and Kant's analytic method alike are aimed at reconstructing the deep structure of the broadly shared views of the subject matter and the basic hypotheses that competent individuals make in that regard.

Yet, beyond these similarities, Kant's analytic method differs significantly from presuppositional interpretation in at least two respects. To begin with, my project is downscaled in its ambitions by comparison with Kant's, since I am only interested in determining the basic commitments presupposed in our discourses on legal obligation. Kant's analytic method, by contrast, is conceived for the very purpose of establishing first principles, those that make up the epistemic foundations on which rests the subject of Kant's inquiry. Indeed, through the analytic method, Kant seeks to uncover the 'laws of the pure use', (that is, the 'sources' or 'grounds of possibility'), of the conceptual construct he is investigating.[16] Kant's analytic method and the arguments produced through it are therefore primarily foundational in nature. And here we have a contrast with presuppositional interpretation, which instead is explorational: like Kant's analytic method, presuppositional interpretation takes a set of premises for granted; but, unlike Kant's analytic method, it focuses on laying bare and explaining what is implicit in those premises, namely, the conditions that need to be satisfied in order for those premises to be intelligible. Which means that on this method – presuppositional interpretation – we do not attempt to rest those premises on any foundation other than what is already implicit in them. So, even if my treatment of legal obligation succeeds in its aims, it does not give us access to any first principle defining what legal obligation constitutively is; it less ambitiously enables us to explain what is implied in the dominant understanding of obligation and what follows from that understanding.

In the second place, the project I undertake is 'earthbound' by comparison with the one Kant pursues through his analytic method. This means that, in contrast to what is the case for Kant's analytical method, the point of entry for presuppositional interpretation is *empirical*, or *a posteriori*. So it cannot in any sense be understood as necessarily valid.

---

[16] Kant, *Prolegomena to Any Future Metaphysics*, 4:274–5 and 365.

In describing the concept of obligation as empirical, I mean that it originates from tenets that *in point of fact* have proved to be largely accepted in the contemporary debate on obligation. The premises of my presuppositional interpretation of legal obligation therefore do not have the status of an a priori notion, as instead is the case with the object of Kant's analytical method. The premises of my argument are rather given in experience and can thus be refuted (also) by recourse to empirical considerations. This means that the initial step in my presuppositional interpretation is a construction whose validity can be challenged. So, as much as the process through which to establish a concept of obligation needs to be rigorous, it is not designed in such a way as to secure a necessarily valid outcome. On the contrary, the concept of obligation one is going to reconstruct remains fallible and revisable to a far greater extent than the expected outcome of Kant's analytic method.

There is a further difference that sets Kant's analytic method apart from my presuppositional interpretation. This difference concerns the basis to which the two methodologies apply and it emerges most clearly when we look at what I would call the common-understanding view of the method that Kant uses in practical philosophy in general and morality in particular. On this view, popular among contemporary Kantians, the starting point for Kant's investigations in the practical realm is not the specialized knowledge of those who have expertise in the subject to be investigated but the common understanding or cognition of anyone who is endowed with the powers of practical reasoning. For the latter is claimed to be understood by Kant as a more reliable knowledge base than that of the practical philosopher.

This reading of Kant's analytic method has been paradigmatically defended by Martin Sticker, who in a series of works argues that, for Kant, the common, pre-philosophical cognition of the subject matter at hand, in any area of practical rationality, is essential to constructing a sound theory of that subject matter.[17] This is understood to mean that Kant's practical philosophy is 'not revisionist with regard to the common conception of morality', its aim being, not to correct or rectify

---

[17] See M. Sticker, 'How Can Common Rational Capacities Confirm the Correctness of the Deduction in Groundwork III – and Why Does It Matter?', *Hegel Society of Great Britain*, 35 (2014), pp. 228–51; M. Sticker, 'The Moral-Psychology of the Common Agent: A Reply to Ido Geiger', *British Journal of the History of Philosophy*, 23 (2015), pp. 976–89; and M. Sticker, 'Kant's Criticism of Common Moral Rational Cognition', *European Journal of Philosophy*, 25 (2016), pp. 85–108.

our common, non-specialist knowledge, but to unpack, clarify, and reveal it:[18] the 'standard view in Kant's scholarship', Sticker argues, is that 'Kant strongly opposes philosophical revisions of the common understanding of morality'.[19] Indeed, practical philosophy, for Kant, begins 'from the pre-theoretical moral convictions and competences of rational human beings'.[20] It is from these powers of practical reasoning and this body of untrained practical cognition, and not from any specialized knowledge, that we must start in building any sound theory of practical philosophy. In support of this view, Sticker points out Kant's belief that, 'under current conditions, the educated are not necessarily better off than those who lack all higher or academic education. In fact, they might be worse off', such that 'uncritical moral theory, instead of setting agents right, "can easily confuse" reasoning "with a host of alien and irrelevant considerations and deflect it from the straight course".'[21] Thus, if 'the pre-philosophical agent is morally competent', it follows that no investigation in the practical sphere can afford to ignore our philosophically unguided cognition.[22] This is taken to mean, on this reading of Kant's practical philosophy, that (a) such unguided cognition must be a core *subject matter* of any investigation in the practical sphere, and that (b) it should also be our *point of entry* into any such investigation, for it is more likely to be reliable and authentic than the philosophically filtered and removed understanding, and therefore more likely to yield an accurate theory of what we are trying to clarify.

Now, insofar as this interpretation correctly tracks down Kant's original project, presuppositional interpretation and analytic method as this is conceived by Kant differs also as far as the entry points of the two methodologies are concerned: whilst Kant's analytic method is understood to apply to the common, qua *non-specialist*, knowledge of the subject matter of one's investigation, presuppositional interpretation takes the understanding shared among *experts* in the relevant field as the starting point of its philosophical treatment of legal obligation.

---

[18] Sticker, 'Kant's Criticism of Common Moral Rational Cognition', pp. 85–6.
[19] Sticker, 'Kant's Criticism of Common Moral Rational Cognition', p. 86.
[20] Sticker, 'The Moral-Psychology of the Common Agent', p. 977. See also Sticker, 'How Can Common Rational Capacities Confirm the Correctness of the Deduction in Groundwork III', esp. pp. 240–3.
[21] Sticker, 'Kant's Criticism of Common Moral Rational Cognition', p. 98. Sticker's quotes are from Kant, *Groundwork of the Metaphysics of Morals*, 4:404.
[22] Sticker, 'The Moral-Psychology of the Common Agent', p. 978.

However, in my opinion it is not so clear that Kant sees our common cognition as a more reliable guide in practical matters than expert knowledge, and hence as the better choice as a port of entry for philosophical investigations. For there are parts of his work where Kant claims that, at least in some domains, commonly held opinions tend to be misleading and less reliable than the experts' view. For instance, in the preface to *Prolegomena to Any Future Metaphysics* Kant assigns different roles to common sense (*Verstand*) and the expert's critical science (*Wissenschaft*), the former being better suited to the practical sphere and the latter to the realm of the speculative and the abstract. As Kant puts it, 'sound common sense and speculative understanding are both useful, but each in its own way, the one, when it is a matter of judgments that find their immediate application in experience, the other, however, when judgments are to be made in a universal mode, out of mere concepts, as in metaphysics, where what calls itself ... sound common sense has no judgment whatsoever'.[23] This is very much in keeping with the previously introduced standard view of Kant's practical philosophy, according to which it is common sense that we must rely on in our investigations in the practical sphere. But in context we can see that Kant's statement is more nuanced and complex, presenting a picture in which these two modes of thought (our common sense and the expert's speculative science) are not understood to work independently of each other but rather interact and function as counterweights. In fact, on the one hand, Kant suggests that common sense, 'a great gift from heaven', can even make inroads into the speculative sphere: he is thus qualifying his neatly laid out scheme, commenting that 'to appeal to ordinary common sense when insight and science run short, *and not before*, is one of the subtle discoveries of recent times, whereby the dullest windbag can confidently take on the most profound thinker and hold his own with him'.[24] But, on the other hand, as is signalled by the italicized phrase, this statement is itself qualified with an additional comment: 'so long as a small residue of insight remains, however, one would do well to avoid resorting to this emergency help' (meaning our common sense). And, on top of that, Kant stresses our need for 'critical reason' as the tool that 'keeps ordinary common sense in check', which in speculative matters 'doesn't

---

[23] Kant, *Prolegomena to Any Future Metaphysics*, 4:260.
[24] Kant, *Prolegomena to Any Future Metaphysics*, 4:259–60.

understand the justification for its own principles'.²⁵ Insofar as this is the case, the reliance on common rational cognition as an adequate premise to philosophical explorations can be argued to be misleading. Likewise, this additional difference between presuppositional interpretation and Kant's analytic method – the difference concerning the base to which the two methodologies apply – should not be overstated.

10.4.1.2 Presuppositional Interpretation and Transcendental Argumentation

The presuppositional interpretation I have used in my exploration of legal obligation should be kept distinct not only from Kant's analytic method but also from another philosophical method that is consolidated especially in the Kantian tradition of philosophy, namely, transcendental argumentation. In this section I will argue that, while presuppositional interpretation is in important ways similar to transcendental argumentation, the two cannot be reduced to each other. To see this, let me have a brief look at this form of argumentation.²⁶

Transcendental argumentation is hardly new to philosophy: it can be traced back to ancient Greece, but not until Kant did it gain prominence, becoming a primary methodological device for constructing philosophical systems. After Kant, transcendental argumentation played an essential role in the German idealist tradition and has also been a favourite tool of contemporary analytic philosophy, especially since the late 1950s.²⁷ The significance of transcendental argumentation for philosophy has not gone unchallenged though. Stefan Körner and Barry Stroud,

---

[25] Kant, *Prolegomena to Any Future Metaphysics*, 4:259–60. A critical stance towards common sense is also expressed in Kant, *Prolegomena to Any Future Metaphysics*, 4:313–14 and 369–71.

[26] For a recent overview of transcendental arguments see R. Stern, 'Transcendental Arguments', in E. N. Zalta (ed.), *The Stanford Encyclopedia of Philosophy* (Summer 2015 ed.), http://plato.stanford.edu/archives/sum2015/entries/transcendental-argumentsStern.

[27] A number of claims central to Kant's philosophical construction are secured by way of transcendental arguments. The 'Transcendental Deduction of the Categories', the 'Second Analogy', and the 'Refutation of Idealism' in the *Critique of Pure Reason*, for instance, are widely considered paradigmatic examples of transcendental argumentation. Particularly influential in that respect in contemporary analytic philosophy have been P. Strawson, *Individuals* (London, Methuen, 1959), P. Strawson, *The Bounds of Sense* (London, Methuen, 1966), H. Putnam, *Reason, Truth and History* (Cambridge, Cambridge University Press, 1981), and D. Davidson, 'The Conditions of Thought', *Grazer Philosophische Studien*, 36 (1989), pp. 193–200.

330   THE METHOD OF PRESUPPOSITIONAL INTERPRETATION

in particular, have been influential in criticizing the anti-sceptical power of transcendental arguments.[28] In reaction to their criticism, a contentious but fruitful debate sprang up between diehard defendants and fierce critics of transcendental argumentation, a debate that has been a source of valuable insights and has helped to keep interest in transcendental arguments alive until today.[29]

In its essence a transcendental argument is described in the literature as a form of argument in which something presented as an undeniable fact or truth (typically some feature of experience, thought, language, belief, intentionality) is claimed to be a sufficient condition for the possibility of something else, to the effect that, if the former obtains, so will the latter. Contained in this concise statement of transcendental argumentation are three elements that need to be emphasized. First, transcendental arguments are concerned with conditions of possibility; second, the link between the condition and what is conditioned by it is understood to be metaphysical, as opposed to being causal, semantic, logical, or of some other nature; and third, the

---

[28] See S. Körner, 'Transcendental Tendencies in Recent Philosophy', *Journal of Philosophy*, 63 (1966), pp. 551–61; S. Körner, 'The Impossibility of Transcendental Deductions', *Monist*, 51 (1967), pp. 317–31; S. Körner, *Fundamental Questions in Philosophy* (Harmondsworth, Penguin, 1969); and B. Stroud, 'Transcendental Arguments', *Journal of Philosophy*, 65 (1968), pp. 241–56.

[29] Among the most significant contributions to this debate are G. Bird, 'Kant's Transcendental Arguments', in E. Schaper and W. Vossenkuhl (eds.), *Reading Kant* (Oxford, Blackwell, 1989), pp. 21–39; E. Förster, 'How Are Transcendental Arguments Possible?', in E. Schaper and W. Vossenkuhl (eds.), *Reading Kant* (Oxford, Blackwell, 1989), pp. 2–20; R. Walker, 'Transcendental Arguments and Scepticism', in E. Schaper and W. Vossenkuhl (eds.), *Reading Kant* (Oxford, Blackwell, 1989), pp. 55–76; R. Walker, 'Kant and Transcendental Arguments', in P. Guyer (ed.), *The Cambridge Companion to Kant and Modern Philosophy* (Cambridge, Cambridge University Press, 2006), pp. 238–68; C. Taylor, 'The Validity of Transcendental Arguments', in *Philosophical Arguments*, (Cambridge (MA), Harvard University Press, 1995), pp. 20–33; Q. Cassam, 'Self-Directed Transcendental Arguments', in R. Stern (ed.), *Transcendental Arguments: Problems and Prospects* (Oxford, Oxford University Press, 1999), pp. 83–110; C. Hookway, 'Modest Sceptical Arguments and Sceptical Doubts: A Reply to Stroud', in R. Stern (ed.), *Transcendental Arguments: Problems and Prospects* (Oxford, Oxford University Press, 1999), pp. 173–87; B. Stroud, 'The Goal of Transcendental Arguments', in R. Stern (ed.), *Transcendental Arguments: Problems and Prospects* (Oxford, Oxford University Press, 1999), pp. 155–72; Stern, *Transcendental Arguments: Answering the Question of Justification*; J. Skidmore, 'Skepticism about Practical Reason: Transcendental Arguments and Their Limits', *Philosophical Studies*, 109 (2002), pp. 121–41; H. Vahid, 'The Nature and Significance of Transcendental Arguments', *Kant-Studien*, 93 (2002), pp. 273–90; and J. Callanan, 'Kant's Transcendental Strategy', *Philosophical Quarterly*, 56 (2006), pp. 360–81.

relation between the elements in the premises of a transcendental argument and those in its conclusion is a priori, vis-à-vis empirical or a posteriori.

This is a minimal definition of what a transcendental argument is, and some philosophers have singled out a couple of other features that are paradigmatic of it even if they are not essential for an argument to be qualified as transcendental. For one thing, transcendental arguments are typically considered to be anti-sceptical in their purpose, their aim being to defeat at least some forms of scepticism. This they do by showing that the propositions the sceptic calls into question are among the necessary conditions of the very possibility of formulating the sceptical doubt. For another thing, transcendental arguments have mainly been of interest in epistemology, especially at the outset, when they were used mainly to make the epistemological claim that it is possible for us to have some kind of objective knowledge that even the sceptic cannot reasonably call into question.[30]

Even with this short introduction we can see that presuppositional interpretation is conceptually akin to methods of inquiry based on transcendental argumentation. This is true with respect to two kinds of transcendental arguments in particular: the modest and the explorational. In literature a transcendental argument is qualified as modest when the conclusion it tries to derive concerns not how things *are* but how they necessarily must *appear* to us, or what we necessarily must believe.[31] A transcendental argument is instead defined as explorational when it is

---

[30] In fairness, transcendental arguments have been used to defend ethical views too. In this context, see K. O. Apel, 'The *A Priori* of the Communication Community and the Foundation of Ethics', in *Towards a Transformation of Philosophy* (London, Routledge, 1980), pp. 225–300; A. Gewirth, *Reason and Morality* (Chicago (IL), University of Chicago Press, 1978); J. Habermas, *Theorie der kommunikativen Handelns* (Frankfurt, Suhrkamp, 1981); J. Habermas, *Moralbewusstssein und kommunikates Handeln* (Frankfurt, Suhrkamp, 1983); W. Kuhlmann, *Reflexive Letztbegründung* (Freiburg, Karl Alber, 1985); W. Kuhlmann, *Unhintergehbarkeit* (Würzburg, Königshausen, 2009); W. Kuhlmann, 'A Plea for Transcendental Philosophy', in G. Gava and R. Stern, *Pragmatism, Kant, and Transcendental Philosophy* (London, Routledge, 2016), pp. 239–58; C. Korsgaard, *The Sources of Normativity* (Cambridge, Cambridge University Press, 1996); Illies, *Grounds of Ethical Judgements*; and B. Rähme, 'Transcendental Arguments, Epistemically Constrained Truth, and Moral Discourse', in G. Gava and R. Stern, *Pragmatism, Kant, and Transcendental Philosophy* (London, Routledge, 2016), pp. 259–85.

[31] So-called modest transcendental arguments make no attempt to close the gap between appearance and reality, so they do not bother with the task of showing what is really the case in the world. This element distinguishes what in literature is known by the name of 'modest' transcendental argument from what is generally qualified as 'ambitious', or 'world-directed', transcendental argument.

aimed at explaining some known fact or some judgement or notion in unassailable ways that even the radical sceptic cannot challenge.[32]

A conceptual continuity can be claimed to exist between presuppositional interpretation and modest transcendental argumentation of the explorational kind, since both argumentative strategies take as their premise a set of propositions which are regarded to be unquestionable (or, at least, are regarded to be such that they cannot be called into question without overthrowing a well-established scheme of thought). And from this premise both arguments derive certain conclusions that, on the one hand, concern the way in which we necessarily have to *reason* about something and, on the other, enrich our knowledge of that thing. In both these strategies, furthermore, the conclusion is argued to be such that it cannot be rationally called into question without forsaking the very framework of thought the discussants implicitly endorse. Nor are these the only similarities between presuppositional interpretation and transcendental argumentation (in some of its variants): the success of both presuppositional interpretation and transcendental argumentation hinges on the tenability of the notion they take as their starting point, a notion that both regard as fundamental, at least within the relevant conceptual framework, since it is taken to be constitutive of a generalized mode of thinking; and both methods offer to clarify the mode of thinking at issue by reconstructing its implicit presuppositions, understood as conditions for the intelligibility of that mode of thinking.

Despite these conceptual continuities, presuppositional interpretation and transcendental argumentation are not reducible to each other, and neither are the theoretical accounts they generate. One major difference lies in what the two accounts take to be their challenge and audience. A theory of legal obligation constructed by a method of transcendental argumentation would address the challenge raised by those who are sceptical about legal obligation.[33] Presuppositional interpretation, by

---

[32] As mentioned in Section 10.3.3, explorational transcendental arguments are contrasted in the literature with retorsive transcendental arguments, which are instead intended to secure, or ground, a judgement and deflect the sceptical challenge by showing that a conclusion in contrast with one or more claims supported by the argument at issue would be either logical or performatively inconsistent. Anyone denying the conclusion backed by a retorsive transcendental argument can thus be accused of either violating the principle of non-contradiction or giving rise to a conflict between what one is claiming (locutionary content) and what is implied by one's speech act (illocutionary force).

[33] This is the dominant view of the use of transcendental arguments. For a statement calling that view into question see, for instance, Callanan, 'Kant's Transcendental Strategy'; and

contrast, addresses the concerns not of doubters but of 'puzzled believers' in legal obligation, namely, those who would not deny that legal obligation has an essential role to play in law, but who are nonetheless at a loss to explain how it should be conceptualized.

This difference is of some moment, for it reflects a structural aspect of the two argumentative strategies: insofar as transcendental arguments address the concerns of a sceptic, their structure is apagogic, or dialectical. No such structure instead characterizes presuppositional interpretation. To briefly elaborate on this point, transcendental arguments are defined by their being concerned with presuppositions claimed to be implicitly endorsed by an interlocutor, the 'opponent' with whom the transcendental arguer is debating. In a transcendental argument the first premise is thus such that this counterparty ought to be expected to accept it; the argument then goes on to show to the counterparty that the necessary condition of that first premise is something they implicitly acknowledge (even if they do not at first realize as much). The structure of transcendental arguments is accordingly second-personal: transcendental arguments engage an interlocutor who is invited to walk down a path along with the transcendental arguer, a path that in the end will show the interlocutor's position to be untenable. This – the built-in interlocutor who needs to be convinced of something – is an essential feature of transcendental argumentation. And here we have a contrast with presuppositional interpretation, in which that element is completely absent: since presuppositional interpretation has no anti-sceptical intent, it does not incorporate any dialectical, or apagogic, element.

Another important difference setting transcendental argumentation apart from presuppositional interpretation concerns the *form* of the two argumentative strategies. A transcendental argument consists in an inference by modus ponens in which the second premise is formulated in contrapositive form. The basic inference associated with transcendental arguments therefore has the following structure: 'necessarily A; if not necessarily B, then A is inconceivable; hence, necessarily B'. In this argumentative scheme, one finds both an arguably uncontroversial statement and a far more controversial, and disputable, claim or set of claims. The latter is argued to hold true, since it is the necessary implicit condition for the conceivability of the former, to the effect that in order

---

G. Gava, 'Kant, The Third Antinomy and Transcendental Arguments', *Pacific Philosophical Quarterly* (2018), doi:10.1111/papq.12267.

for the former to be conceivable, the latter must be accepted (or so the argument goes).

This is *not* the form used in the argumentative structure of presuppositional interpretation. Presuppositional interpretation, as it is here conceived, asks the interlocutor to reflect on the necessary presuppositions of a given concept – here the concept of obligation. The resulting theory, however, is a conception not of that concept but rather of a specific instantiation of such concept – here *legal* obligation – namely, of an idea that in relation to the entry point of the method figures as a species does to a genus. Hence, in my presuppositional interpretation the conclusion of the argument – a theory of legal obligation – does not relate to its premise – the concept of obligation – in the same way that the conclusion of a transcendental argument – what in the argumentative scheme just introduced was labelled 'B' – relates to its premise – namely, to 'A'.

The structural difference between the two forms of argument can be further appreciated by considering that presuppositional interpretation is a two-step process. It first invites us to reflect on the conditions of intelligibility of obligation – on its conceptual presuppositions; then, it instructs us to engage in hermeneutical activities that put us in a position to be able to substantively characterize the obligatory aspect of legal practices. The first step in presuppositional interpretation may well contain elements that typically accompany the transcendental argumentative strategy, and so it bears some conceptual similarity to certain forms of transcendental argumentation. The second step, by contrast, proceeds along lines that have no counterpart in transcendental argumentation. On this basis, it can be concluded that the argumentative strategy underlying a theoretical account of legal obligation based on presuppositional interpretation cannot be reduced to a chain of transcendental arguments, which count as mere accessory parts of presuppositional interpretation, but do not make up the whole of it.

Relatedly, the theoretical accounts yielded by presuppositional interpretation and those yielded by transcendental argumentation stand apart in light of another important way in which the two methods prove to be mutually irreducible. Both presuppositional interpretation and transcendental argumentation make use of some kind of presuppositional analysis: they both take into account the implicit presuppositions that are necessary for the object of inquiry to be conceived in such and such a way. And in both cases the analysis is only a component (though far from an insignificant one) in the theories constructed through the two methods. That is to say, neither presuppositional interpretation nor transcendental argumentation can be reduced to its analysis of implicit conditions or presuppositions. However, the directions in which the two methods proceed in building on the basic level of presuppositional analysis are distinctively different. As has been observed by Corrado Roversi, in addition to presuppositional analysis, 'transcendental arguments require an entire philosophical theory of the epistemic medium (hence, a non-realist philosophy), and the possibility of uncovering implicit presuppositions of the medium. Hence, they are not simply presuppositional-analyses, but *analyses of the implicit presuppositions of an epistemic medium.*'[34] Presuppositional interpretation, by contrast, makes no reference to any comprehensive view of the epistemic medium within which our discourses about legal obligation make sense. Instead, presuppositional interpretation integrates the analysis of the presuppositions of legal obligation (not with a philosophical theory of the epistemic medium, but) with a thick, or substantive, characterization of legal obligation. In other words, the kind of theoretical account of legal obligation that we get with the method of presuppositional interpretation incorporates both an identification of the necessary presuppositions implicit in our concept of obligation and a hermeneutics of the minimal definition of obligation contained in that concept. So, while both presuppositional interpretation and transcendental argumentation build on some form of presuppositional analysis, the two methods follow different trajectories.

This means that the expected outcome of the investigation is also going to be characterized in different ways depending on the method we use: presuppositional interpretation is going to give us a richer conception of legal obligation than the one we can expect to get through a transcendental argumentative strategy, since it combines an analysis of certain presuppositions with a substantive reconstruction of the essential features of the object of inquiry. The conception that presuppositional interpretation is going to generate will specifically and substantively characterize the features of legal obligation that need to be recognized as constitutive of this notion, thus giving detailed content to those features in light of some interpretive hypotheses. As a consequence, presuppositional interpretation is an explicit attempt to move beyond the basic, or fundamental, traits of legal obligation, which we already find

---

[34] C. Roversi, 'Constitutionalism and Transcendental Arguments', *Northern Ireland Legal Quarterly*, 59 (2008), p. 123, original emphasis.

partly summarized in the concept of obligation. A conception of legal obligation framed on the basis of transcendental arguments will instead be programmatically thinner – a bare-bones account of legal obligation – since it will exclusively be concerned with consolidating the very basic, or minimal, traits of legal obligation as specified in our concept of it.

Also different, in fine, will be the nature of the theoretical accounts yielded by the two methodologies. Transcendental argumentation is meant to ground the possibility of some kind of synthetic a priori knowledge about its object, which is likewise understood as an object of synthetic a priori cognition. Transcendental arguments, in other terms, state how certain a priori features of an object of cognition need to be understood. The subject matter of transcendental arguments accordingly consists of non-empirical notions.[35] Presuppositional interpretation, by contrast, takes a set of a posteriori judgements as its starting point: the concept of obligation by its very construction cannot be something we arrive at by way of a priori judgements. As a result, the theoretical construct generated by presuppositional interpretation – namely, a conception of legal obligation – will have an ineradicable empirical component setting it distinctively apart from any construction resulting from the use of transcendental argumentation.

10.4.2 *Presuppositional Interpretation and Conceptual Analysis*

If there is any single style of inquiry, in philosophy and legal theory alike, that has managed to hold sway for generations, especially in the Anglo-American debate, it is conceptual analysis.[36] One may thus wonder why

---

[35] In Christian Illies's words, transcendental arguments are designed so to 'securely establish some *non-empirical* knowledge for use in theoretical or practical matters' (Illies, *Grounds of Ethical Judgements*, p. 30, emphasis added).

[36] Conceptual analysis has a venerable history that some trace back to the foundational moments in philosophy itself, and in particular to Plato. In the early twentieth century it went mainstream, and even though in the 1950s and 1960s it came under the attack of influential thinkers like Willard van Orman Quine and Hilary Putnam, it is still in wide use today. Among the many contemporary contributions to it are G. Bealer, 'The Philosophical Limits of Scientific Essentialism', in J. Tomberlin (ed.), *Philosophical Perspectives* (Atascadero (CA), Ridgeview, 1987), pp. 289–365; G. Bealer, 'Intuition and the Autonomy of Philosophy', in M. DePaul and W. Ramsey (eds.), *Rethinking Intuition* (Oxford, Rowman, 1998), pp. 201–39; D. Chalmers, *The Conscious Mind* (Oxford, Oxford University Press, 1996); F. Jackson, 'Armchair Metaphysics', in *Mind, Method, and Conditionals* (London, Routledge, 1994); F. Jackson, *From Ethics and Metaphysics* (Oxford, Oxford University Press, 1998), and Williamson, *Philosophy of Philosophy*. In

this approach has been rejected here in favour of a presuppositional interpretation of legal obligation. The advantages of relying on conceptual analysis would have been twofold. First, in consideration of the fact that in jurisprudence conceptual analysis can be considered an established paradigm that is widely endorsed, by offering a conceptual analysis of legal obligation I would have contributed to, and associated my project with, a clearly defined and popular tradition in legal theory. Secondly, since presuppositional interpretation, as I conceive it, can be argued to present not only superficial affinities with conceptual analysis and conceptual analysis is a far more consolidated and extensively practised method of inquiry, relying on it, rather than following a slightly divergent and yet less than traditional alternative, would arguably have been a safer path.

legal theory, conceptual analysis finds specific application in what is known as conceptual jurisprudence. Conceptual jurisprudence designates a distinct approach to the study of law and legal notions taken to be fundamental and common to legal orders with a degree of maturity and organization comparable to that displayed by current legal frameworks. The distinctive characteristic of conceptual jurisprudence is its attempt to describe the essential features of all legal systems, or at least all comparably sophisticated legal systems, by providing a philosophically rigorous, morally neutral, and non-empirical explanation for those features (which are in turn treated as the necessary legal constructs) and their mutual relationships. In addition, conceptual jurisprudence should be characterized as an approach primarily devoted to the task of offering an explanation of the nature of law, understood as a set of essential (or non-accidental) features constitutive of law, those in virtue of which law is what it is *in the abstract*, independently of the particular system of laws we may be looking at (so these are features common to all legal systems). In this sense it is in conceptual jurisprudence that we ought to locate the study of legal obligation, since this is a conceptual investigation concerned with the features that would characterize legal obligation regardless of the legal system in which it arises. The theory of legal obligation, as it takes shape in the works of the advocates of conceptual jurisprudence, hence, constitutes an intellectually meticulous treatment purported to offer a morally unbiased elucidation of the concept of duty as it is generated by the law and thus to identify the essential (or necessary) features of the type of obligation that the law engenders. The many systematic contributions to conceptual jurisprudence include H. L. A. Hart, *Concept of Law* (with a Postscript, Oxford, Clarendon, 1994; or. ed. 1961); J. Raz, *The Concept of a Legal System* (Oxford, Oxford University Press, 1970); J. Raz, *The Authority of Law: Essays on Law and Morality* (Oxford, Oxford University Press, 1979); J. Raz, *From Normativity to Responsibility* (Oxford, Oxford University Press, 2011); A. Marmor, *Interpretation and Legal Theory* (Oxford, Oxford University Press, 1992); A. Marmor, *Positive Law and Objective Values* (Oxford, Oxford University Press, 2001); W. Waluchow, *Inclusive Legal Positivism* (Oxford, Oxford University Press, 1994); J. Coleman, *The Practice of Principle* (Oxford, Oxford University Press, 2001); J. Coleman, 'Methodology', in J. Coleman and S. Shapiro, *The Oxford Handbook of Jurisprudence and Philosophy of Law* (Oxford, Oxford University Press, 2002), pp. 311–51; and S. Shapiro, *Legality* (Cambridge (MA), Harvard University Press, 2011).

In addressing this potential objection to my methodological choice, I should first reiterate that conceptual analysis and presuppositional interpretation do indeed bear similarities. To begin with, they both conceive of philosophical research as an activity primarily undertaken from the armchair, so to speak: they are both forms of reflection unaided by experiment and factual observation. This feature markedly distinguishes conceptual analysis and presuppositional interpretation from the empirical investigations now widely used not only in the social sciences but also in the humanities.[37] In addition, not unlike conceptual analysis, presuppositional interpretation is a 'selective' method: far from seeking an exhaustive list of all the components that define a conceptual construct, it selects some constituents of the relevant conceptual construct, shows that those constituents are not only essential but also of particular significance, and then organizes its whole theoretical account around those constituents. Finally, like conceptual analysis, presuppositional interpretation proposes to provide systematic accounts of its subject matter in terms of a limited number of more elemental notions, or fundamental ingredients.[38] In both conceptual analysis and presuppositional interpretation, therefore, theory-construction requires one to operate on a select menu of basic aspects of the object of investigation. For this reason, both conceptual analysis and presuppositional interpretation devote much attention to entailment relations. That is to say, they

---

[37] Naturalistic methods and largely experiment-led research projects have gained some momentum in philosophy, too, especially with works such as S. Stich, 'Reflective Equilibrium, Analytic Epistemology and the Problem of Cognitive Diversity', *Synthese*, 74 (1988), pp. 391–413; S. Stich, 'Reflective Equilibrium and Cognitive Diversity', in M. DePaul and W. Ramsey (eds.), *Rethinking Intuition* (Oxford, Rowman, 1998), pp. 95–112; J. Weinberg, S. Nichols, and S. Stich, 'Normativity and Epistemic Intuitions', *Topoi*, 29 (2001), pp. 429–60; J. Weinberg, S. Nichols, and S. Stich, 'Metaskepticism: Meditations in Ethno-Epistemology', in S. Luper (ed.), *The Skeptics* (Burlington, Ashgate, 2003), pp. 227–47; H. Kornblith, *Knowledge and Its Place in Nature* (Oxford, Oxford University Press, 2002); Kornblith, 'Naturalism and Intuitions', 27–49; S. Nichols and J. Ulatowski, 'Intuitions and Individual Differences: The Knobe Effect Revisited', *Mind and Language*, 22 (2007), 346–65; P. Singer, 'Ethics and Intuitions', *Journal of Ethics*, 9 (2005), pp. 331–52; J. Weinberg, 'How to Challenge Intuitions Empirically without Risking Skepticism', *Midwest Studies in Philosophy*, 31 (2007), pp. 318–43; S. Swain, J. Alexander, and J. Weinberg, 'The Instability of Philosophical Intuitions: Running Hot and Cold on Truetemp', *Philosophy and Philosophical Research*, 76 (2008), 138–55, among others, all of which have strongly criticized the method of conceptual analysis. For a parallel critique of conceptual jurisprudence, see B. Leiter, *Naturalizing Jurisprudence* (Oxford, Oxford University Press, 2007).

[38] For a similar characterization of the purpose of conceptual analysis see Jackson, *From Ethics and Metaphysics*, pp. 2–5.

both seek to explain not only the features of a conceptual construct that are in plain sight but also the more fundamental traits entailed by, and implicit in, those features. In so doing, they are both interested in the internal logic of our thinking about and conceptualizing their subject matter.[39]

These important similarities should not obscure the deeper discontinuity between conceptual analysis and presuppositional interpretation – a discontinuity that is also my reason for choosing the latter. The discontinuity between the two method is ultimately owed to the different roles they allot to intuitions and considered judgements. Indeed, in contrast to presuppositional interpretation, conceptual analysis is more heavily reliant on intuitions and what may be characterized as the folk view of its object of investigation. Although intuitions and the folk view do not enter into conceptual analysis as unassailable elements, nor do they have the final say in determining whether a proposed conceptualization stands, they do have an essential role to play in conceptual analysis in two important respects that have no counterpart in theories constructed by way of presuppositional interpretation.

In the first place, intuitions constitute the essential *input* of conceptual analysis.[40] Intuitions are here understood as instantly convincing judgements that are not deliberately based on any theory and may even be pre-theoretical: they are 'fast, automatic, fluent, and effortless', emerging 'spontaneously, without explicit inference or reasoning'.[41] Conceptual analysis regards these as pieces of evidence, serving a function analogous to that which observation and perception serve in the empirical sciences. For this reason conceptual analysis takes seriously into account whatever

---

[39] This continuity between conceptual analysis and presuppositional interpretation is particularly strong in what may be described as the 'modest' version of conceptual analysis, concerned with the question of how certain issues and phenomena need to be thought and represented. Modest conceptual analysis then provides an account of the way we have to think about certain realities, thus outlining a necessary representation of phenomena. As a result, modest conceptual analysis seeks to determine the structure of our *thinking* about the world, as opposed to the structure, or nature, of the world itself. For a defence of modest conceptual analysis, see Jackson, *From Ethics and Metaphysics*, pp. 28–55.

[40] From now on I will only be referring to intuitions. What I claim in regard to intuitions, however, can be extended to folk views, since both can be understood as judgements that we do not arrive at by inferential reasoning but rather find immediately compelling and intrinsically plausible.

[41] H. De Cruz, 'Where Philosophical Intuitions Come From', *Australasian Journal of Philosophy*, 93 (2015), p. 237.

intuitions about its object of investigation happen to gain currency, even when they appear to contradict theoretical constructions and considered judgements. On this view, any theoretical account needs to be tested against concrete and imagined cases that are meant to elicit our intuitions about the subject matter in question. In this sense, conceptual analysis treats intuitions as reliable sources of knowledge about concepts, by thus appealing to them in validating or invalidating its theoretical constructions.

In this way, conceptual analysis ends up also placing great value on the task of explaining common intuitions and their relevance in ordinary reasoning.[42] Relatedly, a theoretical account is going to consist in large part in a selective restatement of the pre-theoretical insights we have about the object of investigation, namely, in an attempt to align those insights with the constituent features of that object or concept. In this sense, conceptual analysis can be characterized as an intuition-based method, one that 'begins with problems and cases and our intuitions about them, seeks principles that unify and explain the intuitions, and proceeds through adjustment and modification of both the principles and intuitions until consistency and harmony are achieved'.[43]

No such important role is assigned to intuitions in a presuppositional interpretation of a conceptual construct. Presuppositional interpretation is a distinctively theory-driven method, as opposed to an intuition-based one.[44] The starting point of presuppositional interpretation is not a set of intuitions but rather an inference-based and theoretically informed understanding of the subject matter. Here thus the concept of obligation is not understood to summarize the ordinary intuitions that we, or even a subgroup in our community, have about obligations: it rather reasons from the *considered judgements* that experts in the field share. That is to say, the entry point of the theoretical exploration here undertaken incorporates a form of cognition that can be characterized as 'slower, less fluent, deliberate and effortful' by comparison with the form of

---

[42] This aspect of conceptual analysis is discussed, for instance, in Jackson, *From Ethics and Metaphysics*, pp. 21–42; A. Goldman, 'Philosophical Intuitions: Their Target, Their Source and Their Epistemic Status', *Grazer Philosophische Studien*, 74 (2007), pp. 1–26; and Williamson, *Philosophy of Philosophy*, pp. 179–207.

[43] J. McMahan, 'Moral Intuition', in H. LaFollette and I. Persson (ed.), *The Blackwell Guide to Ethical Theory* (London, Blackwell, 2013), p. 106.

[44] The distinction between theory-driven methodology, or 'theoretical approach', and intuition-based methodology, or 'intuitive approach', is borrowed from McMahan, 'Moral Intuition', pp. 103–21.

cognition generated by intuitions.[45] In order to firm up a concept of obligation, in other words, we need to make explicit inferences and thus engage in thorough reflection and reasoning about obligation with a view to consolidating our initial insights. Hence, while presuppositional interpretation deals in our intuitions too, taking also into account those shared by a social group, intuitions do not necessarily figure in the premises of the reasoning carried out on the basis of this method, which in this respect can be described as radically different from conceptual analysis.

In the second place, conceptual analysis relies heavily on intuitions not only at the outset but *throughout* the course of inquiry. In this sense conceptual analysis can be described as doubly intuition-based: it not only (a) starts out from a set of intuitions but also (b) aims to systematize those intuitions, make them rigorous, and possibly correct them by singling out as misguided those that prove to be idiosyncratic, thereby discarding them as not fit to advance our understanding of the concept under investigation, and hence unreliable as a basis for theory-construction. To elaborate on this aspect, conceptual analysis involves a systematic effort to lay out the essential constituents of a given concept by reasoning from our intuitions about the same concept.[46] When we apply conceptual analysis to legal obligation our effort will mainly be devoted to elucidating familiar ideas about that concept. As a result, a conceptual analysis of legal obligation should be expected to proceed more or less as follows. We start out recording our intuitions about legal obligation. These intuitions will provide the source data for the theory of legal obligation we will be constructing. We thus proceed to construct our theory in that fashion, looking to systematize our initial set of intuitions, which may well turn out to contradict one another or to be difficult to fit into a coherent whole. This method can in this sense be understood as a sort of critical and reflective appropriation of our intuitive views about legal obligation. As such, it may well be revisionary and so may lead us to modify or at least qualify our general intuitions about legal obligation. In the end, an investigation of legal obligation based on the method of conceptual analysis is, therefore, intended to yield a sort of map charting a path from intuitions about legal obligation

---

[45] De Cruz, 'Where Philosophical Intuitions Come From', p. 237.
[46] This method is paradigmatically at work in Kenneth Einar Himma's discussion of obligation (see K. E. Himma, 'The Ties That Bind: An Analysis of the Concept of Obligation', *Ratio Juris*, 26 (2013), pp. 16–46).

to considered judgements having that same object (to this end also relying on a method of mutual adjustment between our intuitive views about legal obligation and a theory proposing to account for that concept).

My basic concern with this method of inquiry – and its main difference from presuppositional interpretation – lies in the strong dependence on intuitions that the ensuing theory can be expected to have. I find this feature problematic because intuitions cannot be taken as entirely reliable sources of knowledge: the easy, fluid, automatic, effortless, inference-free, implicit, and spontaneous cognitive processes that accompany the formation of intuitions are prima facie epistemically less authoritative than deliberate forms of reasoning and inference-based explorations of the subject matter, even when this consists of a speculative idea such as obligation. To be sure, even an account of legal obligation arrived at through deliberation and reasoning may turn out to be wrong; but it corrects for this fallibility by making the process systematic. Precisely for this reason it calls into doubt the reliability of a method that places heavy emphasis on intuitions.

What seems theoretically unconvincing about conceptual analysis is in particular the notion that we can make general claims about a question or topic simply by identifying the intuitions we have in that regard and working out their implications, in such a way that those general claims cohere with the intuitions used as their premises and thus explain them. In my view, by contrast, a theory of legal obligation needs not only to systematize and police our intuitions about legal obligation but also to reconstruct and reinterpret the conceptual presuppositions underlying the expert cognition of what is obligatory. From this methodological perspective, our intuitions about obligation can set the boundaries of the investigation, but they do not reliably and exhaustively define the subject matter of inquiry. In other words, our intuition-based understanding of obligation – the set of our intuitions about it – has no explanatory priority in a theoretical construction of legal obligation based on presuppositional interpretation. To be sure, the understanding of obligation, such as it emerges from our intuitions, will constrain a theory based on presuppositional interpretation, since no one can blatantly ignore this understanding of obligation without offering an argument that justifies such a departure from common sense (unless one is going for an error theory of obligation). But the intuition-based understanding of obligation neither primarily nor exhaustively determines the contents of a theoretical account based on presuppositional interpretation.

An account so constructed is instead importantly shaped by thinking about the enabling conditions, or implicit assumptions underpinning the expert understanding, of obligation, and not by engaging with that understanding as such.

As a result, unlike conceptual analysis (and any other intuitionist approach), presuppositional interpretation is not concerned with setting out general principles by which to unify and explain a body of shared intuitions about legal obligation, nor is it concerned with achieving a consistency and harmony between principles and intuitions (by a process of mutual adjustment and modification). It is instead intended as a method for a philosophical exploration of legal obligation, to which end it starts out by reasoning from theory-informed judgements and considerations, understood as sources of knowledge that are more reliable than intuition-based judgements.

In light of the background just covered, it follows that a presuppositional interpretation of legal obligation cannot be reduced to a conceptual analysis of this concept, since in its exploration it is aimed at taking us beyond our intuitions to an extent that conceptual analysis does not contemplate. For in presuppositional interpretation a theoretical account of legal obligation combines three lines of inquiry designed to (i) refine and systematize the intuitive view of obligation in light of a set of considered judgements, as those judgements are made by practical philosophers and legal theorists, (ii) extract the implicit presuppositions of obligation by a philosophical analysis of an acquired sense about obligation that is widespread among experts, and (iii) draw on that theory to substantively reconstruct the kind of obligation law gives rise to (the outcome of which process is a theoretically informed hermeneutics of legal obligation).

In conclusion, the kind of theoretical account we can arrive at by resorting to conceptual analysis cannot be compared to the one achieved by presuppositional interpretation. In contrast to conceptual analysis, which accords great importance to our intuitions, presuppositional interpretation is a largely theory-laden exploration of the subject matter: it heavily relies on inference-based cognitive processes, as opposed to intuition-led procedures of inquiry. Furthermore, presuppositional interpretation takes as its starting point the shared specialists' view of legal obligation, to the effect that common-sense understanding, folk theory, and pre-theoretical accounts of legal obligation – the building blocks of conceptual analysis – are only indirectly relevant to the resulting conception of legal obligation. Finally, presuppositional interpretation consists in a search for the fundamental conditions for the conceivability of its subject matter, a search that cannot be reduced to the attempt, associated with conceptual analysis, to establish individually necessary and jointly sufficient conditions for the possibility of something. These differences that set presuppositional interpretation apart from conceptual analysis in both structure and goals mean that the latter constitutively lacks the resources needed to arrive at the kind of theorization of legal obligation I have been seeking in this book. Hence the justification for working out an alternative method of inquiry and refraining from embarking on a conceptual analysis of legal obligation.

10.4.2.1 Presuppositional Interpretation and the Method of Reflective Equilibrium

In some variants, conceptual analysis specifically takes the form of an activity where one tries to achieve what has been termed 'reflective equilibrium'. In contemporary philosophical jargon, reflective equilibrium consists in going back and forth between common intuitions, understood as sets of empirical data, and theoretical constructions built as philosophical readings of those data.[47] In this process, the results of the inquiry are dependent on the initial shared intuitions, even if these can to some extent be ignored and even revised, especially when they get in the way of our arriving at a systematic and coherent framework

---

[47] The method of reflective equilibrium is theorized in detail in J. Rawls, 'Outline for a Decision Procedure in Ethics', *Philosophical Review*, 60 (1951), pp. 177–97; J. Rawls, 'The Independence of Moral Theory', *Proceedings of the American Philosophical Association*, 48 (1974), 5–22; J. Rawls, *A Theory of Justice* (Cambridge (MA), Harvard University Press, 1999, rev. ed.; or. ed. 1971); J. Rawls, *Justice as Fairness* (Cambridge (MA), Harvard University Press, 2001); N. Daniels, 'Reflective Equilibrium and Archimedean Points', *Canadian Journal of Philosophy*, 10 (1980), pp. 83–103; N. Daniels, 'Wide Reflective Equilibrium and Theory Acceptance in Ethics', in *Justice and Justification: Reflective Equilibrium in Theory and Practice* (Cambridge, Cambridge University Press, 1996); F. Tersman, *Reflective Equilibrium. An Essay in Moral Epistemology* (Stockholm, Almqvist & Wiksell, 1993); F. Tersman, 'The Reliability of Moral Intuitions: A Challenge from Neuroscience', *Australasian Journal of Philosophy*, 86 (2008), pp. 389–405; F. Tersman, 'Recent Work on Reflective Equilibrium and Method in Ethics', *Philosophy Compass*, 18 (2018), pp. 1–10; and G. Brun, 'Reflective Equilibrium without Intuitions', *Ethical Theory and Moral Practice*, 17 (2014), pp. 237–52. Among the critics of reflective equilibrium one can find P. Singer, 'Sidgwick and Reflective Equilibrium', *Monist*, 58 (1974), pp. 490–517; R. Hare, 'Rawls' Theory of Justice', in N. Daniels (ed.), *Reading Rawls* (Oxford, Blackwell, 1975), pp. 81–107; T. Kelly and S. McGrath, 'Is Reflective Equilibrium Enough?', *Philosophical Perspectives*, 24 (2010), pp. 325–59; and T. McPherson, 'The Methodological Irrelevance of Reflective Equilibrium', in C. Daley (ed.), *Palgrave Handbook of Philosophical Methodology* (Basingstoke, Palgrave, 2015), pp. 652–74.

capable of explaining the problem at hand. Considering that reflective equilibrium enjoys significant popularity in the construction of political and legal theory within the tradition of analytic philosophy, it is fitting to integrate my main discussion of the relation between conceptual analysis and presuppositional interpretation with a concise discussion of reflective equilibrium.

As briefly mentioned, the method of reflective equilibrium proceeds from the premise that all the basic beliefs, general principles, specific judgements, and intuitions accepted in a given community need to be submitted to critical scrutiny. Accordingly, a wide-ranging set of accepted propositions about the practical world go into the mix that make up a reflective equilibrium. Once the obvious biases and sources of distortion are weeded out, the remaining elements of the initial set are unified under a scheme of more fundamental explanatory standards designed to account for the intuitions, beliefs, judgements, and principles included in the initial set. Insofar as the relationships that hold between the fundamental explanatory standards unifying the initial set, on the one hand, and the elements of that very set, on the other, prove to be coherent, the explanatory standards so achieved are taken as justified. If, by contrast, the explanatory standards prove to be unable to accommodate deep-rooted and non-idiosyncratic intuitions, beliefs, judgements, and principles included in the initial set, then the explanatory standards will need to be revised in light of the unyielding intuitions, beliefs, judgements, and principles.

The method of reflective equilibrium thus works as a strategy of mutual adjustment between (a) the fundamental standards put forward to explain an array of intuitions, beliefs, judgements, and principles and (b) those propositions themselves, accordingly treated as raw 'empirical' data for those standards to explain. That is, when constructing a theory by reflective equilibrium, we will go back and forth between a constellation of claims and the working hypothesis that can best explain and make sense of those claims. The two sets of elements which reflective equilibrium works on are therefore constantly being adjusted to each other: in using this method to construct theories, our effort will be aimed at finding support for our intuitions, beliefs, judgements, and principles in certain explanatory standards, which we will subsequently test for compatibility with all our intuitions, beliefs, judgements, and principles that are not the outcome of distorting factors.

The outline just offered highlights the specific quality of reflective equilibrium. Stripped of its technicality, the method can be understood as a kind of two-way trip from the particular to the general and back from the general to the particular. This back-and-forth of inferences comes to an end when the fundamental explanatory standards (perhaps needing to be revised) and the initial empirical set of propositions (purified of any idiosyncratic elements) can be said to have reached a balance, where the parts fit together forming a coherent overall picture, such that no further tweaking is needed to that end. The basic insight behind reflective equilibrium thus lies in its idea of what it means to justify a theoretical account of the thing we are investigating: it means achieving a fit or a relation of mutual support among the different elements making up our worldview. And this in turn means that in constructing a theoretical account of something on the basis of a method of reflective equilibrium, our primary task will be to make that account coherent, and hence on reflection stable.

Now, as desirable as it may be to achieve a stable, coherent system in the manner just described, it does not seem a good place to start from if we also want our theory of legal obligation to be comprehensive and genuinely far-reaching. I mean by this that reflective equilibrium may make our practical judgements and intuitions about legal obligation consistent with a theory of legal obligation; but it is not programmatically meant to get us to reflect on the conditions of intelligibility of legal obligation. Presuppositional interpretation, by contrast, enables us to look precisely into those conditions of intelligibility in a systematic fashion. Crucially, this difference between the theoretical accounts that can be produced by reflective equilibrium and presuppositional interpretation is built into the two methods, since it depends on the different kinds of movement the two methods make: the movement of presuppositional interpretation is linear, whereas in reflective equilibrium we have a 'shuttling' movement. To briefly elaborate, in presuppositional interpretation we proceed from the specialists' rational understanding of a subject matter back to its fundamental presuppositions, where the method reaches its point of arrival. Hence, there is no going back and forth between some common understanding of something (the empirical set) and a corresponding theory of that thing (the explanation of the empirical data), as instead would happen with the method of reflective equilibrium. In presuppositional interpretation such back-and-forth is replaced by a one-way movement from an initial set backward to its preconditions of intelligibility. The linear movement of presuppositional interpretation enables one to possibly go even farther into the subject of investigation using this method than using the method of reflective equilibrium. For whereas the latter shuttles to and from between the surface constituents of a concept or object of inquiry, the former drills beneath the surface, underneath the outward features by which that object or concept is defined. Reflective equilibrium thus enables us to systematize and harmonize a vast array of apparent traits ascribable to an object of investigation; but it also seems by its very design unsuitable as a method for exploring the fundamental presuppositions, or conditions of intelligibility, of that object, that is, the conditions that need to be satisfied in order for us to be able to speak intelligibly about that object or concept. Hence my preference for the method of presuppositional interpretation.

10.5 Conclusion

In this chapter I looked at the specific method used to arrive at the account of legal obligation theorized in this book. The account of legal obligation I purported to construct was programmatically aimed at being both rigorous and comprehensive. The rigour of an account depends on whether it validly moves from premises to conclusions. Where the object of the investigation is a practical notion like legal obligation, the premises of the argument are bound to be theoretically charged. But if they are widely accepted among the community, and if the substantive conclusions can be shown to follow from those premises, the entire theoretical construction can be considered rigorous. An account is comprehensive, insofar as the interpretation it can offer of its subject matter – here, legal obligation – should not be confined to analysing the fundamental conditions that need to be met in order for one to be able to intelligibly use that subject matter, but should also provide a philosophical reading of the same subject matter. In this way, we will not run the risk of winding up with a logically well analysed but uninformative account of the relevant notion and so with an account that fails to connect to the social practices out of which it arises.

It is in light of those considerations that I opted to approach the study of legal obligation on the basis of the specific method I call 'presuppositional interpretation'. As the phrase suggests, and as discussed in this chapter, this is in part a study of the conditions or presuppositions absent which it would be impossible to even conceive of legal obligation. Implicit in that description, in the interests of methodological rigour and parsimony, is the concern with *fundamental* conditions of intelligibility. But a theory of this kind would only give us a *thin* account of obligation.

For a thicker, more robust account, the premises of the argument need to be interpreted: this is what happens when the expert understanding of obligation – the premise – is organized into a systematic account of legal obligation at once deep and far-reaching. Through the combination of these two dimensions, I argued in this chapter, presuppositional interpretation has the methodological resources to produce an account of legal obligation that is aptly structured and deep, by so enabling us to comprehensively conceptualize the obligatory dimension of law. In a nutshell, then, the basic claim defended in this chapter was that the method most conducive to advancing our understanding of legal obligation consists in a procedure that combines presuppositional analysis with a hermeneutics of the subject matter. This combined effort was claimed to be able to identify, and give content to, both the essential traits of legal obligation and the necessary conditions under which legal obligation is conceived.

In relation to these conclusions, a final point may be worth noticing, despite the fact that it has not been specifically argued for in the context of this work: nothing in principle seems to prevent one from applying the method of presuppositional interpretation not just to the study of legal obligation but also to the exploration of other concepts, or at least other concepts that bear sufficient similarities (such as fundamental quality, extensions spanning across different domains, essentially contested meaning, wide-ranging usage in diverse disciplines, etc.) with legal obligation. In other terms, here presuppositional interpretation has been argued to be a most suitable method for exploring legal obligation. However, I am inclined to think, its use can be extended beyond the investigation of legal obligation and applied to the explanation of other notions, legal and non-legal alike, as well as to the clarification of issues in fields of study that may have proved to be recalcitrant to alternative methodology of inquiry, namely, that have been given a less than comprehensive, sound, and rigorous elucidation by those methodologies.[48]

---

[48] I am grateful to Daniel Weston for bringing this potential dimension of presuppositional interpretation to my attention. I remain of course solely responsible for the remarks, mistakes and misconceptions contained in this paragraph.

Conclusion

In a nutshell, the main claims defended in this book can be thus summarized. Central to my work was the effort to explain what makes legal obligation distinctive. This effort was undertaken without neglecting to consider that we are, after all, dealing with obligation, and so that we need an understanding of what *obligation* as such is before we can even begin to consider *legal* obligation. Hence the premise from which the entire discussion proceeded, namely, that a theory of legal obligation needs to acknowledge that legal obligation is an instantiation of the wider genus we call obligation by thus incorporating, and being defined by, the concept of obligation as such. It was also pointed out that while this genus (obligation as such) is a normative concept, it needs to be distinguished from other concepts within the normative. That is, obligation is a binding claim on our practical lives: the claim is *normative*, since it specifies a course of action in a realm of possibilities where we could choose to act otherwise; but it is also (and more specifically) *binding*, in that the course of action so specified is not just offered as generic guidance but as something that one is *required* to do.

This initial conceptualization, as it was sketched in Chapter 1, is broad and generic enough to be compatible with several different, and even conflicting, theoretical accounts of what is *legally* obligatory. For this reason, one cannot build too much on the basic account of obligation. Even so, the concept of obligation, as constructed in Chapter 1, is not insignificant: we can use it to guide the discussion in arriving at a comprehensive account of legal obligation. Indeed, as we saw in Chapter 2, this concept of obligation suffices to rule out the 'empirical' model of legal obligation as well as the 'formal' account, neither of which can be relied on to arrive at a satisfactorily comprehensive and theoretically adequate conceptualization of legal obligation.

In Chapters 3–6, I built on this foundation and critically engaged with the main accounts of legal obligation advocated in today's jurisprudence. First, I looked at the social practice account, summarized in the view that we have a legal obligation when a practice gains wide recognition within a social group, becoming something the community expects of its own members. On this view, legal obligation comes down to the legitimate social expectations we have that others behave in certain ways. This account was argued to be inadequate in three ways. To begin with, (a) it secures a disjointed picture of legal obligation at once perspectivized and genuine. But only in the latter sense can legal obligation be understood to carry practical force – purporting to rationally guide and justify conduct – and can accordingly compete with other sources of action-guidance. Moreover, legal obligation in the genuine sense, as conceived in the social practice account, can be criticized as (b) limited in scope, and (c) hardly grounded in social facts alone. Its scope is limited in that it only binds those who are actively engaged in the social practices the law is understood to consist of, and so it only applies to legal officials (those who make, administer, and interpret the law). By contrast, everyone else – the citizenry at large – does not participate in any of those activities and so, strictly, by the terms of the account itself, cannot be held bound. Nor can the account explain legal obligation as a genuinely normative concept grounded just in social facts. For there is no way to squeeze something normative out of a practice on the basis of social facts alone. That is, on the ground that a practice is widespread, people willingly participate in it and those who participate in it expect others to do so too, no obligation can be established.

These shortfalls do not instead affect the interpretivist account, which does, by contrast, recognize the non-social, and indeed moral, component of legal obligation, by presenting it as a genuinely binding demand generated by the law understood as a principled institutional practice. Since on this view legal obligations are not inherent in social practices themselves but result from our interpretation of such practices, this account significantly advances our understanding of legal obligation. Even so, as was observed in Chapter 4, the interpretivist account of legal obligation falls short in another respect. For it waters down and ultimately misunderstands the justificatory component of legal obligation – a component that is not ancillary to legal obligation but *essential* to it. So, while interpretivism correctly sees that the requirements generated by the law are enveloped in a moral casing lacking which they could not be recognized as obligatory in quality, it fails to see that this moral casing cannot be reduced to the surrounding institutional and political morality but must find its basis in practical rationality. The interpretivist account therefore takes a step in the right direction in rejecting the idea that the source of legal obligation lies in social facts alone and arguing that only *principled* practices can ground the obligatory force of legal requirements; but then it fails to push this statement to its logical conclusion, for it recognizes the role of principled practices but not the need for these practices to be put to any independent rationality-led test of critical scrutiny.

As the reader may appreciate, this critique of the interpretivist account of legal obligation is not entirely negative. For implicit in this account is, in the positive, a need to recognize that the connection between legal obligation and practical rationality is not just desirable but constitutive, or conceptually necessary. Recognizing this constitutive connection is essential to the reason account of legal obligation in any of its forms. So it was only natural for this discussion to have come as a follow-up to the critique of the interpretivist account. In laying out the reason account it was argued that legal obligation is best understood not as a concept grounded in social facts or institutional practices but as one constitutively shaped by practical reasons.

This argument was first explored in Chapter 5 under what I called the *conventionalist* reason account, particularly as embodied in the work of Andrei Marmor. Here I claimed that, as much as the conventionalist reason account of legal obligation takes a further step in the right direction by replacing the social practice and interpretivist models with a reason model, the resulting theory of legal obligation is subject to two lines of criticism. First, Marmor conceives of legal obligation as a kind of internal duty endowed with genuine obligatory force. But, as was argued, these two features do not sit well together: it is hard to make the case that a merely internal obligation can be genuine. And yet this is precisely what, on the basic concept of obligation, is required of legal obligations as practical requirements: that they be genuine. The conventionalist reason account therefore fails, in this sense, to capture the full practical import of legal obligation. But there was also a second, and equally serious, flaw that was detected in the conventionalist reason account, at least on one conceivable interpretation of it. Which is to say that it can be understood to support a perspectivized conception of legal obligation. This is a problem because legal obligation so conceived lacks any genuinely normative component. The conventionalist reason account therefore fails to explain legal obligation as a practically rational requirement and so as a standard ultimately capable of determining how we ought to act.

The twofold argument here developed against the conventionalist reason account reveals that the conventionalist turn to reasons for explaining legal obligation is timid and inchoate. And this is why the account fails to grasp the nature of legal obligation. Hence the need to move beyond this account while retaining its distinctive appeal to reasons. So in Chapter 6 I turned to the *exclusionary* reason account, especially as defended by John Finnis, underscoring that while this account does see legal obligation as conceptually linked to practical rationality (thereby providing a better understanding of legal obligation than does the conventionalist reason account), there is a basic tension built into it. For on the one hand, in establishing a conceptual link between legal obligation and practical rationality, the exclusionary reason account posits a continuity of practical rationality as a domain comprising both law and morality, while on the other hand it claims that legal requirements and moral ones are mutually exclusive. What we get in the outcome is a dichotomous picture of legal obligation as an idea governed by conflicting logics.

This analysis and critique of the exclusionary reason account suggest that the reason account needs to be set on new grounds: hence the 'revisionary Kantian conception' (introduced in Chapter 7 and further qualified in Chapter 8), on which legal obligation is a layered notion combining a categorical demand and a rational justification for that demand. Accordingly, an agent may have other inclinations or purposes, but if a course of action is obligatory, those forces are to be set aside as contingencies, and the agent falls under a requirement to act as stated. The rational justification for the stated requirement, for its part, is constitutive of legal obligation in virtue of the normative nature of what is legally obligatory: as was argued, what it means for something to be normative is to serve as a standard by which to guide action, and nothing serves that function without an underlying *reason* for acting as stated (otherwise, we would be looking at an imposition, or a forcible restraint on action, rather than an obligation). In combination, these components of legal obligation – its being categorically mandatory (rather than recommendatory) and backed by reasons (rather than just by force) – account for the distinctively prescriptive quality, or bindingness, of the law, which *constrains* action at the same time as it offers to rationally *justify* its own constraint.

This took us to the discussion in Chapter 9, where I claimed that while reasons play an essential role in explaining legal obligation, the outcome is a special rendering of the reason account that, in showing what uniquely distinguishes legal obligation from other kinds of obligation, cannot be reduced to the robust variant of that account, as it is championed in contemporary jurisprudence. This means that, on the one hand, the revisionary Kantian conception shares with the robust reason account of legal obligation the view that legal and moral obligation are both grounded in practical rationality – an implication of the thesis of the continuity of practical rationality – but, on the other hand, the revisionary Kantian conception emphasizes that there is a distinctive role the law plays in practical human affairs, such that the obligation associated with the law cannot be simply equated with moral obligation. In other words, while the two kinds of obligation share the same nature, or status – both being inexplicable unless they are viewed as activities of practical rationality – these activities respond to different needs, such that legal obligation winds up framing a distinctive set of demands when compared to the claims made by pure practical rationality.

The revisionary Kantian conception thus proceeds from the concept of obligation worked out in Chapter 1 as a basis on which to build in rectifying what have been argued to be the failures of the main competing views of legal obligation found in the literature – namely, the empirical, formal, social practice, and interpretivist accounts, as well as the alternative variants of the reason account (conventionalist, exclusionary, and robust) – so as to explain legal obligation comprehensively rather than neglecting or underplaying this or that aspect of it. But this proved to be an ambitious project, and it needed a method, without which it would not have been possible to construct the revisionary Kantian conception of legal obligation I have put forward, and through which it also became possible to show how the theory informs the substantive conclusions I arrived at. Hence the discussion in Chapter 10, which introduced the method I called 'presuppositional interpretation', distinguishing it from other methods. In particular, two of the most influential alternative methods (transcendental argumentation and conceptual analysis), it was argued, yield a too abstract concept of obligation that, among other things, does not help us understand what is distinctive about legal obligation. Presuppositional interpretation makes it possible to fix this shortcoming by setting itself up as a two-stage process. Those relying on such method begin by setting out the assumptions absent which it would not even be possible to conceive of legal obligation in the first place, and in this way they arrive at an idea of legal obligation that we should all be able to recognize. At this point the idea so obtained can be fleshed out by interpreting it in light of what it does: it is here that the general idea of legal obligation is moulded into a specific conception, in a process through which one obtains a *thick* account of legal obligation, into which substantive views and arguments are built that carry certain conceptual implications, and from which practical consequences can also be derived.

INDEX

accountability, obligation and, 37–8, 41
  legal, 44
action-guiding, law as, 90
  perspectivized obligation and, 101
actions
  general principles of, and practical rationality, 287
  justification of, in revisionary Kantian conception, 243–4
agency
  conceptualization of, 271
  human constitution and, 270–1
Alvarez, Maria, 205
analytical philosophy, 324, 344–5
Anscombe, Elizabeth, 11
Aquinas, 169, 179, 266
Aristotelian tradition, 169, 173, 179
Austin, John, 51, 53, 246
  Hart on, 246–7
authoritative dimension, 1
authority
  common good secured by, 173
  Duff on, 274
  Hurd on, 291–2
  of legal systems, 297–8
authorship, norms of, 251–2
autonomy, 298–9, 302–3
  Kant on, 258–9
  of law, 255
  practical rationality and, 258–9

Baier, Kurt, 227
Bentham, Jeremy, 15–16
  imperatival account and, 51, 53
  on obligation, 246

Beyleveld, D., 68, 263–4, 294–5
  on idealism, 278–9
  on natural law theory, 281–2
  on revisionary Kantian conception, 280, 282–3
  theory of legal obligation of, 278–84
bindingness, 263, 352
  morality and, 253
  of obligations, 33, 242–3
  practical rationality and, 260, 293–4
  rational requirements of, 242–3
Bratman, Michael, 78
  Coleman and, 79–80, 82–3
  Shapiro and, 80–1
Broome, J., 203
Brownsword, R., 68, 263–4, 294–5
  on idealism, 278–9
  on natural law theory, 281–2
  on revisionary Kantian conception, 280, 282–3
  theory of legal obligation of, 278–84
Burton, Steve, 297

Categorical Imperative, 248, 253–5, 257–8
  morality and, 250
categorical justification, 238–9
categoricality, 210–12, 232
  of justificatory reasons, 214–15
  Kant on, 211–12
  motivating reasons and, 213–14
causality, formal account and, 57–8
Christodoulidis, Emilios, 120
civic republicanism, 277

coercion, 50–3, 256–7
  in legal systems, 297–8
  mandatory force and, 230–1
  Mill on, 245
  normativity and, 229–31
  physical, 229–30
  psychological, 229–31
  revisionary Kantian conception and, 232–3
Coleman, Jules, 96
  Bratman and, 79–80, 82–3
  on convention, 140
  on endorsement, 83
  on full-blooded legal obligation, 82–4
  on shared activity, law as, 79–80, 140
common good
  authority securing, 173
  of community, 267–8
  coordination problems and, 173, 182, 187–93
  defining, 273
  Duff on, 273–6
  fairness and, 190–3
  Finnis on, 167–8, 172–5, 178, 182–4, 186, 191, 194
  general norms and, 191–3
  intersubjective reasons and, 274–5
  justification of law and, 275
  legal rationalism and, 275–6
  legal systems and, 273
  practical rationality and, 267–8
  in revisionary Kantian conception, 274–5
  shared values and, 277
  unanimity securing, 173
common-sense understanding, 304–5, 308–9, 342–3
  Kant on, 327–9
community model, Duff on, 277
compulsion, 228
  intersubjective justificatory reasons and, 228–9
  intersubjective reasons and, 228
concept, of obligation, 219, 310, 349
  common-sense understandings of, 304–5
  conceptualization and, 24–5
  contents of, 306–7
  as distinctive category, 304
  folk view of, 305–6
  groupthink in, 307–8
  historically contingent, 27
  intension, extension and, 24
  interpretive, 105, 304
  of mainstream experts, 306–7
  non-deductive, 28–9
  per se, as benchmark, 44–6, 71–2
  presuppositional interpretation in, 311, 313, 321–2
  rational requirements and, 248–9
  received, 312–13
  as specialist, rational, 25–7
  specialists in, 306–7
  theory-dependent, 25–7
  as thin, generic, 26–30, 40–1
Concept of Law (Hart), 2, 20
conceptual analysis, 300–1
  history of, 336–7
  input of, 339–40
  intuitions in, 339–42
  modest, 339
  presuppositional interpretation and, 336–47
  theory-construction in, 338–9
conceptual question, 4
conceptualization, 322–3, 349
  of agency, 271
  concept and, 24–5
  force and, 237–8
  intension, extension and, 24
  of practical deliberation, 270
  presuppositional interpretation in, 311
conceptualization, of obligation, 2–3
concerns, of others, 238–9
conclusive obligation
  categoricality and, 212
  practical rationality and, 146
  presumptive obligation and, 13, 17–18, 41–2, 146, 209–10
  stringency and, 209–10, 212
concurrent, obligations as, 153
conditional obligations, inescapable obligation and, 146–8
constitutivism, 146–8
continuity thesis, 297–9

convention
  constitutive, 139–41, 144
  coordination, 139–41
  deep, 139–41
  features of, Marmor on, 137–8
  games and, 144
  as norm, 141
  surface, 139–41
conventionalism, legal, 351
  Marmor on, 242
  in positivism, legal, 77–8
  practical reasons and, 242
  revisionary Kantian conception and, 242–3
  shared activity and, 77–8
conventionality thesis, 77
coordination problems, 173, 182, 187–93
Cotterrell, Roger, 276–7
Cunliffe, J., 194

Dancy, J., 205, 213
Darwall, S., 35, 37–8
decision-making, 270, 291–2
defeasible force, 263
demandingness. *See* requirement, obligation as
deontic language, 1
Dependence Thesis, 253–4, 256
descriptive, normativity opposed to, 31–2, 99–101
  perspectivized legal obligation and, 99–101
dialogical legal obligation, 193–4. *See also* non-deferential authority
dimension
  authoritative, 1
  normativity and descriptive, 31–2, 99–101
directed obligation, imputed contrasted with, 39–40
dualism, monism and, 132
Duff, Antony, 263–4, 294–5
  on authority, 274
  on common good, 273–6
  on community model, 277
  on justification, 272

revisionary Kantian conception contrasted with system of, 277–8
  on self-interest, 273
  theory of legal obligation of, 272–8
duty
  incentive of, 257–8
  Kant on, 257–8
  Mill on, 245
  obligation and, 260
Dworkin, R.
  early works of, 105
  on genuine obligation, 115
  on integrity, 112–13, 120–1
  on interpretive concept, 105
  interpretivist account and, 62–3, 105–9, 118, 120–1, 127
  as political, interpretivism of, 127
  on political legitimacy, community and, 124
  on political morality, 124

empirical model, 46–7, 71–2
  descriptive in, 47
  imperatival account, 47–53, 72
  normative model compared with, 6, 47, 53–4
  predictive account, 47–50, 72
endorsement, 83, 94–6
epistemic functions, 292
Essert, Christopher, 36, 204, 211, 234
ethical constructivism, 269
evaluative
  in interpretivist account, 63, 110–11, 116
  in interpretivist account, institutional and, 63, 112, 117–18, 133–4
  justificatory reasons as, 205–6
evaluative considerations, 103
evaluative principles
  in interpretivist account, 109–10
  political morality, 110–11
exclusionary reason, 351–2
  conceptual justification for, 186
  dialectical critique of, 185–6, 193, 195–7
  dialogical obligation and, 193–4
  Finnis on, 165, 170, 175–6, 179–80, 185

INDEX   357

moral justification for, 187–90
practical rationality and, 179–83,
   188, 194–5
Raz on, 170–1
expert view, 308–9
identifying, 309
Kant on, 327–9
presuppositional interpretation
   eliciting, 312, 346–7
explanatory reasons, 205, 214–15
as causal account, 207, 214
legal obligation and, 207–8, 214
motivating reasons compared with,
   206–7
explorational presuppositional
   interpretation, 317–18
explorational transcendental
   arguments, 317–18, 331–2
extension, intension and, 24
external freedom, 256–8

family of ideas, obligation as, 18–22
feature model, 237–8
force model contrasted with,
   244
obligations in, 244–5
revisionary Kantian conception and
   incompatibilities with, 245
Finnis, John, 61, 166
on Aquinas, 169, 179
Aristotelian and Thomist tradition
   followed by, 169, 173, 179
on authority, 173
on collateral moral sense, of legal
   obligation, 166
on common good, 167–8, 172–5,
   178, 182–4, 186, 194
on coordination problems, 173, 182,
   191
dialectical critique of, 185–6, 193,
   197
on empirical sense, of legal
   obligation, 166
on exclusionary reason, 165, 170,
   175–6, 179–83, 185
on invariant and variable legal
   obligation, 165, 169–72, 175–6,
   179–83, 196, 198, 200

on legal sense, of legal obligation,
   166–72, 175–87, 192–8
on moral sense, of legal obligation,
   166–72, 175–9, 181–7, 192–4, 196
Natural Law and Natural Rights, 164
obligation *simpliciter and*, 165–6, 197
practical force and, 164
practical rationality and, 165, 167–9,
   171–3, 175–83, 185–6, 196–8,
   295–6
on promissory obligation, 166–8
rational necessity and, 164
Raz and, 170–1
on systemic, law as, 174–5, 194
on unanimity, 173
will-dependence and, 164, 168–9
force mode, 261
Hart on, 247
force model, 237–8, 243–7
feature model contrasted with, 244
Hart on, 247
justification in, 243–4
obligations in, 244
Pink on, 244
formal account, 6–7, 54–5, 72–3
causality and, 57–8
as intra-systemic, 55–6
Kelsenian, 55–8
as normative and formal, 55
freedom
external, 256–8
internal, 256–8
Kant on, 258–9
practical rationality and, 258–60
protection of, 257–8
full-blooded legal obligation, 81–2, 84,
   94–5, 102–3
Coleman on, 82–4
endorsement in, 83, 94–6
genuine quality in, 84–5
as limited, 87–90
perspectivized obligation compared
   with, 86
reasons in, 83–4
Fuller, L., 192

Gaut, Berys, 268–9
Gauthier, D., 35

general idea, obligation as, 6
generality, 263
generic consistency, principle of, 280
  legal systems conforming to, 280–1
Generic View, of obligation, 21
genocide, 121–2
German idealism, 329–30
Gewirth, Alan, 280, 283–4
Gilbert, Margaret, 34
  Marmor on, 138
Green, Leslie, on social practice-rule, 246–7
Greenberg, Mark, 115
Greenspan, Patricia, 215–16
Groundwork for the Metaphysics of Morals (Kant), 323–4
Guest, Stephen, 111

Hage, Jaap, 30–1
Hart, H. L. A., 2, 20, 79
  on Austin, 246–7
  on force model, 247
  legal positivism of, 77, 96–7
  on obligation, 246–7
  social practice account of, 58–60, 69, 96–7
Hart-Raz debate, 51–2
hermeneutical presuppositional interpretation, 316
Hershowitz, Scott, 99–100
Hieronymi, P., 205
Himma, Kenneth Einar, 30, 211, 341
  on wrongness, 37
Hohfeld, Wesley N., 15–16
Holmes, Oliver Wendell, 48–9
human constitution
  practical rationality and, 271–2
  reflectivity in, 271–2
  self-determination in, 271–2
humanization
  practical deliberation and, 270–1
  in revisionary Kantian conception, 272
Hurd, H., 290–1
  on action, 291
  on authority, 291–2

idealism, German, 329–30
idealism, legal, 235–6
  Beyleveld on, 278–9
  Brownsword on, 278–9
impartiality, subjective reasons and, 239
imperatival account, 47–8, 50, 72
  Austin and, 51, 53
  Bentham and, 51, 53
  coercion in, 50–3
  of Kramer, 51–3
  ought, must in, 52–3
  sovereign in, 51
imperativeness, 225–6
imperium model of law, 276–7
imputed obligation, directed contrasted with, 39–40
Independence Thesis, 253–4, 256
inescapable obligation, 146–8
instrumental principle, 251–2
integrity
  critical morality and, 124–5
  Dworkin on, 112–13, 120–1
  in interpretivist account, 112–14, 119–21, 124–5
  pure and inclusive, 120–1
intension, extension and, 24
interdisciplinary approach, 22–4, 41–2
internal freedom, 256–8
internal obligations
  bindingness of, non-genuine, 155–61
  Marmor on, 136–7, 142–6, 148–53, 155–61, 164
  perspectivized obligation and, 156–8
interpretivist account, 7–8, 62–4, 73, 104, 106, 350–1
  acceptability and acceptance in, 123
  critical morality and, 123–5
  critique of, 116–25
  Dworkin and, 62–3, 105–9, 115, 118, 120–1, 127
  evaluative principles in, 109–11, 116, 133–4
  evolving, 106–8
  of fit, predicament in, 118–19
  as genuine, obligations in, 115–17
  historical background in, 112–14, 117–18, 121

institutional and evaluative in, 63, 110–12, 117–18, 133–4
integrity in, 112–14, 119–21, 124–5
interpretive facts in, 111–14, 116
justification in, 114–19, 123–34
legal obligations, rights central to, 108
normative facts in, 116
originality of, 104–5
political morality in, 105–15, 117–18, 121–34, 200
practical rationality and, 132
practically rational considerations and, 7–8, 120–34
reason account and, 64, 136
as reconstructive, interpretation in, 110, 113–14, 120–1, 123
revisionary Kantian conception and, 200
settled iniquities and, 120
social facts in, 111–12
social practice account compared with, 132–4
of Stavropoulos, 105–10, 114–15
as substantive, 111
theoretical significance of, 105–6
wicked legal systems and, 121–2
intersubjective morality, 239
intersubjective reasons, 217, 262
broadness of, 221–3
common good and, 274–5
compulsion and, 228–9
criticism of, 222–3
equality, impartiality of, 220–1
force of, 244
impersonal concerns reflected by, 220
justification, 225–9, 232
mandatory force of, 223–7, 232
moral deliberation and, 239–40
non-self-centred stances and, 240
obligation-generating reasons and, 241–2
overridingness of, 240–1
in practical justification, 221–3, 225
in practical normativity, 226
practical rationality and, 223–5, 231–2

as right, 222–3
subjective reasons and, 217–18, 220–1, 223–5, 231–2
supererogatory strength of, 223–4, 226–7
wrongness and, 222–5
intra-categorical presuppositional interpretation, 318–22
intra-systemic obligation
Finnis on, 166–72, 175–9
in formal account, 55–6
intuitions, 339
in conceptual analysis, 339–42
formation of, 342
in presuppositional interpretation, 340–1, 343–4
in reflective equilibrium, 346–7
source data and, 341–2
invariant, legal obligation as, 165, 171–2, 175–6
dialogical obligation and, 193–4
moral justification for, 188
is
empirical model pertaining to, 47
ought and, 30, 72

judgments, *a posteriori*, 336
jurisprudes, practice of, 250
justification, 297
categorical, 238–9
compulsion and, 228–9
conclusive, practical rationality as, 127–9
Duff on, 272
in force model, 243–4
in interpretivist account, 114–19, 123–5, 127–34
intersubjective, 225–9, 231–2
of law and common good, 275
of legal systems, 297–8
non-prudential, 225–7, 231–2
practical, intersubjective reasons in, 221–2, 225
practical rationality and, 135
practical reasons as, 205–6
in revisionary Kantian conception, practical, 200–1, 270

justificatory reasons, 205–8
  as categorical, 214–15
  legal obligation defined by, 214–16
  normativity and, 231–2
  practical normativity and, 214–16

Kant. See also revisionary Kantian conception
  on autonomy, 258–9
  Categorical Imperative of, 211
  on categoricality, 211–12
  on common-sense understanding, 327–9
  Doctrine of Right, 20–1
  on expert view, 327–9
  on freedom, 258–9
  Groundwork for the Metaphysics of Morals, 323–4
  on legal naturalism, 255
  on legal positivism, 255
  on maxims, 248
  Metaphysics of Morals, 248–50
  methodological concerns of, 302–3
  obligation *simpliciter* and, 20–1, 232
  original view of legal obligation, 237–8
  practical philosophy of, 247–8, 253, 261
  on practical rationality, 249
  practical rationality and, 232
  on principles, 248
  Prolegomena to Any Future Metaphysics, 327–9
  on rights, 250
Kant's analytic method, 9–10, 324
  presuppositional interpretation and, 323–9
  purpose of, 324–5
  structure in, 324–5
Kelsen, Hans, 55–8
  on legal empowerment, 56–7
  on legal norm, 55–6
  on normativity, nomological conception of, 57–8
  on technical and moral legal obligation, 177–8
knowledge, synthetic *a priori*, 336
Körner, Stefan, 329–30

Korsgaard, Christine, on practical rationality, 270–1
Kramer, M.
  imperatival account of, 51–3
  predictive account and, 53
Kutz, C., 80

Law and Economics Movement, 49–50
law conception, of moral theory, 10–11
legal empowerment, 56–7
legal existence, obligatoriness and, 97–8
legal norms, 274–5, 292
legal obligation as variable, in revisionary Kantian conception, 200–1
legal rationalism, 204
  common good and, 275–6
legal realism, 48–9
legal sense, of legal obligation
  as conceptually separate, 186
  dialectical relations of, 185–6, 193, 195–6
  dialogical relation of, 193–4
  Finnis on, 166–72, 175–86, 192–8
  Kelsen and Raz on, 177–8
  morally justified separation of, 187–90
legal systems
  coercion in, 297–8
  common good and, 273
  compliance under, 273–4
  justification of, 297–8
  practical rationality in, 288–9
  principle of generic consistency and, 280–1
legal-moral obligations, purely moral obligations and, 279–80
Lewis, David, Marmor on, 139

mandatory force, 232
  coercion and, 230–1
  imperativeness and, 225–6
  of intersubjective reasons, 223–7, 232
  normativity and, 230–1
Marmor, Andrei, 351
  bindingness and, 145–63
  conditional, legal obligations as, for, 144–7, 151–3, 161–2

on constitutive conventions, 139–41, 144
on convention, features of, 137–8
conventionalist reason account of, 136–45
on coordination convention, 139–41
on deep conventions, 139–41
on external obligations, 136–7, 142–5, 148–9
on games, 144–5
on Gilbert, 138
on internal obligations, 136–7, 142–6, 148–53, 155–61, 164
on legal conventionalism, 242
on Lewis, 139
minimalist reason account of, 142, 162–3
on normative institution, law as, 137
on normative reasons, conventions and, 136
on norms, conventions as, 141
objections to, 145–55, 161–3
as perspectivized, legal obligation for, 136–7, 155–61
practical rationality and, 145–50, 153–5, 162
Raz and, 142
revisionary Kantian conception and, 200
shared activity, law as, and, 136–7, 140, 158–9
social practice account and, 136–7, 140, 142, 161
on surface conventions, 139–41
maxims, Kant on, 248
Metaphysics of Morals (Kant), 248–50
Mill, John Stuart
on coercion, 245
on duty, 245
on obligation, 245
minimum wage, 287–8
model. *See also* empirical model; force mode; normative model
Duff on community, 277
feature, 237–8, 244–5
value-conferring, 268–9
modest conceptual analysis, 339

modest transcendental arguments, 331–2
monism, dualism and, 132
moral domain, 241
moral enterprises, 278–9
moral nature, of legal obligation, 238–43
moral sense, of legal obligation
as conceptually separate, 186
dialectical relations of, 185–6, 193
dialogical relation of, 193–4
Finnis on, 166–72, 175–9, 181–6, 192–4, 196
Kelsen and Raz on, 177
morally justified separation of, 187–90
moral theory, legal obligation and, 10–11
morality
bindingness of law and, 253
categorical, 239
categorical imperative and, 250
defining, 241
intersubjective, 239
law and, 250, 252–5, 260–1
non-conventionality of, 242
overridingness as essential feature of, 241
practical rationality and, 250, 252–5
motivating reasons, 205, 216
explanatory reasons compared with, 206–7
as hermeneutical, 206–7
legal obligation and, 207–8
not categorical, 213–15
as psychological, 206–7, 213–15
Murphy, Liam, 132
Murphy, Mark, 281–2

Nagel, T., 132
Natural Law and Natural Rights (Finnis), 164
natural law theory
Beyleveld on, 281–2
Brownsword on, 281–2
jurisprudence and, 266–7
legal positivism and, 284
rationalism and, 266, 268–9

natural law theory (cont.)
  revisionary Kantian conception
    converging with, 272
naturalism, legal, Kant on, 255
necessitation, 263
non-deferential authority, 194
non-hypotheticalness, 232
  categoricality as, 211
  of justificatory reasons, 214–15
  motivating reasons and, 213–14
  practical reasons and, 212–14
  stringency as, 210–13
non-prudential justification, 226, 231–2
normative model, 46–7, 71–2. *See also* social practice account
  as analytical, not contingent, 54
  empirical model compared with, 6, 47, 53–4
  formal account of, 6–7, 54–8, 72–3
  interpretivist account of, 6–8, 62–4, 73
  reason account of, 6–8, 64–71, 73
  social practice account of, 6–7, 58–61, 73
  versions of, 6–7
normative pressure, of obligation, 33–5, 208–10
normativity
  causality and, 57–8
  coercion and, 229–30
  descriptive dimension and, 31–2, 99–101
  general norms, 191–3
  justificatory reasons and, 214–16, 231–2
  legal obligation and practical, 44
  mandatory force and, 230–1
  nomological, Kelsen on, 57–8
  obligation and practical, 30–2, 41, 100–1, 201–2
  ought-to-do and ought-to-be in practical, 30–1
  reason as fundamental to, 202–3
  reasons and, 201–5, 234–5
  in revisionary Kantian conception, 234–5
norms, of authorship, 251–2

obligation, legal. *See specific topics*
obligation *simpliciter*, 6, 11, 13–14, 16
  Finnis and, 165–6, 197
  Kant and, 20–1
  obligation, varieties of, and, 18–22
  perspectivized obligation and, 101
  practical rationality requiring, 165
  in presuppositional interpretation, 303–9
  revisionary Kantian conception and, 8, 199
  as stringent, 208
obligation-generating reasons, intersubjectivity of, 241–2
oneness-of-obligation thesis, 249, 251–2
  practical rationality and vindication of, 252–3
Orman Quine, Willard van, 336–7
ought, 30
  binding, obligation as, 33
  in imperatival account, must and, 52–3
  is and, 30, 32, 47, 72
  ought-to-do and ought-to-be, 30–1
overridingness
  of intersubjective reasons, 240–1
  morality and, 241
Owens, D., 34

Paulson, Stanley, 56
Peirce, Charles Sanders, 28
Perry, Stephen, 35
perspectivized legal obligation, 81–2, 85–6, 102, 200–1
  critique of, 98–102
  as descriptive, not normative, 99–101
  as external, 100
  Marmor and, 136–7, 155–61
  as normatively inert, 99–101
  presumptive standards compared with, 159–61
perspectivized obligation, obligation *simpliciter and*, 101
physical necessitation, 229
Pink, Thomas, 31
  on force model, 244
planning theory of law, 81, 85–6

Plato, 336-7
pluralism, 283-4
political morality
  critical morality and, 123-5
  Dworkin on, 124
  integrity and, 112-14
  in interpretivist account, 105-15, 117-18, 121-34, 200
  obligations and, as genuine, 115
  practical rationality and, 126-31
  Stavropoulous on, 114
political obligation, 3-4
positivism, legal, 75, 77-8
  Hartian, 77, 96-7
  Kant on, 255
  legal conventionalism in, 77-8
  natural law theory and, 284
  of Shapiro, 80-1
  shared activity, law as, and, 75, 77-8, 80-1, 96-7
possibility, grounds of, 325
practical, theoretical and, 32
practical authority, law and, 5
practical deliberation
  conceptualization of, 270
  humanization and, 270-1
practical institution, law as, 89-90, 97-8
practical justification, intersubjective reasons in, 221-3
practical normativity
  intersubjective, 226
  justificatory reasons and, 214-16
  obligation and, 30-2, 203-4
  practical reasons and, 207-8
practical rationality, 351-3
  action-guiding principles of, 286-7
  autonomy and, 258-9
  Baier on, 227
  bindingness and, 260, 293-4
  common good and, 267-8
  as conclusive justification, 127-9
  continuity thesis of, 297-9
  conventionalist reason account and, 145-50, 153-5
  defining, 260
  dialectical relationship with law of, 295-6

exclusionary reason and, 170-1, 175-6, 179-83, 188, 194-5
  Finnis and, 165, 167-9, 171-3, 175-82, 185-6, 196-8, 295-6
  as foundation, 267-8
  freedom and, 258-60, 283
  general principles of action in, 287
  human constitution and, 271-2
  as inclusionary, 165
  inconclusive, 290
  inescapable obligation and, 146-7
  interpretivist account and, 7-8, 120-34
  intersubjective, 223-5, 231-2, 290-1, 295
  justification and, 135
  Kant on, 249
  Korsgaard on, 270-1
  law and, 171-2, 250, 253-5
  legal instantiations of, 252
  in legal systems, 288-9
  meaning of, 204-5
  monist and dualist conceptions of, 132
  morality and, 250, 252-5
  obligation and, 248, 252-3, 265
  obligation *simpliciter* as requirement of, 165
  oneness-of-obligation vindicated by, 252-3
  political morality and, 126-31
  presumptive obligations and conclusive, 146
  qua morals, 250-2
  rational obligations and, 290
  in reason account, 135
  reasons thesis and, 203-5
  in revisionary Kantian conception, 232, 235-6, 267-70, 286-7
  self-sufficiency of, 293
  specificity of, 126
  standards in, 271-2, 288-9
practical reasonableness, 268-9, 296-7
practical reasoning, 297-8
practical reasons
  classes of, 205, 207-8
  as explanations, 205-8, 214-15
  as justifications, 205-8, 214-16

practical reasons (cont.)
  legal conventionalism and, 242
  meaning of, 204–5
  as motivations, 205–8, 213–16
  non-hypotheticalness and, 212–14
  Raz on, 205–6
  stringency and, 208
practical significance, legal obligation theory and, 11–12
predictive account, 47–50, 72
  Kramer and, 53
  Law and Economics Movement, 49–50
  legal realism, 48–9
presumptive obligation
  conclusive obligation and, 13, 17–18, 41–2, 146, 209–10
  perspectivized obligation compared with, 159–61
  practical rationality and, 146
presuppositional interpretation, 9–10, 300, 353
  abstract concepts understood through, 306
  as belief-oriented method, 318–19
  challenges to, 321
  conceivability of legal obligation in, 320
  in concept of obligation, 311, 313, 321–2
  conceptual analysis and, 336–47
  in conceptualization, 311
  entry point of, 303–9, 340–1
  epistemic medium in, 334–5
  expected outcome of, 312–14
  expert view elicited by, 312, 346–7
  explorational, 317–18
  form of, 333–4
  hermeneutical, 316
  intelligibility in, 315–16, 346–8
  intra-categorical, 318–22
  intuitions in, 340–1, 343–4
  Kant's analytic method and, 323–9
  limits of, 319
  nature of, 314–22
  non-trivial conception of, 318
  obligation *simpliciter* in, 303–9
  procedure of, 310–12

rationale behind, 322–3
reflective equilibrium and, 344–7
regressive, 314–16
in revisionary Kantian conception, 9–10, 201
as selective method, 338–9
structure of, 303–14, 334
as syncretic method, 300–1
theory-construction in, 338–9
transcendental arguments and, 329–36
as two-step method of inquiry, 310–12
Weston on, 348
pretheoretical determinations, 306–7
prima facie obligation. *See* presumptive obligation
Principle of Generic Consistency, 68
principles
  community of, 124
  Kant on, 248
pro tanto obligation. *See* presumptive obligation
pro tanto wrongs, 263
Prolegomena to Any Future Metaphysics (Kant), 327–9
promissory obligation, 166–8
prudential rationality, 218–19, 222–3
  supererogatory strength and, 223–4
prudential reasons, revisionary Kantian conception and, 241–2
psychological necessitation, 229
public sphere, 296–7
public wrongs, 292
purely moral obligations, legal-moral obligations and, 279–80
purely morally legitimate, 278–9
Putnam, Hilary, 336–7

Railton, P., 211
rational morality, 266
  defining, 285
rational obligations, 284–5
  defining, 285
  minimum wage and, 287–8
  practical rationality and, 290

in revisionary Kantian conception, 285–6, 293–4
taxation and, 287–8
rational obligatoriness, 260–1
rational requirements, 263
rational structures, 270
rationalism
  ethical, legal idealism and, 235–6
  natural law theory and, 266, 268–9
  revisionary Kantian conception and, 232–6
  in robust reason account, 235
  strict legal, 235–6
Raz, Joseph, 35
  on exclusionary reason, 170–1
  Kramer critique of, 51–3
  Marmor and, 142
  reason account of, 65–6, 69
  on reasons, 201–2, 205–6
  on technical and moral legal obligation, 177–8
realist view, 278–9
reason, as fundamental normative concept, 202–3
reason account, 8, 64–5, 164, 234
  exclusionary, 8, 65–7, 73, 164
  interpretivist account and, 64, 135–6
  minimalist, of Marmor, 142, 162–3
  non-conventionalist, 68–71
  practical rationality in, 135
  of Raz, 65–6, 69
  robust, 8, 65, 67–8, 73, 235, 263–4
  social practice account and, 135–6
reason account, conventionalist, 8, 65, 73, 164
  inescapable obligation and, 146–8
  of Marmor, 136–45, 200
  practical rationality and, 145–7, 149
  revisionary Kantian conception and, 200
  social practice account and, 136, 140
reasons
  discovery of, 201
  intersubjective, 220–5
  justificatory reasons as, 215
  normativity and, 201–5, 234–5
  Raz on, 201–2
  reasons thesis, 202–5
  subjective, 217–20
reasons thesis
  legal rationalism and, 204
  practical rationality and, 203–5
  as thin, claim of, 204
recognitional account, 268–9
recommendatory force, 219–20, 222–3
Reeve, A., 194
reflective equilibrium
  defining, 344–5
  intuitions in, 346–7
  presuppositional interpretation and, 344–7
reflectivity, in human constitution, 271–2
regressive presuppositional interpretation, 314–16
regulative standards, 1
relational, qua personal obligation as, 38–40
requirement, obligation as, 32–5, 41, 231–2
  legal, 44
  physical necessitation and, 229–30
  psychological necessitation and, 229–31
  wrongness and, 35–6, 44
retorsive transcendental arguments, 317–18, 332
revisionary Kantian conception, 8–9, 199–200, 237–8, 247–62, 265–6, 352–3
  across domains, oneness of, 232
  Beyleveld on, 280, 282–3
  Brownsword on, 280, 282–3
  coercion and, 232–3
  common good in, 274–5
  components of, 296–7
  conventionalist reason account and, 200
  exclusionary reason account and, 200
  feature model and incompatibilities with, 245
  general practical justification in, 200–1
  genuinely binding, 200–1
  humanization in, 272

revisionary Kantian conception (cont.)
  interpretivist account and, 200
  intrinsically rational, 200–1, 204, 234–5
  justification in, 200–1, 270
  justification of actions in, 243–4
  legal conventionalism and, 242–3
  legal obligation account of Duff and, 277–8
  natural law theory converging with, 272
  non-reductivist, 232–5
  normativity in, 234–5
  obligation *simpliciter* and, 8, 199
  practical rationality in, 232, 235–6, 267–70, 286–7
  presuppositional interpretation in, 9–10, 201
  prudential reasons and, 241–2
  rational obligations in, 285–6, 293–4
  rationalism and, 232–6
  as revisionary, 232
  robust reason account and, 284–5
  social practice account and, 200–1
  thick, theoretically demanding, 201
  variable, 200–1
  voluntarism and, 233
right
  intersubjective reasons as, 222–3
  Kant on, 250
road traffic, 290
robust reason account, 8, 65, 67–8, 73, 263–72, 294–5
  revisionary Kantian conception and, 284–5
Rodriguez-Blanco, Veronica, 100
Roversi, Corrado, 334–5
rule-based account, 246–7

Sanchez Brigido, R., 80
sanction theory, 228, 246–7
sanction-based account, 246–7
Scanlon, Thomas, 202–3
scepticism, in transcendental arguments, 331
Schauer, F., 192
self-determination, in human constitution, 271–2

self-interest, 241–2
  Duff on, 273
Shapiro, Scott, 80–1
  convention and, 140
  on perspectivized legal obligation, 85–6
  planning theory of, 81, 85–6
shared activity, law as, 60–1, 74–7, 84
  Bratman and, 78–81, 95
  Coleman on, 79–80, 82, 84
  commitment in, 87–8
  evaluative considerations and, 92–6, 102
  existence, obligatoriness in, 97–8
  full-blooded obligation in, 81–90, 94–6, 102
  legal conventionalism and, 77–8
  legal obligees in, 88–90
  legal positivism of, 75, 77–8, 80–1, 96–7, 140
  as limited theory, 86–92, 102
  Marmor compared with, 136–7, 140, 158–9
  perspectivized obligation in, 81–2, 85–6, 98–102
  as practical institution, law in, 89–90, 97–8
  Shapiro on, 80–1, 140
  social action, theory of, and, 78–81
  social fact thesis in, 75, 92–8
  as social practice account, incoherence of, 86–7, 92–8, 102–3
  thick account of, 79–80
  thin accounts of, 80–1
  as voluntarist, 87
shared values, 276–7
  common good and, 277
social action, theory of, 78–9
  Bratman, 78
social fact thesis
  evaluative considerations and, 92–6
  existence, obligatoriness and, 97–8
  law as shared activity and, 75, 92–8
social practice account, 6–7, 58, 73, 102
  Bratman and, 78–81, 95
  Coleman on, 79–80, 82, 84, 140
  endorsement in, 83, 94–6

evaluative considerations and, 92–6, 102, 104
existence rather than obligatoriness in, 97–8
full-blooded obligation in, 81–90, 94–6, 102
of Hart, 58–60, 69
incoherence of shared activity in, 86–7, 92–8, 102–3
interpretivism compared with, 132–4
law as shared activity in, 60–1
as limited theory, 86–92
Marmor and, 136–7, 140, 142
perspectivized obligation in, 81–2, 85–6, 98–102
as practical institution, law in, 89–90, 97–8
reason account and, 8, 135–6
revisionary Kantian conception and, 200–1
Shapiro on, 80–1
social fact thesis in, 75, 92–8, 104
theory of social action and, 78–81
as voluntarist, 87, 94–5
will theory in, 61
social practice-rule, Green on, 246–7
Stavropoulos, Nicos, 107–8
  genuine obligation and, 115
  on moral relevance, legal relevance and, 114
  on normative facts, legal obligation and, 115
  political morality and, 105–10
Sticker, Martin, 326–7
Strawson, Peter, 37
stress tests, 309–10
stringency, 208
  conclusiveness contrasted with, 209–10, 212
  of justificatory reasons, 214–15
  as non-hypothetical, categorical, 210–13
  not inviolable, 208–10
  overridingness contrasted with, 209–10
  severity contrasted with, 210
strong natural law thesis, 281–2, 284

Stroud, Barry, 329–30
subjective reasons, 217–18
  impartiality and, 239
  intersubjective reasons and, 217–18, 220–5, 231–2
  legal obligation and, 219–20
  as prudential practical thinking, 218–19
  recommendatory force of, 219–20
supererogatory strength
  of intersubjective reasons, 223–4, 226–7
  prudential rationality and, 223–4

taxation, 287–8
technical sense, of legal obligation. *See* legal sense, of legal obligation
theoretical, practical and, 32
theoretical account, of obligation, 2–3, 10–11
Third Reich, 121–2
Thomist tradition, 173
thoughts, fundamental connections between, 319
transcendental arguments, 300–1
  defining, 330–1
  dialectical structure of, 333
  epistemic medium in, 334–5
  explorational, 317–18, 331–2
  form of, 333–4
  history of, 329–30
  modest, 331–2
  presuppositional interpretation and, 329–36
  retorsive, 317–18, 332
  scepticism in, 331
  theoretical accounts yielded by, 334–5

uncertainty, 290–1
unity-within-difference, 253–5
Universal Principle of Right, 256–8
universal truths, 321
universalization requirement, 251–2

value-conferring model, 268–9
vegetarianism, 218–21

voluntarism
    revisionary Kantian conception and, 233
    social practice account as, 87, 94–5

Weinrib, Ernest, 11–12
Weston, Daniel, 348
wicked legal systems, 121–2

will theory, 61, 70
Wodak, D., 21
wrongness, 36–7. *See also* right
    accountability and, 37–8
    intersubjective reasons and, 222–4
    obligation and, 35–6, 44
    reasonable, advisable, compared with, 36